Stewart Binns began h[...]
becoming a teacher and [...]
and began a successful career in television, during [...]
many awards including a BAFTA for his 'in-colour' documentary
series, 'Britain at War'. Stewart has since published several fiction
and non-fiction books.

Praise for

BARBAROSSA

'A masterful narrative, deeply enriched by extraordinary research
and a profound analysis of the soul of Russia'
Nick Hewer

'This is a truly astounding book, packed with searing
hitherto-unpublished testimony about what it was like to
endure, and ultimately defeat, the most formidable invasion
in the history of mankind.'
Andrew Roberts,
author of *Churchill: Walking with Destiny*

'This is an admirable book. How can anyone write an
all-encompassing narrative of these times in a mere 305 pages?
Binns has managed to do it beautifully, capturing the story,
the rationale for the response by the Soviet people in general to
mobilise willingly against the invader, whatever their view of their
own dictator and his murderous cronies, and the sheer military,
industrial and human enormity of the subject.'
Aspects of History

'This compact and well-written account clearly demonstrates the
close links between the military events at the front, the suffering
of the civilian population and the genocide of the Jews.'
TLS

Also by Stewart Binns

BARBAROSSA

AND THE BLOODIEST WAR IN HISTORY

STEWART BINNS

WILDFIRE

First published in 2021 by
WILDFIRE
an imprint of HEADLINE PUBLISHING GROUP

First published in paperback in 2022 by
WILDFIRE
an imprint of HEADLINE PUBLISHING GROUP

1

Cataloguing in Publication Data is available from the British Library

ISBN 978 1 4722 7629 2

Map illustrations © Tim Peters

Designed and typeset by EM&EN
Printed and bound in Great Britain by Clays Ltd, Elcograf S.p.A.

HEADLINE PUBLISHING GROUP
An Hachette UK Company
Carmelite House
50 Victoria Embankment
London EC4Y 0DZ

www.headline.co.uk
www.hachette.co.uk

To the millions of East Europeans of many nationalities
who stood in the way of the most brutal assault
in modern history

CONTENTS

PART FIVE: GÖTTERDÄMMERUNG

LIST OF IMAGES

With thanks:

I would like to thank Cathie Arrington of Headline for her invaluable expertise in gathering the photographic imagery for Barbarossa, and my friend Alex Kalinin, who unearthed many important routes to discovering outstanding images in the Russian archives.

1. With Joseph Stalin looking over his shoulder, Soviet Foreign Minister, Vyacheslav Molotov, signs the Nazi-Soviet Pact, Moscow, 23 August 1939. (Niday Picture Library / Alamy Stock Photo)
2. The horrific devastation of Barbarossa. Countless villages are destroyed as the Wehrmacht advances into the Soviet Union in the summer and autumn of 1941. (Sueddeutsche Zeitung Photo / Alamy Stock Photo)
3. With men of the German Einsatzgruppe A looking on, an unnamed Lithuanian nationalist uses a club to beat to death his fellow Jewish citizens in Kaunas, Lithuania, June 1941. The identity of the murderer has never been established definitively, or whether he was the infamous 'Death Dealer of Kaunas'. The image is thought to have been captured by Wehrmacht photographer, Wilhelm Gunsilius. It may well be a scene from the notorious Lietūkis Garage Massacre. (Bundesarkiv. B 162 Bild-04145)
4. Red Army soldiers captured by the Wehrmacht are burying their dead, Bialystok, Belarus, July 1941. (INTERFOTO / Alamy Stock Photo)

CHRONOLOGY

1939

August	23	Germany and the Soviet Union sign the Nazi–Soviet Non-Aggression Pact
September	1	Germany invades Poland
	3	Britain and France declare war on Germany
	17	Soviet invasion of Poland

1940

May	10	Germany invades France, Belgium and the Netherlands
	26	Evacuation begins of Allied troops from Dunkirk, France
June	10	Italy declares war on France and Great Britain
	22	France surrenders to Germany

1941

May	22	Operation Barbarossa launched
July	1	German Army enters Latvian capital, Riga
	10	Battle of Smolensk begins
August	8	Battle of Kiev begins

September	8	Siege of Leningrad begins
October	2	Operation Typhoon, German advance on Moscow
	18	Axis Campaign in Crimea begins
	20	First Battle of Kharkov
November	16	After the Axis invasion of the Crimea, the siege of Sevastopol begins
December	6	The German advance on Moscow is halted

1942

January	8	Several Red Army attempts to push back the Wehrmacht's Central Front begin
May	12	Second Battle of Kharkov
June	28	Operation Blue, the Axis summer offensive to capture the oilfields in the Caucasus and destroy Stalingrad, begins
July	25	Rostov-on-Don falls to Axis forces; the Battle of the Caucasus begins
August	23	The Battle of Stalingrad begins
November	19	Operation Uranus launched; Romanian and Hungarian armies destroyed; 300,000 Axis troops trapped at Stalingrad
December	12	Operation Winter Storm fails to relieve Stalingrad
	15	Operation Saturn, a Soviet offensive, destroys the Axis position in the Caucasus and Donbass

1943

February	3	Axis forces in Stalingrad capitulate
	16	Third Battle of Kharkov; Wehrmacht traps overextended Red Army

July   5   Battle of Kursk, the largest tank battle in history

August   3   Battle of Belgorod
               23   Fourth Battle of Kharkov
               26   Battle of the Dnieper begins

September   14   Third Phase, Battle of Smolensk

November   3   Battle of Kiev

December   24   The Carpathian Offensive begins

1944

January   18   The siege of Leningrad lifted

April   8   Battle of the Crimea

June   23   Operation Bagration; destruction of German Army
                     Group Centre

August   1   Warsaw Uprising
               20   Romania and Bulgaria fall to the Allies

December   29   Battle of Budapest

1945

January   12   Vistula–Oder Offensive
               13   East Prussian Offensive

February   10   East Pomeranian Offensive

April   16   Battle of Berlin
               30   Suicide of Hitler

May   7   Unconditional surrender of Germany in Rheims
                8   Unconditional surrender of Germany in Berlin

MAPS

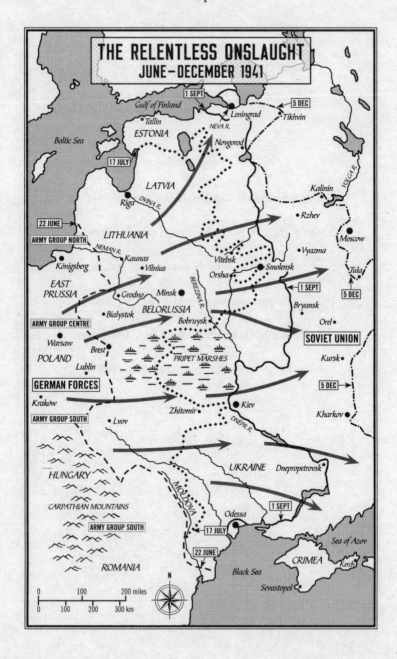

THE RELENTLESS ONSLAUGHT
JUNE–DECEMBER 1941

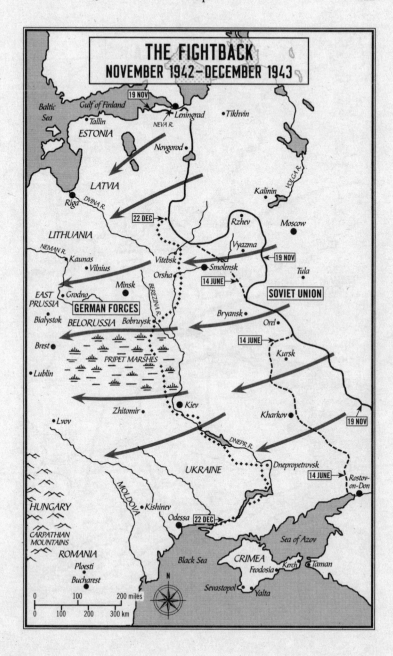

THE FIGHTBACK
NOVEMBER 1942–DECEMBER 1943

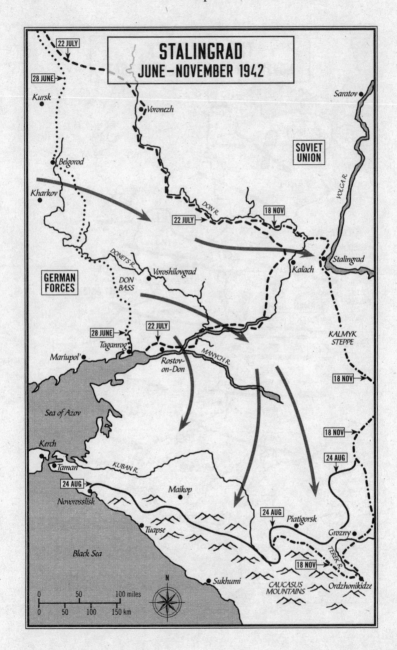

STALINGRAD
JUNE–NOVEMBER 1942

22 JULY

28 JUNE

Kursk

Voronezh

Saratov

SOVIET UNION

Belgorod

Kharkov

VOLGA R.

DON R.

22 JULY

18 NOV

DONETS R.

Voroshilovgrad

Stalingrad

GERMAN FORCES

DON BASS

Kalach

28 JUNE

22 JULY

Taganrog

Mariupol'

Rostov-on-Don

MANYCH R.

KALMYK STEPPE

18 NOV

Sea of Azov

18 NOV

Kerch

24 AUG

KUBAN R.

Taman

24 AUG

Novorosslisk

Maikop

18 NOV

24 AUG

Piatigorsk

Grozny

Tuapse

24 AUG

TEREK R.

18 NOV

Black Sea

Sukhumi

CAUCASUS MOUNTAINS

Ordzhonikidze

0   50   100 miles

0   50   100   150 km

N

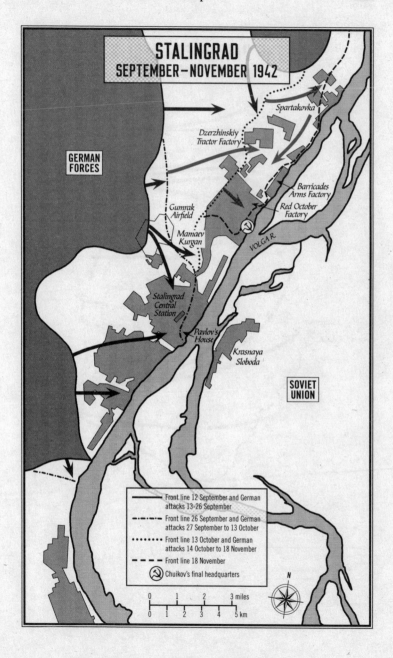

STALINGRAD
SEPTEMBER–NOVEMBER 1942

GERMAN FORCES

Spartakovka

Dzerzhinskiy Tractor Factory

Barricades Arms Factory

Red October Factory

Gumrak Airfield

Mamaev Kurgan

VOLGA R.

Stalingrad Central Station

Pavlov's House

Krasnaya Sloboda

SOVIET UNION

Front line 12 September and German attacks 13–26 September

Front line 26 September and German attacks 27 September to 13 October

Front line 13 October and German attacks 14 October to 18 November

Front line 18 November

Chuikov's final headquarters

0   1   2   3 miles

0   1   2   3   4   5 km

N

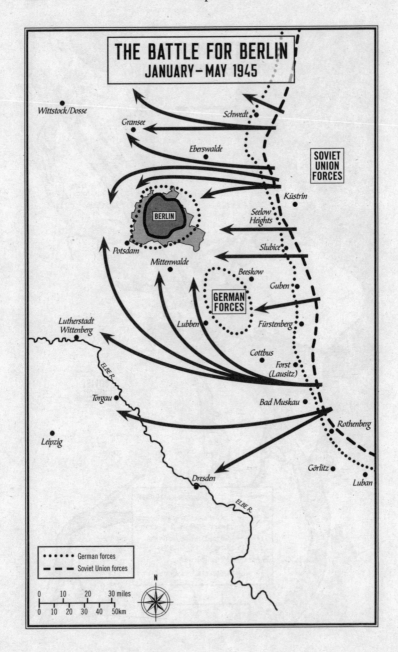

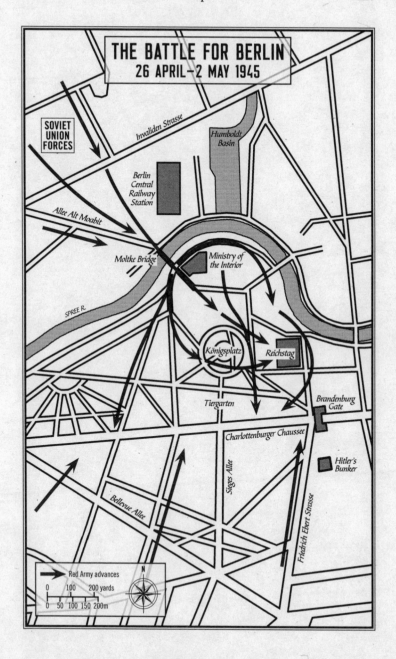

THE BATTLE FOR BERLIN
26 APRIL–2 MAY 1945

SOVIET
UNION
FORCES

Invaliden Strasse

Humboldt
Basin

Berlin
Central
Railway
Station

Allee Alt Moabit

Moltke Bridge

Ministry of
the Interior

SPREE R.

Königsplatz

Reichstag

Tiergarten

Brandenburg
Gate

Charlottenburger Chaussee

Hitler's
Bunker

Sieges Allee

Bellevue Allee

Friedrich Ebert Strasse

Red Army advances

0   100   200 yards

0   50 100 150 200m

N

AUTHOR'S NOTE

Grappling with the statistics of war is never easy. The mayhem of the battlefield, the traumas of death, injury, desertion and destruction, make it impossible to create accurate numbers for the arithmetic of war. When deep layers of Soviet and Nazi propaganda, and not a little post-war disguise, deception and shame, are added into the equations, the figures become even less reliable. Such was the scale of the war on the Eastern Front, we will never have reliable figures. Pointedly, most of the human statistics of the war – mortality, casualties – are rounded to the nearest million. Inevitably, this lack of definitive evidence has led to wide discrepancies in the historical accounts and not a little of both exaggeration and underestimation. In attempting to steer through this challenge, I have tried to find a considered consensus. However, there is at least one thing that can be stated without fear of contradiction; the dreadful tally of death and destruction, of injury and desolation, beggars belief.

I have also aimed to be consistent with my rendering of the Cyrillic alphabet (the alphabet of several contemporary Eurasian languages, including Russian) into English. There is not one single rule of thumb to be used in translation. However, I have tried my best to follow a standard approach. Where I have erred, I beg my Russian friends for their forgiveness in distorting their language.

PREFACE: THE 'SOUL' OF RUSSIA

I first went to Russia, the Soviet Union as it then was, in the summer of 1969. We were four students in a Mini, one of whom, fortunately, was a fluent Russian speaker. Without her, we may never have returned. The visit, with its many escapades and dramas, gave me a host of vivid memories that have stayed with me for over fifty years.

I have been back several times, including recently in researching this book, and have seen the country transformed from a vast Soviet Empire, not far removed from the rigours of Stalinism, to a new, far less idealistic, much more nationalistic, Russian Federation, which is flexing its new muscles on the international stage.

My 1969 visit was a six-week summer adventure that began on the Finnish border, at Vyborg, and ended on the Romanian border, on the Black Sea. It took in Leningrad (now St Petersburg), Novgorod, Moscow, Orel, Kiev and Odessa. They were the heady days of 'flower power' and radical student politics in the West, but such things were far removed from the communist strictures and banalities of the Soviet Union.

Our arrival in Vyborg was a real eye-opener. The Finnish side of the Soviet border enjoyed all the accoutrements and comforts of the Swinging Sixties Western lifestyle. But those disappeared immediately as we crossed into a no-man's-land of tank traps and watchtowers. It was eerie; we saw no people, buildings or vehicles for several miles, just swathes of clear space cut through the dense pine forest. The Soviet border guards we soon encountered in their remote border huts were grim-faced, clearly not enamoured by the arrival of four hippies who had interrupted their midday slumbers.

We were made to eat or throw away all the gorgeous fruit we had bought at Helsinki's wonderful harbour market. When we offered the guards our fruit, we got a stern, one-word reply: '*Nyet!*' Our little Mini was all but stripped down and thoroughly searched, which led to much consternation as the more mechanically minded guards lifted the bonnet and pondered over Alec Issigonis' revolutionary and space-saving transverse engine, with its front-wheel-drive layout.

When we arrived at Vyborg in the gloom of dusk, it looked almost medieval. Peasants in smocks and shawls trudged along the unpaved roads. Street lighting was sporadic and dim, the buildings spartan and crumbling. The police station, where we had to report upon arrival, was full of stony-faced soldiers and even more stern-featured security men. Vyborg was, after all, a grim border town at the epicentre of centuries-old tension and conflict between Finns, Swedes and Russians.

The local campsite, where the only other guests were Russians, was somewhat rudimentary, with a unisex latrine that was no more than an open cesspit with a horizontal tree branch upon which to perch. We were all anxious – what on earth had we let ourselves in for!

But it got better. The days were warm and sunny, and people strolled in the evenings and at weekends in their Sunday best. We experienced the Soviet Union enjoying a brief period of stability and modest prosperity, ushered in by the reforms Leonid Brezhnev had introduced since taking over as Soviet leader, just five years before our inauspicious arrival.

Cynics might say there was little to compare with the amenities and entertainments available in the West. The few cafes that existed stocked little except black bread, dry cakes and pickled gherkins. Fruit must have existed somewhere in a country with vast tracts of fertile land, but it was nowhere to be seen in the northern towns and cities.

Vodka and beer were plentiful and abject drunkenness commonplace; vodka for the men, beer for the women. The fact that the two male members of our quartet, both blonds with long hair down their backs, eschewed the vodka and drank the beer, while the two females drank the vodka, raised many an eyebrow. The alcohol clearly went a long way to ameliorate the sheer drabness of people, places and life in general.

There appeared to be no 'fashion', just plain, standard-issue clothing; no neon; virtually no cars, except black limousines for the Party hierarchy; and any personal 'luxuries' had been hidden away or sold by their owners long ago.

There were several other revelations, too, some confirming well-known stereotypes. Most of the members of the road gangs were, indeed, women – and women of such proportions that arguing with them about the right of way, or a stop sign, would not have been wise. Similarly, there were cohorts of very large, heavily muscled men walking the streets, who would have found ample employment on the doors of Soho's clubs and bars. Bespectacled intellectuals, complete with goatee beards and mariner's caps, bearing more than a passing resemblance to Vladimir Ilyich Ulyanov – Lenin – could be found quietly reading heavy tomes in the parks, or on the buses and trains. An equally large group could be seen, heads down in earnest contemplation, grappling with complex openings or end-games, in huge open-air chess gatherings.

There were police everywhere; we had to report to them at every location in which we stayed. We were followed on several occasions and came across large groups of soldiers with seemingly little to do. Although there was a mild aura of oppression, there seemed to be no violence or disruption, save for the many drunks to be found prostrate in the parks, on the streets and in the Metro carriages.

Not everything about Soviet life was negative. Education and medical care were free and of an excellent standard; rents were low, and public transport almost free. Everyone had a job, even if just a token one, like the countless war widows who sat all day at the bottom of the escalators on Moscow's Metro, its stations a stunning Stalinist architectural achievement designed to embody *svet* ('radiance and brilliance').

We found a few remarkable comforts, even to relatively affluent Western students. Public water fountains were plentiful, each with glasses laid out on shelves, small jets of water to rinse them, and dispensers of fruit juice with which to fill them. The price? Just a kopek, next to nothing. It was the same on the buses, trams and Metro; there were no ticket collectors, just an honesty box for a couple of kopeks. In 1969, one kopek – one-hundredth of a Russian rouble – was worth just over a penny.

Small ice-cream carts could be found on many street corners. The Russians love ice cream. In Soviet days it was said there were only three reasons to travel to the Soviet Union: the ballet, the state circus and ice cream. In the 1930s, the state had decreed that only natural ingredients could be used in the making of ice cream, and the result was a very milky, very delicious treat, served between biscuits and beautifully wrapped in silver foil. The price: three kopeks. Thruppence!

When we left the Soviet Union, across the Danube in what is now Moldova, we travelled through Romania, Bulgaria and Yugoslavia, each of which had its own distinct version of Soviet communism. Romania was perhaps even duller and drabber, but at least it had Castle Dracula. Bulgaria was similarly gloomy, but it had Varna, the Black Sea, and sandy beaches. Tito's Yugoslavia was far more relaxed, and it had the Adriatic. It also had fruit, and – a little bit of heaven after several weeks of black bread – French fries!

Years later, during my career as a documentary film-maker, my travels took me to many parts of Soviet Eastern Europe and to the Soviet Union. I was able to revisit most of the places I had first visited in 1969, but after their regimes had changed. I had the unnerving experience of walking across Checkpoint Charlie from an affluent, cosmopolitan West Berlin to an all but deserted, and distinctly oppressive, East Berlin. The same night, I wandered down the famous Unter den Linden to the towering Brandenburg Gate. The entire boulevard was devoid of people and bathed in an eerie half-light of sporadic street lighting. Normal life did not seem to exist. Even though this was a major city, where were the bars, cafes, restaurants? More to the point, where were the East Berliners?

The scene made me think about the previous fifty years of history and everything that had happened between Germany and the Soviet Union. East Berlin was still wrapped in a cocoon born of the Second World War; it was an uncanny experience.

A central part of my work was the search for archive films of the twentieth century – especially rare colour film – which took me to Moscow several times. Those treasure hunts, and the friends and colleagues I encountered along the way, made me appreciate several things about the psychology of the Russian people. Not only do they adore their history and take great pride in their achievements, but they also have an impressive intellectual pedigree. Music, literature, art and academic curiosity figure prominently in their lives. Their archives, often stored in somewhat tired buildings, are kept immaculately, and the information needed to make use of their content is meticulously recorded. The procedures involved in working in Russia can be somewhat bureaucratic, but, unlike in many countries, at least there are procedures. Moreover, there is no shortage of devoted historians, translators and lovers of old film, willing and eager to assist with extremely diligent research.

By the 1980s, the cracks in the edifice of Soviet communism were as wide as Red Square, and its satellite states were in a sorry state of downtrodden resentment. I remember being in Sofia in 1987. After a goodbye lunch of clear, greasy soup enhanced by a few slivers of mutton – and, yes, accompanied by black bread – we toured the city as my hosts tried to buy me a bottle of excellent local wine as a present to take home. Alas, and to their considerable embarrassment, we were unable to find even a single bottle in the entire city. Bulgaria was at that time the fourth largest exporter of wine in the world, and yet none was available in the humble shops of its capital city. Bulgaria had been an ally of Germany during the war, but it was currently existing in quite stifling and straightened circumstances, under the dominance of Moscow. It was impossible to see the country as anything but a beleaguered child of the Second World War.

Russia and Eastern Europe are quite different places now – and, sadly, in Russia, they eat the same ice cream as the rest of the world. Although much of the Soviet Empire was lost in the wake of its collapse in 1991, the new Russian Federation is still a vast state, much of it remote and still beset by rural poverty. Even in the cities, massive swathes of poorly built residential tower blocks are the norm, where modest lives are lived in stark contrast with the enormous wealth of those who have benefitted from the country's vast reserves of oil and gas. Decades of state socialism have been replaced by an unbridled clamour for wealth under the watchful eye of Vladimir Putin.

Moscow's streets swarm with luxurious cars; restaurants and bars abound, full of bright young things, eating and drinking well, where pasta, pizza and American steaks have supplanted borscht and stroganoff. Long gone are the black bread and pickled cucumbers; the shops are now full of every delicacy, the finest Swiss watches and the latest designer clothes and handbags.

But through all the changes in modern Russian history – from medieval tsars to communist dictators; from Gorbachev to Yeltsin to Putin; through revolutions, wars and purges; in suffering and in death – the Russian people have remained the same.

Theirs is a long and complex history. It is the story of a vast and diverse continental empire stretching across half the globe – an empire of multiple nationalities, cultures and languages – rather than the story of a unified nation. It reflects the ethnic mix of the many peoples who have crossed the wide expanses of 'Mother Russia'. The original Slavs came from the east, but the ninth and tenth centuries saw Viking migrations from the north, along the country's huge rivers, bringing trade and new rulers who held sway from the Baltic to the Black Sea. The trade routes established links to the Byzantine Empire and opened Russia to the rest of the world. In the thirteenth century, the Mongols invaded, destroying many cities, including Kiev and Moscow, before eventually being expelled by Ivan the Great, whose grandson became the first Tsar of Russia in 1547.

The harsh climate and environment in which they live, and the many adversities they have faced over the centuries, have made the Russian people resolute and, at times, taciturn. But beneath the rugged facade, which visitors may see as cheerless, even rude, there is genuine warmth, a generosity, and a strong belief in the common good. It is not a communist vision of the 'common good' – although it formed part of the people's ready acceptance of socialism – but more a collective willpower, a belief in the strength of the culture and traditions of Mother Russia. They call it the 'soul' of Russia, and it is expressed in its music, dance, literature and architecture. Many have searched for Russia's soul, including Gogol and Tolstoy. Dostoevsky said of it, 'It's frightening how free a Russian man's spirit is, how strong is his will!'

Such generalisations veer towards stereotypes, but they are more revealing than the harsh perceptions frequently held in the West, derived from the Cold War and the autocracy of Vladimir Putin. Overall, regardless of what their leaders have desired, the Russian mentality has shown itself not to be aggressive. It is passive, even fatalistic. The Russian people are stoics, not warmongers.

But when threatened, their collective will imparts great strength; their soul allows them to endure and to resist. These are the qualities they brought to bear in their enormous struggle during the Second World War, empowering them to survive and, ultimately, to win the bloodiest war in history.

I have grown fond of the Russian 'soul'. This book is, in part, my homage to those intangible phenomena that define it.

Stewart Binns

INTRODUCTION: DRAWING THE IDEOLOGICAL BATTLE LINES

This account of the extraordinary events that took place on the Eastern Front of the Second World War, between 1941 and 1945, will examine the conflict exclusively from the point of view of those who faced the German onslaught, both combatants and non-combatants. Whether they be Russian, or one of the many other nationalities drawn into the fight, it will be their letters, diaries and first-hand accounts that will underpin this book's narrative.

The story of the Eastern Front is not well known outside contemporary Russia and Germany. The Western nations were only indirectly involved, and their historians have tended to concentrate on the events that involved Britain, the USA and their Commonwealth allies, rather than the war in the east. There are some notable exceptions, the horrors of the Battle of Stalingrad being one such example. However, even in most accounts of that almighty battle, the central focus has been on the catastrophic defeat of the Wehrmacht, Germany's forces, rather than the heroic victory of the Red Army of the Soviet Union.

It is important to put the enormous conflict on the Eastern Front into the broader perspective of Russia's recent history. At the start of the twentieth century, Russia had been ruled by Romanov tsars for three centuries. The Romanovs had modernised the country in the seventeenth and eighteenth centuries, laying the foundations for a vast Russian Empire that extended from the Baltic to Alaska, and building a new capital, St Petersburg.

During the enlightened reign of Catherine the Great, Russia's power and influence grew throughout the eighteenth century. Its empire extended westwards into Poland, Prussia and the Habsburg Empire and southwards as far as the Crimea, making it a world power of some significance. Inevitably, Russia's size and status brought it into conflict with its equally formidable neighbours – the Ottoman Empire, Britain and France – and resulted in crippling defeat in the Crimean War in 1856.

In 1914, in defence of Serbia, Russia joined Britain and France in the Great War against Germany and its allies, Austria-Hungary and the Ottoman Empire. The Great War had a disastrous impact on Russia. Militarily, feudal Russia was no match for industrialised Germany, and Russian casualties were greater than those sustained by any nation in any previous war. Food and fuel shortages escalated, and inflation spiralled. Coupled with long-term unrest after centuries of oppression from medieval tsars, revolutionary change was inevitable.

In 1917, amidst great turmoil and violence, Lenin led his revolutionary socialist Bolshevik Party to power in a coup. A protracted civil war, during which opponents of the Bolsheviks were supported by Western allies – including Germany, Britain and the United States – broke out later that year, with Lenin's Red Army eventually claiming victory. Lenin declared the establishment of the Soviet Union in 1922, which, as Chairman of the Council of the People's Commissars, he ruled until his death in 1924.

Lenin was succeeded as leader not by a Russian but by a Georgian, Joseph Stalin, who consolidated his dictatorial rule through draconian economic policies and vicious purges, which included mass executions and imprisonments. The purges were a harrowing time for those who lived through them.

Lyubov Shaporina was part of the Soviet Union's pre-revolutionary intelligentsia, a prime target for Stalin's terrors. The founder of the Leningrad Puppet Theatre, she was married to composer Yuri Shaporin. In her diary from the time, she recalls the run-up to the elections for the new Supreme Soviet legislature on 12 December 1937. The elections followed the adoption of Stalin's new Soviet Constitution, which had been declared in 1936.

'Leningrad USSR

On the 22nd [November] *I woke up at about three and couldn't go back to sleep till after five. There were no trams, it was completely quiet outside. Suddenly I heard a burst of gunfire. And then another. The shooting continued in bursts every ten to twenty minutes until just after five.*

I opened the window and listened, trying to decide where the shots were coming from. What could it mean? The Peter and Paul Fortress is nearby, that was the only place where shooting could be coming from. Were people being executed?

That is what they call an election campaign. And our consciousness is so deadened that sensations just glide across its hard, glossy surface, leaving no impression. To spend all night hearing living people, and undoubtedly innocent people, being shot to death and not lose your mind. And afterwards just fall asleep . . . How terrible.

Irina Detskaya came home from school and said, "They told us there are mass arrests going on right now. We need to rid ourselves of undesirable elements before the election." [. . .]'

In callously deceitful contrast, just three weeks later, on 11 December, the eve of the election, Comrade Stalin gave a speech to voters in Moscow's Bolshoi Theatre. It was greeted by a loud ovation, lasting for several minutes, with cries of 'Long live great Stalin, Hurrah!', 'Hurrah for Comrade Stalin, the creator of the Soviet Constitution, the most democratic in the world!', 'Long live Comrade Stalin, leader of the oppressed throughout the world. Hurrah!'

Stalin's words in his election speech were the height of duplicity.

For my part, I would like to assure you, comrades, that you may safely rely on Comrade Stalin . . . You may take it for granted that Comrade Stalin will be able to discharge his duty to the people, to the working class, to the peasantry and to the intelligentsia . . . The forthcoming elections are not merely elections, comrades, they are really a national holiday of our workers, our peasants and our intelligentsia. Never in the history of the world have there been such free and democratic elections, never! History knows no other example like it . . . our universal elections will be carried out as the freest elections and the most democratic compared with elections in any other country in the world.

In 1938, Shaporina reflected on the show trials conducted after the arrest of several senior Red Army officers: *'The great, great Dostoevsky. We now see, not in a dream, but right before our eyes, the herd of devils that entered into the swine. We see them as we've never seen them before. Never have people worked so hard to destroy their homeland . . . The really dangerous ones are Stalin and Voroshilov* [People's Commissar for the Defence of the Soviet Union] *. . . It is unbelievable to be living in the middle of it all. It's like walking around in a slaughterhouse, with the air saturated with the smell of blood and carrion.'*

Volha Barouskaya is the last living witness to the mass executions that were commonplace during Stalin's Great Purge. She was ninety years old when she told her story, in 2017. In 1938, she was an eleven-year-old girl picking wild berries in the Kurapaty Woods near Minsk, Belorussia, when she stumbled across a mass execution: *'I was very scared when I heard women yelling. "Why are you doing this to us? My God, what have we done? What are we guilty of?" I can't even describe how loud they were yelling. There were lots of tears. People in uniform put them on their knees, facing the pit. The executioners started from behind, and then came the bang-bang-bang, like peas on a frying pan . . . They fell, they fell, they fell . . . I was lucky, I found somewhere to hide in a wolf's den. Many people died there. My mother told me never to breathe a word about it.'*

Barouskaya kept her secret until 1988, when the burial site was discovered. It is estimated to be the resting place of at least 30,000 people, murdered by Stalin's secret police, the NKVD (People's Commissariat for Internal Affairs).

Stalin had an executioner-in-chief, Nikolai Yezhov, during his Great Purge. Less than five feet tall, Yezhov was called the 'bloodthirsty dwarf'. As head of the NKVD, he had free rein to eliminate anyone who stood in Stalin's way, and, for that matter, thousands more who were just in the wrong place at the wrong time. A man totally without compassion or remorse, he wrote: *'There will be some innocent victims in this fight against Fascist agents. We are launching a major attack on the Enemy; let there be no resentment if we bump someone with an elbow. Better that ten innocent people should suffer than one spy gets away. When you chop wood, chips fly.'*

Yezhov was a relentless sadist, who often carried out his own tortures. In 1937 and 1938 alone, he oversaw at least 1.3 million arrests and 681,692 executions for 'crimes against the state'. He was responsible for the administration of a system of Soviet labour camps, known as 'gulags', whose population swelled by 685,201 under his jurisdiction, nearly tripling in size in just two years. At least 140,000 of these prisoners (and probably many more) died of malnutrition, exhaustion and the dreadful conditions in the camps; many did not even survive the tortuous journeys to get to them.

Perhaps inevitably, Yezhov fell foul of Stalin's murderous regime. Having vigorously pursued his task of liquidating those who Stalin wished to remove by the end of 1938, he was replaced as head of the NKVD by Lavrentiy Beria, the party chief in Georgia, who had only narrowly escaped Yezhov's death warrant by making a personal appeal to Stalin.

Beria was not far off being Yezhov's clone; another sadist, he enjoyed the torture and pain of his victims and had a particular penchant for beating and raping young women. Beria had Yezhov arrested and, after a secret trial, Stalin's former henchman was dragged, shouting and screaming, to his execution in a basement room he himself had had designed for that purpose. He had specified a sloping floor so that blood could easily be sluiced away. His demise was kept so secret that, for several years afterwards, it was reported that he was being kept in an 'asylum for the insane'.

Despite the terrors, ruthless despots have their uses. Just as Hitler and Mussolini were admired in their countries, building roads and making the railways run on time, Stalin's draconian rule transformed the country from an agrarian economy into a military and industrial power capable of withstanding the immense challenges of the Second World War.

Importantly for any appreciation of the psychology of Russian leaders and the Russian people, it is crucial to remember that throughout the long history of Mother Russia, her vast empire has been repeatedly attacked by her neighbours. These challenges have come not only from the west, but also from the east and the south. At various times, Japan, Britain, France, Germany, Finland, Sweden and the Ottomans have challenged Russia's vast borders.

It is also important to note that Russia is not one homogeneous nation. Its disparate ethnic groups, nationalities, religions, languages and cultures – especially when the Russian Empire was at its greatest extent – have also brought significant dissent and opposition within its borders. Today, following the dissolution of the old Soviet Empire and the independence of fifteen new nations, from the Baltic to the Pamirs of Central Asia, 80 per cent of the population of the Russian Federation are ethnic Russians, but there are significant numbers of Tatars, Ukrainians, Bashkirs, Chuvash, Chechen and Armenians, all of whom live within the Russian Federation.

•

Wars change history; that is why the protagonists fight them. Wars transform nations, change continents, and sometimes shift the axis of the global balance of power for generations to come.

The horrors of the religious wars of the Crusades left a legacy of bitterness that still resonates in the Middle East to this day. Not only did the wars of Qin Shi Huang give us his mausoleum and its guardians, the Terracotta Army, but they also gave birth to the empire that is modern China. The Napoleonic Wars created twentieth-century Europe, while the Spanish Wars of Conquest against the Aztec and Inca empires laid the foundations of South America, as did the French and British colonial wars in Africa, South-East Asia and the Indian subcontinent.

The Eastern Front has left a long legacy. It was the crucial theatre of a war that created post-war Europe, heralded the Cold War and was the prelude to the precarious stalemate that exists today in the political stand-off between the United States, Russia and China. Our twenty-first-century world has just entered a new era of uncertainty and anxiety, and the seeds of the current tensions were sown on the battlefields of the bloodiest war in history.

Wars are sometimes just, but never pure; never clean. They are bestial, a shocking illustration of the cold heart of humanity at its worst. But they can also exemplify courage, heroism and self-sacrifice. They are never easy to understand, or to explain.

The war on the Eastern Front between 1941 and 1945, which began with Operation Barbarossa in the early hours of Sunday 22 June 1941, was the epitome of human savagery let loose on an unprecedented scale. But it was also an extraordinary example of the strength and resolve of the human spirit, the power of the collective will and a belief in the common good. It led to an astonishing victory, but it was won at a terrible price.

The casualty figures from the war are staggering. The figure for German military losses, so imprecise that it is rounded to the nearest 100,000, was 5.1 million. A further 4.5 million were captured, most of whom never made it home. Soviet military losses were even higher. Such were the chaotic circumstances that estimates vary between 8.7 million and 10 million. A further 5.7 million were captured, most of whom were executed, starved, or perished in labour camps. The figures for civilian deaths are an even bigger guess, but they were at least 20 million, perhaps even 25 million. In total, at least 40 million died – approximately two-thirds of the global deaths in the whole of the Second World War. It cost more lives, both military and civilian, than any other conflict in history.

The war on the Eastern Front, what the Russians call the 'Great Patriotic War', was a war of ideological extremism, of racial hatred, of atrocities that almost defy description, and of battles that are some of the largest and most bloodthirsty ever fought.

From its outset, Germany's Führer, Adolf Hitler, intended his campaign to be a *Vernichtungskrieg* (a 'war of annihilation'). He believed that for Germany to fulfil its destiny it needed *Lebensraum* ('living space'), and to solve the 'Jewish Problem' by eliminating the Jews he hated so much. His loathing of Jews was pathological. He believed them to be responsible for Germany's woes, and was convinced they were at the heart of two ideologies he despised: Bolshevism in the Soviet Union, and social democracy in Europe and the United States. His campaign also had a pragmatic necessity. He needed oil to fuel his machines of war, and the Soviet Union had oil in abundance.

Hitler described the vast, fertile lands to the east as 'Germany's India', and called it the 'Wild East', analogous with America's Wild West. The Wild East was the key to creating the 'Greater Germany' he craved, a vast homeland for the German people, the *Volk* he revered.

In Hitler's convoluted psyche there was a historical imperative that he was compelled to follow: in order to achieve the global domination he craved, he had to conquer the huge lands to his east – and destroy their inhabitants. These *Untermenschen* ('sub-humans' or 'inferior people') would provide the slave labour he needed. The abundant resources would create the raw materials to drive his economy. Then, armed with his Greater German Empire, he would bring to heel his greatest rivals: Britain and the United States.

The conquest of the Soviet Union was not an end in itself, merely a means to an end. Frighteningly, in Hitler's diabolical logic, his *Ostkrieg* ('East War') would be only a precursor to an even mightier struggle to come: the capitulation of the Western democracies, either by their submission to his rule, or by their total destruction.

Hitler did not lack a knowledge or understanding of history, but he did ignore its lessons. After his victories in Western Europe, buoyed by power, he saw himself as an Alexander or a Napoleon, with the world at his feet, forgetting that neither Alexander's nor Napoleon's maraudings ended well.

His expansionist obsessions – which would prove to be delusions – led to global catastrophe. As a result of his war in the east, almost an entire generation was wiped out, vast tracts of land were laid to waste and entire industries were destroyed. He turned his personal dreams into nightmares for his people. Eight out of every ten German soldiers who died during the Second World War died on the Eastern Front. His vainglorious 'Thousand Year Reich' ended in the rubble and stench of Germany's devastated cities and in the total humiliation of its people.

Even today, over seventy-five years since the end of the conflict, German wounds have not fully healed; the memories linger still, and they are beginning to polarise the country. The guilt, shame and remorse that are still felt by many stand in stark contrast to potent opposing views, which claim that Germany has paid its price, needs to forget its past and must assert itself once more.

The war left the Soviet Union in ruins, leading to years of stagnation and the traumas of the Cold War. Having defeated Germany's foreign dictator, Adolf Hitler, the Soviet people continued to live under the heel of their own home-grown tyrant, Joseph Stalin. He dominated his people for another eight years, who then had to live on under an oppressive and increasingly inefficient Soviet regime until 1991. Ultimately, the mighty Soviet Empire went into rapid decline and ended in a sudden and spectacular downfall. We hear the echoes of the collapse every day in our news: in Ukraine, in Syria, in new forms of sophisticated espionage, and even in the US presidential elections. Contemporary Russian nationalism is rooted in the bitter memories of the Motherland being despoiled by countless invaders, who were the precursors of Hitler's Wehrmacht and the murderous ideology embodied by Operation Barbarossa.

•

In the summer of 1941, the Russian Revolution and the Civil War that followed it, ending in 1922, had happened less than twenty years earlier. Despite the brutality of the communist regime in Moscow's Kremlin, huge progress had been made in industry and infrastructure. Illiteracy had been eliminated, life expectancy had reached Western European levels, women had been granted equal status with men, and many of the inefficiencies and economic disasters that would loom in later years had yet to come to pass.

It is also largely forgotten that the Soviet Union's military resources in 1941, in terms of materiel and soldiers, were significant – and were, indeed, in large part superior to those of Germany. The Red Army had more than 300 divisions, boasted 5.5 million soldiers, was well equipped, and supported from the skies above by the world's largest air force.

In short, despite Stalin's gulags and mass murders, there was sufficient pride, courage and determination in the hearts and minds of a people only recently freed from centuries of oppression by the tsars of the Romanov dynasty, to enable them to defeat the Nazi invaders. However, it was a victory won at a terrible price – both for the victors and the vanquished.

As an ex-soldier of modest calibre – and like most people with some experience of military matters and the psychology of soldiering – I remain intrigued by two enduring puzzles. First of all, from where and from what depths of human endurance and courage did the defenders of their Eastern European homelands find the strength to resist such a brutal onslaught as Barbarossa? It is perhaps an even more fascinating conundrum, given that the catastrophic first few months of the war were such a disaster when, in the main, the Red Army was in total disarray. Similarly, when glorious victories turned into humiliating defeats, from where did Germany, its soldiers and civilians, find the resolve to continue to fight all the way to Hitler's bunker in the heart of Berlin?

This book draws on intimate, first-hand accounts, several of which have not been published before, written by people who lived through the war, offering us a unique insight into this extraordinary conflict. Their letters and diaries, many of which have lain unremembered and unread in archives and museums, record the agonies they endured, and provide an intimate account of what it was like to live and die during those most terrible times. By giving their authors a voice, it attempts to arrive at an answer to these two fundamental questions.

Sadly, as we shall see, one everlasting truth permeates all the accounts: suffering never seems to be very far away for the people of Russia.

PART ONE

INVASION

1

A PACT WITH SATAN TO DRIVE OUT THE DEVIL

AUGUST 1939-JUNE 1941

Historians have been prone to link together Adolf Hitler, Germany's Führer, and Joseph Stalin, the Soviet Union's communist tsar, as the twentieth century's 'terrible twins' of evil. But to pair them as two identical monsters is far too simplistic; they were as different as they were similar.

Stalin's original Georgian name was Dzhugashvili. He changed it to Stalin in 1912. The name derives from the Russian for steel (*stal*), thus 'Man of Steel'. He also had the nickname 'Koba', which he picked up in his youth after a Robin Hood character in the 1882 novel *Patricide* by Alexander Kazbegi. Stalin purported to be an ideological Marxist, philosophically determined to create a truly egalitarian society, even if he had to murder hundreds of thousands of his own people to achieve his socialist Utopia. He was not the first so inclined, nor would he be the last.

Conversely, Hitler was totally committed to theories, often melded together as Social Darwinism, which espouse the idea that, throughout history, races have struggled with other races in a survival battle that will ultimately produce a 'master race'. In particular, Hitler was convinced that this human struggle had reached a pinnacle of evolution and that his Germanic peoples were the *Herrenvolk* ('master race'), the high point of human progress, and that their destiny was to conquer the world.

Through ruthless opportunism, Stalin quickly rose from rural poverty in Georgia to supreme leadership of the Soviet Kremlin. Once in power, he used the formidable apparatus of a police state to liquidate millions of opponents, including any who stood in the way of communist purity. Millions more died in famines, and huge numbers were transported to forced labour camps – the gulags – from which many never emerged.

Hitler's rise to power was equally rapid. He was also utterly ruthless in dealing with opponents, but it was his racial fanaticism – his loathing of Jews, Slavs and many others he regarded as inferior – that made him uniquely evil, even when compared with Stalin. Hitler referred to those he despised as 'vermin'; he regarded them as 'infestations' that had to be eliminated without mercy. So virulent was his loathing and so potent was his oratory that his views permeated German society, swelling into a plague of hatred that distorted civilised life like nothing before or since.

These 'terrible twins', two malevolent leaders of such monstrous proportions, were preparing to confront one another in a military campaign that would produce the bloodiest war in history.

•

Strangely, the background to this most gruesome of wars was an extraordinary expression of peace, even if an entirely amoral one. In August 1939, despite their ideological differences, strategic pragmatism, as it often does, led to a remarkable deal between Hitler and Stalin. It was best described as 'a pact with Satan to drive out the Devil', uniting them in a macabre display of mock friendship.

The countdown to the Second World War had begun in March 1936, when German troops rolled into the Rhineland, which had been demilitarised by the Versailles Treaty at the end of the Great War. Benito Mussolini, Hitler's ally, had already sent his troops into Ethiopia, and in the summer of 1937 Japan's army was on the march in China. Fascist militarism was rampant across the globe.

In March 1938, Hitler strode into Austria, an Anschluss ('connection') that united the German-speaking country of his birth with the German 'Fatherland'. Six months later, at the end of September, still plagued by bitter memories of the Great War, France and Britain allowed Hitler to occupy the Sudetenland, a German-speaking part of Czechoslovakia.

The poet Hannah Senesh was living in Budapest, Hungary, when Hitler occupied the Sudetenland. She was just seventeen and still at school.

'September 1938, Budapest

We're living through incredibly tense days. The question is: will there be war? The entire world is united in fearful suspense. The Devil take the Sudeten Germans and all the other Germans, along with the Führer. Why is it necessary to ruin the world, turn it topsy-turvy, when everything could be so pleasant? Or is that impossible? Is it contrary to the nature of man?'

Senesh kept her diary throughout the war. A passionate Zionist, she fled to Palestine in 1939, while her homeland, Hungary, was the first country to join the Axis powers – Germany, Italy and Japan – in June 1941. She was recruited by Britain's Special Operations Executive and in March 1944 parachuted into Yugoslavia to assist anti-Nazi forces in the rescue of Hungarian Jews about to be deported to Auschwitz. She was arrested at the Hungarian border by the Hungarian police, who found her British military transmitter. She was imprisoned, stripped, tied to a chair, then whipped and clubbed for three days. She lost several teeth as a result of the beating.

Transferred to a Budapest prison, she was repeatedly interrogated and tortured, but only revealed her name and refused to provide the transmitter code, even when her mother was also arrested. They threatened to kill her mother if she did not cooperate, but still she refused.

She kept a diary until her last day. One of the entries reads: *'In the month of July, I shall be twenty-three. I played a number in a game. The dice have rolled. I have lost.'*

Senesh was executed by firing squad on 7 November 1944.

•

Hitler's annexation of the whole of Czechoslovakia in March 1939 and his triumphant entry into Prague were further steps in a dominoes cascade of aggression that few wanted to acknowledge was happening. War was all but inevitable.

It was clear that Hitler's next planned conquest would be his neighbour Poland. To thwart him, on 31 March, France and Britain promised to guarantee Poland's security and independence. However, Hitler was ahead of the game. Even though he had called the Soviet Union 'the greatest danger for the culture and civilisation of mankind which has ever threatened it since the collapse of the . . . ancient world', his greater ambition compelled him, for the time being, to put to one side his virulent hostility towards communism in order to secure his eastern border.

Through the spring and summer of 1939, Hitler berated the Polish government in Warsaw, demanding that Germany be allowed to reclaim the port of Danzig, a former German city internationalised by the Treaty of Versailles. He also claimed that ethnic Germans living in Western Poland were being mistreated and demanded they be liberated.

However, despite Stalin's purges of his military elites in 1937 and 1938, which had seriously weakened his forces, Hitler and his generals were wary of a scenario that would repeat the nightmare of the Great War – a conflict on two fronts, where Germany and its allies fought Russian troops in the east and French and British troops in the west.

To avoid such an alarming outcome, in August 1939, Hitler's Foreign Minister, Joachim von Ribbentrop, flew from Berlin to Moscow. He was soon inside the Kremlin's towering walls, face-to-face with Stalin and Soviet Foreign Minister, Vyacheslav Molotov, who had been working with Ribbentrop to negotiate an agreement. Ribbentrop carried a proposal from Hitler, suggesting that both countries commit to a non-aggression pact that would last a hundred years; Stalin replied that ten years would be enough! He just needed time to continue the build-up of his armed forces in readiness for the future conflict with Germany that he knew was inevitable.

The proposal contained a secret protocol, which, in colloquial parlance, was a territorial 'stitch-up'. It specified the spheres of influence in Eastern Europe that both parties would accept. Germany would occupy Western Poland, including Warsaw, while the Soviet

Union would acquire the eastern half of Poland, along with the Baltic States.

The protocol was startlingly blunt.

1. In the event of a territorial and political rearrangement in the areas belonging to the Baltic States (Finland, Estonia, Latvia, Lithuania), the northern boundary of Lithuania shall represent the boundary of the spheres of interest of Germany and the USSR. In this respect, the interests in the Vilna [Vilnius] area are recognised by each party.

2. In the event of a territorial and political rearrangement of the area belonging to the Polish state, the spheres of influence of Germany and the USSR shall be bounded approximately by the rivers Narew, Vistula and San.

3. With regard to South-Eastern Europe, attention is called by the Soviet side to its interests in Bessarabia [between Moldova and Ukraine]. The German side declares its complete political disinterest in these areas.

4. This protocol shall be treated by both parties as strictly secret.

Satan had bought himself the time he needed to expand his armed forces, while the Devil had secured his eastern border until such time as he was ready to launch his mighty onslaught eastwards.

Sergo Beria, the son of Lavrentiy Beria, the head of the NKVD from 1938, wrote an account of his father's life, which was published in English in 2000. A teenager at the outbreak of war, Sergo was close to his father and privy to the machinations of life in the Kremlin. Although much of the book attempts to bolster the claim that his father, 'Stalin's Butcher', was not the evil apparatchik condemned by history, it does offer a unique view of the intrigues, jealousies and plots that typified life inside the Soviet Politburo (the executive committee of the communist regime) during the war.

The younger Beria offers us an insight into Stalin's manoeuvring around the non-aggression pact with Germany, amidst the power politics operating in Europe at the time:

'*Down to the last moment my father tried to persuade Stalin not to sign the German–Soviet Pact. The Germans were negotiating with Britain through Sweden, and with us. When Stalin concluded that the British and French were deceiving us, he wound up the whole business in 48 hours, without consulting the Politburo. The Politburo was far from unanimously enthusiastic, but Stalin explained that war with Germany was inevitable and that this pact was only provisional. It was necessary to win time and to make sure that the USSR would not have to face Hitler alone.*'

Valentin Berezhkov, Stalin's interpreter in both German and English, wrote about his time with Stalin in detail in his 1994 memoir, *At Stalin's Side*. In it, he confirms the Machiavellian nature of Satan's pact with the Devil: '*Stalin was reasoning, Germany's readiness to sign the pact clearly showed that its government had decided to attack not the East, but the West. This conflict could turn out to be quite protracted, which would enable the Soviet Union to stay out of it until Stalin concluded it was time to get involved. In terms of that time and place, this was a logical way of thinking. Every country that was potentially a target for Nazi aggression was reasoning roughly along the same lines.*'

Soviet General Georgy Zhukov, who would soon become a key player in the war to come, dismissed Britain and France's diplomacy in 1939 as both naive and cowardly: '*While bombs had not yet begun to explode in their own home, the class interests of the long-standing allies in the struggle against the first socialist state boiled down to one and the same thing – they kept bowing to Hitler.*'

He later quoted Alfred Jodl, Hitler's leading general, speaking at his war crimes trial at Nuremburg in 1945: '*If we did not collapse already in 1939 that was due to the fact that during the Polish Campaign, the approximately 110 French and British divisions in the West were held completely inactive against 23 German divisions.*'

Dawid Sierakowiak, a fourteen-year-old son of a Jewish family in Łódź, Poland, saw the events of 1939 very differently. With thousands of his fellow Poles, he was one of the first of millions who stood in the way of the terror to come: '*Terrible, interesting, strange news! The Germans are concluding a non-aggression pact with*

*the Soviets! What a turnabout! What a capitulation of Nazi ideology!
The Soviets apparently do not want to interfere in European politics . . .
Mobilisation! We don't know if this is the real thing or not, but nearly
every recruit is mobilising. Many of our neighbours have already gone . . .
There's not the least hint of defeatism. There are tens of thousands of
volunteers . . . old Jews, young women, Hasidic Jews, all citizens (except
Germans) are rushing to volunteer. The bloody Hun will not pass!'*

Still believing, somewhat naively, that France and Great Britain
would not meet their treaty obligations to Poland, and knowing
he had nothing to fear from the Soviet Army, Hitler ordered his
troops to strike eastwards into Poland on 1 September 1939. Two
days later, France and Great Britain declared war on Germany. The
catastrophe that was the Second World War had begun.

Sierakowiak witnessed the German invasion.

*'Friday 1st September: The German army has crossed the border
in several places. Things are boiling around the world. We are waiting
for France and England to join the war, maybe even the United States.
Meanwhile, we're repelling German attacks quite well. I shall go to bed
half-dressed.'*

Sierakowiak's optimism soon evaporated. Hitler's *Blitzkrieg*
('lightning war') overwhelmed Polish forces in the west.

*'September 6th: Oh God, what's going on! Panic, departures en
masse, defeatism. The city, abandoned by its institutions and the police,
awaits the imminent arrival of the German army in terror. People are
running nervously from place to place, anxiously carrying around their
worn-out possessions. There is crying and lamenting in the streets. Reservists and recruits are running away. Following them are women carrying
bundles on their backs, filled with clothes, bedding and food. Even small
children are running.*

*September 12th: Jews are being seized, beaten and robbed. The store
where my father works was robbed as the local Germans freely indulge
their whims. People speak about the way Jews are treated at work. Some
are treated decently but others are sadistically abused. Some Jews were
ordered to stop working, to remove their clothes and stand and face the
wall, at which point they said they would be shot. Shots were fired in*

their direction, and although nobody was killed, it was repeated several times.'

Stalin's invasion of Poland from the east began on 17 September. Caught in a vice between two hugely powerful aggressors, Poland fell in just thirty-five days.

Sierakowiak kept his diary until August 1943, when he died of tuberculosis in the Łódź Ghetto. His last entry reads: *'I so very much want to live and survive.'* His sister died in the concentration camp at Auschwitz-Birkenau.

For the rest of 1939 and into 1940, both Germany and the Soviet Union used their pact to consolidate their positions. In Britain and France, the period became known as the 'Phoney War', during which, from their perspective, little of military consequence appeared to be happening. But it was far from 'phoney' elsewhere.

At the end of November, the Red Army invaded Finland, opening what became known as the 'Winter War'. The conflict continued until the middle of March 1940, when a peace treaty was signed – the Moscow Peace Treaty – in which Finland conceded 11 per cent of its territory and over 30 per cent of its economic resources. Hostilities would later reignite as part of the German attack on the Soviet Union in June 1941, when Finnish forces invaded Soviet-occupied Finnish territory.

The Phoney War came to a dramatic end in the spring of 1940, when German forces struck in Western Europe. Norway and Denmark were invaded on 9 April, and on 10 May the Wehrmacht rolled into the Netherlands, Belgium and Luxembourg. Hitler outflanked the Maginot Line, France's elaborate defensive fortifications, by attacking north of it, through the heavily forested and difficult terrain of the Ardennes.

The Dutch Army surrendered on 14 May, the Belgians on the 28th. By 9 June, Norway had fallen. On the 14th, German soldiers were marching along Paris's Champs-Élysées in triumph. Marshal Pétain's Vichy France was declared on 22 June and on the following day, Adolf Hitler strutted around the tourist sites of Paris as a conquering hero. As he did so, he may well have been imagining that his next pompous swagger would be across the cobblestones of Moscow's Red Square.

As Western Europe was falling under Nazi control, one of the worst atrocities of the war was taking place in the east. After the Red Army had annexed Eastern Poland, the NKVD took thousands of prisoners, many of them Polish soldiers, but it also rounded up hundreds of intellectuals, clergymen, landowners – and any others it disliked. On 5 March 1940, following a recommendation to Stalin from Beria, a document was signed ordering the execution of 25,700 Polish 'nationalists and counter-revolutionaries'.

The executions were mainly carried out in the Katyn Forest, which is now in the Russian Federation, twelve miles west of Smolensk. The death toll by firing squad was at least 22,000. A mass grave of 3,000 Polish officers was discovered in 1942, during the German occupation of the area. When Germany announced the gruesome find and accused the Soviet Union of the crime, the Kremlin denied it. Soviet deceit was compounded when the area of Katyn was liberated by the Red Army, in 1943, and it 'rediscovered' the atrocity. The Kremlin at once laid the blame at the door of the retreating Wehrmacht.

Despite much speculation, denials and counter-denials, this remained the official position until the 1990s, when future Russian President Boris Yeltsin released top-secret files to Polish President, Lech Walesa. The documents finally revealed that the massacre had been an NKVD crime.

STRICTLY CONFIDENTIAL

All-Union Communist Party (Bolsheviks).

CENTRAL COMMITTEE

No. P13/144

Com. Beria.

March 5, 1940

Resolution of March 5, 1940

144. The matter from the NKVD USSR.

I.   Instruct the NKVD USSR:

1) the cases of 14,700 people remaining in the prisoner-of-war camps – former Polish Army officers, government officials, landowners, policemen, intelligence agents, military policemen, settlers and jailers,

2) and also the cases of arrested and remaining in prisons in the western districts of Ukraine and Belorussia people in the number of 11,000 – members of various counter-revolutionary spy and sabotage organizations, former landowners, factory owners, former Polish Army officers, government officials and fugitives – to be considered in a special manner with the obligatory sentence of capital punishment – shooting.

II.   The consideration of the cases to be carried out without the convicts being summoned and without revealing the charges; with no statements concerning the conclusion of the investigation and the bills of indictment given to them. To be carried out in the following manner:

a) people remaining in the prisoner-of-war camps – on the basis of information provided by the Directorate of Prisoner-of-War Affairs NKVD USSR,

b) people arrested – on the basis of case information provided by the NKVD of the Ukrainian SSR and NKVD of the Belorussian SSR.

III.   The responsibility for consideration of the cases and the passing of the resolution to be laid on a troika that consists of C. C. Merkulov, Kobulov and Bashtakov (Head, 1st Special Division of the NKVD USSR).

The Secretary of the CC

Stalin had signed the order, but there were many more with blood on their hands. Included in the documents was Beria's death warrant.

2

FACING THE BLITZKRIEG

JUNE 1941

One of the most crucial factors in securing the remarkable escape of the greater part of the British Expeditionary Force from the beaches and port of Dunkirk in May–June 1940 was Adolf Hitler's obsession with the capture of Paris. He was desperate to humiliate the French, just as they had humbled Germany at the end of the Great War. Twice he halted his panzers (tanks), giving the BEF and its French allies time to organise effective defensive positions around the retreat to the coast. He also made the mistake of listening to his Reichsmarschall, Hermann Göring, who failed to deliver on his promise that his Luftwaffe would destroy the BEF.

Hitler hoped that Britain would, eventually, become party to his megalomaniac vision of world domination by the Aryan races. However, Hitler's analysis of Britain's position was not only ideological but also pragmatic. He assumed that a direct attack on Britain would, almost certainly, bring the United States into the war and, coupled with the resources of Britain's Commonwealth, would, at least in the short term, represent too formidable an opponent, even for the all-conquering Wehrmacht. Although it is often difficult to unravel the volatile logic of Hitler's decision making, it is clear that his desire to destroy Bolshevism, solve the 'Jewish Problem', and create his *Lebensraum* for the German people, found a match in playing a long game with Britain and the United States.

In fact, at the end of the war, in his *Testament*, written in his Berlin bunker in April 1945, Hitler outlined what his thinking had been at the time.

The weight of the human and materiel potential of the USA,
the development of military technology . . . the threatening
proximity of the British coast, all this compelled us to try with
all means to avoid a prolonged war. Time, always time! Would
increasingly work against us. The only way to force the English
to make peace was to take away their hopes of confronting
us on the Continent through the annihilation of the Red
Army. For us there remained no other choice but to strike the
Russian factor out of the European equation.

For Hitler, the logic was clear. He was convinced that, without
Russia as an ally in the European theatre, pragmatism would
prevail within the British establishment and its leaders would sue
for peace, leaving the United States isolated and in an increasingly
perilous position as the Axis powers of Germany, Italy and Japan
slowly but inevitably wore it down.

So, the die was cast; the might of Germany's war machine
would be hurled against the Soviet Union. Planning, under the
code-name 'Operation Otto', began in July 1940. 'Otto' had been
the code-name for the Austrian *Anschluss*, named after Otto von
Habsburg, the Austro-Hungarian crown prince. Hitler authorised
the plan on 18 December 1940. Its objective was bold: it would
result in the total domination of European Russia all the way to
a line stretching from Arkhangel on the White Sea in the Arctic
north, via Kotlas, Kirov and Kazan and then along the Volga River
to Astrakhan on the Caspian Sea to the south. The original estimate
was that it would take the Wehrmacht between nine and seventeen
weeks to achieve its goal.

Dissatisfied with Otto, Hitler demanded a new plan and
renamed it 'Operation Barbarossa', after the great German folk hero
the Holy Roman Emperor, Frederick I, Barbarossa ('Red Beard').

In March 1941, Hitler issued the 'Barbarossa Decree', which
would prove to be a death warrant for tens of millions. In it he
declared that war against Soviet Russia would be a war of extermination, in which, in order to ensure a long-lasting German
victory, both the political and intellectual elites of Russia would

be eradicated by German forces. He specified that executions would not be a matter for military courts, but for the 'organised action of the military'. The decree exempted punishable offences committed by enemy civilians (in Russia) from the jurisdiction of usual military justice. Suspects were to be brought before an officer who would decide if they were to be shot. The decree, one of the most notorious in military history, was carte blanche for brutal and murderous war crimes on a vast scale.

Throughout 1941, Hitler moved more and more men and armaments to the Soviet border. Initially scheduled for an attack in May, Hitler delayed until June, largely because of the Axis invasion of Yugoslavia. Planning for the invasion was detailed and thorough. By the eve of the attack, Germany had assembled the greatest invasion force in the history of warfare. Its state of readiness was a masterpiece of military planning: 3.8 million military personnel, 3,500 tanks and over 3,000 aircraft were primed and ready to roll.

In an invasion characterised by its motorised blitzkrieg strategy, it was nevertheless inevitable that the support infantry would have to cover the vast distances into the Soviet Union on foot. The German High Command was aware that it was short of motorised transport vehicles, necessitating the addition of over 600,000 horses to the invasion inventory. They were used as draught animals for supply lines and for moving artillery. Horses died in the same huge numbers as men and, in the increasingly dire circumstances that unfolded, often became part of the rations of hungry soldiers. Although small in number, cavalry units fought throughout the campaigns of the Eastern Front. By 1945, the Wehrmacht and Waffen SS had six cavalry divisions, while the Red Army had nineteen cavalry corps at the outbreak of hostilities (at least 300,000 horses), and each regular rifle division had at least 3,000 horses as draught animals. The total must have been at least 3.5 million horses engaged on both sides of the conflict.

Hitler organised his forces into three army groups to attack in the north, centre and south, consisting of seven field armies and four panzer groups. His German units were supported by Romanian, Italian, Hungarian, Slovak and Spanish units.

Fully aware of the vast lines of communication that would be required if the German onslaught was to reach its objectives, Hitler's generals knew that a lightning war was the only way victory could be achieved. Many generals tried to convince Hitler that territory was the key, especially Moscow, but the Führer, overconfident after his successes in the west, was certain that the destruction of the Red Army was the primary objective.

The situation within the planning rooms of the Kremlin could not have offered a more startling contrast. During Stalin's purges in the late 1930s, which had not ended by the time of the German invasion, huge numbers of the officer corps of the Red Army had been executed or imprisoned. Their replacements, appointed by Stalin for political reasons, often lacked military competence. Of the five marshals of the Soviet Union appointed in 1935, only two, Kliment Voroshilov and Demyon Budyonny, survived Stalin's purges. Fifteen of the 16 army commanders, 50 of the 57 corps commanders, 154 of the 186 divisional commanders, and 401 of the 456 colonels were killed, and many other officers dismissed. In total, about 30,000 Red Army personnel were executed.

As General Georgy Zhukov explained in his memoirs, Soviet High Command knew what they faced on their border: '*In the spring of 1941, the Nazis had no fear of any serious action by their western opponents. For that reason, the bulk of the German armed forces was concentrated all the way from the Baltic to the Black Sea. Towards June 1941, Germany's armed strength totalled some 8,500,000, an increase of 3,500,000 since 1940, the number of divisions reaching 214.*'

But the Red Army's defence against such a formidable foe largely depended on Stalin's judgement, which was far from infallible, as Zhukov noted: '*Stalin was convinced that the Nazis would first try to seize Ukraine for its grain, the Donets Coal Basin, and, later, Caucasian oil. Stalin was the greatest authority for all of us. It never occurred to any of us to question his opinion. Yet his conjecture as to the main strike of the invader proved incorrect.*'

Facing German forces, the Soviet defenders had only partially completed a mobilisation plan, organised into four fronts, that was not scheduled to end until 1942. In total, the Soviet defenders consisted of 2.7 million troops, 30,000 artillery and mortar weapons, 11,000 armoured vehicles and 7,000 aircraft. Although it was on a formidable scale, much of the materiel was approaching obsolescence, while many of the troops were poorly trained or very raw recruits. However, unlike the Wehrmacht, the Red Army had considerable reserves of manpower under training, far to the east.

Although many intelligence reports warned of the impending German attack, Stalin, for reasons still debated by historians, hesitated. There is no doubt that he feared that the Red Army was not ready to repel an invasion on such a scale. For the same reason, he was also reluctant to provoke Hitler into attacking by making overt defensive plans. However, in the end, his indecisiveness would prove costly.

3

A WARM SUNNY MORNING

JUNE 1941

The long hot days of the midsummer of 1941 on the expansive open spaces of Eastern Europe and Western Russia provided an unlikely setting for the horrors to come. After so much winter gloom, the blossoming of summer is a special time for those who live in those vast tracts of land. Perhaps the warmth in the air and the promise of nature's abundance to come lulled the people into a false sense of security.

On Sunday 22 June, Nikolai Evseev, an officer in the Red Navy, stationed with the Black Sea Fleet in Sevastopol in the Crimea, wrote in his diary: *'A wonderful Crimean evening. All the streets and boulevards in the city were lit. The white houses were bathed in light, the clubs and theatres beckoned the sailors on shore leave to come inside. As always, the famous Primorsky Boulevard was full of people out for a stroll. Music was playing. There were jokes and happy laughter on the evening before the holiday.'*

Then, with German planes swooping towards the harbour, Evseev wrote: *'Are those planes ours?'*

The answer came from a fellow sailor: *'Our anti-aircraft batteries are firing live rounds and those bombs don't look like dummies.'*

Much further north, in the Belorussian capital, Minsk, Colonel-General Dimitri Pavlov, commander-in-chief of the Western Military District, was at Minsk's officers' club watching a comedy. What was about to unfold for him, and his Motherland, was far from funny; his tragic story would soon become the Russian experience on the Eastern Front in miniature.

Pavlov's forces faced Barbarossa's *Schwerpunkt* ('main effort'), intended to strike at the strategic and emotional heart of the Soviet Union, following a route travelled by previous marauding armies: Brest, Minsk, Smolensk, Moscow. In the centre of Barbarossa's attack were several of the Wehrmacht's elite units. Pavlov had no clue as to what was about to engulf him and his men.

Even though an intelligence officer brought him news that German troops appeared to be preparing for an attack, Pavlov carried on watching the play at his officers' club. But he then spent the night in hurried discussions with his senior officers before, at one in the morning, he received a telephone call from Moscow.

On the line was Soviet Defence Commissar Semyon Timo-shenko, who told him: *'Get the staff together this morning because something unpleasant may happen. If there is any specific provocation, ring me.'* There have been many casual understatements in the history of warfare, but Timoshenko's must be one of the most blasé. Within a few minutes, bombs were raining down over the Soviet Union's major cities, engulfing them in flames.

At 03:15, at the border bridge on the Bug River at Koden, Eastern Poland, German border guards summoned their Soviet opposite numbers – with whom, of course, there was a non-aggression pact – telling them that they needed to exchange important information. When the Soviet soldiers duly appeared, they were machine-gunned by German assault troops. It was a telling illustration of how the war on the Eastern Front would be conducted.

It is one of the most distressing aspects of human conflict that, in battle, places and circumstances that are the most ordinary suddenly become the most extraordinary. So it was in the expansive rural tedium of the Bug Basin in the early-morning mists of that June morning. Koden on the Bug, a definitive point between east and west, had seen armies pass by before, but nothing – not even Napoleon's *Grande Armée* – on the scale of the juggernaut of armour and men that went past it in those fateful hours.

For those who dared look out from their humble wooden homes, or watch from a distance while hiding in the fields and woods, they would have seen flocks of gull-grey Stuka dive-bombers howling overhead; long columns of panzers, many of them Czech

T-35 tanks acquired and adapted after the annexation of Czecho-slovakia in 1939; hundreds of horse-drawn supply wagons; and, in their immaculate field-green uniforms, countless marching landsers (common soldiers), the pride of the Wehrmacht. Their uniforms would not be immaculate for long – nor would their behaviour.

Dimitri Masslinikov was with the Red Army's 13th Rifle Regiment, stationed on the right flank of Bialystok as the panzers rolled towards them: '*Our defences were poor. Most were hardly finished. We never stood a chance. They blew away most of our artillery from the air and were across the bridges before our engineers could destroy them. They came on so quickly, we had two choices: stand and fight and face certain death, or retreat to fight another day. What would you have done?*'

In Minsk, General Pavlov's men were in the path of 18 German divisions, including 5 panzer divisions: almost 200,000 men and 1,600 tanks. One of his generals, Vasily Kuznetsov, in command of the 3rd Army, was overwhelmed in the attack and completely surrounded. He rang Pavlov, who recalled: '*Kuznetsov informed me with a tremble in his voice that the only thing that was left of the 56th Rifle Division was its number.*'

Pavlov sent his deputy, Lieutenant General Ivan Boldin, to the 10th Army headquarters in Bialystok. Boldin reported that the area was in utter chaos: '*The atmosphere was incredibly hot, and the air reeked of burning. My truck made slow progress through bewildered lines of refugees. Then came a small motorcade, led by a ZIS-101* [a high-powered official limousine]. *The broad leaves of an aspidistra were protruding from one of the windows. It was the car of a local top official. Inside were two women and two children. They could have ditched the plant and made room for another human being. As the women looked away in shame, a plane dipped low above the road and there were three cracks of machine-gun fire. The women and children were all dead. Sticking out of the window, only the evergreen leaves of the aspidistra were still alive.*'

Nearby Grodno and Brest had fallen, and the 10th Army had been obliterated. But Boldin managed to escape eastwards with a motley collection of around 1,600 men who scavenged and skirmished for seven weeks before reaching the main body of the Red

Army near Smolensk. Pavlov was relieved of his command on 1 July 1941. He was arrested and accused of criminal incompetence. He and his deputies were charged with 'failure to perform their duties' rather than treason. On 22 July, the same day the sentence was handed down, Pavlov's property was confiscated; he was deprived of military rank, shot by the NKVD, and buried in a landfill near Moscow. Except for Ivan Boldin, death penalties were also passed down for all the front's other commanders, including Pavlov's Chief of Staff, Major General Vladimir Klimovskikh.

In Moscow, when he heard multiple reports of the attack, Zhukov called Stalin at 03:30.

'*No one answered. I kept calling. Finally, I heard the sleep-laden voice of the general on duty at the security section. I asked him to call Stalin to the phone.*

"*What? Now? Comrade Stalin is asleep.*"

"*Wake him at once. The Germans are bombing our towns!*" *About three minutes later, Stalin picked up the phone. I reported the situation and requested permission to begin retaliatory action. Stalin was silent. I heard the sound of his breathing.* "*Did you hear me?*"

Silence again. At last Stalin answered. "*Where is the Defence Commissar?*" [Timoshenko]

"*Talking with the Kiev District.*"

"*You and him come to the Kremlin, and summon the Politburo.*" [...]'

The first news of the invasion reached the people of Moscow just after noon on 22 June. It was a warm sunny day and Muscovites were looking forward to a Sunday stroll in the balmy weather. The announcement came in a radio broadcast over the city's loudspeakers by the Kremlin's Foreign Minister, Vyacheslav Molotov.

Citizens of the Soviet Union. The Soviet government and its head, Comrade Stalin, have ordered me to make the following announcement: Today, at four o'clock in the morning, German troops have entered our country, without making any demands on the Soviet Union and without a declaration of war. They have attacked our borders in many places and have subjected our towns – Zhitomir, Kiev, Sevastopol, Kaunas, and some others – to aerial bombardments during which more than two hundred people have been killed or wounded. This attack is unheard of and is a treacherous act that has no equal in the history of civilised peoples.

Molotov ended his broadcast with a call to arms which encapsulated the long historical context of the bitter war to come.

It is not the first time that our people face an arrogant aggressor. During Napoleon's Russian campaign, our people reacted with the War of the Fatherland; Napoleon suffered a defeat and went down. That shall also happen to the arrogant Hitler who has unleashed a new campaign against our country. The Red Army and our population shall once more wage a triumphant war for our homeland, for honour and for freedom. The government calls on you, citizens of the Soviet Union, to close ranks around our triumphant Bolshevist Party, around our Soviet government and around our great leader, Comrade Stalin. Our cause is just. The enemy shall be defeated. Victory shall be ours.

It is interesting to note that the first Russian casualty figures issued by Molotov for the opening day of the conflict were 'two hundred'. In fact, estimates suggest that, by noon, they were likely to have been in the tens of thousands.

Today, long after the events and after so many years of state secrecy, it is difficult to be certain about how the mass of the Soviet citizenry reacted to the news of the invasion, but most historians agree that there was a huge groundswell of patriotism. There must also have been, in private thoughts and hushed conversations, hopes and dreams that a German conquest might free them from the oppression of Stalinist communism. There were countless anti-communists, and many more in the non-Russian Soviet republics, who resented rule from Moscow.

Elena Skrjabina, the daughter of a pre-Revolution politician, was at home in Leningrad when Molotov spoke, and she recorded her thoughts in her diary: *'Molotov sounded hesitant and hasty, as if he was out of breath. His encouraging appeal was quite inappropriate. I had the feeling that a monster was approaching, slowly, threateningly, frightening everybody to death. Panic spread around the city, they rushed to the shops to buy anything they saw. They were running around like mad. I tried to withdraw some money, but the banks were empty, payments had been stopped. The June day blazed; the heat was unbearable. Somebody fainted, others were cursing. In the evening, everything became strangely quiet. It seemed that everyone had hidden somewhere, possessed by terror.'*

Despite all the hardships and cruelty inflicted upon them during the previous decade by Stalin and his regime, there was a wave of patriotic fervour among ordinary Soviet soldiers and civilians, as outlined in Catherine Merridale's excellent 2005 account, *Ivan's War*. One veteran told her: *'I was a boy, fifteen years old. I had lived my whole life in a Siberian village. I'd never even seen Moscow. But still, it came from somewhere, that patriotism. I knew I would volunteer straight away.'*

Using words that could have been taken directly from the Communist Party's propaganda lexicon, another veteran said: *'I lived through German rule in Ukraine in 1918 and 1919. We'll drive that bloodstained Hitler out, bag and baggage. I declare myself mobilised and ask to be sent to the front to destroy the German bandits.'*

Another worker declared: *'We will put up with any hardships to help our Red Army to ensure that the Soviet people utterly destroy the fascists.'*

A printer echoed the sentiment: *'Our indignation has no limits. Hitler has violated the sacred borders of the first socialist country in the world ... We will win because there is no power in the world that can vanquish a people risen up in patriotic war.'*

In the city of Kursk, the local Communist Party called an emergency midnight meeting on 22 June. Every member was present and arrived on time. In appropriate language, the meeting's minutes read: *'The feeling of unlimited love for their Motherland, for the Party and for Stalin, and the people's deep outrage and hatred of bestial fascism were reflected in every speech the members made.'*

Misha Volkov worked in Kiev's metal industry. He had already served in the military, so he was one of the first to be mobilised.

On 24 June, he was ordered to join a unit in Lvov, a city in Western Ukraine which had been ceded to the Soviet Union as part of the 1939 Nazi–Soviet Pact. The arrangement had created an incendiary situation in the city, which had a Jewish population of over 160,000 and was a hotbed of Ukrainian nationalism.

The inevitable chaos of an urgent mass mobilisation, made worse by mayhem in the Kremlin, meant that there were no rallying points for the mobilised men. They had no accommodation, no food, and no transport to take them to the front. In a truly Kafkaesque dilemma, conscripts who thus had no means of reaching their units could be condemned as deserters – punishable by firing squad.

Using his own initiative, Volkov managed to get on a train to the west and along the way acquired a small group of twenty men who chose him as their commanding officer. As he approached Lvov, he wrote: *'We passed columns of refugees from Lvov and other cities in Western Ukraine. They told us that there was street fighting in Lvov and that life in the city had come to a standstill.'*

Discovering that the unit he was supposed to join had fled, Volkov's little band remained in the city for three days, awaiting new orders. But none came, so they had no choice but to walk eastwards to see if they could find elements of the Red Army: *'We walked without a break for forty-eight hours. There was nothing to eat and we were very thirsty. We walked through woods, ravines, through mud; we fell into potholes. Ten people got left behind, they didn't have the strength to go on.'*

After over a hundred miles, the bedraggled group reached their main unit: *'I still can't understand where I got the strength from, where I found the stamina, especially as I had no time to toughen up.'*

A few days later, as German forces approached Lvov, the NKVD murdered the entire population of the city's three prisons. After the city fell on 29 June, Ukrainian nationalists went on the rampage, aided by German soldiers, blaming Jews for the killings of the prisoners. Jews were humiliated, abused, raped and murdered in their thousands. It was an ominous foretaste of what was to come, not just in Ukraine, but across the entire front.

The poet and author Konstantin Simonov was a war correspondent close to the German advance at the end of June, when he was caught up in the rapid retreat of the Red Army: *'After about three hours, above the forest, a group of about fifteen planes passed over. We jumped up, pleased that our planes had finally arrived. But they poured a good portion of lead on us. Several people next to me were injured. We thought it was an accident, a mistake, but the planes turned around and passed over the forest for a second and a third time.*

They flew at a height of twenty-five to thirty metres. Large red stars on their wings were perfectly visible to us. When they went over the forest for the third time, someone managed to bring one down with a machine gun. A lot of people ran to the edge of the forest where the plane was burning. Those who ran there said that they pulled out the corpse of a half-burned German pilot from the cockpit.

I still don't understand how it happened. The only possible explanation is that the Germans during the first days captured several planes and taught their pilots to fly them. It was very depressing.'

As he retreated towards Smolensk in early July, Simonov stopped at a peasant's hut, which housed an old couple, living on their own. The old grandmother gave them all fresh milk.

'[. . .] "We have given everything to the war, our sons and grandchildren. Will the Germans come here soon?"

"We don't know," we said, although we knew it would be soon.

"It must be soon," said the grandmother. "You are drinking the last milk. We gave the cow to the collective farm. There are few people in the village. Everyone is leaving."

"And you?" we asked.

"Where are we to go? We will be here. And the Germans will come."

The old grandfather was silent. He seemed not to care that he was very old; and, if he could, he would die there and then. He sat on the bench in silence and shook everything with his ancient grey hair, as he kept repeating, "Yes, yes, they will come, they will come." [. . .]'

Simonov was soon overwhelmed by a deep-seated sense of nostalgia for his Motherland.

'Moving east, we drove into such a wilderness there were no refugees, just lonely villages, home to a few peasant women. They brought out cold

milk from their cellars and blessed us, "God save you. May God help you." Offers of money for the milk were rejected out of hand.

The villages were small, and near them, next to the rickety church, were large cemeteries with identical old wooden crosses. The discrepancy between the small number of huts in the villages and the high number of crosses shocked me. I realised then how strong are the feelings I have for my homeland; how much I feel this land of mine, and how deeply these people who live there are embedded into its earth. The sorrows of the first two weeks of the war convinced me that the Germans would come here, but it was impossible to imagine this as German land. Whatever would become of it in the future, it would remain Russian. So many unknown ancestors, grandfathers and great-grandfathers were buried in these cemeteries, that this land is Russian, not only from above, but also from many fathoms deep below.'

As he travelled further eastwards, passing more and more civilians along the road, Simonov was struck by yet more profound generosity. He came across a small peasant boy and two older girls collecting wild strawberries. They were certainly from families with few possessions and meagre supplies of food, but the children gave Simonov and his colleagues all their strawberries and refused any payment: 'It was so poignant, and even more sad when I thought about what would happen to these kids in a week.

When we were driving back through Krasnopolie, we saw two women holding children in their arms. The kids waved their hands at us. I don't know why, but at that very moment my eyes filled with tears and I almost screamed with anger. Of course, children always wave at people passing by, but there was something in their simple gesture that made me want to cry out in rage.'

There was another phenomenon in this war of hate that Simonov heard about when they arrived at a heavily armed Red Army defensive position south of Orsha, a city in Eastern Belarus on the banks of the Dnieper River. When he and his party arrived, they were met by an indignant colonel, furious about what had just happened to his men: 'Bitter and angry, the colonel said that the right flank of his battalion, which had surrounded a German force in a nearby village, was about to move in and finish them off when several white *flags were raised at once. An overjoyed commander and his men then advanced to take in hand the Germans in an open field. At that moment, and without warning, German mortars and machine guns opened up and mowed down three-quarters of the battalion in a few seconds. The remnants of the battalion had no choice but to retreat.'*

The incident was just one of many that were beginning to form the insidious psychology of hatred that would characterise the war.

By the middle of July, Simonov found himself east of Mogilev, another Eastern Belorussian city. Behind him, a collection of scattered units, led by Major General Mikhail Romanov, was holding Mogilev, but was completely surrounded, having been outflanked by panzers crossing the Dnieper north and south of the city. Romanov and his men held on for ten days until they ran out of ammunition. He and 35,000 of his men were taken prisoner, after which he was sent to the Hammelburg prisoner of war camp in Bavaria, where he died six months later.

The Wehrmacht's panzer advance was relentless, so much so that the infantry found it all but impossible to keep pace. Many infantry divisions were marching more than twenty miles a day, a pace that took Soviet planners by complete surprise. On 14 July, Simonov was approaching Cherikov on the Sozh River. He was sure that the Germans were still at Chausy, twenty miles behind him: *'We took a truck and drove along a forest path and on to the road leading to Cherikov. As soon as we turned at the edge of the forest, a man jumped out and held on to the side of the truck. He had a stunned, terrified face, so distorted by fear. Then he jumped off. I don't know what happened to him.*

We drove down towards the river. Suddenly the driver prodded me in the side, "Look!" I will never forget what I saw. Right below us, between us and the river, perpendicular to us, like a row of toys, half a dozen German tanks. How did they get there? Who knows! But now, in the early evening, rising up from the calmly flowing river, over which burst a pink sunset, two hundred yards from us, German tanks at neat intervals, like on a military parade – astonishing and frightening.'

Simonov and his group managed to get away and cross the Sozh downstream. But he was left with an overpowering sense of menace: *'It was a hot summer day. The road was completely peaceful. There were villages on either side, where there was no hint of war. The news of the German breakthrough had not yet reached here, and no one could have imagined that in a few days these places would become the front line. There was a painful paradox between what we had seen in recent days and this peaceful, innocent rural silence. All these things, one after another, put me into such a terrible mood, one that I have never had before. It seemed that the Germans were pushing, pushing, and pushing forward; when would they stop? I had an overwhelming sense of acute pity and love for everything that was here, for these village huts, for women, for children playing near the road, for grass, for birch trees, for all Russia. We drove on in silence; we were silent for a long time.'*

4

CRISIS IN THE KREMLIN

JUNE 1941

So severe was the scale of the Soviet losses and the speed of the German advance in the first few days of the war, it led to a sort of paralytic shock within the walls of the Kremlin. How destabilising it was – especially its impact on Stalin's decision making – is the subject of much historical debate. The discussion remains inconclusive because much of the historical record has been hidden behind state secrecy for many decades, and also because of the simple fact that most of the individual recollections have been grounded in vanity, jealousy and enmity.

However, one crucial decision was taken very early. It was based on calculated pragmatism rather than defeatism, but it was vital for the future conduct of the war. On 24 June, just two days after the invasion, a 'Soviet (Council) for Evacuation' was created, to 'relocate powerful human and material resources from threatened regions to the east, to the rear of the country'. In effect, this meant beyond the Ural Mountains and even further.

During the following six months, 2,593 industrial enterprises were evacuated, of which 1,360 were armaments-related. In most cases, between 30 and 40 per cent of their skilled workforces and key technicians went with them. The relocation was often chaotic, and the new sites sometimes not ready, but approximately 1.5 million railway wagons rolled eastwards. This meant the country could rebuild a war economy to fight a long and brutal war, a total war that would consume weapons, munitions, tanks and aircraft at an astonishing rate.

Contrary to the opinion of some historians, there is little evidence that Stalin suffered a nervous breakdown in the dark days at the end of June. Records show that his office was a hive of activity. He worked long hours, saw a host of people, and made numerous senior appointments. However, there are strong hints that, whether to buy time, send confusing signals to Berlin, or in a serious approach, at some point between the 25th and the 27th, Stalin had Lavrentiy Beria put out feelers to Hitler about a possible peace deal. Under Beria's orders, Pavel Sudoplatov, a senior officer in Soviet Intelligence, met with Ivan Stamenov, the Bulgarian Ambassador, at the Aravgi, a Georgian restaurant in the centre of Moscow. Sudoplatov asked the ambassador if Hitler would stop penetration of the USSR in exchange for ceding to Germany a large part of the west of the country. There is evidence that another approach was made later in the year.

Nothing came of the suggestion, nor is it known if the offer ever reached Berlin. Similarly, we will never know how genuine Stalin's offer was. Neither should we assume it was indicative of defeatism in Stalin's mind or among his senior coterie. The Kremlin was under immense pressure, yet throughout those long summer days, any sense of 'panic' was surely more to do with haste than fear.

As with Soviet industry, in the Politburo Central Committee's Order No. 34, issued on 27 June, all the state's precious metals, gemstones, diamonds and other assets, including the treasures of Leningrad's Hermitage Museum, were to be transported to safe storage beyond the Urals. Was this blind panic, or simply shrewd contingency planning?

If there was a moment when Stalin came close to breaking point, there is strong evidence that it may have happened on 27 June, with the news of the imminent fall of Minsk, the capital of Belorussia. A meeting was called at the Commissariat of Defence; among those present was Politburo member and wily old Bolshevik, the Armenian Anastas Mikoyan, about whom one veteran Soviet diplomat said, 'The rascal was able to walk through Red Square on a rainy day without an umbrella and would not get wet. He could dodge the raindrops.'

Mikoyan's recollection of the meeting was precise: *'They began by asking Zhukov questions, then realised that the military were totally in the dark. They couldn't tell them anything: where our army was . . . where the Germans were . . . how far the Germans had advanced . . . Nothing was clear. Zhukov was so shaken up that he was on the verge of tears.'*

The situation drove Stalin into a rage. He is said to have berated Zhukov as the bearer of bad news and stormed out of the meeting, saying, 'Lenin founded our state and now we've fucked it up!'

Beria's version of the meeting was slightly different: *'Stalin would not calm down, furious at the helplessness of our armies. "Why? Why? Where is your accursed working class?" [. . .]'*

Beria then claims that he said to Stalin: *'If these men had been property owners, they would have fought like lions and tigers in the first days of the war.'*

There is no doubt that Stalin then retreated to his dacha for at least forty-eight hours, during which it is speculated that he succumbed to a fit of deep depression. Mikoyan described in detail the bizarre events of 30 June, when he and several members of the Politburo drove out to see Stalin: *'We decided to visit him. He was in his so-called "nearer" dacha, Kuntsevo, in the forest of Poklonnaia Gora. We found Stalin in a small dining room, sitting in an armchair. He looked at us quizzically and said, "Why have you come?" One could sense that he was worried, but that he was taking care to appear calm. Molotov, as our spokesman, said that it was necessary to put power into one organ that would be called upon to decide all the questions of operations and to organise the mobilisation of all the country's forces for the resistance against the occupiers. That kind of organ had to be headed by Stalin. Stalin looked somewhat astonished, but after a brief pause said, "Very well." [. . .]'*

Stalin had probably expected a coup, perhaps even a bullet, but neither happened. The Politburo had blinked first. Had Stalin collapsed? Perhaps, but the truth is, we will never know. In his excellent book about the war in the east, *Absolute War*, Chris Bellamy quotes the tactic of Ancient Chinese general and philosopher Sun Tzu when confronting an enemy: 'Pretend inferiority and encourage his arrogance.' Stalin was certainly shrewd enough to use such a ploy.

That evening, the People's Commissariat for Defence (GKO) was formed. It was a war cabinet, chaired by Stalin, and included Molotov, Kliment Voroshilov (Marshal of the Red Army), Georgy Malenkov (senior politician) and Beria. It had only two stated aims: to concentrate all state power in its hands, and to oblige all citizens and all military organisations to obey its orders without question. It was certainly a draconian step but one that would prove to be highly effective. A tier below the GKO was 'Stavka', the High Command of the Soviet armed forces, headed by Marshal Semyon Timoshenko and the redoubtable Georgy Zhukov, head of the Army's General Staff.

One of the sources of rumour about Stalin's state of mind was the fact that he did not, even in those most perilous days, speak to his people. He corrected that on 3 July. However, by then, the situation had worsened significantly. In the north, Vilnius, the capital of Lithuania, had fallen on 24 June. Riga, the capital of Latvia, fell on 1 July, over 250 miles from the border of 21 June. In the south, the advance had engulfed Rovno, in Ukraine, 200 miles from the border. Even greater distances had been covered in the centre. Not only had Minsk fallen, but to its south-east, the panzers had reached Bobruysk in Belorussia, more than 450 miles from the frontier.

Sergo Beria was blunt about his country's response to the crisis: *'Stalin and our military men had not appreciated that our senior officers were unable to command troops. The Germans broke through our lines not because we lacked weapons or men, but because our army had never fought . . . It was not the German attack that took Stalin by surprise but the collapse of our troops . . . In the first days of the war our army's communications were non-existent. This was not, as has been alleged, the result of operations by German commandos but quite simply the usual Russian "balls-up"!'*

To all objective observers, and certainly within the Wehrmacht, it must have appeared that, as in Western Europe a year earlier, an overwhelming German victory was assured, and the obliteration of the Soviet Union imminent.

What was not known at the time, except by a murderous few, was how complete the intended annihilation of the country and its people was planned to be.

It is irrefutable that the Soviet Union was ill-prepared for war. In his later reflections on the first days of the conflict, Zhukov is frank about the shortcomings of the Soviet military and its strategic planners: *'We did not foresee the large-scale surprise offensive launched at once in all major strategic directions. We did not envisage the nature of the strike in its enormity . . . [We did not] expect the enemy to concentrate such huge numbers of armour and motorised troops, and their commitment on the first day of action in powerful compact groupings, in all strategic directions, with the aim of striking powerful wedging blows.'*

Although Zhukov's candour is admirable, his words are also a lamentable confession that not only had the Soviet Stavka not learned the lessons of the Wehrmacht's victories in the west, they had forgotten the basic principles of war.

As an ardent communist, Zhukov's memoirs contain frequent references to the power of the Bolshevik ideal in bolstering the country's morale and will to survive: *'There were over 563,000 Communists in the Red Army and Navy at the outbreak of the war and more than a third of the entire Army personnel were Komsomol* [The All-Union Leninist Young Communist League] *members. Some 1,100,000 Communists went to the front lines in the first six months of the war. On many occasions, I met and talked with newly arrived political soldiers. They showed a kind of special and unshakable confidence in our victory. "We'll make it!" they used to say. And I always felt that these were not mere words, but a way of thinking and a reflection of genuine Soviet patriotism.'*

Although Zhukov's words are clearly championing standard Soviet propaganda, it is apparent that he believes them to reflect the truth. He also talks sympathetically about the courage of young Soviets: *'In early July, when the enemy had occupied Minsk, an intelligence and saboteur group was to be sent behind enemy lines. It was made up by two girls and two boys, all members of the Komsomol who had a good command of German. When I asked them if they were scared, with*

*a faint smile, they replied, "Of course, we are – a bit. Bad deal if we're
captured. If we're not, then everything will be alright." [. . .]'*

Zhukov does not reveal what became of them; it is unlikely
that he ever knew. However, so dire would be the circumstances
the young volunteers would encounter behind enemy lines, their
chances of ever seeing home again were slim.

The situation in those first few days of the war was so critical, it was clear that for Mother Russia to survive, it needed a
saviour, a figurehead, around whom the country could unite – like
Churchill in Britain, or Roosevelt in the United States. To the surprise of many, Stalin's speech of 3 July offered strong hints that the
menacing autocrat might be the country's redeemer. He delivered
a tour de force.

> Comrades! Citizens! Brothers and sisters! Soldiers of our army
> and navy!
>
> To you I turn, my friends.
>
> The treacherous military attack by Hitler-Germany on our
> Motherland, which was launched on June 22nd, continues.

He was candid about the scale of the losses.

> The enemy continues to advance and throws new troops into
> battle. Hitler's forces have succeeded in conquering Lithuania,
> a considerable part of Latvia, the western part of Belorussia
> and part of Western Ukraine. The Fascist air force expands
> the range of its bombers and subjects Murmansk, Orsha,
> Mogilyow, Smolensk, Kiev, Odessa and Sevastopol to bombard-
> ments. A danger hangs over our Motherland.

He then invoked history, just as Molotov had done, eleven days
earlier.

> The army of Napoleon was thought to be invincible and yet
> it was defeated. The German army of Kaiser Wilhelm was also
> considered invincible during the First Imperial War, yet it was
> defeated more than once by Russian and Anglo-French troops
> and ultimately destroyed by Anglo-French armies.

Stalin appealed to his people's pride and reminded them of the ethnic diversity of the Soviet Union.

> The enemy is cruel and unrelenting. His goal is the conquest of our territory, drenched with our sweat, and the appropriation of our grain and our oil, harvested by our hard work. His goal is the destruction of the culture and the national government systems of the Russians, Ukrainians, Belorussians, Lithuanians, Latvians, Estonians, Uzbeks, Tatars, Moldavians, Georgians, Armenians, Azerbaijanians and the other free peoples of the Soviet Union ... Therefore, it means the life or death of the Soviet state, the life or death of the peoples of the Soviet Union, and it concerns the question of whether the Soviet peoples remain free or will be subdued.

He issued an ominous warning.

> Furthermore, it is necessary that there shall be no place in our ranks for lamenters, panic mongers, cowards and deserters, that our people know no fear in battle and that they shall participate in our national war of liberation against the Fascist suppressors in a sacrificial spirit. The Red Army, the Red Navy and all citizens of the Soviet Union must defend every inch of Soviet territory, fight till the last drop of blood, and show our towns and villages the manliness, the spirit of enterprise and the cleverness that are peculiar to our people.

Significantly, he then set the war in the east in the context of the global struggle against fascism and praised his allies, Britain and the United States.

> Our war for freedom will blend with the struggle of the European and American populations for their independence, for democratic freedom. In this connection, the historical statement of the British Prime Minister, Mister Churchill, about aid to the Soviet Union and the declaration of the American government about its willingness to come to the aid of our nation cannot evoke anything else but feelings of gratitude in the hearts of the Soviet peoples.

All our efforts in support of our heroic Red Army and our illustrious Red Navy.

All efforts by the population for the destruction of the enemy.

Forward, for our victory.

It was a long and powerful speech, delivered with passion and emotion. Stalin spoke not as an aloof leader locked away in the Kremlin, but, like his listeners, as a Soviet citizen. Most importantly, his words had a significant impact on the Red Army. When Stalin spoke, Colonel Ivan Fedyuninsky was commander of the 15th Rifle Corps, part of the 5th Army in the Kiev Military District: *'It is hard to describe the enormous enthusiasm and patriotic uplift. We suddenly seemed to feel stronger.'*

For her 1985 classic account of women in the Red Army, published in English under the title *War's Unwomanly Face*, 2015 Nobel Prize winner Svetlana Alexievich interviewed Elena Kudina, who was a driver in the Red Army. Like many others, she lived in fear of the consequences of speaking out, and of what the NKVD could do: *'But when Stalin began to speak . . . He addressed us as "Brothers and sisters". Then everybody forgot their grievances . . . We had an uncle sitting in a labour camp, Mama's brother, a railroad worker, an old communist. He had been arrested at work . . . You know who arrested him? The NKVD . . . Our beloved uncle, and we knew he wasn't guilty of anything. He was decorated after the Civil War . . . But after Stalin's speech Mama said, "We'll defend the Motherland, and sort it out later." Everybody loved the Motherland. I ran to the recruiting office at once. I couldn't wait.'*

War correspondent Konstantin Simonov wrote: *'Stalin did not describe the situation as tragic. The truth he told was a bitter truth, but at last it was uttered, and people felt that they stood more firmly on the ground* [with] *a tense expectation of change for the better.'*

Stalin was not Churchill, the inspirational orator, the writer of speeches that gave the 'British lion' its roar, but there is no doubt his speech on 3 July made a difference. However, matters would get much worse before they improved.

Nikolai Moskvin was a *politruk* – a political commissar – based in Belorussia. On 4 July, at which point he had not heard his leader's speech, he wrote: *'Our situation is very bad. How could it have turned out that we, preparing to fight on enemy soil,* [must] *consider that we might have to mount a defence. Something is up with the doctrine of our armed forces.'*

A little later, on 15 July, after seeing a transcript of Stalin's speech, which he was required to read to his men, he still despaired: *'It is possible that we are not completely beaten yet, but it is extremely difficult. The enemy's aviation is destroying absolutely everything. The roads are littered with the bodies of our soldiers and the civilian population. Towns and villages are burning. The Germans are everywhere – in front, behind, on our flank . . . What am I to say to our boys? We keep retreating. How can I get their approval? How? Am I to say that Comrade Stalin is with us? That Napoleon was ruined, and that Hitler and his generals will find their graves with us?'*

That night, Moskvin lost thirteen men, deserters, who slinked away into the Ukrainian forests: *'It seems that I didn't do a good job convincing them!'*

Gabriel Temkin, a Jewish refugee from Poland who was living in Bialystok, right on the border, at the beginning of the invasion, witnessed the parlous state of the Red Army as they passed by: *'Some in trucks, many on foot, their outdated rifles hanging loosely over their shoulders. Their uniforms worn out, covered with dust, not a smile on their mostly despondent faces with sunken cheeks.'*

Colonel Fedyuninsky was also concerned about the situation: *'Sometimes bottlenecks were formed by troops, artillery, motor vehicles and field kitchens, and then the Nazi planes had the time of their life . . . Often our troops could not dig in, because they did not have the simplest implements. Occasionally, trenches had to be dug with helmets, since there were no spades.'*

Anastas Mikoyan wrote about the surprise in the Kremlin when it emerged that there were reports of a shortage of rifles at the front: *'We thought we surely had enough for the whole army. But it turned out that a portion of our divisions had been assembled according to peacetime norms. Divisions that had been equipped with adequate numbers of rifles for wartime held on to them, but they were all close to the front. When the Germans crossed the border and began to advance, they simply captured them. As a result, reservists going to the front ended up with no rifles at all.'*

In order to survive, the Soviet Union needed an almost miraculous set of circumstances to come to pass: for Hitler to make catastrophic blunders; for the Wehrmacht to run out of steam, and certainly of materiel and reinforcements; for Russia's weather ('General Winter' and 'Marshal Mud') to play a decisive role; for the Red Army to find extraordinary levels of courage and resolve; for Soviet civilians (farmers, factory workers and planners) to produce the resources to support the war effort; for the military leadership to find strategies and tactics to win the major battles to come; and for the Soviet Union's allies to send enormous amounts of basic supplies to bolster the war effort.

Remarkably, all the above happened. But it was a close-run thing.

It would take four years of agony and despair before all the elements came together to create an astonishing outcome.

5

SMOLENSK

JULY–SEPTEMBER 1941

The first hint that a miraculous set of circumstances might be written in the heavens occurred at the First Battle of Smolensk, which began on 10 July. Smolensk is only 250 miles west of Moscow and has seen many battles in its history. The battle for the city in 1941 marked the second phase of Operation Barbarossa.

General Zhukov summed up the importance of the encounter: *'The enemy aimed to cut the Western Front in two by committing powerful shock forces to encircle the main Soviet force at Smolensk, and thereby open the road to Moscow. A furious battle ensued beside the ancient Russian city, which had once risen as a next-to-impregnable obstacle to Napoleon's armies heading for Moscow.'*

Initially, the Wehrmacht's successes continued and reports going back to Moscow were particularly inauspicious. The head of the Belorussian Communist Party, Panteleimon Ponomarenko, who was already organising Belorussian partisan resistance, wrote to Stalin: *'The retreat has caused blind panic. The soldiers are tired to death, even sleeping under artillery fire ... At the first bombardment, the formations collapse, many just run away to the woods. The whole area of woodland in the frontline region is full of refugees. Many throw away their weapons and go home.'*

An ordinary Soviet rifleman who, for obvious reasons, preferred to remain anonymous, told a similar story from the battlefield: *'Our unit was surrounded. The politruk mustered the remaining troops and ordered us to leave the encirclement in groups. I and two others from our unit changed into civilian clothes and decided to go home where we used to live. We took this decision because, according to rumour, the German troops moving towards us had advanced far away to the east.'*

As early as the first day of the invasion, the Supreme Soviet had already granted the Red Army the power to punish desertion through three-man military tribunals, which had the right to order the death penalty.

Nikolai Moskvin shot his first deserter in July. The man was a Ukrainian, who was urging his comrades to surrender. He then confronted Moskvin: *'He made a salute to, I suppose, Hitler, shouldered his rifle and walked off towards the scrub. Red Army private Shulyak* [a fellow Ukrainian] *brought him down with a bullet in the back. The deserter shouted, "They'll kill the lot of you," and, turning to me, "and you, you bloodstained commissar, they'll hang you first." [. . .]'*

Moskvin then despatched the deserter with his revolver: *'The boys understood. A dog's death for a dog.'*

The situation seemed hopeless. But because of the strategic importance of the city, on 4 July Stavka had ordered that the Dnieper River, which flows through Smolensk, and the Dvina, which is to the city's north-west, should be defended. Two days later, the Soviet Stavka launched a massive counter-attack against the advancing Wehrmacht forces. The attack included the fresh troops of the 19th Army, which had just arrived by train from the east.

Although it was fresh to the conflict and led by an experienced general, the 19th was severely mauled, as were several other Red Army units in the counter-attacks around Smolensk. However, the attacks had damaged the Wehrmacht's panzer numbers significantly and challenged the perception in its ranks, and among its generals, that the war was already won.

The loss of panzers was particularly critical. By 16 July, the Wehrmacht's 18th Panzer Division had only 12 operational tanks remaining from the 218 with which it had started on 22 June. The huge loss led a senior Wehrmacht officer to express one of the most memorable quotes of the entire war, when he said that the loss of tanks needed to be reduced, 'if we do not intend to win ourselves to death'.

A new piece of Soviet military hardware made its appearance on 14 July. Deployed for the first time at Orsha in Belorussia, it had a devastating impact. Its first barrage destroyed several freight trains containing ammunition, fuel and tanks. A second barrage destroyed a bridge across the Orshica River, on the road from Minsk to Moscow. The weapon would play a significant role in future conflagrations.

The Soviets called it *Katyusha* ('Little Kate'). Kate was a truck-mounted, portable bank of multiple (sixteen) rocket launchers. She could unleash enormous firepower very quickly, especially if used in a battery of several units in parallel. German soldiers feared the rocket launchers and, because of the terrifying noise they made and their resemblance to organ pipes, called them 'Stalin's Organs'. They became one of the emblematic symbols of Soviet weaponry and part of the country's warrior folklore.

General Andrei Yeremenko, who had replaced the disgraced Dimitri Pavlov as Commander of the Western Military District, enthused about their impact: *'We first tried this superb weapon northwest of Smolensk . . . the earth shook. Like red-tailed comets, the rockets were hurled into the air. The frequent and dazzling explosions, the like of which had never been seen, struck the imagination. The Germans fled in panic.'*

Zhukov's memoirs reflect the importance of the Red Army's resistance at Smolensk: *'On July 16th almost the whole of Smolensk fell into German hands. The 16th and 20th Armies were encircled in the northern part of the city. But they did not lay down their arms and fought for nearly ten days. On July 26th, most of the troops of the 16th and 20th Armies managed to break out of the encirclement and reached the eastern bank of the Dnieper where they joined the Front's main forces . . . The Battle of Smolensk holds an important place among the operations of 1941. Although it had been impossible to smash the enemy, the enemy's shock forces were worn to a frazzle and visibly weakened. The Red Army and the people of Smolensk displayed great bravery during the battle. Heavy fighting developed around every street and every house.'*

The fighting in Smolensk was a portent of what was to come in many other places throughout the war.

The Red Army finally lost control of the Smolensk area at the end of July, leaving the road to Moscow at the mercy of the German forces. Ukrainian Nikolai Amosoff was a surgeon in the front-line field hospital PPG-2266. He kept a diary throughout the war. In early August, he was stationed eighty miles south-east of Smolensk.

'*Soviet Army*

5 kms west of Roslavl,

We are retreating all along the front – if there is such a thing as a 'front'. The communiques stress the enemy's losses in millions. So why are the Germans advancing with such apparent ease? How could we have been caught so much by surprise? Had we no intelligence service? Of course, no one discusses such matters. Even those who dislike and dread Stalin have learned to trust him. Propaganda? Yes and no. He has succeeded in transforming the country, though often by savage methods. We have built mighty industries out of nothing. Our men are brave. They have always been brave. Suicidal Russian courage, some call it. But why are we retreating? Why don't we attack?'

Soviet resistance was still undermined by low morale within large sections of the army. Many men, overwhelmed by the horror of the war, would go to any lengths to get away from the cauldron of the battlefield. Red Army officer Vasili Chekalov kept a diary from the early days of the war. He wrote an entry in late August 1941.

'*We were near a small village and discovered a wounded rifleman. We suspected a self-inflicted gunshot. When asked which way the bullet went in, outside or from the palm of his hand, he said, "I don't know," and then claimed that it went in from the outside. When asked how such a strange wound could happen, he explained that during the shelling he covered his head with his hands, lying on the ground, and at that moment he was wounded. The uncertainty with which he spoke underpinned our suspicions.*

When his commander asked why he had done it, he replied, "I have a wife, a child at home . . . I was scared, Comrade General . . ." One of our men, almost in tears, said to him, "And you think I have no wife and children. We all have those for whom we must fight." I could not contain my feelings and shouted at him, "You're a scoundrel and a traitor!"

One of our men stood up and said to our general, "Comrade General of the army, let me take him away." The detainee began to beg the general for clemency. Pointing at us, the general said, "I can't do anything. Here are your comrades; they must decide."

I felt no pity. I said, "He will not be able to fight, because he shot his hand. Stalin in his order requires to shoot anyone running from the battlefield. That's what he's done. He needs to be shot, Comrade General." One of the men offered to shoot the man and said to him, "To the right, march!" Realising that it was pointless, the man no longer begged for clemency. A minute later, a single shot rang out from behind the hut, followed by two short bursts of machine-gun fire. The executioner came out from behind the hut and reported, "He tried to run. I shot him and gave him two bursts to be sure." [. . .]'

However, led by the experienced veteran Marshal Timoshenko, such was the impact of the repeated Soviet counter-attacks that Hitler decided, in Führer Directives 33 and 34, to halt the drive towards Moscow. In its place, he ordered the reinforcement of the attacks northwards and southwards, towards Leningrad and into Ukraine respectively. It was a change of mind that his generals cautioned against and would prove to be an error of judgement that may well have cost him the opportunity to march across the shiny black cobbles of Red Square.

The importance of Hitler's decision was not lost on General Zhukov: 'That the enemy's offensive was halted at Smolensk for a while was an important strategic success. As a result, we gained time and were able to raise strategic reserves and carry out defensive works on the Moscow sector . . . Hitler's leadership and the German troops now had a taste of the gallantry and mass heroism of Soviet soldiers and saw that the farther inland they advanced, the harder the struggle became for them.'

Typical of the gallantry referred to by Zhukov were the actions of Major-General Lev Dovator's Cavalry Group – the 50th and 53rd Divisions. Unlike the aristocratic Prussian Junker leaders of the Wehrmacht, Dovator was from Belorussian Jewish peasant stock and a committed Bolshevik. He was ordered to deploy his Cossack cavalry to break through the German lines and wreak havoc to the rear. Perhaps somewhat embellished in the telling by the press, the action soon became part of Red Army legend.

> Dovator broke through the German positions and for 10 days smashed the German rear. During this time, they killed more than 2,500 troops of the Wehrmacht, and destroyed 200 vehicles and 7 tanks. The Germans reported 'tens of thousands of wild Cossacks', although the actual number of units amounted to three thousand cavalry. Part of the force were artists from the Moscow Circus, who were able to shoot standing on the back of a galloping horse or from under its belly.

Not surprisingly, amidst the cowardice and desertion, there were many examples of heroism like that of Dovator's Cossacks. But, regrettably, there were also 'heroic actions' that became cherished in Soviet folklore which were, instead, creations of Soviet propaganda. One such was 'Panfilov's Twenty-Eight Guardsmen', a tale that led to streets being named after them, statues erected in their honour and movies made to commemorate their bravery.

The story, related by an overenthusiastic journalist from the Red Army newspaper *Krasnaya Zvezda* (*Red Star*), described how twenty-eight of the Red Army's 316th Rifle Division, led by Major-General Ivan Panfilov, died while destroying eighteen German panzers and repelling a front-on attack. Following the article and subsequent acclaim, they each received the title Hero of the Soviet Union. Sadly, a 1948 investigation concluded that the Last Stand of Panfilov's Twenty-Eight 'did not occur, it was a pure fantasy'.

Panfilov had had nothing to do with the fabrication, and had indeed led his men in several courageous rear-guard actions. In recognition of his heroism in defending Mother Russia, he was awarded his third Order of the Red Banner, and his 316th was given the honour of being redesignated the 8th Guards Rifle Division. In a ceremony to mark the double distinction, attended by several of his men and a group of journalists, he was in the middle of an address when a mortar attack was launched. Panfilov was killed outright by a mortar fragment.

There was really no need to make up heroic stories. There were real heroes aplenty to admire. Captain Nikolai Gastello, a Soviet Air Force pilot, who flew in a long-range bomber regiment, was one of them. On 26 June, four days after the invasion, Gastello bombed a German position near the village of Dekshany in Belorussia. His plane was hit by flak, leading to his wing fuel tank being ruptured and engulfed in flames. He then flew his doomed aircraft into a Panzer column, performing the first 'fire taran' (ramming by fire) of the war. He was made a posthumous Hero of the Soviet Union and became a popular legend.

Not only had resolute Soviet resistance compromised the objectives of Barbarossa, but the problem of military logistics – the bane of all generals – had begun to have an impact on the forward momentum of the Wehrmacht. A constant resupply of fuel, ammunition and the basics of a soldier's life are vital in any war. With the Wehrmacht's infantry advancing on foot, and its supplies largely horse-drawn, the old axiom 'an army marches on its stomach' became significant. Food and fodder became difficult to find, especially with the Red Army and the Soviet citizenry operating a scorched earth policy.

As the Wehrmacht advanced, its supply lines got longer, but the Red Army's got shorter. For example, the 2nd Panzer Group's bridgehead over the vital Desna River at Yel'nya, almost fifty miles east of Smolensk, was 450 miles from the nearest railhead. Also, Wehrmacht losses – casualties, missing, prisoners – in the first six weeks of the war numbered 213,000, but only 47,000 new troops replaced them.

There had also been a subtle but important shift in the minds of the men of the Red Army. As more and more evidence emerged about the murderous behaviour of the Wehrmacht towards both Soviet soldiers and civilians, what had been fear turned into hatred; and hatred is as much an incitement to fight as fear is an inducement to capitulate.

Hitler's contempt for Bolshevism persuaded him that it was such a flawed ideology that as soon as the people living under its regime saw the opportunity to reject it, they would. He believed that, as soon as people saw how vulnerable it was, the entire Soviet system would collapse – and with it, the Red Army. But he had miscalculated.

Even though there were millions who had no love for communism, the Party, Stalin and the Kremlin, and all their repressive evils, there were just as many who still carried the idealistic torch that Lenin had held aloft in 1917. His 'new world', free of the oppression of the tsars, the aristocracy and the grinding poverty that had been prevalent for centuries, was a dream still very potent for peasants and workers alike. Hitler had also misjudged the raw power of national patriotism, the love of Mother Russia, which the communist regime had managed to harness to the cause of fighting anyone who dared to threaten their homeland.

Crucially for the outcome of the entire war, on 7 September, Zhukov was able to issue a despatch to all Soviet officers and men after the success of the 24th Army in the Yel'nya Offensive. It contained several vital words, including 'victory' and 'beaten': *'After unrelenting and bitter battles, brave units of our 24th Army have achieved a great victory. In the Yel'nya region* [thirty miles south-east of Smolensk] *German forces have been dealt a crushing blow. The enemy has been beaten.'*

Again, the guile of propaganda determined the tone of Zhukov's words but, despite huge Soviet losses, some of the Wehrmacht's crack troops had taken a step backwards; it was a 'victory' and, in this particular instance, they had been 'beaten'. It was the Wehrmacht's first retreat of the war. The Chief of Staff of the *Oberkommando des Heeres* (OKH – Supreme Command of the German Army) had already admitted on 11 August, 'We have underestimated the Russian colossus.'

However, Smolensk was but a hiatus in the relentless onslaught of German forces. Circumstances would become significantly worse before they got any better. All the Baltic States were in German hands, as was Belarus and most of Ukraine. Kiev fell on 19 September, a defeat that led to mass slaughter in the city. On 24 September, an ammunition depot exploded, creating a large fireball in which several Wehrmacht officers were killed. The German occupiers blamed 'partisans and Jews' for the fire and proceeded to arrest and murder people in their thousands.

While mayhem reigned in Kiev, the Wehrmacht's panzers were pushing south and east inexorably. Muscovite Nikolai Inozemtzev was just twenty-one years old at the outbreak of the war. He kept a diary from September 1941. His first entry, recorded near to Podgorodnoe in Ukraine, begins innocuously: *'September 27, 1941. Nice sunny day. Time flows as usual.'*

But his tone soon changes: *'The order comes: "Under the cover of machine guns, companies to stand down from battle formation and begin to withdraw." In an adjacent area, German tanks have broken through. This is the End!*

We travelled all night. We are overtaken by convoys of vehicles, cavalry units and motorised artillery. Suddenly, a deafening explosion was heard from behind, most of the horizon was lit with pink tones. Following the first explosion, a whole string of smaller ones followed, destroying ammunition depots. Machine-gun fire is approaching. The Germans are pushing more and more. This chatter of machine guns is like a toothache; it won't go away.

The brain-drilling noise of diving planes, the yellow-black ends of the wings overhead; the earth shook several times. We rise. The column of vehicles is burning. Shells fly towards us, they hiss, plop into the wet ground, the fragments of their shells burst. Panic!

Two people are seriously injured. What do we do with them? One is an old telephone operator, Grigorchuk. The other is just a boy, Korolev. They are given two flasks of vodka and dragged into a shelter.

We found a lieutenant lying on the ground, leaning on his hand. I shouted, "Eh, stop resting, let's go!" He stared at us but did not say a word. We moved closer. He had an honest, pleasant face, his chin rested on his smeared hand. In the other hand was an open folder. I said to him, "Come on, my friend, you can't help us by lying there." I looked closer. On the left side of his chest was a small patch of blood. He had been shot in the heart and died instantly.'

In the north, Leningrad was under severe threat. It had already lost its direct supply routes into the city when the railway at Mga fell, on 30 August. On 1 September, the first long-range artillery shells fell on the city.

Having decided to halt the advance on Moscow in July, in favour of attacks on Leningrad in the north and Ukraine in the south, Hitler now changed his mind again. His generals, increasingly perplexed and even angry about shifts in their Führer's strategic priorities, began to call them 'fatal errors' – errors that would cost Germany not only the campaign in the east, but the entire war.

At the beginning of September Hitler ordered a renewal of the push towards Moscow. Aware that taking the city, street by street, house by house, would be costly for his troops, and with the bitter cold of a northern winter not far off, he decided to starve the 'Venice of the North' into submission. The epic siege of Leningrad had begun.

6

LENINGRAD: THE GREAT SIEGE BEGINS

JULY–OCTOBER 1941

The tragedy that was to befall Leningrad began to unfold in the early days of Barbarossa. It was one of the most heartbreaking stories of the entire conflict on the Eastern Front. Realising that the Soviet Union's second city, and its most iconic, would be a priority target for Hitler, the Leningrad Military Council (LMC), headed by the city's Communist Party Chief, Andrei Zhdanov, began planning the defence of the city as early as 29 June.

Unfortunately, most of the city's defensive positions faced north, towards Karelia, where the threat was from the Finns – Russia's traditional enemies and Hitler's allies – who had lost Karelia to the Soviet Union's Red Army as a result of the Winter War of 1939–40. However, even including the conquered territory, the Finnish border was only sixty miles from the outskirts of Leningrad. Also, the LMC did not anticipate that the German Army would reach Leningrad, so its defensive focus was facing the wrong way in the autumn of 1941.

Not surprisingly, Finland attacked Karelia on 10 July, and quickly regained the territory it had lost in 1939. Fortunately, having reclaimed Karelia, the Finnish Army advanced no further. Even so, the new border was little more than twenty miles from the city at its nearest point.

The military situation around Leningrad worsened in September. Wehrmacht panzers made a dash for new ground on 9 September, and by the 12th they had taken Krasnoye Selo, a suburban town just ten miles from Leningrad's centre. By the evening of the 12th, motorised Wehrmacht units reached the

Pulkovo Heights, from where they could see the city, less than seven miles away.

However, as in many other places throughout the country, the closer the Wehrmacht got to Russia's heartland the more the will to resist stiffened. Valeri Krukov was born in 1908, when Russia was still ruled by the Romanov tsars. He was typical of the countless ordinary citizens who would fight for what they thought was a brave new world: *'We lived in a little wooden house in Muravyevskaya Street. There was nothing around but bare fields. In winter huge snowdrifts built up. In spring the roads were impassable. My mother could barely make ends meet. My father earned very little. He had a scar on his face, thanks to a Cossack whip, a souvenir from the 1905 uprising . . . Then the October Revolution [1917] came; everything changed. A miracle was performed by the Soviet system: tarmac roads, fine apartment blocks, shops . . . We were given a heated flat. How clean the streets were – a miracle! Even the people changed, fitter and stronger . . . My father retired and got the pension our constitution guaranteed . . . Then came the summer of 1941. On Sunday morning the radio suddenly announced special news. Then came the fatal announcement. Comrade Molotov was to speak. The Germans had invaded our country! War!'*

Krukov had a lot to lose and he was not going to let it go without a fight, especially when he heard that his family had been trapped behind the German lines: *'I joined a battalion of volunteers and left the city to fight. We reached the Pulkovo Heights. There we fought like demons . . . Those German savages were burning everything. They want to give us nothing but grief. Therefore, we will stand indomitably and hold our line.'*

Valeri Krukov survived the war; his family were never heard of again.

Not everyone was like Krukov. For many, their families had lost too much in the great levelling of Soviet society, or the purges had come too close, or they had just been unlucky enough to be in the wrong place at the wrong time. In reigns of terror, where brutality spreads like a contagion and the worst in the human psyche comes to the surface, a simple affront, a petty jealousy, a whispered rumour can lead to imprisonment, torture, or even death.

Elena Skrjabina kept her diary going throughout Leningrad's long siege. One day she wrote about her friend's husband suddenly reappearing after two months in a gulag. He was a changed man: *'A strained relationship has grown up between them. He is fearful, crushed, afraid to speak. They beat him often, demanding some sort of confession of his "crimes". He has a broken rib and is deaf in one ear.'*

On 8 July, Skrjabina's co-worker disappeared – part of mass arrests undertaken by the NKVD to root out anyone disloyal to the state. Her co-worker's brother had been drafted into the army, while she was caring for an ageing mother, a tubercular sister and had a three-year-old daughter: *'They came at night, searched, found nothing, confiscated nothing, but took her away anyway.'* Skrjabina's co-worker was never seen again.

Yuri Ryabinkin was a fifteen-year-old schoolboy in 1941. He was too young to remember the October Revolution and too bright to fall for Soviet propaganda: *'Every leader in every paper shouts out, "We shall not surrender Leningrad! We shall defend it to the last!" But our Army has not won any victories and there are not enough weapons. The militiamen in the streets and the People's Volunteers are armed with rifles of alarming vintage. The Germans roll forward with their tanks and we are taught to fight them with a few grenades and bottles of incendiary fuel!'*

Ryabinkin continued to write throughout the winter of 1941. However, his health deteriorated and by January his writing became increasingly desperate. His last entry, dated 6 January, reads: *'Where's Mama? Where is she? . . . She has wild nervous fits because she can't stand my appearance, that of a weak, hungry, tormented person who can barely move from one place to the next . . . Oh Lord, what's happening to me?'*

Despairing of the situation in the north, Stalin sent Zhukov to take control of the defence of Leningrad on 13 September. He immediately ordered all-out counter-attacks, no matter what the cost. Typically, he told his senior commanders that anyone who retreated would be shot, as would their families. The counter-attacks failed; their only outcome was thousands of Red Army casualties.

Zhukov, perhaps trying to make a point to Stalin – and to the GKO and Stavka in the Kremlin – persisted and mustered what was left of Leningrad's reserves to mount another attack.

Although the Wehrmacht had failed to get as close to Leningrad as it had hoped, it had encircled the city and held it in an iron fist. Four Soviet armies – the 8th, 23rd, 42nd and 55th – a total of 20 divisions, over 300,000 men and at least 3 million civilians were trapped with little prospect of escape, and with winter only a few weeks away

The city's supply of food was only sufficient for one month, but this was reduced even further when the Luftwaffe bombed at least forty sheds of the Badaev food warehouses on 8 September. Important reserves of flour and sugar were lost.

Elena Skrjabina described the worsening hunger: *'The destruction of the Badaev warehouses can already be felt. The daily ration has been lowered. We are approaching the greatest horror. It gets harder every day. Everyone is preoccupied with only one thought: where to get something edible so as not to starve to death. We have returned to prehistoric times. Life has been reduced to one thing – the hunt for food.'*

Until the ice of winter took hold, it was possible to transport food in barges across Lake Ladoga, to the north of the city. However, the barges could only handle about 22,000 tons of food – 8,000 tons short of the city's monthly needs.

It took sixteen hours for a convoy of barges to cross from the Soviet-occupied mainland to the railway station at Osinovets Lighthouse, east of the city. In a relentless bombing campaign, the Luftwaffe destroyed 24 of the 31 barges and 6 steamers in the coming months, leaving the population facing mass starvation.

While the Red Army units worked continuously to strengthen the city's defences, Andrei Zhdanov, in a pragmatic, even ruthless, policy concentrated on relocating Leningrad's major resources rather than its beleaguered citizens. Factory equipment vital to the war effort, as well as key technicians – more than 10,000 of them – were sent out on the barges as a priority. Even though many thousands of children were evacuated, in the main, civilians would have to wait. A large percentage of them were women – their men away fighting – for whom it would be a long winter of extraordinary hardship.

Those children who were evacuated often faced perils as great as those in the city. The evacuations began in the middle of August, but many had to travel without their mothers. That was a trauma too great to bear for many families, especially when it was discovered that the destinations for many of the children were inside areas already occupied by the German units encircling the city.

Dimitri Likhachev, a medieval scholar, lived through the siege with his wife and twin daughters. He had survived the Solovki prison camp, established in 1923, which became a model for the regime's gulags, but had returned to Leningrad, where he joined Pushkin House, the Institute of Russian Literature. He began his diary in the late summer of 1941, when the evacuation of children had begun.

'The rumours of children's evacuation were frightening. We decided not to send our children, not to be separated from them. It was clear that the evacuation of children was in total disarray. Indeed, we later discovered that many children who were sent to Novgorod were simply delivered straight into German captivity, to meet the Germans. Also, in Lubani, when the Germans appeared nearby, the women who had accompanied the children grabbed their own children and fled, leaving the other children behind. They wandered, hungry, crying . . . too young to give their names. When they were eventually found, much later, they had lost their parents for ever.'

The greatest tragedy happened at Lychkovo, 250 miles southeast of Leningrad, on 18 August.

Maria Mostovskaya was helping with the evacuation of hundreds of pre-school children: *'Suddenly we heard that the Germans were dropping paratroopers, trying to cut us off. We used military vehicles, anything we could get our hands on, and ferried the kids to another station, Lychkovo.'*

The children had not been at Lychkovo Station for long when Luftwaffe dive-bombers appeared. Nine-year-old Ivan Fedulov and a group of older boys were loading luggage on the platform: '*A plane flew right over us, along the length of the train, dropping bomb after bomb, with terrifying methodical precision. When the smoke cleared carriages were scattered everywhere, as if they had been knocked off the track by a giant hand.*'

There were body parts everywhere. Fedulov ran into a nearby field with a group of survivors. The children were dressed in their Sunday best, and could not be mistaken for anything other than children: '*A plane circled and came back. Then it began machine-gunning the children. It was flying so low, I could see the pilot's face – totally impassive.*'

Alexandra Aresenyeva was on the train: '*The station was on fire. Bodies were strewn everywhere. It was absolutely horrifying. The chief of the evacuation was sitting on a stump, clasping his head in his hands. He had lost his family.*'

It is not known how many children were killed at Lychkovo, but twelve carriages were destroyed, so it must have been many hundreds. They were buried in a mass grave close to the station, mostly unidentified. All paperwork listing their names was destroyed in the attack.

The situation worsened as winter approached. Dimitri Likhachev recorded the dangers faced by the citizens in his diary entry for 8 September: '*One day, returning from the Pushkin House, I noticed several buses on Lakhtin Street. Women poured out of them with a lot of kids. It turned out that the Germans had suddenly approached the Putilov factory and shelled the area with mortars. The residents were urgently moved. These families, all from the southern districts of Leningrad, all soon died.*'

By early October, it became obvious that Hitler had decided to order his army to dig in and starve the city to death, and some units were withdrawn to reinforce his assault on Moscow. For those within the city the situation looked bleak. The average daily temperature had already dropped from its July level of 14°C to 4°C. Within a month it would be –2°C, and in December –6°C. The first snows had fallen and by December it would snow at least every other day, possibly more frequently. Leningraders were used to snow and low temperatures, but not in a city threatened by fuel and food shortages.

In Jonathan Dimbleby's *Russia*, the book he wrote to accompany his BBC TV series of the same name, he recounted extracts from NKVD files that had been compiled from secretly intercepted letters written by ordinary Leningraders.

> Our beloved Leningrad has turned into a heap of dirt and corpses. There is no light, no fuel, the water is frozen, the rubbish isn't cleared. And, most important, we're tormented by hunger.

> With every day that passes, life in Leningrad gets worse. Flour dust, which used to be used for making wallpaper paste, cannot be bought for love nor money.

> I was witness to a scene when a cabbie's horse collapsed on the street from malnutrition. People ran over to it with axes and knives and began cutting it up into pieces and carrying them home. It's awful. These people had the look of executioners about them.

> We've become a herd of hungry beasts. You walk along the streets and come across people swaying like drunks, collapsing and dying. We've become used to such sights and pay no attention because today they are dying but tomorrow it will be me.

> Leningrad has become a mortuary; the streets have become avenues of the dead, in cavalcades of corpses. In every house, the cellar is a dump for corpses.

Reduced to anonymity by decades of censorship, these testimonies have lost none of their power. They are a terrible foretaste of what was to unfold in the months to come.

7

LENINGRAD: STARVATION

DECEMBER 1941–JANUARY 1944

By December 1941, the city of Leningrad was starving to death. Tsar Peter the Great's Venice of the North was disintegrating, captured in the vice-like grip of the German Army. On 19 September the Wehrmacht's once unyielding advance had been halted, six miles short of the city. The city's 872-day ordeal had begun.

On 22 September, refusing to use its Soviet name, Hitler declared: 'St Petersburg must be erased from the face of the earth. We have no interest in saving the lives of the civilian population.' In a speech in Munich on 8 November, he bellowed: 'Leningrad must die of starvation!' Hitler had pronounced the city's death sentence.

With December's harsh winter set hard, the siege was three months old and the city was beginning to resemble a mortuary in limbo, with half the people dead, the other half barely alive. People no longer walked, they shuffled, like zombies, their limbs moving robotically, lacking the fluid motion of a well-nourished body and an alert brain.

The only food available was 125 grams of black bread per day, of which half was made up of sawdust and other inedible supplements, including dust from the floors of warehouses. The temperature dropped to –30°C. There was no fuel for public or private transport. Malnutrition meant that a distance of a few hundred yards to a food distribution kiosk was too far for all except the young and the strong.

Unable to capture the city, the Germans resorted to an aerial bombing campaign and artillery bombardment to reduce it to rubble and make its inhabitants cower. Tens of thousands of incendiary devices and thousands of high-explosive bombs rained down on the hovels of the poor and on its many once sumptuous palaces. Over 16,000 people were killed by the bombing, more than 30,000 wounded. Literary critic and historian Lydia Ginzburg's diary was published in 1984 and translated into English, as *Notes from the Blockade*, in 1995.

> You begin to realise that as you sit at home in your room you are suspended in space, with other people similarly suspended over your head and beneath your feet. You know this, of course – you have heard furniture being moved about upstairs, even wood being chopped. But that's all in the abstract . . . Now the truth is demonstrated in dizzying, graphic fashion. There are skeleton buildings which have kept their facade . . . The sky shows through the empty window sockets of the upper storeys. And there are buildings, especially small ones, whose beams and floors have collapsed under their crumbling roofs. They hang at an angle and look as if they are sliding downwards, perpetually falling like a waterfall.

With her city besieged and the whistle, thud and roar of explosions falling upon her, the poet Olga Berggolts wrote of how it felt to be under constant bombardment: *'One wanted to squeeze oneself into the ground. This one's for me. You die and it passes, but a minute later it comes again, and you die, are resurrected, sigh with relief, only to die repeatedly. How long will this last . . . Kill me all at once, not bit by bit, several times a day.'*

Dimitri Likhachev recorded the daily destruction that was being unleashed on the city: *'Houses burned for weeks. There was nothing to put them out. In every house there were emaciated who could not move, and they burned alive. There was one terrible case, a big new house on Suvorovskiy, which had been turned into a hospital. It was hit by a bomb, which broke through all the floors, destroying the stairs. The fire started from below; it was impossible to get out of the building. The wounded were thrown out of the window; it is better to break your bones than burn to death.*

There was a two-storey house on Grand Avenue, on the corner of Lenin Street. There was a bakery downstairs. A shell pierced the whole house from top to bottom and exploded in the bakery. Dozens of people were killed. The basement was flooded with blood.

The wife of the head of the dining room, Sergeychuk, had her head blown off. She was riding in a tram. Leningrad's old tram cars had benches along the windows. The explosion knocked out the windows and decapitated everyone seated.'

The city had just one lifeline: the now legendary *Doroga Zhizni* ('Road of Life'). Only operational in the depths of winter, it was a thirty-mile-long umbilical cord of ice that provided a meagre hope of survival. The Road of Life began to operate on 19 November 1941, when the first supplies were carried over the frozen Lake Ladoga on horse-drawn sleighs. German bombardments and ruptures in the ice meant that supplies were minimal and intermittent. It was only in mid-December, with the construction of a railroad directly connecting the western shore of Lake Ladoga to Leningrad, that the ice road began to receive supplies carried by trucks. But on the first crossing, 157 supply trucks fell through the ice and sank to the bottom of the lake – a depth of 700 feet at its deepest point.

After sustaining massive initial supply losses in November and December, the Road of Life slowly began to show signs of improvement by January and February 1942, but it was too late to stave off the privations of those two terrible months. Through the incompetence of the authorities, precious food that arrived from late December onwards – 4,000 lorries carrying 700 tons of food a day – did not reach ordinary Leningraders quickly enough.

During the winter of 1941/42 the ice corridor operated for 152 days, until late April. About 514,000 city inhabitants, 35,000 wounded soldiers, industrial equipment from 86 plants and factories, as well as art and museum collections, were all evacuated from Leningrad during the first winter of the siege. Eventually, the total number of people evacuated from the siege of Leningrad along the miracle on ice was about 1.3 million, mostly women and children.

Vera Rogova was one of its traffic wardens: *'We were stationed at 500-metre intervals along the road. It was difficult and dangerous work.*

Out on the flat, open expanse of the lake it was bitterly cold, with tem-
peratures dropping to minus 40 Celsius. There was nowhere to take cover
from German attacks. We did what we could – putting medical units
along the road to help the wounded or anyone suffering from frostbite,
and setting up anti-aircraft guns to provide some sort of protection. But
conditions were terrible.'

Despite the adversities, Vera found that recruiting volunteers
and maintaining morale was not a problem: *'We all took a military*
oath, but it was not really necessary. Everyone felt the urgency of the
situation. We all knew that Leningrad was starving to death. The drivers
drove bumper to bumper. They were trying to get as much food into the
city as possible.'

Ivan Krylov worked as a loader on the eastern shore of Lake
Ladoga: *'We laboured day and night. It was exhausting work . . . The*
Germans constantly tried to bomb our supply columns, seven or eight
air raids a day. We just kept working through them, regardless of the
explosions around us . . . We had all heard of the reduction of the food
ration, so we kept going. We really felt that the ice road would save
people's lives.'

With the Road of Life yet to have any discernible effect,
Christmas 1941 passed with only a flicker of celebration. There
were church services, but religious observations were of little consequence with the pangs of hunger tormenting bloated bellies.
Such was the volume of deaths, even funerals became redundant.
On New Year's Eve, the German Army bombed the city. They also
made a deadly addition to the Luftwaffe's bombing of the Road of
Life. When they realised that many desperate citizens were trying
to cross the ice of Lake Ladoga on foot, they began to drop what
appeared to be tins of food. However, they were not rations, they
were mines which exploded when touched. There was no festive
goodwill on the Eastern Front.

The power stations ran out of fuel, so the power supply in the
city failed. The water-pumping stations were no longer able to
pump water to the bakeries, and without water the bakers could
not bake bread. The fire department had to bring in hand pumps
and, armed with pails, 4,000 Young Communist League volunteers,

the only people strong enough to do it, formed human chains to draw water by hand from the Neva River to the bakeries.

The poet Vera Inber made a diary entry on 25 January: '7 p.m. The situation is catastrophic. People have now fallen on the wooden fence around the hospital and are using it for kindling. There is no water. Our water supply: half a tea kettle (we keep it on the warm stove), half a pan for washing, and a quarter of a bottle for tomorrow. That's all.'

Her entry for the next day reads: 'I cried for the first time from grief and bitterness. I upset the cereal in the stove. Ilya swallowed a few spoonfuls mixed with ashes. No bread yet.'

Dimitri Likhachev, too, recorded the extreme conditions in which they were living: 'The bathrooms didn't work. People wrapped what they made in paper and threw it outside. So it was dangerous to walk near the houses. Trails of excrements were trodden into the pavements. Fortunately, one only needed to do one's business occasionally, perhaps once a week, even once every ten days. The body digested everything.'

The death toll in January reached 100,000 per month, mostly from starvation. People died on the streets; bodies, no more than bundles of rags, were commonplace. Anna Govorov kept a diary throughout the siege: 'The first time I saw a body, I mistook him for a disabled veteran from the Vostochny Front [The Eastern Front in the Great War] huddled in a doorway. He didn't raise his hand for money, which was strange. Then I looked at his face and it was like dull porcelain. I knew then he was dead. When I got home, I got out my fur coat and sold it on the streets for a few roubles. I thought I could buy food with it. But I was stupid; there was no food to buy.'

Translator and librarian Aleksandra Liubovskaia wrote that she felt like Mary washing Jesus when she bathed her emaciated son, and described her shock that men and women had become 'so identical . . . Everyone is shrivelled, their breasts sunken in, their stomachs enormous, and instead of arms and legs, just bones poke out through wrinkles.'

Dimitri Likhachev described how: 'I saw nurses dragging the corpses of the dead into hospital basements. I remember that one was still very young. His face was black. The nurse explained to me that it *is necessary to pull the corpses down while they are still warm. When the corpse gets cold, lice crawl out. The city was infected with lice; the starving are not capable of hygiene!'*

Theatre producer Alexander Dymov wrote: *'We lead a primitive life, without water, without light, without warmth. Hundreds of people, carrying pitchers or kettles, queue despondently at a tap in a laundry. They stand there for hours.'*

But Dymov refused to give up hope, nor did he lose his sense of humour. One evening, he decided to respond to the pangs of hunger he was feeling in his stomach by writing it a letter of complaint. At the same time, he cast his words in a mocking tone, ridiculing the censorship rules of the Soviet state.

'Much respected Citizen Editor, Comrade Stomach,

I am weak and feeble. I have great difficulty even dragging my feet and my face has long got out of the habit of smiling. I have been hungry for a long time, but I am fighting, fighting not to fall, for death quickly tramples the fallen. So far, I am hanging on, and even continuing to fight. And I have not yet stopped thinking or reading books. You, Citizen Editor, prevent me from doing all this. Every moment I am conscious of your power, of your oppression, your interference in my internal affairs . . . I refuse to think of nothing but gorging myself. I want to dream of the future, a beautiful future, not being stuffed to the brim with potatoes, bread and sunflower oil. You need to understand that I want to stay a human being . . . Abdicate your role of dictator. Go about your modest business conscientiously – after all, now you haven't that much work to do.

Accept my sincere respects,

Your obedient servant,

A. Dymov.'

Domestic pets had long since disappeared. When the ration for service dogs ended on 1 December, dogs had become a prized commodity. Vera Inber's friend Irina had a pet Airedale terrier. One day, Vera met Irina, who was taking her dog to the toxicologist to put him to sleep: *'But first I'll give him one good meal. I have a crust of bread left. And what happens next, I don't want to know. But of course, he'll be eaten. I know my co-workers have been waiting a long time for this.'*

People began to stew the pages of books and boil leather belts to make soup. They ate rats. Anything that moved was a potential meal, and much more nourishing than paper and leather. Reports of cannibalism soon appeared in the records of the NKVD, which were not published until 2004.

It is, of course, a taboo subject, and the scale of the consumption of dead bodies – and, indeed, the murder of individuals for food – during the siege is the subject of much debate, and its extent will never be known. Nevertheless, as more and more letters and diaries are read, it becomes clear that cannibalism was widespread during the dark days of December 1941 to February 1942. A diary entry by optical engineer Dmitri Lazarev recalls his daughter and niece reciting a chilling nursery rhyme, adapted from a pre-war song.

> *'A dystrophic walked along*
> *With a dull look.*
> *In a basket he carried a corpse's arse.*
> *I'm having human flesh for lunch,*
> *This piece will do!*
> *Ugh, hungry sorrow!*
> *And for supper, clearly*
> *I'll need a little baby.*
> *I'll take the neighbours',*
> *Steal him out of his cradle.'*

In January, Lazarev had to bury his father-in-law: *'Finally, we were at the gates of the mortuary, a former woodshed. Opening the door, we saw a pile of corpses . . . We began our ascent to the top of the pile, climbing over frozen and slippery-as-ice stomachs, backs and heads. Despite the cold, the stench was overpowering . . . We felt a dull indifference to the death of a loved one. The way back was easier. We even stopped for a minute, struck by the unusual beauty of a besieged, silhouetted Leningrad in the moonlit night.'*

Dimitri Likhachev recorded the grim reality: *'The cannibalism has begun! Soft body parts were cut off the corpses lying in the streets.*

First the corpses were undressed, then cut to the bone, there was almost no meat on them; naked corpses were terrible. Cannibalism can't be judged indiscriminately. For the most part it was not conscious. The one who cut the corpse rarely ate the meat himself. He either sold the meat, deceiving the buyer, or fed it to his loved ones to save their lives. After all, when a child is dying and you know that only meat can save him, you will take meat off the corpse.

There were also some villains who killed people to get their meat for sale. The following horror was discovered in the huge red house of the former Humane Society. Someone was supposedly selling potatoes. The buyer was offered to look under the sofa where the potatoes were lying, and when he bent down, he was hit in the back of the head with an axe. The crime was discovered by a buyer who noticed unwashed blood on the floor. The bones of many people were found.'

Equally shocking was the incidence of murder for ration cards, money and clothing. A conservative estimate of the official murder rate was six per day throughout 1942. Anna Govorov heard of one unfortunate victim: *'Comrade Ivanov was killed today. I heard that two men and a woman attacked him with shovels. They beat him to death and stole his coat, his shoes and all his money. They looked and looked for his ration card but couldn't find it. He had let his sister borrow it because she is very sick. He was too old to defend himself. The poor man is now lying in the street. We will go and collect him later and bury him in the mass grave in the park.'*

A web of dingy streets behind the city's Haymarket, which had, before the Revolution, been the gathering place for criminals and prostitutes, once again became a focus for ne'er-do-wells and the desperate. Bread was the currency. For bread, anything was for sale: women's bodies or men's lives. The naive brought watches, diamond rings and furs, but got only a crust of bread in return.

Gangs roamed the city at night, looking for anyone foolish enough to be on the streets in the blackness of a winter night. Few who ventured out were ever seen again. Those buying little black-market meat patties in the Haymarket convinced themselves that the crucial ingredient was rat or dog. No one wanted to think that they may be consuming a fellow comrade.

As the corpses mounted in the cemeteries around the city, the sappers from the army units defending the perimeter were sent in to bury them. They noticed that many of the bodies had pieces missing and, like prime cuts of beef, it was usually thighs, upper arms or whole shoulders that had gone missing. Grotesque as it sounds, there was no law which forbade the dismemberment of corpses, nor the consumption of the products of the necro-butchery.

Elena Taranukhina, a teenager who was digging trenches when the siege began, remembered the courtyard at the back of her apartment filling with corpses. Two of the bodies, young women, had had their breasts hacked off. Taranukhina even feared that, delirious with hunger, her mother would attack and eat her own granddaughter: *'I came back from the queues and saw my mother bathing my daughter. But there was no water in the bath. I arrived just in time. It's difficult to say that she was going to eat my daughter alive. She kept saying what a fatty child she was. Within hours of that my mother had died.'*

Maria Ivanova, a housing administrator, was asked to visit a family by a neighbour who said that the mother had been acting strangely. The family had included several children, but she found only two. *'The rest have died,'* claimed the mother. But there were no registrations of death. There was a pot boiling on the stove. Ivanova was told it was mutton, but when she stirred the contents, a human hand appeared.

Army supply officer Vasily Yershov reported that organised gangs of cannibals were at work on Leningrad's streets. One group, medical workers, including several doctors, had even infiltrated a hospital. Another gang, twenty strong, was abducting and slaughtering military couriers coming into the city. Many witnesses have said that, in early February, with law and order on the brink of collapse, the one thing that saved the city from anarchy was that people did not have the strength to take to the streets in vast numbers.

The only water available came from ice holes in the city's rivers and canals. But the ice around the holes was strewn with the bodies of people who could survive no longer or had frozen to death trying to collect water. The rivers were also a convenient means of disposing of the dead.

It did not take long for epidemics to break out; in particular, dysentery and typhus. Diarrhoea was endemic and was called 'starvation diarrhoea'. Dysentery killed Dimitri Likhachev's father. As he took his body to be buried, he was passed by a truck full of corpses, many of them loaded upright: *'I remember the body of a woman: naked, brown, thin, upright, hands raised. The lorry was going at speed, leaving her hair streaming in the wind. It looked as if she was making a speech – calling out, waving her arms – a ghastly, defiled corpse with open, glassy eyes.'*

One of the most poignant accounts of the war came from Tanya Savicheva, who kept a diary during the siege. It has only eight pages but is one of the most powerful illustrations of the suffering inflicted on the city. It chronicles the deaths of her entire family.

'Zhenya died on December 28th at 12 noon, 1941
Grandma died on the 25th of January at 3 o'clock, 1942
Leka died March 17th, at 5 o'clock in the morning, 1942
Uncle Vasya died on April 13th at 2 o'clock in the morning, 1942
Uncle Lesha May 10th, at 4 o'clock in the afternoon, 1942
Mama on May 13th at 7:30 in the morning, 1942
The Savichevs are dead
Everyone is dead
Only Tanya is left – Tanya Savicheva'

Tanya survived the siege but died of intestinal tuberculosis on 1 July 1944, aged fourteen, the last of her family.

Dimitri Likhachev wrote about the paradox of human morality: *'In hunger people showed their true selves: some were wonderful, unparalleled heroes; others were villains, scoundrels, murderers, cannibals. There was no middle ground.*

The human brain was the last to die. When the hands and feet ceased to function, the fingers did not button, there was no strength to close the mouth. When the skin darkened and tightened, it barely covered the skull with exposed, laughing teeth. The brain continued to work. People wrote diaries, philosophical works, scientific papers "from the heart"; they showed extraordinary resolve, not yielding to pressure, not succumbing to what they endured.'

In the end, despite the horrors, despite the depravity, the city and its people survived. They did so because, as much as humans can be cruel, and utterly selfish, they can also be caring, compassionate and totally selfless. The collective will of the ordinary people triumphed over the incompetence of their leaders and the malevolence of those who strove to exploit their plight.

People remembered their heritage. Pride in their city and their love for Mother Russia fortified them. They read Tolstoy in groups, recited poetry and sang songs together. Dedicated to the people of his native city, Shostakovich wrote his 7th symphony, 'Leningrad', in December 1941. The Leningrad premiere, at the Grand Philharmonia Hall, was performed on 9 August 1942 by the surviving musicians of the Leningrad Radio Orchestra, supplemented with military performers. Most of the musicians were suffering from malnutrition, which made rehearsing difficult. They often collapsed during rehearsals; three died. The orchestra was able to play the symphony all the way through only once before the concert.

Despite the poor condition of the performers, the concert was a huge success, prompting floods of tears during an hour-long ovation. The conductor, Karl Eliasberg, said, 'In that moment, we triumphed over the soulless Nazi war machine.'

Loudspeakers broadcast the performance throughout the city, in what was called a 'tactical strike against German morale', reaching the German forces around its periphery. One German soldier is reputed to have said that he and his fellow soldiers 'listened to the symphony of heroes'.

Twelve-year-old Andrei Krukov was left abandoned when his father died of exhaustion after bringing food for his family. Andrei survived thanks to the kindness of strangers: *'The suffering was on an unprecedented scale – yet, astonishingly, Leningrad did not succumb. People somehow had the strength to reach out to help others, and by doing this, something mysterious yet deeply powerful came into being. We were fighting a battle to keep a human face, to stay human beings. And we won it.'*

The writer Pavel Luknitsky wrote during the darkest days of the siege: *'Such was the image of my own unhappy, proud, besieged city. I am happy that I did not run away, that I share its fate, that I am a witness, a participant, and a witness to all its misfortunes. And if I live, I will remember them – I will never forget my beloved Leningrad in the winter of 1941–42.'*

The horror of the siege would go on through another winter, but supplies via the Road of Life meant that conditions were never again as bad as they were in the long, dark months of 1941/42. A land corridor was opened in January 1943, and the siege was finally lifted when the German Army was pushed back in January 1944.

Apart from the Soviet military casualties sustained in the defence of the city, estimated to have been at least 1 million, it is thought that over 650,000 civilians died during the siege of Leningrad.

Leningrad's harrowing story, and its extraordinary fight for survival, encapsulates the characteristics of the entire conflict, the story of the war itself.

PART TWO

EXTERMINATION

8

THE 'BRUTAL DOG' LET LOOSE

JULY 1941

With a perverted pride, the *Brutaler Hund* ('Brutal Dog') of the Eastern Front was a name coined for himself by one of the commandants of Hitler's death squads during the war. Its vicious arrogance encapsulates the psychology of hate that characterised Hitler's deviant Nazi ideology and led to the wholesale abuse and murder of millions of prisoners and non-combatants during the conflict.

The Führer's undeniable charisma as a cult figure, revered as a Teutonic god incarnate, and for his National Socialism to be worshipped as a pseudo-religion. A speech made in February 1937 by the fanatical Nazi Robert Ley, the head of the German Labour Front, gives a perfect illustration of Hitler's malign grip on the minds of the German people.

> Adolf Hitler! We are linked and united with you alone! In this hour we seek to renew our vow to you: we believe on this earth in Adolf Hitler alone. We believe that National Socialism alone is the redemptive faith for our people . . . And we believe that . . . Almighty God has sent us Adolf Hitler, so that Germany shall have eternal security.

Armed with this messianic power, Hitler and his disciples were able to imprint the Führer's malevolent thoughts and impulses on to significant numbers of the population, who embraced his ideology with a herd-like enthusiasm. The police and the armed forces were particularly galvanized by his rhetoric. Not only did swathes of the existing police and Wehrmacht embrace Hitler's fanaticism, but also new macabre institutions like the Gestapo and the *Schutzstaffel* (the SS). At the head of these organisations Hitler had the perfect henchman Heinrich Himmler, who became the second most powerful man in Germany and who oversaw Hitler's vicious extermination policies.

Hitler's menace was first felt with unbridled ferocity within German society itself. As early as July 1933, only a few months after his appointment as German Chancellor, all other political parties and the trade unions were suppressed, the press and radio brought under state control, and most elements of a free society neutralised. Significantly, in 1934, all German civil servants and armed forces personnel swore an oath, not to the state, not to the constitution, but to Hitler. His rule was absolute. Germany was about to acquire a terrible legacy that still troubles its citizens today.

Operating beyond the law, the infamous Gestapo – an abbreviation of *Geheime Staatspolizei* (Secret State Police) – became responsible for the ruthless eradication of any opponents of the Nazi regime. Left-wing elements within National Socialism, embodied by Ernst Röhm and his SA – *Sturmabteilung* (Storm Detachment) – were destroyed in the 1934 'Night of the Long Knives', a killing spree in which Hitler participated personally. In addition, dissident clergy, opposition trade unionists, army officers, journalists – indeed, anyone who dared speak out against the Nazis and their ideology – were rounded up and executed. Approximately 77,000 German citizens were killed for various forms of 'resistance' during Hitler's rule of Germany.

Concentration camps appeared as early as 1933. The first, Dachau, only ten miles north of Munich, opened in March, and was filled with a range of people who contradicted Hitler's ideology, as well as those groups he loathed: communists, socialists, Roma, Jehovah's Witnesses, homosexuals and those considered to be 'deviant' or engaging in 'anti-social behaviour'.

The policy of *Aktion T4* was introduced throughout Germany and German-occupied territories in September 1939. The policy allowed for the 'mercy killing' of various categories of people deemed to be 'incurably sick'. The disabled, those in psychiatric hospitals and asylums, anyone with a deformity or congenital condition, were all subject to examination, experimentation and euthanasia under *Aktion T4*.

Hospitals, nursing homes, old people's homes and sanatoria were required to report all patients who had been institutionalised for five years or more. This included all who had been committed as 'criminally insane', who were of 'non-Aryan race' or who had been diagnosed with any of a long list of conditions. The conditions included schizophrenia, epilepsy, Huntington's chorea, advanced syphilis, senile dementia, paralysis, encephalitis and 'terminal neurological conditions generally'. Based on the savage notion of 'racial hygiene', as many as 300,000 people were killed between 1939 and 1945 throughout Europe.

The target of Hitler's most potent venom was Germany's Jews, and those living in countries under the heel of the Wehrmacht. In January 1933, some 522,000 Jews lived in Germany; as soon as Hitler grabbed power and implemented his racist ideology, the Jewish community was increasingly targeted. The persecution of Jews became an official national policy.

In 1935 and 1936, the pace of anti-Semitic oppression increased. Jews were banned from all professional jobs, effectively preventing them from participating in education, politics, higher education, the armed forces and industry. In 1935, the Nuremburg Race Laws forbade any sexual contact between 'Aryan' and 'non-Aryan' people. The SA (*Sturmabteilung*) initiated *Kristallnacht* ('Night of Broken Glass') on 9–10 November 1938, when Jewish shops and offices were vandalised, and many synagogues were destroyed by fire. As many as 60 per cent, around 304,000 people, emigrated during the first six years of the Nazi dictatorship. Only 214,000 Jews were left in Germany on the eve of the Second World War.

Beginning in late 1941, the remaining Jewish community was subjected to systematic removal to ghettos and, ultimately, to death camps in Eastern Europe. In May 1943, Germany was declared *Judenrein* ('clean of Jews'). By the end of the war, it is estimated that between 160,000 and 180,000 German Jews had been killed by the Nazi regime and its collaborators.

Hitler's treatment of the Jews of Germany would be extended to the Jews of Eastern Europe, and to all other *Untermenschen*, when Barbarossa was unleashed in June 1941.

The teeth of the Brutal Dog were the notorious *Einsatzgruppen* ('deployment groups'), formed in 1938 under the direction of *SS-Obergruppenführer* Reinhard Heydrich and operated by the SS. Heydrich was another of the Führer's most savage henchmen, someone Hitler himself described as 'the man with the iron heart'.

In preparation for the invasion of Poland in September 1939, the *Einsatzgruppen* were reassigned to combat suspected enemies of the German state behind the advancing Wehrmacht. Seven *Einsatzgruppen* and their sub-units, *Einsatzkommandos*, totalling 4,250 men, were placed under the operational command of Heydrich. He directed a campaign involving the widespread arrest and execution of individuals considered a threat to the establishment of German control, including Polish nationalists, Roman Catholic clergy, Jews, and members of the Polish nobility and intelligentsia. By December 1939, these SS units, aided by ethnic German auxiliaries, had murdered 50,000 Poles, including 7,000 Polish Jews. By the time of Operation Barbarossa, Germany's pitiless beast of war was already off the leash.

Euphoric with the news of the Wehrmacht's early successes, Hitler took the opportunity afforded by the capture of millions of Soviet citizens to launch his extermination policies on an industrial scale. With ruthless efficiency, gruesome experiments began with the aim of determining the most efficient way of killing people on a vast scale. This fuelled the genocide that was to become the most horrific hallmark of the Second World War; the 6 million dead in the Holocaust that followed was the inevitable conclusion.

•

The *Einsatzgruppen* went to work within days of the launch of Barbarossa. The rounding-up of 'undesirables', 'suspicious elements', 'hostiles' and Jews of all sorts – 'wandering', 'rebellious', 'activist', 'intellectual', but eventually just 'Jews' – became routine, as did their mass slaughter. The policy was indiscriminate; men, women and children all suffered the same fate. Thousands were simply rounded up and shot.

Yitskhok Rudachevski was a thirteen-year-old Jewish boy in Vilnius, the capital of Lithuania, when the city fell to the Wehrmacht on 24 June. He kept a diary from inside one of the city's ghettos: *'June 1941. The first great tragedy. People are harnessed to bundles which they drag across the pavement. People fall, bundles scatter . . . I think of nothing: not what I am losing, not what I have just lost, not what is in store for me. I feel that an insult, a hurt is burning inside me. Here is the ghetto gate. I feel that I have been robbed, my freedom is being robbed from me, my home, and the familiar Vilna [Vilnius] streets I love so much. I have been cut off from all that is dear and precious to me.'*

His diary entry for 30 September reads: *'It is Yom Kippur Eve. A sad mood suffuses the ghetto . . . This holiday is drenched in blood and sorrow which is solemnized in the ghetto, and now penetrates my heart. In the evening I felt so sad at heart. People sit at home and weep. They remind themselves of the past . . . Drenching each other with tears as they embrace . . . I run out into the streets and there it is also the same: sorrow flows over the little streets, the ghetto is drenched in tears. The hearts which have turned to stone in the grip of ghetto woes and did not have time to weep their fill have now in this evening of lamentation poured out all their bitterness . . . The evening was dreary and darkly sad for me.'*

After the liquidation of the Vilnius Ghetto on 23 September 1943, Yitskhok, his family and his uncle's family all went into hiding. Two weeks later, their hiding place was discovered, and they were taken to Ponar, a village near Vilnius, where they were all murdered and buried in mass graves. It is estimated that at least 70,000 Jews, 20,000 Polish intelligentsia and 8,000 Soviet POWs were murdered at Ponar between 1941 and 1944.

It is one of history's saddest truths that hatred spreads like a disease and is highly contagious. However, there have been few infections quite as virulent as the spread of Nazi repression and genocide in the occupied territories. Among the first recorded atrocities of the Eastern Front was one perpetrated not by German death squads, but by their all-too-willing local supporters.

On 25 June, a 600-strong rogue unit of Lithuanian nationalists, led by Algirdas Klimaitis, a vicious attack on the Jews of Kaunas, Lithuania's second city, began. They were supported by *Einsatz-gruppe A*, fresh from its killing sprees in occupied Poland.

One of the most shameful incidents occurred in what was later known as the Lietūkis Garage Massacre. Carried out before the invading Germans had set up their administration, Jews were forced to gather in the courtyard of a garage in the centre of the city. Gentile Lithuanian children were lifted on to the shoulders of their parents to catch a glimpse of the 'Death Dealer of Kaunas'. Although the depths of this man's depravity are known, his identity has never been established. An anonymous witness described the incident, an account almost too graphic to repeat: '*On the concrete forecourt of the petrol station a blond man of medium height, aged about twenty-five, stood leaning on a wooden club, resting. The club was as thick as his arm and came up to his chest. At his feet lay about fifteen to twenty dead or dying people. Water flowed continuously from a hose washing blood away into the drainage gully. Just a few steps behind this man some twenty men, guarded by armed civilians, stood waiting for their cruel execution in silent submission. In response to a cursory wave the next man stepped forward silently and was beaten to death with the wooden club in the most bestial manner, each blow accompanied by enthusiastic shouts from the audience. Once the mound of the bodies at his feet had reach fifty, the Death Dealer fetched an accordion, climbed to the top of the pile of the corpses, and played the Lithuanian national anthem.*'

Laimonas Noreika was a resident of Kaunas and witnessed another example of the horror perpetrated at the garage: '*Those horrific events have been burned on to my memory and will remain there until my dying day. In the middle of the yard, in broad daylight and in full view of the assembled crowd, a group of well-dressed, spruce, intelligent-looking people held iron bars which they used to viciously beat another group of similarly well-dressed, spruce, intelligent people. The assailants relentlessly battered the Jews until they fell to the ground. They kept hitting them until, finally, they lay inert. Then, using a hosepipe, they doused them with water until they came around, following which the abuse would start all over again. And so it went on and on until the hapless victims lay dead. Bodies began to pile up everywhere. I stood next to the fence and watched it all until, finally, my brother Albertas pulled me away.'*

Another outrage occurred in Slobodka, the Jewish suburb of Kaunas. Rabbi Ephraim Oshry, despite starvation and repeated beatings, was one of the few European rabbis to survive the Kaunas Ghetto, where his wife and children were killed. In 1995, he wrote *Annihilation of Lithuanian Jewry*. He described what happened when the German death squad arrived in Slobodka: *'There were Germans present on the bridge to Slobodka, but it was the Lithuanian volunteers who killed the Jews. The Rabbi of Slobodka, Rav Zalman Osovsky, was tied hand and foot to a chair, then his head was laid upon an open volume of the Gemara [a part of the Talmud – the holy book of Judaism] and [they] sawed his head off, after which they murdered his wife and son. His head was placed in a window of the residence, bearing a sign, "This is what we'll do to all the Jews." [. . .]'*

Macha Rolnikas was fourteen when the Wehrmacht marched into Vilnius. Not only was she Jewish, her father was a liberal lawyer who often defended communists, so she and her family were prominent targets for the *Einsatzgruppen*. She started writing her diary as soon as the German occupation began. She describes just one of the many harrowing scenes as the city's Jews were persecuted by both the Germans and their fellow Lithuanians: *'A woman crawling on all fours. Her hair is tangled, her clothes are dirty from dragging herself along the ground, her eyes wide open, her face grimacing. Her bulging belly is resting on the ground. Covered with sweat, she stops every few minutes and, like an animal, pricks up her ears; is danger awaiting her somewhere? She is losing strength. A great pain seizes her, shooting pains into her breast. She knows that her last moments are approaching, she is going to give birth. All night long, rolled up like a ball, exhausted, full of pain, she felt the looming delivery. She turns over and over in pain, writhing like a snake. She startles and death comes and interrupts her anguish at the same moment that her little girl comes into this world of pain and shadow. She is taken into the ghetto and named Ghettala. Poor girl.'*

A similar saga of horror unfolded in Latvia, especially its capital, Riga. As in the other Baltic States, there was little affection for the Soviet system. Balts are not Russian, and most Baltic peoples thought of the Red Army as an army of occupation. Not unexpectedly, many Latvians welcomed the Wehrmacht's panzers when they rolled into Riga on 1 July.

Within three months, more than 6,000 people, mostly Jews, had been killed in Riga and its surroundings. Large groups of prisoners were taken out of the Central Prison by truck to Bikernieki Forest, where they were shot. On 2 July, armed Latvian youths dragged Jews out of their homes and attacked them. Some were beaten to death, others shot.

By the middle of October, up to 30,000 Jews had been killed – nearly half of the approximately 66,000 Jews who had not been able to flee the country before the German occupation. By the end of the month, all the remaining Jews of Riga and its suburbs had been confined to a ghetto within the city's gates.

Riga's agony culminated in what is known as the Rumbula Massacre. It took place on 30 November 1941. Two days beforehand, orders were received that all able-bodied men and female seamstresses should be relocated to a different ghetto, to provide 'useful' slave labour. The remaining population consisted of children, the elderly and 'less useful' women.

Early in the morning of 30 November, men of *Einsatzgruppe A* and Latvian officers forcefully removed them from their homes. Those who were too old or sick to leave were murdered on the spot. Once the victims had been gathered, they were herded into 12 groups of 1,000 people each and paraded through the streets. Anyone who could not keep up the pace was also shot, as were those who attempted to escape.

Frida Michelson survived the massacre by diving into the snow and pretending to be dead: *'The columns of people were moving on and on, sometimes at a half-run, marching, trotting, without end. There one, there another, would fall and they would walk right over them, constantly being urged on by the policemen, "Faster, faster!" with their whips and rifle butts. [It was] about midday when the horror of the march ended . . . Now the street was quiet, nothing moved. Corpses were scattered all over, rivulets of blood still oozing from the lifeless bodies. They were mostly old people, pregnant women, children, handicapped – all those who could not keep up with the inhuman tempo of the march.'*

At least 1,000 Jews were murdered before they even arrived at the designated killing ground – three mass burial pits in the Rumbula Forest, dug by Jewish forced labourers. Upon arrival, the Jews were forced to stand at the edge of the pit, where they were shot by teams of *Einsatzgruppen* soldiers. Each person was shot once, in the back of the head, but as the day wore on and the light grew worse, the executioners sometimes missed, meaning that victims often survived. But they would soon envy the dead, as they were crushed to death by the weight of new corpses above them.

Max Kaufmann, another survivor of Riga, described the horrors he witnessed: *'The bloody evacuations began on the night of November 29th. Thousands of totally drunk Latvian and German guards in uniform swarmed into the large ghetto and started hunting Jews. Like wild animals they broke into apartments. Many Jews were beaten and some murdered. Children were torn from their parents, and some were thrown out of windows by the guards. Jews were ordered to dress quickly and fall into columns. Under German leadership these were surrounded and heavily guarded by Latvians. At the Rumbula railroad station, adjoining the forest, graves had already been prepared by Soviet prisoners of war under German guidance. In bitter cold, men, women and children were ordered to undress, after which they were horribly beaten, pushed to the edges of the graves and slaughtered. Thousands of victims had to wait their turn in the meantime and watch the mass killings. The bloodbath ceased after several days . . . The earth still heaved for a long time because of the many half-dead people.'*

A further death march took place on 8 December. Estimates suggest that the number of survivors from the first atrocity was about 30 people out of almost 12,000. Around 25,000 people were murdered in total in both marches.

In 1944, to destroy the evidence, the Germans forced prisoners to reopen the mass graves in the Rumbula Forest and burn the bodies. Once they had completed their task, the prisoners were executed. In the same year, thousands of Jews were killed in the remaining Latvian concentration camp at Kaiserwald, or sent to the Stutthof concentration camp in Germany. By the time the Red Army liberated Riga, in October 1944, almost all of Latvia's Jews had been murdered; no more than a few hundred are believed to have survived.

•

For the Jews of Estonia, there could not have been a greater contrast between life before and after German occupation. In 1936, the British-based Jewish newspaper *The Jewish Chronicle* reported that:

> Estonia is the only country in Eastern Europe where neither the Government nor the people practise any discrimination against Jews and where Jews are left in peace and are allowed to lead a free and unmolested life and fashion it in accord with their national and cultural principles.

Before the war, there were approximately 4,300 Jews in Estonia. Following the 1940 Soviet occupation, as in the other Baltic States, several hundred Jews were deported to Siberia, along with other Estonians to whom the Soviets took a dislike: politicians, dissidents, intellectuals – all 'enemies of the people'.

A further 3,000 Estonian Jews, aware of the fate that awaited them from the Nazi death squads, escaped. Almost all who remained, about 1,000 people, were killed by *Einsatzgruppe A* – with the active support of local collaborators – before the end of 1941. The Roma people of Estonia were also murdered. At least 6,000 ethnic Estonians and 1,000 ethnic Russians who were accused of being communist sympathisers, or were the relatives of communist sympathisers, were also executed. Of the 1,000 Jews who remained in Estonia, fewer than a dozen are known to have survived the war.

There are few recorded witnesses to the fate of those who died in Estonia. One woman, known only as 'E.S.', described the arrest of her Jewish husband: *'When I came home, there were two men in our apartment from the police, who said they were taking my husband to the police station. I ran after them and went to the chief officer and asked for permission to see my husband. He said that he could not give me permission but added, in a low voice, that I should come the next morning when the prisoners would be taken to prison and perhaps I could see my husband in the corridor. I returned the next morning as I had been advised, and it was the last time I saw my husband. On September 15th, I went to the German police to get information about my husband. I was told he had been shot. I asked the reason since he had not been a communist but a businessman. The answer was: "Er war doch ein Jude." ["But he was a Jew."]'*

The most infamous killing field in Estonia was Kalevi-Liiva, an area of sand dunes near the Baltic coast, close to the Jägala concentration camp. The site was the execution and burial site for trainloads of Central European Jews transported to Estonia for extermination. Other victims included Roma people and Estonian and Russian political prisoners. The executions were mainly carried out by Estonian collaborators under German supervision.

At least two trainloads of Jews arrived, carrying over 2,000 people, mainly German and Czechoslovak Jews. About 450 were selected for forced labour; the rest were transferred by bus to Kalevi-Liiva and immediately executed. Estimates vary about the total number of victims. However, the two memorial stones on the site state 6,000 Jews and 2,000 Roma.

The number of killing squads escalated throughout Eastern Europe as the Wehrmacht gained more and more territory. Over 10,000 SS troops were added to the death squads, joined by police units and local auxiliaries. It is estimated that by the end of 1941, over 50,000 men were committed to the mass executions.

The people of German-occupied Belarus, especially its Jewish population, were caught in the jaws of the Nazis' Brutal Dog. On 18 July 1941, Heydrich ordered that all male Jews in the occupied territory aged between fifteen and forty-five were to be shot on sight as 'Soviet partisans'. By August, the victims included women, children and the elderly.

Einsatzgruppen soldiers conducted the first wave of killings, but the newly formed Belorussian Auxiliary Police – a collaborationist force established in early July – became more involved. They knew, far better than the Germans, who was Jewish and who was not. The Jews were separated from the general population and confined to makeshift ghettos. Because the Soviet leadership fled from Minsk without ordering an evacuation, most Jewish inhabitants were captured. There were 100,000 prisoners held in the Minsk Ghetto, 25,000 in Bobruisk, 20,000 in Vitebsk, 12,000 in Mogilev, 10,000 in Gomel and 10,000 in Slutsk. There were also many smaller ghettos.

In November 1941, 12,000 Jews were rounded up in the Minsk Ghetto to make room for the 25,000 foreign Jews designated for expulsion from Germany, Austria and the Protectorate of Bohemia and Moravia. On the morning of 7 November 1941, the first group of prisoners was formed into columns and ordered to march while smiling for the cameras. Once beyond Minsk, 6,624 Jews were taken by lorries to the nearby village of Tuchinka and shot by members of *Einsatzgruppe A*. The next group of over 5,000 Jews followed them to Tuchinka on 20 November 1941. No fewer than 800,000 Jews perished in the territory of modern-day Belarus.

There were many tragic local and individual stories that unfolded in Belarus. One particularly poignant example involved the 'Martyrs of Nowogródek' (then in occupied Poland – now Navahrudak, in Belarus). The Sisters of the Holy Family of Nazareth had arrived in Nowogródek in 1929, at the request of the local bishop. They soon became an important part of the life of the town.

Of the 20,000 inhabitants of the town before the war, approximately half were Jews. The Germans murdered about 9,500 of them and sent the remaining 550 to slave labour camps. Arrests of Polish dissidents followed, and several executions were carried out. The women of the town asked the Sisters to pray for the prisoners' release.

The Superior of the community, Sister Maria Stella, responded by saying: '*My God, if sacrifice of life is needed, accept it from us and spare those who have families. We are even praying for this intention.*' Almost immediately, the Germans' plans for the prisoners were changed; they were deported to work camps in Germany, and some of them were even released. When the life of the local priest was under threat, the Sisters repeated their pledge, saying: '*There is a greater need for a priest on this earth than for us. We pray that God will take us in his place if sacrifice of life is needed.'*

Without warning, the nuns were summoned by the Gestapo to report to the local police station, where they were held overnight. The next morning, they were driven to a secluded spot in the woods where the eleven women were machine-gunned and buried in a common grave.

Maria 'Masha' Bruskina was one of many thousands of partisans who were killed fighting the German invaders. She was a member of the Minsk Resistance and worked as a nurse at a hospital, caring for wounded members of the Red Army. She also helped them escape by smuggling civilian clothes and false identity papers into the hospital.

One of her patients informed on her and she was arrested in October 1941. After her arrest, Bruskina wrote to her mother: *'I am tormented by the thought that I have caused you great worry. Don't worry. Nothing bad has happened to me. I swear to you that you will have no further unpleasantness because of me. If you can, please send me my dress, my green blouse and white socks. I want to be dressed decently when I leave here.'*

To make an example of Bruskina, it was decided that she should suffer a public hanging. Before the execution, she was marched through the streets with a placard around her neck, which read 'We are partisans and have shot at German troops'.

She was hanged on Sunday 26 October 1941. The Germans let her body hang for three days before allowing it to be cut down and buried. Pyotr Borisenko witnessed the execution: *'When they put her on the stool, the girl turned her face towards the fence. The executioners wanted her to stand with her face to the crowd, but she turned away. No matter how much they pushed her and tried to turn her, she remained standing with her back to the crowd. Only then did they kick away the stool from under her.'*

•

The single most brutal example of mass murder took place in a ravine on the outskirts of Kiev called Babi Yar. Over a seven-day period in September 1941, *Einsatzgruppe C* killed at least 34,000 Ukrainian Jews, although Soviet estimates put the number at nearer 100,000.

The Wehrmacht occupied Kiev on 19 September. A few days later, an explosion damaged a command post in the city, killing several German soldiers. The Jewish community was blamed, wrongly, for the explosion. It provided a convenient excuse for a wanton act of killing on a scale not seen before. All local Jews were required by order to report to central Kiev. The Germans were expecting a few thousand but were surprised when thousands more appeared with all their belongings. Not aware of what was happening elsewhere, the hapless victims had believed the information that were they going to be 'relocated'.

On 29 and 30 September, 34,000 Jews were marched in small groups to Babi Yar, stripped naked and machine-gunned into the ravine, which was immediately covered over. Some of the victims were still alive. Over the next two years, the mass grave expanded with the addition of many more victims – mainly Jews, but also communist officials and Soviet prisoners of war.

A lorry driver called Hofer later described what he saw: '*I watched what happened when the Jews – men, women and children – arrived. The Ukrainians led them past a number of different places where, one after the other, they had to give up their luggage, then their coats, shoes and over-garments and also underwear. They also had to leave their valuables in a designated place. There was a special pile for each article of clothing. It all happened very quickly and anyone who hesitated was kicked or pushed by the Ukrainians to keep them moving. Once undressed, they were led into the ravine which was about 150 metres long and 30 metres wide and a good 15 metres deep . . . When they reached the bottom of the ravine, they were seized by the German soldiers and made to lie down on top of Jews who had already been shot . . . The corpses were literally in layers. A marksman came along and shot each Jew in the neck.*'

Only a handful of survivors, thought to be fewer than thirty, got out of the Babi Yar ravine alive. Dina Pronicheva, an actress at the Kiev Young Viewers Theatre, was one of them. When she arrived at Babi Yar, with her mother, she showed her passport, which identified her as a Russian (because she had a Russian husband). It was to no avail. The German officer said: *'Dina is not a Russian name, you're a Kike. Take her away.'*

In her testimony to the investigation into the massacre after the war, Pronicheva described how she survived: *'The policeman ordered me to strip and pushed me to a precipice, where another group of people was awaiting their fate. But before the shots resounded, I fell into the pit. I fell on the [bodies] of those already murdered . . . People started to fall on top of me.*

I pretended to be dead. Those who had been killed or wounded were lying under me and on top of me – many were still breathing, others were moaning . . . The shooting was continuing, and people kept falling. I threw bodies off me, afraid of being buried alive. I did so in a way that would not attract the attention of the policemen. Suddenly all became quiet. It was getting dark. Germans armed with sub-machine guns walked around, finishing off the wounded.

Then I felt we were being covered with earth. I closed my eyes so that the soil would not get into them, and when it became dark and silent, literally the silence of death, I opened my eyes and threw the sand off me, making sure that no one was close by, no one was around, no one was watching me. I saw the pit with thousands of dead bodies. I was overcome by terror. In some places the earth was heaving – people half alive were [still] breathing. I stood up and ran.'

Raya Dashkevich was another survivor: *'I stood at my father's side and held my three-year-old little brother, Petenka, in my arms. We were shot right at the precipice of Babi Yar. My father fell down and then my older sister, Sima. People fell like small stones thrown by some hand. I don't know when I was shot but I regained consciousness at night in the ravine. There were dead bodies all around; streams of blood were flowing on all sides. I was only wounded and started to climb from under the pile of bodies, which surrounded me on all sides. Soon I got out and started to crawl, not knowing where I was going. Several times I lost consciousness but revived and crawled forward again until I saw lights from a house. After I knocked, an old woman opened the door. She looked at me and I saw the horror in her eyes, and I passed out.'*

The woman tended her for three days, then sent her away for fear of Nazi reprisals. She sought refuge with a Ukrainian priest, Ivan Bondarenko, who had hidden Jews from pogroms before the 1917 Revolution. He took her in, gave her a false baptismal certificate and sheltered her throughout the war.

As the Wehrmacht retreated from the Soviet Union in 1944, they attempted to destroy the evidence of the slaughter. Bulldozers were brought in; heavy machinery was used to crush the remains. Funeral pyres were lit, the flames from which were visible in Kiev. When the work was finished, most of the workers – prisoners who had been brought in from the nearby Syrets concentration camp – were killed. It is estimated that at least 90 per cent of the corpses were eradicated.

There would be many more appalling examples of mass slaughter, including the Odessa Massacre of 22 to 24 October 1941, mainly perpetrated by Romanian soldiers and local ethnic Germans. Several occupying Romanians had been killed when a mine left by the retreating Red Army exploded. After blaming Jews and communists, the invaders went on a rampage of killing. Tens of thousands were shot, hanged or burned alive.

By the late autumn of 1941, the enormous escalation in brutality and mass murder had already killed hundreds of thousands, many of them Jews. The seeds of the horror had been sown in Germany eight years earlier, but it had grown like an epidemic. It had now become a plague of hatred.

Svetlana Alexievich interviewed a group of female medical veterans in a Moscow hotel in the early 1980s. They had gathered for their annual reunion. One of them spoke bluntly about where hate comes from: '*The Germans didn't take women soldiers prisoner . . . They shot them at once, or led them before their lined-up soldiers, "Look, they're not women, they're monsters." We always kept two bullets for ourselves, yes, two, in case one misfired. One day, one of our nurses was captured . . . A day later, we took back that village. We found her: eyes put out; breasts cut off. They had impaled her on a stake . . . She was nineteen years old. In her knapsack we found letters home and a green rubber bird. A child's toy.*'

9

MOSCOW: ENEMY AT THE GATES

OCTOBER 1941

The Battle of Moscow began with Hitler's change of mind about his priorities in the war on the Eastern Front. It was confirmed in a Führer directive ordering an all-out attack on Moscow, the Soviet Union's capital city. Convinced that his judgement was infallible, and certain that his armed forces were impossible to defeat, he was sure that he could take Moscow before winter tightened its grip. Despite delaying the final assault, he was confident that he would soon be standing before the great gates of the Kremlin as a Teutonic hero of the Fatherland.

Called 'Operation Typhoon', it began on 2 October. The Soviet defenders faced one of the largest gatherings of fighting men and weapons of war ever assembled: 78 divisions, 1,930,000 men, 14,000 artillery pieces, more than 1,000 tanks and 1,390 combat aircraft. It began 300 miles south-west of Moscow with an attack by the Wehrmacht's 2nd Panzer Group, with over 200 tanks. They made dramatic progress; Sevsk, Dmitrovsk and Kromy fell within days. Soon, the crucial rail junction at Orel was all but defenceless. The panzers had covered over 150 miles in just four days and lost only 41 men killed and 120 wounded. Further to the north-west, panzers took Bryansk and Karachev by 6 October, encircling over 700,000 Red Army soldiers.

More panzers then attacked from the Desna River and turned north-west towards Vyazma, an important rail junction between Smolensk and Moscow. At the same time, supported by a large force of infantry, the main thrust towards Moscow was launched. By 7 October, panzer spearheads met and took Vyazma. Once again, tens of thousands of Red Army soldiers became trapped in German-occupied territory as the panzers advanced at an alarming rate. At that point, three entire panzer armies, almost 1,000 tanks, were massing together, poised to make a decisive strike against Moscow

On the same day, Soviet General Konstantin Rokossovskiy had an encounter that he recorded in his diary, the details of which he never forgot. Polish by birth, he had fought in the Great War and the Russian Civil War, like most of the Soviet military hierarchy, and had worked his way up through the ranks of the Red Army. A victim of Stalin's Great Purge in the 1930s, during which he was imprisoned and tortured, he was reinstated in 1940 because of the alarming shortage of experienced senior army officers.

Rokossovskiy was near the main railway line to Moscow at Tumanovo, twenty-five miles east of Vyazma, when he sought information about the whereabouts of the Germans in a peasants' house in a small village. After a small boy and his mother told him what they knew, a bedridden veteran, who had been wounded twice in the Great War, spoke to him from the shadows in the corner of the room. He was a grey-bearded old man, the grandfather of the family: *'What's going on, Comrade Commander? . . . You're getting away yourselves and leaving us behind. We've given all we have to help the Red Army; we'd spare the last shirt from our back if it would help. I'm an old soldier myself. I fought the Germans, and we didn't let them into Russia. What are you doing now?'*

Rokossovskiy was stunned by the old man's comment: *'His words were a slap in the face.'*

As the general left, the old man continued: *'If I were well, I'd go and defend Russia myself.'*

The situation became chaotic for the Red Army. Its western defences had been completely overrun by the speed of the panzer attacks, with most of its infantry trapped in 'pockets' where they would be gradually overwhelmed by the Wehrmacht's support infantry.

Major Ivan Shabalin was a state security officer in the NKVD, attached to the headquarters of the 50th Army as it was encircled by German panzers near Bryansk.

'14.10.41. *The enemy has encircled us. Incessant gunfire. Cannon, mortar, and sub-machine gun exchanges. Danger and fear all day long. And this is not to mention the swamp, the forest, and the problem of passing the night. I have not slept for two nights.*

15.10.41. Terrifying! I wander around, dead bodies, horrors everywhere. I am hungry and have had no sleep again. Our destruction is obvious. The army is beaten, its supply train is destroyed. The army has disintegrated.'

While the politicians fretted and the generals searched for answers, the serving soldiers of the Red Army were in disarray. Fyodor Bogratyov was in an engineer battalion and had been constructing defensive positions on the Moscow–Minsk highway, each of which was immediately overrun by the German advance. By the middle of October, his unit was in headlong retreat, less than a hundred miles from Moscow: '*We drove along a major road. We passed six settlements; they were all burned from the bombing. We arrived at an army headquarters, where they had presumed that we were missing or in captivity. Again, we were given a new task: to carry out defensive work in a nearby village.*

We arrived, quartered and drank tea. Then a messenger arrived, shouting, "To the trucks!! We're surrounded!" German tanks were on top of us, firing at us with their cannons and machine guns. We didn't have time to get on the trucks with our comrades. We ran into the woods and got rid of everything, except plans and other secret documents. We spent the night in the woods then began to walk towards Moscow.

We soon found a truck, but all roads were clogged: military, civilians, horses, cows and other animals. Twelve people were seriously injured in our truck: they lost legs, arms, and other injuries. The commissar was shot in the chest and died. There was a shortage of fuel, roads were damaged. There was mud, rain and the cold of October. The wounded were just left by the side of the road. Everything was on fire.'

Bogratyov arrived in Moscow a few days later. He made only a brief entry in his diary: '*In Moscow, panic; it is difficult to understand what is happening.*'

Horrified by the poor performance on the front line, Stalin recalled Zhukov from Leningrad and dismissed General Ivan

Konev, Commander of the Western Front. As he had with General Pavlov in June, Stalin ordered Konev's execution, but Zhukov persuaded Stalin to change his mind and instead reinstate him as a theatre commander.

When Zhukov reached Moscow, Stalin was at home suffering from a heavy cold: *'He didn't look very well and received me curtly and called my attention to a map. "Look at this. A very grave situation has developed. I can't get a detailed report from the Western and Reserve Fronts. You are to go at once to investigate the situation thoroughly. Phone me at any hour of the day or night."* [. . .]'

When Zhukov reached the battle area, he found he was in familiar territory: *'As we drove across the Protva River, I recalled my youth. I knew the area very well. I had walked through it many times. My village, Strelkovka, was just ten miles from the Reserve Front HQ at the Obninskoye railway station. My mother, sister and her four children were there. There was no time to see them. What would happen to them if the fascists came to the village? What would they do to a Red Army general's family? Shoot them, surely. "First chance I get," I thought, "I'll have them brought to Moscow."* [. . .]'

It would prove to be a fortunate prod for Zhukov. He did have his family relocated to Moscow, sixty miles to the north. Two weeks later, Strelkovka was overrun by the Germans, along with large parts of the Protva River basin.

A few days later, Zhukov was near Medyn, an abandoned town close to the advancing panzers: *'I saw only an old woman rummaging through the ruins of a house that had been turned into a pile of rubble by a bomb. "What's the matter with you, granny?" Without a word of reply she went back to digging at the rubble. Another woman emerged from the ruins. "Don't ask her. She's gone mad with grief. There was an air raid the day before yesterday. The Germans bombed and machine-gunned us. This woman lived here with her grandchildren. She was at the well getting a pail of water when a bomb hit the house right in front of her eyes. The children were killed." The tears streamed down her cheeks as she talked.'*

With the Wehrmacht advancing towards Moscow at an alarming rate and German air raids bombarding the city, there was panic in

Moscow, both within the government and on the streets. Rumours of the imminent appearance of German tanks circulated like wild-fire. It was said that roads to the east were full of official cars carrying bureaucrats, party officials and their families in their thousands.

On 8 October, the GKO had ordered the creation of a *Pyatërka* ('Gang of Five'). These senior officials would 'prepare to take the industrial enterprises of Moscow out of commission'. A total of 1,119 enterprises were identified for destruction: 412 were designated as of 'defence significance' and were to be blown up; a further 707, deemed less 'defence' focused, were to be damaged or set ablaze. Other establishments were listed: dairies, bakeries, meat warehouses, railway, bus and trolleybus facilities and power stations. It was an operation just like the one Fyodor Rostopchin, the Governor of Moscow, had prepared for Napoleon's conquering French army in 1812. He had evacuated the city, opened its prisons, stripped it of anything useful and burned most of it to the ground. Similarly, should the Wehrmacht breach the city's defences, *Pyatërka* began a rigorous scorched earth policy to greet them at the gates of the city and render it an empty shell not worth capturing.

On 13 October, Stalin ordered that the city's major theatres be evacuated, a sure signal to Muscovites that the situation was dire. Key buildings were mined, including the iconic one loved by everyone, the Bolshoi Theatre. When the Germans reached the village of Borodino, less than eighty miles from Moscow, scene of the great and bloody battle during Napoleon's invasion of 1812, the decision was taken to evacuate the city. Most of the government was relocated to Kuibyshev, a city at the confluence of the Samara and Volga rivers, 650 miles south-east of Moscow.

Significantly, Stalin stayed in the city. Whether this was a valiant act to remain as the visible leader of his people in their capital city, or born of his insecurity, fearing that those left behind, particularly his generals, might unseat him, is the subject of much debate. Either way, his presence was important to the country's morale. It is also worth considering that should Moscow have fallen to the Wehrmacht, it would have been straightforward to use a light plane, with Red Square as an improvised runway, to fly Stalin from Moscow at the last moment. Sergo Beria claims that his father was the only member of the Politburo who advised Stalin to remain in Moscow: '*My father told me that he had said to Stalin, "If you go, Moscow will be lost. To ensure your safety, we can turn Red Square into an airstrip. The army and the people must know that you are in Moscow." [. . .]*'

Tellingly, Beria evacuated himself to the Caucasus. Valentin Berezhkov was scathing about Beria's motives, saying that he left '*ostensibly to coordinate the supplies of oil for the army, but in reality, he wanted to sit out the time of danger far away from Moscow*'.

Fear and panic led to looting on Moscow's streets, which reached a peak on 16 and 17 October. People leaving the city were attacked and their belongings stolen. Workers left their factories and went on the rampage. There was little response from the Party hierarchy, many of whom had already left, or were in a state of paralysis caused by the dire circumstances they faced. However, a city-wide curfew was introduced before the end of the month.

An elite unit of the NKVD was deployed to key points around the city. One of them was Mikhail Ivanovich, a sniper who was positioned in the famous GUM building in Red Square. His targets were foreign invaders, or any Soviet citizens who flouted the law or threatened the state. Ivanovich was coldly ruthless about his duties: '*It was necessary, absolutely necessary to establish order. And yes, we did shoot people who refused to quit the shops and offices where food and other goods were stored.*'

During these ominous autumn weeks, there is no doubt that, in stark contrast with the courage of many, there existed widespread dissent and considerable opposition. During October, over 125,000 people were arrested in Moscow for 'breaches of military regulations'. Over 12,000 more were charged with attempting to avoid military service. There are no reliable statistics for the punishments meted out for these 'crimes'; what figures do exist vary widely and many grind one propaganda axe or other. However, given that dozens of leading military and civilian officials were still being executed for their 'failures', it is likely that punishments were severe, including local imprisonment, incarceration in distant gulags, and the ultimate threat – a firing squad.

Panic was also widespread. Tellingly, an NKVD report on the situation at the HQ of the Communist Party Central Committee in Moscow presented the situation in the starkest of terms: *'The building was all but deserted, with whole floors unguarded; important pieces of equipment, including fire-fighting apparatus and gas masks, were strewn all over the floor. Vital paperwork, including top-secret documents, were scattered across desks and chairs.'*

With little protection from air-raid bombardments available within the walls of the Kremlin, Stalin moved his office to the nearby Air Defence Headquarters. When an air raid threatened, and sometimes at night, he took the lift down to one of Moscow's new Metro stations, where he slept in quite primitive conditions with just a mattress on the floor and a piece of plywood to separate him from passing trains.

Irina Tupikova was at school in Moscow in 1941. Her father was an officer in the NKVD and unable to leave the city. Irina and her mother chose not to be evacuated: *'It was a very nervous time. Everything was closed, people just stayed at home, or dashed out to grab food when the shops got new deliveries. At night, there was an eerie silence, except when there was an air raid of course, just a few soldiers on the streets. We all prayed that Comrade Stalin would stay. Most people said that if he went east, Moscow would fall.'*

Yelena Rzhevskaya, born into a Jewish family in Belorussia in 1919, was a philosophy student at Moscow State University in 1941. Like many others, she wanted to fight, but she was sent to a munitions factory and later studied to become a nurse. However, her fluency in German meant that she was transferred to a school for interpreters, after which she was transferred to the Red Army, a move that took her all the way to Hitler's bunker in Berlin, in 1945. Rzhevskaya kept a diary throughout the war: *'I was still in Moscow on October 1st. Columns of volunteers – students, workers, academics – streamed along Leningrad Prospekt on their way to the front to defend Moscow. The Moscow Conservatory marched past, our famous musicians. Everybody was marching out to defend Moscow . . . My first duty was to keep watch from the rooftop of a high neighbouring building and put out any incendiary bombs. I had a supply of sand but had not yet been told what to do with it . . . A blacked-out city, everything swallowed up in darkness, lit only by the snaking of tracer bullets. It is all so peculiar, so unfathomable, so monstrously beautiful and breathtaking.'*

By 10 October, Rzhevskaya had passed the test to become a translator and was ready to leave Moscow on the first stage of her long journey to Berlin: *'A steamer was moored waiting for us, and we sailed out along the Moscow–Volga canal. There was already fighting on the approaches to Moscow . . . Aggravation, unease, but also curiosity: might something happen to us? We were hungry, we had a sense of fore-boding, and we did not know where we were being taken because that was a military secret.'*

Georgy Zhukov wrote glowingly, and with not a little hyper-bole, about his countrymen's efforts in defence of Moscow: *'Something like 250,000 people, with three-quarters of them women and teenagers, erected 72,000 metres of anti-tank ditches, some 80,000 metres of escarpments and 52,000 metres of communication trenches. All in all, they moved more than 3,000,000 cubic metres of earth by hand.'*

That is the equivalent of 170 football pitches six feet deep!

Zhukov heaped yet more praise on his comrades: *'The Moscow Motor Works started making machine guns, the trolleybus depot, hand grenades, all garages were busy repairing tanks, and the Rot Front Confectionary and other fancy goods enterprises were now making anti-tank grenades and detonators . . . In the critical days of October, the Military Council of the Western Front issued an appeal: "Comrades! In this grim hour of mortal danger to our state, the life of every soldier belongs to the Motherland. She demands of each of us the utmost effort, courage, forti-tude and heroism. The Motherland calls on us to rise like an unbreakable wall in the way of the fascist hordes and to defend our beloved Moscow. Vigilance, iron discipline, organisation, resolute action, an unbending will to win and readiness for self-sacrifice are required today more than ever before." [. . .]'*

The Military Council's words were propagandist in the extreme, and potentially naive, but the truth is, tens of millions of men and women, both military and civilian, answered the call and gave their lives.

10

MOSCOW: 'MARSHAL MUD' AND 'GENERAL WINTER'

OCTOBER–DECEMBER 1941

As October wore on, the Wehrmacht's window of opportunity to storm Moscow was beginning to close. No matter how successful the next few months might be, German forces would still fall short of their grossly optimistic initial objective of reaching the White Sea in the north and holding a line all the way to the Caspian Sea in the south. Even so, the OKH (Supreme Command of the German Army) still believed that it was possible to take Leningrad, Moscow and Stalingrad before deep winter set in. Such a success would not end the war, but it would put the Wehrmacht in a powerful position to resume the drive eastwards in the spring of 1942. It is difficult to know whether such optimism was the result of the desire to appease Hitler, or a misjudgement based on overambition – especially as most of the German generals wrote accounts after the war which totally contradicted the expressed conviction of their words and deeds during the conflict.

There had already been several mistakes and miscalculations, the most notable of which was the OKH's underestimation of the Soviet Union's ability to replace at an impressive rate their lost soldiers and destroyed materiel. The German commanders also seem to have chosen to ignore the difficulties of sustaining enormously long lines of supply and communications across the vast distances of their advances. That was quite apart from the issue of the different railway gauges used by the protagonists. In many cases, in order for the Soviet rail network to be made effective for the Wehrmacht, German engineers had to replace huge sections of rail lines or transfer the materiel to different rolling stock. The maximum the

Eisenbahnpioniere ('railway pioneers') could achieve was fifteen miles a day, which meant it took at least two to three weeks for the rail lines to catch up with the blitzkrieg advances.

Good roads were rare in the vast expanse of the Soviet Union. For the invaders, progress had to be achieved over unmade roads, which presented different challenges in each of Eastern Europe's intense seasons. Summer had brought jarring ruts and swirling dust, which hobbled horses, broke axles and blinded troops. Now, autumn brought heavy rain and cloying mud and an affirmation of the old Russian saying: 'In the autumn, a spoonful of water makes a bucketful of mud.' Soon, winter would bring snow, ice and temperatures so cold that the oil in the sumps of the panzers' engines would freeze. The ill-clad landsers on the ground would soon feel the excruciating effects on their fingers and toes of the depths of the Soviet winter.

On cue, October brought a brief period of salvation for the defenders of Moscow – *rasputitsa*, the 'season of mud'. The renowned author Vasily Grossman, one of whose works, *Life and Fate*, is regarded as a contemporary Russian masterpiece, became a special correspondent for the Red Army newspaper *Krasnaya Zvezda* ('Red Star'). He witnessed the impact of *rasputitsa* near the crucial city of Tula, 120 miles south of Moscow: '*I don't think anyone has ever seen such terrible mud. There's rain, snow, hailstones, a liquid bottomless swamp, black pastry mixed by thousands and thousands of boots, wheels, caterpillars. And everyone is happy again. The Germans must get stuck in our hellish autumn.*'

The Wehrmacht advance slowed, but it was still unyielding. Grossman went on to describe the awful conditions for the wretched civilians trapped in the mayhem: '*Life for the people was terrible. At night, the sky became red from dozens of distant fires, and a grey screen of smoke hung all along the horizon during the day. Women with children in their arms, old men, herds of sheep, cows and horses were moving east . . . Thousands of German aircraft droned in the sky continually. The earth moaned under the steel caterpillars of German tracked vehicles. They crawled through marshes and rivers, tortured the earth, and crushed human bodies . . . The head of a driver of a heavy tank*

*had been blown off by a shell. The tank came back driving itself because
the dead driver was pressing the accelerator. The tank drove through the
forest, breaking trees, and reached our village. The dead driver was still
in it.'*

The fighting on the western approaches to Moscow in October
was ferocious. Attacks and counter-attacks followed one another
in quick succession, until, on 16 October, seventy miles from
Moscow, the vital town of Mozhaisk fell. The Red Army had made
Mozhaisk a fulcrum of a key defensive line and the headquarters of
its Western Front Command.

It is estimated that in the defence of Moscow during October,
over 660,000 Red Army soldiers were surrounded and taken prisoner. However, most continued to fight, even in hopeless positions.
Most importantly, every day that delayed the advance of the Wehrmacht allowed the Red Army to bring forward ever greater reserves
of men and materiel, resources not available to the Germans. Each
delay also counted down the days to the onset of winter.

Stories about the Wehrmacht's treatment of Soviet prisoners
stiffened the resolve of those trying to hold their positions. Misha
Volkov, one of the first to answer the mobilisation call in June
when he escaped from the traumas of Lvov, eventually got news of
his wife's whereabouts. He was still fighting on the front line in
defence of Moscow. Like all Red Army soldiers, he knew what his
fate would be if captured: *'However much they write in the newspapers
about their atrocities, the reality is much worse. I've been in some of the
places where the beasts have been. I've seen the burned-out towns and
villages, the corpses of women and children . . . The spirit of these places
has affected me, and it has grown in all our soldiers.'* The desire for
revenge was quickly becoming the biggest boost to Soviet morale,
outweighing fear, patriotism and discipline.

Both sides of the conflict began to prepare for winter. The
first German winter greatcoats were ordered, but there were only
enough for 20 per cent of the troops. The Wehrmacht tried to close
the gaps between its infantry and armoured units, and to replenish
its supplies. For the Red Army it was another period of regrouping,
reinforcing and consolidating defensive positions.

With Japanese eyes focused southwards towards the Philippines and Indonesia, and intelligence reports indicating that Japan would not overtly support the German assault on the Soviet Union from the east, Stalin was able to release huge numbers of men from his forces in the Far East. Whole divisions started to arrive in Moscow every two days. By the end of October, 13 rifle divisions and 5 tank brigades had been brought to the defence of Moscow.

The numbers involved in the struggle became significant. At the beginning of November, the Red Army had 269 divisions available, with 2.2 million men, but within a month, the number would be 343 divisions, with over 4 million men. Significantly, no one at Rastenburg, in East Prussia – Hitler's 'Wolf's Lair', his Eastern Front Headquarters – nor any of his generals believed it possible that the Soviets were capable of finding men and materiel on such a scale. Conversely, the Wehrmacht's effective number was only 83 divisions, 2.7 million men, and there would be few reinforcements.

The city of Tula, 120 miles south of Moscow, became a pivotal battleground. On 29 October, a German attack by 60 panzers and 2 regiments of infantry almost broke through into the city. However, it was brought to a halt by a fierce artillery barrage and the courageous actions of depleted Red Army units, supported by large numbers of civilians and NKVD. Although the encounters were fierce and panzers circled the city for a further five weeks, it did not fall, creating a crucial Soviet bastion against Operation Typhoon.

Zhukov was being given the time he needed to stiffen Moscow's defences: *'Losses were being replaced, arms and ammunition were being supplied, as well as engineering, communications and other technical facilities. From November 1st to the 15th, the Western Front was reinforced with 100,000 officers and men, 300 tanks and 2,000 guns.'*

Vasily Grossman was near the Tula battleground. He described an encounter with a seventy-year-old woman living alone in her cold and dark *izba*, a traditional log farmhouse, near the city: *'With a tsarina-like generosity she gives all that she has. A dozen logs that would have lasted her for a week, a handful of salt, leaving not a single grain for herself, half a bucket of potatoes. Having graced us with food,*

1. Soviet Foreign Minister, Vyacheslav Molotov, signs the Nazi–Soviet Pact, Moscow, 23 August 1939.

2. The horrific devastation of Barbarossa.

3. An unnamed Lithuanian nationalist uses a club to beat to death his fellow Jewish citizens in Kaunas, Lithuania, June 1941.

4. Red Army soldiers captured by the Wehrmacht are burying their dead,
Bialystok, Belarus, July 1941.

5. The ravine of Babi Yar, Kiev, Ukraine, where 33,771 Jews are murdered in a single operation. 29–30 September 1941.

6. The execution of partisan Hero of the Soviet Union,
Zoya Kosmodemyanskaya.

7. A German victim of the Red Army's 'General Winter', frozen in the snow,
January 1942.

8. Burying the dead, the shocking reality of the Siege of Leningrad, the Volkovo Cemetery, 3 February 1942.

warmth, light and soft beds, she retreats to the cold part of the izba and begins singing. If we do win this terrible, cruel war, it will be because there are such noble hearts in our nation, such righteous people, souls of immense generosity, who are losing their lives for the sake of their nation with the same generosity with which this old woman from Tula has given us all that she had. The regal generosity of this pauper has shaken all of us. In the morning we leave her all our supplies, and our drivers, in a frenzy of kindness, loot the whole area and bring her so much firewood and potatoes that she will be able to last until spring on them. "What an old woman," our driver says when we set off.'

Early November brought an important symbolic moment in the conflict. It is hard to know how important symbolic gestures can be amidst the horrors of war. Nevertheless, Soviet folklore makes much of the grand gesture ordered by Stalin on 6 November.

On 30 October, Stalin had asked his commanders if the military situation would permit him to hold the annual Red Square military parade on 7 November. The parade marks the anniversary of the October 1917 Bolshevik Revolution (on 25 October, according to the old Julian calendar, but 7 November according to the Gregorian calendar, adopted by the Soviet Union in 1918).

One of his generals said it could not be done, but Stalin insisted. If there was an air raid, he suggested, any dead or injured could be quickly removed and the parade would continue regardless. The troops and their armour would march through Red Square and straight to the front with his words ringing in their ears. Invoking the likes of Pushkin, Tolstoy, Tchaikovsky, Alexander Nevsky and General Kutuzov, he proclaimed: 'May you be blessed by great Lenin's victorious banner! Death to the German invaders! Long live our glorious country, its freedom and independence! Under the banner of Lenin – onward to victory!'

The parade, which included the new T-34 medium tank and the Kliment Voroshilov heavy tank – two weapons that would have a major impact in the battles to come – was a propaganda master-stroke.

Sergo Beria was a witness to the parade: *'I returned to the capital on 7th November, just in time to attend the great military parade. This has remained etched in my memory. The whole world thought Moscow had fallen, and here was Stalin reviewing his troops! The parade took place in the morning. The Germans did not start bombing the city until the afternoon. The review restored the people's courage. It had a colossal effect.*' The 7 November spectacle reinvigorated the committed, persuaded the waverers and silenced the doubters.

Not only did the Wehrmacht face a newly powerful and hate-filled enemy, and suffer from the mistakes and miscalculations of its Führer and his increasingly beleaguered High Command, but it was also unlucky. The winter of 1941/42 was an unusually cold one. In fact, it was one of the coldest winters on record across most of Europe. In the Moscow area during the three winter months, the air temperature was between 5°C and 7°C below normal, while at nearby Kalinin and Yachroma the temperature dropped to –50°C. (However, it should be stressed that, for propaganda reasons, German and Soviet accounts of the severity of the winter of 1941/42 differ markedly.)

Many accounts of the Battle of Moscow have emphasised the onset of winter as one of the main reasons for the failure of Operation Typhoon. However, it should be said that the severe cold began in the middle of November and reached a peak of intensity on 4 December. In truth, 'Marshall Mud' was at least as significant as the snow and ice of 'General Winter' in impairing the progress of the German attack.

Having patched up its units as best it could, the Wehrmacht launched a renewed attack towards Moscow, which began on 15 November. The offensive involved two pincer movements designed to encircle Moscow from the rear. To the north, its panzers would strike towards the Moscow–Volga Canal, directly north of the city, and create a bridgehead across it. To the south, they would bypass the irritation of Tula towards the main rail line at Kashira and Mikhailov, before swinging north towards Podolsk and Kolomna and encircle Moscow from the south-east.

The intensity of the assault was evaluated on the pages of *Pravda*, the Communist Party's official organ, by its military correspondent Oleg Kurganov.

The enemy knows that December can bring ferocious frosts, and impenetrable snowdrifts and blizzards. Therefore, the fascists will not spare one of their soldiers, one piece of equipment. They will throw regiment after regiment into combat. The cruellest battles, requiring enormous exertions of strength and will from our people, will take place.

Kurganov could not have been more accurate in his words. The fighting was as intense as any since the beginning of Barbarossa, in June. However, these new encounters took place in the icy depths of winter. German soldiers had to steal winter clothing from dead and captured Soviet soldiers; the oil in the sumps of their vehicles froze; their weapons jammed in the cold; and they began to die from exposure to the appalling conditions, rather than enemy fire.

Despite everything, various German units did get very close to Moscow. It was reported that some were able to see the towers of the Kremlin through their binoculars. But they got no further. Operation Typhoon ground to a halt within a few miles of the cobblestones of Red Square. The reasons usually given by Western historians include Hitler's meddling, the OKH's over-optimistic ambition, failures in logistical support, and Russia's 'General Winter' and 'Marshal Mud'. Not surprisingly, Zhukov saw it differently: *'Bourgeois historians put all the blame on mud and lack of roads. But I was there to see thousands upon thousands of Moscow women dig anti-tank ditches and trenches, put up barricades and carry sandbags. Mud stuck to their feet and the wheelbarrows in which they carried earth ... It was neither rain nor snow that stopped the fascist troops near Moscow. The grouping of picked Nazi troops, over one million strong, was routed by the courage, iron staunchness and valour of the Soviet troops which had the people, Moscow and their country behind them.'*

It is also worth noting that, despite Zhukov's rhetoric, behind many of the Red Army's fighting units were 'barrier troops' – NKVD detachments whose purpose was to maintain military discipline. According to an official letter addressed in October 1941 to Lavrentiy Beria, in the period between the beginning of Operation Barbarossa and early December 1941, a total of 657,364 servicemen had fallen behind their lines and fled from the front. Of those, 25,878 were arrested, and the remaining 631,486 were formed into units and sent back to the front. Among those arrested were 1,505 spies, 308 saboteurs, 2,621 traitors, 2,643 'cowards and alarmists', 3,987 distributors of 'provocative rumours' and 4,371 others. In total, 10,201 of them were shot, amounting to 40 per cent of those arrested. As we have already seen, the Russians do not do war by halves.

Zhukov knew that the moment to strike back at the 'invincible' Wehrmacht had arrived. On 29 November, he called Stalin and asked for orders to launch a counter-attack that he had planned for some weeks: *'Stalin asked, "Are you sure that the enemy has reached a critical point and is in no position to bring some new large force into action?" "The enemy has been bled white."* . . . *Later at night on November 29th, we were informed that the Supreme Command had decided to launch the counter-offensive.'*

It took several days to put the plan into effect: *'Deep snow greatly hampered the concentration and regrouping of troops. However, by the morning of December 6th we were ready to launch the counter-offensive. A large-scale battle developed.'*

It was indeed an encounter on a massive scale. The Wehrmacht was soon in disarray and sustaining heavy losses in trying to withstand the Red Army's audacious, indeed epic, cavalry attacks, its clever use of mobile light tanks, and its deployment of well-clad fresh troops. In one of the many cavalry advances, General Lev Dovator, one of the heroes of Smolensk in July, led an attack by the Cossacks of his 2nd Guards Cavalry Division from the front, but was killed near the town of Ruza, sixty miles west of Moscow.

Hitler's attempt to win the 'decisive' battle, by taking Moscow, had failed. He had hoped that its capture would lead to the collapse of his enemy. But, as Napoleon had discovered before him, that was unlikely. Even if he had strutted across Red Square to look with contempt upon the mummified Lenin in his marble mausoleum – and almost certainly have his embalmed corpse destroyed – he would simply have been in control of an empty city, with Stalin and the Red Army continuing the fight, far to the east.

Even the strategy of besieging the Soviet Union's great cities was flawed, as Leningrad, Moscow and Stalingrad would prove. They would suck in men and materiel and act like inverse traps, where the besiegers would eventually become the besieged.

The blow to the Wehrmacht by the reversal of Operation Typhoon was both real and symbolic. Its façade of invincibility had been shown to be a myth, and its losses were catastrophic: over 100,000 casualties, 500 tanks and 1,000 artillery pieces. In effect, Barbarossa was over, but not the war. The Wehrmacht was only a wounded beast – one which, through extraordinary discipline and doggedness, had plenty of fight left in it. Hitler did learn some lessons from Typhoon and purged many of his senior generals. Neither he nor his beloved Wehrmacht were done yet.

Hitler's hubristic tenacity was matched by a newly emboldened Stalin. Zhukov recalls the moment when Stalin, the tentative defender, became the rampant aggressor: *'Late on January 5th* [1942] *I was summoned to the Stavka . . . Stalin said, "The Germans are taken aback after their defeat near Moscow . . . Now is the time to take the general offensive. The enemy expects to hold it up until the spring, to gather his forces and again launch active operations. He wants to win time and some breathing space. Our objective,"* he said, pacing up and down his study as was his wont, *"is to deny the Germans any breathing space, to drive them westward without let-up, to make them up their reserves before spring comes . . . By that time, we'll have fresh reserves, while the Germans will have none."* [. . .]'

Most of Stalin's generals, including Zhukov, advised caution. But the Supreme Commander would not hear of delay beyond April. It seemed 1942 would be another year of blood and iron.

11

EYES SOUTH

JANUARY–JUNE 1942

Events on the southern front during the initial phase of Operation Barbarossa are often neglected because of the dramatic happenings in the north, around Leningrad, and in the centre, towards Moscow. However, in terms of Hitler's strategic objectives – his *Lebensraum*, and the resources needed to support it – the south was much more important.

Although the Wehrmacht failed to meet its original highly ambitious objective in the south – the aim of reaching Astrakhan, the Caucasus and the Caspian Sea – it did conquer Ukraine, the Crimea, the Donets Basin (Donbass) and the 'Gateway to the Caucasus', Rostov-on-Don. In fact, if one includes the administrations of its Axis allies, and additionally incorporates the North African territories of Vichy France, the Third Reich was an immense empire in January 1942.

Despite the scale of Germany's advances, the Kerch Peninsula of the Crimea was an important target in Stalin's fanciful master-plan to throw the Germans out of the Soviet Union by the end of the year. His blood was up; there was no stopping the Supreme Commander, not even the oceans of blood that would inevitably be shed by his own people.

As early as 26 December 1941, the Soviets had launched an amphibious attack to break the siege of the city of Sevastopol, which had been surrounded by the Germans since the end of October.

The landings took place at Kerch, a city as far to the east of the Crimea as Sevastopol is to the west, and at Feodosia, a town to the west of the Kerch Peninsula. However, the Red Army's bold adventure was ill-prepared and badly executed. Feodosia was retaken on 15 January and, despite several attempts during February, March and April, Soviet forays to break out from its bridgehead at Kerch all failed.

By the beginning of May, Axis forces were ready for a sustained attack to drive the Red Army out of the east of the Crimea. It was code-named *Trappenjagd* ('Bustard Hunt') and was conducted by five German infantry divisions, two and a half divisions of Romanian mountain troops, and a division of panzers.

The Germans won another astonishing victory in less than two weeks. An entire Soviet army, many of them Georgians, was pushed back by the German panzers to the Sea of Azov, where it was destroyed. Kerch was overrun by the German infantry, backed up by significant artillery and Luftwaffe support. The Red Army's casualties were 30,000 dead and 150,000 taken prisoner. In a hasty evacuation attempt it got off only 37,000 men, but lost all its armaments and over 400 aircraft.

Konstantin Simonov witnessed the fighting around Kerch: '*Everyone had to go forward, forward.*' But he was horrified that behind the attack, '*there was no support, no transport, no reserves, no field hospitals; they were not needed, those at the front were either going to die or be taken prisoner. I saw more bodies on the ground than anywhere else in the war and watched as more soldiers stepped over the bodies of their comrades to face the same fate.*'

The end of the Soviet bridgehead at Kerch led to one of the most tragic events in an already brutal war. Several thousand soldiers and civilians left behind at Kerch took refuge in a large limestone cave system known as the Great and Small Adzhimushkay catacombs. It is estimated that more than 13,000 people fled there.

The catacombs were difficult to defend. There were no supplies prepared, and all the wells for water were located outside the caves, so water had to be retrieved by armed sorties. Most of those trapped died a slow death, deep underground, as they ran out of ammunition, food and water. Those trapped resorted to eating their horses and collecting drips of water from the roof of the caves.

The German forces surrounded the area with barbed-wire fencing, blocked the entrances and exits, bombed the entombed defenders, and used gas to poison them.

At the end of October, German forces entered the catacombs and captured the remaining defenders. From the initial 13,000 who had sought refuge, the estimates for the number of survivors of the siege after five months underground, and their subsequent treatment by the Germans, vary from as few as fifty to perhaps 300.

•

Further north, Kharkov in Ukraine was another important objective for Stalin's 1942 offensive. It had been captured by the Wehrmacht on 24 October 1941, leaving the city in ruins. After the occupying Germans had stripped the city of food, widespread starvation ensued, especially during the long winter to come. The Jews of the city suffered a more immediate fate: 20,000 were killed, initially by shooting, then by carbon monoxide poisoning and suffocation in a sealed 'gas van' that toured the city, killing groups of fifty at a time. Leading local communists also suffered summary executions; their bodies were left hanging from balconies to cow the population.

Stalin became impatient in his demands for the retaking of Kharkov, but his commanders' requirements, particularly those of Marshal Timoshenko for men and materiel, delayed the date of the offensive until 12 May.

After an encouraging start, the offensive was halted after only three days by massive Luftwaffe air attacks and a German pincer movement, on 17 May, which cut off three Soviet armies. The Soviet force was devastated. After six days of encirclement, resistance came to an end as the Red Army formations were either killed or taken prisoner. The losses were horrendous: 277,000 casualties (170,000 killed, missing or captured; 107,000 wounded); 1,250 tanks destroyed; 542 aircraft destroyed; 57,000 horses killed. In just over two weeks, one of Stalin's primary ambitions had led to an unmitigated disaster.

Vladimir Gelfand was in charge of a mortar battery and kept a diary throughout the war: '*Singles, small groups and large divisions.*

All have a worn and exhausted appearance. Many were dressed in civilian clothes, most had dropped their weapons, some commanders tore off their insignia. What a disgrace! What an unexpected and sad discrepancy with newspaper data. Woe to me, a fighter, a commander, a Komsomol member, a patriot of his country. My heart shrinks from shame and powerlessness in this shameful flight. I have to admit that we are unorganised, we do not have the proper discipline.

The high command fled on their machines, betrayed the masses of the Red Army, despite the distance from this front. All ferries and bridges are destroyed, property and cattle, broken and mutilated, lying on the road. Looting thrives, cowardice reigns. The military oath and the order of Stalin are trampled at every step.'

Back in Ukraine, with the obstacle of the Red Army's invasion of Kerch dealt with, the Wehrmacht resumed its attempts to take Sevastopol, the last Soviet enclave in the Crimea. It had been an exceedingly tough nut to crack since the forces of Barbarossa arrived in the Crimea at the end of October 1941. The Axis (German and Romanian) assault, code-named *Störfang* ('Sturgeon Catch'), began on 2 June 1942. The Red Army and the Black Sea Fleet held out for several weeks under intense bombardment. The Luftwaffe flew over 23,000 sorties and dropped 20,000 tons of bombs in June alone, while the German Army launched almost 50,000 tons of artillery ammunition during *Störfang*. At the end of the siege, there were only eleven undamaged buildings left in the whole of Sevastopol.

Nikolai Evseev, the officer in the Black Sea Fleet who had described the Luftwaffe's bombing of Sevastopol in June 1941, was, a year later, still with his ship as the city succumbed to the German aerial onslaught. He described *'a hellish cacophony . . . and the heavier the bombing, the greater and stronger became our rage and hatred for the enemy'*. He watched as his city was destroyed, its inhabitants blown to pieces in their homes and on the streets. *'Heat! We were all desperately thirsty. But no one had any water.'* As in Kerch, many hid in the caves and tunnels under the port, where they could only daydream about their favourite drinks: *'Lemonade, kvass, seltzer water, beer and, if you please, ice cream. But we agreed on one thing. We'd drink anything, even if it were polluted, even if it had been flowing through the corpses . . . We had been drinking water from under corpses for several days.'* The corpses were bodies that had been discarded into the tanks and reservoirs around the city. *'We never managed to clear them out.'*

As if they had not suffered enough, one of the most extraordinary weapons ever made was used to intimidate the beleaguered people of Sevastopol. Built by the ancient armaments dynasty Krupp, it was called *Schwerer Gustav* ('Heavy Gustav'), but nicknamed 'Dora' by its artillerymen. Built originally to smash the French defences on the Maginot Line, it was the largest gun ever used in combat. Once assembled, Dora was over 140 feet long, 23 feet wide, and weighed 1,329 tons. Protected by two flak battalions, Dora sat nineteen miles north-east of Sevastopol on double railway tracks. The behemoth's operation required 1,500 men, one colonel and one major-general. Her 107-foot, 800-mm barrel fired 5-ton high-explosive or 7-ton armour-piercing shells a distance of twenty-nine or twenty-four miles respectively. During the siege, Dora fired over forty shells at Sevastopol, one of which passed through water and a hundred feet of rock to pulverise a Soviet ammunition dump beneath Severnaya Bay. The monster took four hours to calibrate for each firing and the Germans soon realised that it was resource-intensive and impractical to deploy – in truth, not much better than an extravagant vanity project for Adolf Hitler. One general said it was an engineering wonder, but militarily 'useless'. It is thought the mighty weapon was destroyed in the final days of the war.

Colonel Ivan Laskin was in command of the Red Army's 172nd Rifle Division in Sevastopol as it faced the onslaught on their position from land and air: *'Shells whined overhead and exploded on all sides. A whirlwind of fire was raging at all our positions. Enormous clods of earth and uprooted trees flew into the air. An enormous dark grey cloud of smoke and dust rose higher and higher and finally eclipsed the sun. In my sector, the Germans outnumbered us nine to one in manpower and ten to one in artillery, not to speak of tanks, because we had none.'*

One of the most heartrending stories from the appalling siege was that of a small group of sailors from the Black Sea Fleet who were defending a position near the village of Kamyshly. They all died during the attack. One of them left a note: *'Russia my country, my native land! Dear Comrade Stalin! I, a Black Sea sailor, and a son of Lenin's Komsomol, fought as my heart told me to fight. I will slay the beasts if my heart beats in my breast. Now I am dying, but I know we shall win. Sailors of the Black Sea Navy! Fight harder still, kill the mad fascist dogs! I have been faithful to my soldier's oath – Kalyuzhny.'*

As the Axis forces advanced, more Soviet defenders, soldiers and civilians retreated into the network of caves and tunnels under the city. Deep below ground, the network had water, food, power and medical facilities, but those who sought refuge there never came out. Stalin ordered that the remaining Soviet defenders fight to the last man. They did as they were ordered and fought on until, several weeks later, like rats in a sewer, they were blown up, poisoned by gas, or starved to death. The last two radio messages sent out by the defenders read:

> There are forty-six of us left. The Germans are hammering at our armoured doors and calling on us to surrender. We have opened up the inspection hatch to fire twice on them.

> There are twenty-six of us left. We're getting ready to blow ourselves up. Farewell.

Above ground, some survivors tried to get away by sea. It was a pitiful scene, described by an unnamed witness: *'They ran with maddened eyes, with tunics torn and flopping; panic-stricken, bewildered, miserable, frightened people. They seized feverishly any kind of craft they could – rafts, rubber floats, automobile tires – and flung themselves into the sea.'*

Boris Borisov, Chairman of Sevastopol's Defence Committee, who later wrote several books about the defence of the city, recounted the unfortunate story of two young Komsomol defenders, Nadya Krayevaya and her friend Sasha Bagrii: *'Taking rifles and cartridges from dead soldiers, they tried to break through to the Crimean hills to join the partisans. As the Germans started their final attack, the shots from the Russians became fewer and fewer . . . Most of the survivors counter-attacked with nothing but their bayonets. Nadya was killed. The last that was heard of Sasha was that he was seen, scarcely able to move, in a column of prisoners. Then he was seen, half dead and spitting blood, first at Bakhchysarai, then at Simferopol. And there, traitors denounced him to the Germans. And the Germans did not forgive all that he had done for his country and for Sevastopol . . .'*

On 4 July 1942, the Soviet defenders surrendered the city. The Red Army's Coastal Army was annihilated, with 118,000 men killed, wounded or captured in the final assault. The Black Sea Fleet suffered a further 80,000 casualties.

With the Soviet presence in the Crimea extinguished and Stalin's exalted hopes thwarted, Hitler could revert to one of Barbarossa's primary objectives – the Soviet Union's vast oilfields in the Caucasus. There was little the Red Army could do to prevent the Caucasus from falling. It was midsummer. Stalin's bravura had cost the Red Army dearly; morale was collapsing once again. If Hitler got control of the oilfields, how could they survive?

A young rifleman, Oleksiy Gudzovsky, captured the dreadful mood: *'The majority of our commanding officers are cowards. Surely, we did not need to run away, we could have stood our ground and faced them. Give us an order to go west! To hell with retreating! I'm sick to death of pulling back from the places where I grew up.'* He died shortly after he wrote these words.

An unnamed rifleman admitted to cynicism as he encountered helpless civilians snared by the conflict: *'They shared their last crusts with us. I ate that bread and knew that in an hour I'd be leaving, retreating. But I said nothing! I didn't have the right! . . . If we had told them, they would have run away as well, and then there would have been bottlenecks along the road for us.'*

His words bear poignant witness to the desolation of defeat.

12

THE FULCRUM

JUNE–JULY 1942

In April 1942, Hitler had made his priority for the summer abundantly clear: 'If I don't get the oil of Maikop and Grozny, then I must liquidate the war.' Having been precise about his need, he then made a series of decisions that undermined his primary goal.

Germany was an oil-poor nation, but during the 1939 German–Soviet Pact, Hitler was able to obtain the oil he needed for his war effort in the West from the Soviet Union's huge oil reserves – which, in the main, came from the Caucasus. By 1940, Germany was receiving 50,000 tons of oil per month from the Soviet Union. Without that oil, the blitzkrieg offensives that overran Western Europe could not have happened.

Over the winter of 1941, Hitler seemed to realise that instead of wasting more resources in trying to capture symbolic strongholds like Leningrad and Moscow and attempting to pursue and totally destroy the Red Army, he should make a dash for the oilfields of the Caucasus. In fact, his supply and communication lines were too stretched and his manpower too depleted to do otherwise.

If he could grab the oil, he would not only have it for himself, but he would also deny it to the Soviets. The Caucasus was also the key to the Persian Corridor, the main route via which the Soviet Union's allies, particularly Britain and the United States, sent vital supplies – everything from weapons to food. The route ran by sea around the Cape of Good Hope, into the Persian Gulf, then through Iran and into Soviet Azerbaijan. If Hitler could close the corridor, it would be a major blow to the Soviets' ability to keep their war machine running effectively. Typically, Hitler even thought of continuing beyond the Caucasus into Iran and Iraq, where he would be able to undermine Britain's position in the Middle East.

However, there was a fundamental weakness on the northern and eastern flanks of an assault on the south. Although it might prove straightforward for the mobile panzers to devour the ground to the south, for every mile they advanced, their long lines of communication would be under constant threat. The Soviets had significant strongholds, offering reserves of men and materiel, across the Don and Volga rivers to the north and east. There was also the looming presence of Stalingrad, yet another strategic and symbolic prize, the kind of trophy Hitler found irresistible. Crucially, the city was a major industrial centre; it sat on a strategic bend on the Volga and was within forty miles of an important location on the Don.

Despite warnings from his generals that he must secure his eastern flank before going too far south, Hitler ignored the advice and disregarded the risks. He was determined to split his forces. He committed one group to a thrust south-east, towards Stalingrad, and the other to a drive due south, towards the oilfields.

The ambition was crystallised in *Fall Blau* ('Operation Blue') and made clear in Führer Directive 41, launched on 28 June. The fateful two-pronged attack comprised: Operation *Edelweiss*, towards the oilfields, and Operation *Fischreiher* ('Heron'), towards Stalingrad.

Hitler was rolling the dice once more. With America by then in the war, after the Japanese attack on Pearl Harbor nearly seven months earlier, it was perhaps the last time he would roll with a free hand. It was a second Barbarossa – audacious, but full of risk – and this time there would be no redemption from failure. Hitler gambled: if he could gain control of the riches of the Soviet south, he might just be able to realise his dream, his Euro-Asian power-house, his *Lebensraum*, his Teutonic paradise that would allow him to challenge his Anglo-Saxon enemies, Britain and America, and, in due course, to rule the world.

In fact, although it was not obvious at the time, the mid-point of 1942 was the fulcrum of the war. We will never know if Hitler saw the situation in those starkest of terms, but during the hot summer

months of 1942, across the historical divide between Eastern
Europe and Western Asia, it was death or glory for his Third Reich.

On 28 July, Stalin issued Order No. 227, his *Ni shagu nazad!*
('Not one step back!) order. Distributed to every unit in the Soviet
armed forces and read out to all of them, it was blunt in its honesty
and chilling in its warnings for all those who would not accept its
command.

> The people of our country, for all the love and respect that
> they have for the Red Army, are beginning to feel disappoint-
> ment in it; they are losing faith in it, and many curse the Red
> Army for giving our people over to the yoke of the German
> oppressors while the Army runs away to the east. Some foolish
> people at the front comfort themselves by saying that we can
> always retreat further east, since we have much territory, much
> land and manpower, and that we will always have more than
> enough grain. They say this to excuse their shameful conduct
> at the front.
>
> But such talk is lies and falsehood, and only helps our
> enemies. After the loss of Ukraine, Belorussia, the Baltic lands,
> the Donbass, and other regions, we have much less territory,
> far fewer people, much less grain and metal, fewer factories
> and industrial plants. To retreat any further would be to ruin
> ourselves and our Motherland. Every little scrap of land that
> we give up strengthens our enemy and weakens our defence,
> our Motherland. And so, the time for retreating is over. Not
> one step back! That must now be our watchword.
>
> Can we take the blows of the enemy and push them back
> to the west? Yes, we can, because our factories in the rear are
> doing excellent work and the front is receiving ever more air-
> craft, tanks, artillery and mortars. Is there something we lack?
> We lack order and discipline. This is our main shortcoming.
> We must establish the strictest order and iron discipline in
> our army if we want to rescue the situation and defend our
> Motherland. Panickers and cowards will be eliminated on the
> spot. Commanders of companies, battalions, regiments and

divisions, along with their commissars and political workers, will be considered traitors to the Motherland if they retreat without orders from above.

There can have been few more forthright and threatening words issued by a leader in wartime. The order led to the formation of *Shtrafbats* ('punishment battalions'), 800-strong units of disgraced soldiers who could 'purge themselves with blood' by undertaking dangerous or even suicidal attacks. It is thought that tens of thousands of soldiers fought in these battalions from 1942 onwards. Given that it is also estimated that few of them survived the war, it seems that the 'redemption through blood' policy was distinctly successful. Should any members of the *Shtrafbats* feel inclined to reject the offer of salvation, Order No. 227 also reinforced the need for NKVD 'barrier troops' to use whatever methods they deemed necessary to 'persuade' those who were recalcitrant to do their duty.

Like Stalin's speech at the beginning of the war, and his Red Square parade in November 1941, Order No. 227 galvanised the Soviet cause. Its oddly contradictory mix of patriotism and draconian threat seemed to appeal to the hearts and minds of his people in one of their darkest hours. Nikolai Moskvin summed up the reaction to Stalin's order: '*He openly recognises the catastrophic situation in the south. My head is full of one idea. Who is guilty for this? The political information men keep asking if there isn't some treachery at work in all this. I think so too. But at least Stalin is on our side . . . So, not a step back! It's timely and it's just.*'

Albina Gantimurova was a sergeant-major and served as a Red Army scout. He witnessed the methods employed by the NKVD: '*Stalin's famous order No. 227: "Not a Step Back!" If you turn back, you're shot! Shot right there. Or court-martialled and sent to the punishment battalions. Those who wound up there were as good as dead. Behind us moved the retreat-blocking battalions . . . Our own shot at our own . . . An ordinary clearing . . . It's wet, muddy after rain. A young soldier is on his knees. A cultivated boy from Leningrad. They had already taken his rifle. We all lined up. We hear him beg . . . He begs not to be shot; his mother is at home, alone. He begins to cry. And they shoot him on the*

*spot – right in the forehead. A show execution: this is what will happen
to people who waver. Even for a single moment! A single moment!'*

In addition to Stalin's daunting entreaties, the country was
developing a potent psychological defence mechanism that rose,
ever higher, on a popular tide. Based on first-hand accounts of
German brutality, it had grown slowly. By the middle of 1942, it
had become a cult of hate.

A profound loathing for all things German blazed in the
hearts of the Soviet people. It was a furnace of revulsion fuelled
by propagandists, who used their talents with words to stoke the
hearth of hatred; a hatred that would have dire consequences as
the war ended.

The poet Konstantin Simonov wrote 'Kill Him' in August 1942.
His words were included in a Soviet propaganda poster.

> If you don't want to give away
> To a German, with his black gun,
> Your house, your wife, your mother
> And everything we call our native land.
> Then know your homeland won't be saved
> If you yourself do not save it.
> And know the enemy won't be killed,
> If you yourself do not kill him.

Alexei Surkov, known as 'the Soldiers' Poet', wrote 'I Hate',
which was published in *Pravda* and widely read by soldiers at the
front. It ended with the following words.

> My heart is as hard as stone,
> My grievances and memories are countless.
> With these hands of mine
> I have lifted the corpses of little children . . .
> I hate them deeply
> For those hours of sleepless gloom.
> I hate them because in one year
> My temples have grown white
> My house has been defiled by the Prussians,

Their drunken laughter dims my reason.
And with these hands of mine
I want to strangle every one of them.

Ilya Ehrenburg took the literary campaign – effectively a 'hate campaign' – against the Germans to an even higher level of vitriol. Ehrenburg's words were published in *Red Star*, the Red Army's newspaper, on 13 August 1942, and would have been read by every soldier throughout the country:

One can bear anything: the plague, and hunger and death. But one cannot bear the Germans. One cannot bear these fish-eyed oafs contemptuously snorting at everything Russian . . . We cannot live as long as these grey-green slugs live . . . Kill them all and dig them into the earth . . . We shall kill them all, but we must do it quickly; or they will desecrate the whole of Russia and torture to death millions more people.

On another day, adopting the same *Untermensch* mentality espoused by his enemy, he wrote:

The Germans are not human. Let us not speak. Let us not be indignant. Let us kill. If you do not kill Germans, the Germans will kill you. He will carry away your family, and torture them in his damned Germany . . . If you have killed one German, kill another. There is nothing merrier than German corpses.

Another product of the enmity towards Germany grew to be of enormous importance to the outcome of the war. It was a phenomenon that blossomed behind the Wehrmacht lines as it advanced. It, too, was born of hatred – a predictable emotional reaction, given the behaviour of the Germans as they passed through conquered territory. Elena Kovalevskaya was a partisan in Belorussia: '*I discovered what hatred was . . . How can they walk on our land! Who are they? Why are they here? A column of prisoners passes. They were driven like cattle and hundreds of corpses are left on the road . . . Hundreds . . . Those who fell down exhausted were shot on the spot. It was impossible to bury them, there were so many. I met my half-sister. Their village had*

been burned down. She had three sons, but they were no more. Their
house had been burned down with the children in it. She used to sit on
the ground and rock from side to side, rocking her grief. We all left for
the forest: Papa, my brothers and I. Nobody urged us, nobody forced us,
we went on our own. Mama stayed with the cow.'

So significant was this part of the war, it took on a designation all its own: the 'Partisan War'. Spontaneous partisan units, widely dispersed and uncoordinated, had sprung up during the first days of the war. Stranded or oppressed civilians coalesced with escaped or marooned soldiers to fight the invader. By the middle of 1942, they had become large in number, efficiently organised, well equipped, and their activities were synchronised effectively.

On 30 May 1942, a Central Headquarters for the Partisan Movement (CHQPM) was created in Moscow. Its responsibility was to coordinate and control the entire Soviet partisan structure. Many leaders of the partisans were summoned to Moscow and met Stalin, who agreed to their requests for weapons, ammunition, clothing and medical supplies.

However, before launching into a tale of heroic patriotism as these brave partisans fought the hated invader, it should be stressed that a major part of their activities – both in intent and in actuality – was often neither patriotic nor heroic. Their actions often involved violent clashes with local pro-Nazi groups, local ethnic Germans, pro-independence nationalists and pro-Western nationalist partisans, especially in Ukraine and, later in the war, in Poland, Belorussia and the Baltic States.

One of the best-known units of the partisan movement was that of Sydir Kovpak. From a poor peasant background in Ukraine, Kovpak was twice decorated in person by Tsar Nicholas II during the Great War. After the Russian Revolution he became a Bolshevik and fought in the Civil War, following which he became head of the local government in the town of Putyvl, in north-east Ukraine.

Not long after the German invasion in 1941, units led by Sydir Kovpak, who was by then fifty-four years old, began to wage guerrilla attacks against Axis forces, which soon spread deep into German-occupied territory. They also fought against anti-Soviet elements of the nationalist Ukrainian Insurgent Army; a large force estimated to be tens of thousands strong. Kovpak insisted on an oath of loyalty among his partisans: *'As a guerrilla, I swear before all the Soviet people, the Party and the government, that I will fight for the liberation of my country from the yoke of Fascism to the complete destruction of it.'* Kovpak's group, at least 1,500 strong, continued to harass the Germans until they retreated to Germany.

General Zhukov was in no doubt about the value of Soviet partisans during the war: *'According to incomplete figures, hundreds of thousands of people's avengers fought in organised partisan detachments in the enemy-occupied territory: 220,000 in Ukraine and 370,000 in Belorussia. The enemy command was forced to set up a second front in his own rear to fight the partisans, thus engaging considerable forces. That factor seriously told on the general condition of the German front and, in the long run, on the outcome of the war.'*

Another, almost legendary, partisan was Dmitri Medvedev. He was born into a steelworker's family in Bryansk, south-west of Moscow. A Civil War veteran and former NKVD intelligence officer, by 1941 he had retired, but after the German invasion he was reinstated and sent to his native Bryansk region to organise resistance behind enemy lines.

During the spring of 1942, Medvedev was given a new assignment, to move his operation to Ukraine. In June, his unit, *Pobeditel'i* ('The Victorious'), was parachuted into Ukraine, where, between June 1942 and March 1944, it is estimated to have initiated over 120 enemy engagements. It 'liquidated' up to 2,000 German soldiers and officers, including 11 generals and other high-ranking officials, and destroyed 81 freight trains.

In his memoirs, Medvedev was clear about the role of his partisans: *'Our role is to distract, annoy and enrage the enemy, like a horsefly on a hot day. Every time the German donkey swishes his tail to remove us, he's not focused on killing Russians. Mind you, horseflies are not deadly, but we are!'*

Medvedev also organised a secret hiding place for 160 rescued Jewish women, children and elderly, who had fled from Jewish ghettos. After the Red Army entered Western Ukraine in the spring of 1944 the *Pobeditel'i* became part of the regular army and Medvedev was made a Hero of the Soviet Union.

There were also several notable female partisans whose heroic activities led to them being made Heroes of the Soviet Union. Of the 10 million Soviet soldiers who fought on the Eastern Front, 800,000 of them were women. At the beginning of the war, enthusiastic women were turned away from recruiting offices and given jobs in munitions, or digging defensive ditches.

Sergeant Klara Tikhonovich became an ant-aircraft gunner, despite the military authorities' initial reluctance: '*I heard words . . . Poison . . . Words like stones . . . It was men's desire to go and fight. Can a woman kill? Those were abnormal, defective women . . . No! A thousand times no! No, it's a human desire. The war was going on, I lived a girl's life . . . Then a neighbour got a letter. Her husband was wounded and in hospital. I thought, he's wounded, who will replace him? One came back without a leg. Who will replace him? I wrote letters. I begged. That's how we were brought up, that nothing in our country should happen without us. We had been taught to love it, to admire it. Since there's a war, it's our duty to help in some way. There's a need for nurses, so we must become nurses. There's a need for anti-aircraft gunners, so we must become anti-aircraft gunners.*'

However, that changed, partly through the persistence of the women and partly because of the growing demand for reinforcements. Also, within the socialist ideology of the Soviet Union, women were designated as equals, a fact that was significant in allowing them to make the transition to the front line.

Antonia Kondrashova fought with the Bytoshsky Partisan Brigade. She described some of the German atrocities that fuelled the partisans' hatred: '*My mother was taken by the Gestapo. My brother managed to escape, but my mother was taken away. They tortured her about my whereabouts. For two years she was held there. Along with other women, the fascists made her lead the way during their operations. They feared our mines and always drove local people ahead of them. More than once, waiting in ambush, we suddenly saw women followed by the fascists. More than once I saw my mother. I hated them. My hatred helped me.*

To this day the scream of a child thrown down a well still rings in my ears. Have you ever heard that scream? The child is falling, screaming, screaming as if from somewhere under the ground, from another world. And to see a young fellow cut up with a saw ... Our partisan ... After that, when you go on a mission, your heart seeks only one thing: to kill them, kill as many as possible, annihilate them in the cruellest way ... In 1943, the fascists shot my mother ...

You can't imagine how hard it is to live with. And the longer I live, the harder it gets. Sometimes you wake up, feeling you can't breathe. The smell of burning chokes you ... You don't know the smell of a burning body; an anxious and sweet smell. That smell ... burning people ... And so you wake up in the night, run and fetch your cologne, and it seems that in the cologne, too, there's that smell. Everywhere. Now I like to read books about life after death. What's there? Who will I meet? I want to meet Mama, but I'm afraid of it, because I think my mother died because of me.'

For those who had to live within German-occupied territory, life was unbearable. Alexandra Khramova was a partisan, Secretary of the Underground Regional Party Committee of Antopol, a town in the south-west of Belorussia: *'There was a woman, Zajarskaya. She had a daughter, Valeria, who was seven. We had to blow up the [German] mess hall. We decided to plant a mine in the stove, but it had to be carried there. The mother said her daughter would bring the mine. She put the mine in a basket and covered it. So the little girl brought the mine to the mess hall. People say that the maternal instinct is stronger than anything. No, ideas are stronger! And faith is stronger! I'm certain that if it weren't for such a girl and such a mama, we wouldn't have been victorious. Yes, life is a good thing. Excellent! But there are things that are dearer.'*

Paulina Kasperovich was also a Belorussian partisan: *'We had the Chimuk brothers in our detachment ... They ran into an ambush in their village, took refuge in a barn, there was shooting, the barn set on fire. They went on shooting until they ran out of ammunition ... Then they came out burned ... They were driven around the village in a cart to see who would recognise them. As their own. So that people would give themselves away.*

The entire village stood there. Their father and mother stood there; nobody made a sound. What a heart that mother must have had not to cry out. Not to call out. She knew that if she began to weep, the whole village would be burned down. For one German killed, they used to burn an entire village. She knew ... There exist awards for everything, but no award, not even the highest Star of Hero of the Soviet Union, is enough for that mother ... For her silence.'

In total, 92 women were made Heroes of the Soviet Union, 50 of them posthumously. Of the 92 awards, 27 were given to partisans. One of the most courageous was Yelena Kolesova. Born in 1920, she worked as a gym teacher at a school in Leningrad. After the German invasion, she began working in the construction of defensive fortifications until, after repeatedly applying to join the Red Army but being rejected, she was allowed to join a *Spetsnaz* 'special forces' unit, No. 9903. After training, which consisted of only a three-day crash course in explosives and weapons, she was deployed in October 1941 to carry out sabotage and gather intelligence on the outskirts of Moscow. During that mission she was captured by the Germans, but after being held for two days, she managed to escape.

Kolesova was then made commander of a small group of several women whose job was to sabotage infrastructure around Minsk. They instructed civilians in explosives, derailed trains, bombed supply warehouses and destroyed military vehicles. They were totally ruthless, enticing German soldiers into the forest by pretending to be unmarried local women looking for a good time, only to ambush and execute them. Such was the destructiveness of Kolesova's unit, German intelligence was convinced that it was several hundred strong. In fact, it had fewer than a dozen members.

Kolesova was killed in action in September 1942 while leading a raid on a fortress in Krupki, in Belorussia. She parachuted in with ten comrades, but they had had no parachute training and four of them were killed making the drop. Kolesova was mortally wounded while trying to take out a machine-gun post. Her dying wish was to be buried with the other members of her unit who had died in the raid, a request that was granted. She was made a Hero of the Soviet Union in 1944.

One of her unnamed male comrades said of her: *'She was the bravest soldier I knew, not the bravest female soldier, the bravest soldier of them all!'*

One of the most tragic partisan stories concerns a young woman, barely old enough to fight, eighteen-year-old Zoya Kosmodemyanskaya. In October 1941, while still a high-school student in Moscow, she volunteered and was accepted for a partisan unit: *'What can I do when the enemy is so close? If they came here, I would not be able to continue living.'*

During one mission, three of her female colleagues failed to return. Kosmodemyanskaya asked her commander for permission to go back and see if they were wounded. She went alone, despite continued German activity in the area, and did not return for several hours. Her colleagues were sure she was dead. But she did return. Her hands were covered with blood. Her three colleagues had been killed but she had taken all their weapons and ammunition and brought them back.

She later went on a mission to a village called Petrischevo, where she was captured. Soviet newspapers wrote an account of her brutal torture, when she was beaten multiple times by heavy leather belts. Despite prolonged interrogation by a German officer, she remained defiant throughout.

She was later tortured again and then, the next morning, taken to makeshift gallows to be hanged in front of the entire village. Her final words were: *'Comrades! Why are you looking so sad? Be brave, fight, beat the Germans, burn, trample them! I'm not afraid to die, comrades. It is happiness to die for one's people.'*

To the Germans, she said: *'You hang me now, but I'm not alone. There are two hundred million of us. You can't hang us all. They will avenge me.'*

With the noose around her neck, in the moment before the hanging, she cried out: *'Farewell, comrades! Fight, do not be afraid! Stalin is with us! Stalin will come!'*

The Germans left her body hanging on the gallows for several weeks. From time to time, passing German soldiers, usually drunk, would defile her corpse. Clothes were removed, breasts were hacked off, and what was left used for bayonet practice. Eventually, the body was thrown into a pit. A *Pravda* journalist, Pyotr Lidov, found her body when the village was retaken by a Soviet counter offensive. He wrote:

> Her eyes, arched by the black wings of her eyebrows, were closed; her long lashes lay on her olive-skinned cheeks, her lips were tightly pressed, and her high forehead had a purple tinge of suffocation. Her handsome Russian face still preserved its integrity and freshness of line. An imprint of profound rest lay upon it.

Kosmodemyanskaya was the first woman to be made a Hero of the Soviet Union, and became a national war hero.

13

PROTECT THE OIL

JULY–NOVEMBER 1942

After its launch on 28 June, *Fall Blau* started well for the Axis forces. Supported by over 2,000 aircraft and almost 2,000 panzers and artillery, the 1.3 million-man German Army Group South advanced over thirty miles on the first day. During July and August, they captured 625,000 Soviet prisoners, destroyed 7,000 tanks, 6,000 artillery pieces and 400 aircraft. The numbers were not as high as 1941, but they were significant.

General Ivan Tyulenev, Commander of the Red Army's Transcaucasian Front, described the chaos that ensued. As during the blitzkrieg of 1941, Soviet civilians bore the brunt: '*Even the smallest railway stations were cluttered with thousands of refugees. Weeping women and children were desperately hoping to be taken across the Caspian* [Sea]. *A danger of epidemics arose. The local Party organisations made a frantic effort to ship them to Krasnovodsk on the other side of the Caspian.*'

German losses were also high. But more importantly, despite Stalin's 'Not one step back!' order, the Red Army was making tactical withdrawals to more defendable positions. This meant that although the Axis advance was swallowing large tracts of territory, the Red Army was maintaining much of its strength and securing better and better defensive positions. At the same time, the German lines of communication and supply were becoming longer and longer, and thus increasingly vulnerable.

Among a host of Red Army soldiers standing in the way of the Axis forces was a forty-two-year-old army veteran, General Vasili Chuikov. The eighth of twelve children from a peasant family in a small village south of Moscow, he started adult life as a factory worker in Leningrad (then, as now, called St Petersburg), then fought in the Russian Civil War. He rose through the ranks of the Red Army, commanded the 4th Army in the Soviet invasion of Poland in 1939, and fought in the Russo-Finnish 'Winter War' of 1940.

Chuikov became fluent in Mandarin Chinese at the prestigious Frunze Military Academy, where he excelled, and was appointed military attaché in China. He then became an adviser to Chiang Kai-shek, the Chinese nationalist leader, before being recalled to Moscow in July 1942. He was given command of the Soviet 64th Army on the west bank of the Don. He wrote detailed accounts of his time in the Red Army, with which he served all the way to Berlin in 1945. Like Zhukov, Chuikov was a new breed of general: battle-hardened, professional and ruthless; a dog of war, like the enemy he faced. A strong disciplinarian, he was not averse to carrying out acts of punishment personally.

Within days of taking command at the end of July, his 64th Army initially suffered defeat after defeat. He later wrote: *'Many years have passed since all this happened, but I am still not ashamed to remember my baptism of fire on the Don.'*

Despite Soviet military setbacks, Chuikov was encouraged by the many acts of heroism he witnessed on the front line. He recorded the bravery of Lieutenant Nedelin, an officer in an artillery battery, who described the experience of being under fire: *'Early on the morning of July 22nd, a big column of tanks appeared and not far behind was a column of trucks with supplies and fuel. A duel began between our four guns and their twenty tanks. There was nowhere to withdraw to, we couldn't move across the open steppe under constant bombardment. We thought it over and decided to stay where we were and fight to the last shell.*

Everything was blowing up with a thunderous noise all about us. The thick steppe grass was on fire. The flames took away the camouflage over our guns, leaving us exposed. About 4 p.m. the gun commanders began to report that they were running out of shells. The battery had six shells left . . . three . . . and finally, the last one. Then on our side, everything fell silent. But even after we had stopped firing, the enemy again plastered us with a great tornado of firing and only then came to attack us.

A few dozen rifle bullets against an avalanche of tanks were quite pointless. We stayed in our emplacements, covered in earth, and waited for the end to come. The tanks came right up to the dugouts, still firing. Our battery commander was killed. Only a few men were still alive. I don't remember anything else; I was wounded by fragments from a shell which burst no more than a couple of yards away . . .'

Chuikov does not tell us how Lieutenant Nedelin escaped from his devastated artillery battery, or what became of him. He does, however, remind us that he was one of the countless heroes who stood in the way of the Axis advance.

Critical at this point was the Battle of Kalach, in what is known as the Don Bend. The town sits on the eastern side of the Don, just above the point where the Don swings sharply westwards. It is only forty-five miles from modern-day Volgograd (Stalingrad in 1942).

On 25 July Chuikov's army was positioned on the opposite bank of the Don from Kalach, with orders to hold the Axis advance. Initially, the 64th Army was all but surrounded. However, a Soviet counter-attack forced the Germans back. Following a resupply, the Axis forces attacked the flanks of the Soviet bridgehead, successfully collapsing it.

The Axis victory put it in a position to cross the Don River and advance on Stalingrad and the Volga. The defeated men of the 64th Army who managed to escape across the Don at Kalach began the long trudge towards the city that had been given Stalin's name in 1925. Vasily Grossman witnessed the retreat: 'Those were hard and dreadful days . . . The army was retreating. Men's faces were gloomy. Dust covered their clothes and weapons. It got into people's nostrils and throats. It made one's lips dry and cracked. It was a terrible dust, the dust of retreat. It ate up the men's faith, it extinguished the warmth of people's hearts.

The first units of the retreating army entered Stalingrad. Trucks with grey-faced wounded men, vehicles with crumpled wings, with holes from bullets and shells. And the war's breath entered the city and scorched it. Fear found its way into a lot of hearts and many eyes looked across the

Volga. It seemed to these people that they didn't have to defend the Volga, but that the Volga had to defend them.'

The retreat along the Don led to one of the many legendary stories of the war. On 2 August, the 13th Kuban Cossack Cavalry Division was ordered to attack the village of Kushchevskaya. The objective was to take out the Wehrmacht's panzers. While the Red Army attack included Soviet tanks, the Cossacks concentrated on attacking German support infantry. Zinaida and Olga Vasilyevna, the two daughters of Belorussian partisan leader Vasily Korzh, rode with the Cossacks. Both were teenaged medical orderlies.

Zinaida Vasilyevna described the sisters' experience of what was a classical cavalry charge into the teeth of an armoured Wehrmacht formation: 'The first baptism in combat. It was the famous cavalry charge of the Kuban Cossacks. It was a dreadful battle for Olga and me because we were still very afraid . . . When the cavalrymen went in it was like an avalanche: capes flying, sabres bared, horses snorting against tanks and artillery. It was like an otherworldly dream. There were lots of fascists, more than us. They walked next to their tanks with their machine guns at the ready. But they couldn't hold on against our avalanche. They abandoned their machine guns and fled. What a sight.'

Vasili Chuikov was part of the retreat and stopped at the Yurkin State Farm near the village of Abganerovo: 'We stopped for a snack near a burned-out T-34 tank. We started eating. However, right in front of me, not more than a yard away, I saw a blackened and decayed human hand sticking up out of the grass. Suddenly, we had no appetite and got back in our truck.' There would soon be many more rotting corpses. The almighty battle for the city would soon begin.

To the south-west, in its dash for oil, the Wehrmacht had made the kind of progress it had made in the summer of 1941. Rostov-on-Don had fallen on 25 July, Krasnador and the oilfields at Maikop were seized on 9 August and those at Elista on the 13th. Astrakhan, the heart of the Lower Volga, was less than 200 miles away from Elista, and the Caspian Sea at Lagan was even closer.

Another stark reminder of the horrors of 1941 was the number of Red Army fallen, lying dead along the route of the German advance. Over 340,000 Soviet soldiers would die in defence of their nation's oil. One of them, an unnamed artilleryman, had written to his loved one just before his death. His letter was found on his body by a partisan. It was dated 22 July 1942. Sadly, there was no envelope with the letter, nor did it bear the name of its intended recipient. It is a poignant symbol not only of another death among millions but also of the countless emotional expressions that disappeared into the void of war.

> A year has passed, every day of which sowed death around me; every hour carried more and more intense experiences. More than once during this time it seemed to me that the eyeless face of death was approaching me. Death was sometimes so close that I wanted to reach out and push her away. Many of my comrades, my close friends with whom I shared the hardships and petty joys of combat life, are no longer alive. I lost them.
>
> I have lost a family, a father and a mother whose fate is unknown to me, and if sometimes I ask myself how and why I am still alive, I find no words to answer. But still I live and there is still a soldier in me. I'm still holding my weapon, my strength, my will is not broken yet. The soldier has few joys in his life, and they are, for the most part, primitive. The soldier's greatest joy, the heady joy of victory, is not familiar to me. Many villages and cities abandoned to the uncertainty of the enemy leave a heavy sense of loss. There is so much grief. And when it is hard to think about what I have lost, or when I think my life could end in a matter of minutes, I think of you.

As the Wehrmacht's panzers and support infantry pushed further south, two things began to change. The terrain was transformed from the endlessly flat Nogai Steppe to the increasingly precipitous foothills of the Caucasus Mountains. The Terek River was also a major obstacle; the river's currents were strong and fast-flowing. Not only was it difficult for the Germans to create bridgeheads, but the Red Army's resistance was stiffening yet again; its leadership was becoming more strategic, and its organisation and tactics were improving by the day.

A Wehrmacht bridgehead across the Terek was finally established after the fall of Mozdok on 25 August, but another new and surprising military development emerged. On the night of 6 September, a Soviet U-2 biplane scored a direct hit on the Wehrmacht's pontoon bridge with a 50kg bomb. It was an excellent aerial sortie and a superb bombing strike. But it was unusual in one specific respect; the pilot was a twenty-year-old woman called Marina Chechneva.

Chechneva was one of a new breed of airborne warriors. She was a pilot in the all-female 588th Night Bomber Regiment of the Soviet Air Force. A typical attack technique of the night bombers involved idling the engine near the target and gliding to the bomb-release point, with only wind noise left to reveal their presence. German soldiers likened the sound to broomsticks and named the pilots 'Night Witches'. Because of the modest weight of their bombs and the low altitude of their attacks, the pilots of the night bomber did not carry parachutes until 1944.

Chechneva was born to a working-class family in 1922 and, at the age of sixteen, enrolled in a flying club, where she learned sport flying. She became an instructor pilot at the Central Flying Club in Moscow between 1939 and 1941 and joined the Communist Party in 1942.

When the Germans invaded in 1941, the club evacuated to Stalingrad. In the October, Chechneva was permitted to join the new women's aviation group formed by pioneer Marina Raskova. After undergoing further training at Engels Military Aviation School, she was assigned to the 588th Night Bomber Regiment. The unit later received a prestigious Guards designation and was renamed the 46th Guards Night Bomber Regiment. After her exploits in the Caucasus, Chechneva was promoted to flight commander and later squadron commander.

Chechneva made 810 bombing sorties during more than 1,000 flight hours. She destroyed 6 warehouses, 5 river crossings, 4 anti-aircraft artillery batteries, 4 searchlights and a train, and instructed 40 navigators and pilots for the war effort. After the war she wrote: *'I felt nothing for the Germans I was attacking. They were violating our homeland, destroying us, committing terrible crimes. It was a fight to the death, and I was happy to kill as many of them as I could. There is no sympathy in war.'*

Female pilots were initially barred from combat in the Soviet Air Force, but experienced navigator Marina Raskova, who had set a pre-war aviation distance world record, was able to change the ruling by using her position and personal contacts in the higher echelons in Moscow. She campaigned until she obtained permission to form female combat units. On 8 October 1941, an order was issued to deploy three women's Air Force units, including the 588th Regiment. The Regiment's motto was: 'You are a woman and you should be proud of that.'

At the Engels School of Aviation, they underwent intensive training in flying, mechanics and navigation. Their ill-fitting uniforms were hand-me-downs from the men of the Air Force, and they flew in obsolete wooden biplanes. The women flew over 24,000 missions in combat during the war and produced 23 recipients of the honour Hero of the Soviet Union, when the average number of recipients per regiment was only around three.

Lieutenant Polina Gelman, too short to be a pilot because she could not reach the pedals, served as a navigator, and was made a Hero of the Soviet Union in 1946: *'We had been fighting for one thousand nights – one thousand nights in combat. Every day the girls became more courageous. To fly a combat mission is not a trip under the moon . . . Every attack, every bombing is a dance with death. Despite this, every girl knew the danger, and none ever refused to fly her mission or used a pretext to avoid participating in a bombing. Our feelings were that we were doing a simple job, just a job to save our country, to liberate it from the enemy.'*

Guards Lieutenant Alexandra Popova flew from 1942 onwards: *'The planes they gave us were Po-2s* [Polikarpov Po-2]. *Small, slow. They flew only at low level, hedgehopping. They were made out of plywood, covered with aircraft fabric. One direct hit and it caught fire and burned up completely in the air. The only solid metal part was the M-11 motor. Towards the end of the war, we were issued parachutes, and a machine gun was fitted in the pilot's cabin. Before that, we had no weapons, except for the four bombs under our wings. That's all. Nowadays, they'd call us kamikazes, and maybe we were. Yes! We were! But victory was valued more than our lives.'*

Popova lost many colleagues. The fighting took a heavy toll: *'You approach a target, and you're shaking all over because below it's all gunfire: fighter planes are shooting, anti-aircraft guns are shooting. We did up to twelve flights a night. And the work our armourers did! They had to attach four bombs to the aircraft by hand – eight hundred pounds. They did it all night: one plane takes off, another lands. The body reorganised itself so much during the war that we weren't women ... We didn't have periods ... After the war, not all of us could have children.'*

In the ground war, well-trained Soviet troops began to arrive by sea and in parachute drops near the coast of the Caspian Sea. Sterner Soviet defence, partisan sabotage operations along German supply lines, and the long distances from its depots and manufacturing base reduced the effectiveness of the Wehrmacht attacks. The completion of its strategic objective of capturing the main Caucasus oilfield at Baku seemed increasingly unlikely. Luftwaffe support had been a vital instrument until now in the Axis advance, but airborne attacks on Baku were prevented by the insufficient range of the German fighters.

As in the defence of other Soviet cities, after embarrassing early losses, the resolve of ordinary citizens and soldiers had made a difference. In the words of a Luftwaffe pilot captured and interrogated by General Chuikov during the early days of the fighting on the Don: *'The Führer made a mistake about Russia. He and many other Germans did not expect the Russians to have such staying power.'*

General Tyulenev was unstinting in his praise of the work done to bolster the defences of the Caucasus: *'The entire Caucasian theatre of war became a complex of defences. People worked till they nearly collapsed, with bloody rags around their blistered hands. Sometimes they had little or nothing to eat for days, but they still went on with the work, even at night, and despite the air raids ... 100,000 defensive works were completed: 70,000 pillboxes, 500 miles of anti-tank ditches, 200 miles of anti-infantry obstacles, and 1,000 miles of trenches. 9,150,000 working days were committed to the task.'*

Yet another Hitler 'masterstroke' began to stall. His megalo-mania and paranoia deepened; his moods were darkening, his temper getting ever shorter. In what should have been a moment of symbolic delight when, on 21 August, news reached the Führer that a detachment of mountaineers had climbed the snow-capped Caucasus summit of Mount Elbrus, the highest mountain in Europe, to place a swastika at its top, he flew into a rage. He screamed that the achievement was a 'mad stunt' and threatened to court-martial those involved.

Those who witnessed the outburst later viewed it as a watershed which exposed Hitler's realisation that his cause was lost. Realising that the oil of the Chechen city of Grozny was beyond his grasp, Hitler ordered that the Luftwaffe destroy its oilfields, which they did on 10 and 12 October. Like many other actions, it was a flawed and ill-considered strategic decision. Although the loss of the oil of the Caucasus was critical to him, Stalin had alternative supplies of oil, east of the Urals.

One boon for the Wehrmacht was that anti-Soviet sympathies in the region meant that it was able to recruit many volunteers, despite Hitler's initial reluctance. It is estimated that 80,000 Cossacks fought for the Germans, along with many other local nationalities, as *Osttruppen* ('East Troops'), including many of the region's Muslims.

As in all the other battlefronts of the war, in the wake of the advance into the Caucasus came *Einsatzgruppe D*. As early as 5 August, it used its mobile extermination trucks to gas 600 mentally ill patients in Stavropol. After that, it is estimated that it murdered up to 35,000, mainly Jewish, civilians between July 1942 and January 1943.

Under severe pressure in the Caucasus, the Wehrmacht was eventually forced to retreat. It managed to get back across the Don bridges in early February 1943, from where it fought a defensive campaign until it retreated to the Crimea in October 1943.

Hitler's mad grab for oil had failed.

PART THREE

THE MOTHER OF ALL BATTLES

14

STALINGRAD: THE GREAT BATTLE BEGINS

SEPTEMBER 1942

After it was named 'Stalin's City', in 1925, the city bore the name for only a few decades. Before that, it carried its ancient name, Tsaritsyn. In 1961, it became Volgograd when the Soviet Union was 'de-Stalinised' under Khrushchev. Even so, the name 'Stalingrad' is forever seared into the consciousness of military historians and anyone with an interest in modern history.

It is remembered for a titanic battle: a battle unique in history; a battle that changed the course of the greatest conflict in history; a battle that exemplified the horrors of war like no other; and a battle that exemplified courage, valour and heroism.

The stark facts of the Battle of Stalingrad are almost too extraordinary to comprehend. It lasted for five months, one week and three days. There were over 840,000 Axis (German, Italian, Hungarian, Romanian) casualties (killed, wounded or captured) and at least 1,130,000 Soviet casualties (480,000 killed or missing, and 650,000 wounded or diseased); a total close to 2 million. These figures do not include innumerable civilian casualties; their toll is unknown.

In the 1960s, Andrei Borodin, former Director of the Museum of the Defence of Stalingrad, was tasked with compiling an accurate figure for Red Army losses. He attempted to assess the horror of Stalingrad in statistical terms, when not only people, but documents, files and paperwork had disappeared into oblivion. He gave a telling summation:

Nothing but tears. Regiments disappeared along with all their paperwork. There was no accounting of losses. This was just a meat grinder. Divisions would be destroyed in just three days. It is not given to us to understand this nightmare.

Like so many decisions taken by Hitler and Stalin during the war, symbolism and pride played a significant part in defining the reasoning behind the horrendous battle for this industrial city on the west bank of the Volga. The fact that it was named after the Soviet leader must have enticed Hitler to destroy it and, for the same reason, convinced Stalin to defend it. Hitler proclaimed that, because Stalingrad's population was 'thoroughly communistic' and 'especially dangerous', after its capture its male citizens were to be killed, and all women and children were to be deported.

Hitler's decision to divide his Army Group South, so that a significant part of it was diverted to take Stalingrad, while the rest marauded through the Caucasus in search of oil, would prove catastrophic. Not only did it fly in the face of his primary objective of seizing a crucial supply of oil, but it halved his strength, which, ultimately, would deny him both the oil he craved and the city he coveted. This calamitous misjudgement would eventually cost him the war.

After a gradual advance on the city, from July onwards, the Battle for Stalingrad began in earnest on 23 August 1942, with the heavy bombing of the city. Some 1,000 tons of bombs were dropped in forty-eight hours, more than in London at the height of the Blitz.

Stalin had refused to evacuate the civilian population from the city, meaning that at least 400,000 civilians were trapped within its boundaries. Accurate records do not exist but it is more than likely that most of them were killed. Much of the city was turned to rubble, although some factories continued production until, in desperation, the workers joined in the fighting.

The Dzerzhinsky Tractor Factory continued to turn out T-34 tanks until German troops burst into the workshop itself. Civilians, including women and children, were put to work building trenches and defensive fortifications. The massive Luftwaffe air raids of 23 and 24 August created a devastating firestorm, killing thousands.

Vasili Chekalov had survived the early days of the war in Leningrad and in the defence of Moscow. He was in Stalingrad on the 23rd: *'The day passed quietly. Nothing seemed to precede the beginning of the violent events. The city lived its normal life; institutions worked; children played. Around 4 o'clock events began to develop violently. The first bombs dropped on residential buildings of the city. One of the bombs hit a hospital near me. Walking wounded already had time to leave their beds and were crowded down the stairs. This most brutal extermination of civilians lasted up to two hours a night. The heat destroyed whole quarters of the city. There was no one to extinguish the flames, nothing could be done. The entire city was lit up by the glow of the fires.'*

Vasili Chuikov described the events of that day: *'August 23rd proved to be a tragic day for the city, when, with several infantry and panzer divisions, and with enormous losses, the enemy managed to break through to the Volga north of the city. With the deliberate intention of sowing panic, they launched 2,000 bombers on the city. Never in the entire war had the enemy attacked in such strength from the air. The city was enveloped in flames. Everything was blazing, collapsing. Death and disaster descended on thousands of families.'*

Misha Volkov, having survived the traumas of Ukraine in June 1941 and taken part in the defence of Moscow in October, was in Stalingrad with his unit at the end of August. He wrote to his wife: *'For the past few days and still right now, I am in the front line. I don't have time to tell you what's going on, but I can tell you that what's around me is hell. There's wailing and roaring all around, the sky is splitting with the din. One shell burst just three metres from me, and I was splattered with mud, but I'm still in one piece. But as to what will happen, I can give you no guarantees.'*

It is not known what became of Misha Volkov. He may have survived Stalingrad, but most of those who were there in August never made it to the end of the year.

The Volga has a special place in Russian history and folklore. Its downstream area is said to be the cradle of Indo-European civilisation. Countless tribes have traversed it: Turkic, Germanic, Finnic, Nordic, Mongol. If Mother Russia has a home, it is the Volga Basin.

The 'Song of the Volga Boatmen' is as anthemic as any national melody. When it is sung, all Russians weep.

For the Germans to have reached the Volga, over 1,600 miles from Berlin, was like a dagger in the heart of Mother Russia. Vasily Grossman was in Dubrovka, a town on the bank of the river, twenty-five miles north of Stalingrad: *'Now there is nowhere further to retreat. Every step back is now a big and probably fatal mistake. The civilians in the villages beside the Volga feel it as well as the armies that are defending it and Stalingrad ... The war has reached the Volga! That trickster* [Hitler] *has reached the heart of our land.'*

A few days later, Grossman was caught in an air raid: *'A clear, cold morning in Dubrovka. There is a bang, clinking of broken glass ... Screams and weeping over the Volga. A girl in a bright yellow dress is screaming, "Mama, Mama!" A man is wailing like a woman. His wife's arm has been torn off. A woman sick with typhoid has been hit in the stomach by a shell fragment. Carts are moving, blood dripping from them. And the screaming, the crying over the Volga.'*

The geography of the city of Stalingrad, a narrow, urban and industrial strip, twenty-five miles long and just five miles wide, hard against the wide Volga, made blitzkrieg irrelevant. The city would have to be taken street by street with full-frontal panzer and infantry engagements, followed by vicious close-quarters, hand-to-hand fighting.

Among the early Soviet heroes of the battle were the gunners of the 1077th Anti-Aircraft Regiment. As German panzers approached Gumrak Airfield, north-west of the city, the 1077th reoriented their guns to their lowest elevation to engage the tanks, 'shot for shot', for several hours. Eventually, all the anti-aircraft positions were destroyed and overrun. When the Germans reached the Soviet positions, they were shocked to discover that many of their adversaries had been young female volunteers. They had had little training and were armed only with flak rounds, which were designed to destroy the flimsy bodies of aeroplanes, not the heavy armour of tanks. The actions of the women, some only just out of school, soon became part of Red Army folklore.

Vasili Chuikov described the courage of those who defended the city: *'Sixteen guardsmen, led by Lieutenant Kochetkov, were ordered to defend a hillock on the outskirts of the city. Armed with only rifles and grenades. They held off four infantry attacks and an assault by machine-gunners. At dawn the next day, twelve enemy tanks attacked . . . A battle to the death began. One of the defenders threw himself under one of the tanks with a handful of grenades. A second man followed, then a third, and a fourth. Only four defenders were still alive, but the Lieutenant was dying. The other three placed him under cover before they too threw themselves under the oncoming tanks. Six tanks were destroyed by the sixteen guardsmen. Kochetkov lived long enough to tell the story before he died.*

In another sector, twenty-five miles west of Stalingrad, led by a Komsomol member called Leonid Kovalev, thirty-three soldiers of the 62nd Army found themselves completely encircled. Seventy German tanks stormed their position. Their provisions ran out; they had no water. They did not waver. In the battle that followed, they burned out twenty-seven tanks and killed more than 150 of the enemy.'

As well as the tales of heroism, recounted with patriotic hyperbole by Chuikov and others, there were also many examples of fear and cowardice, and of the brutal treatment meted out by NKVD detachments to those who wavered. At least 13,500 Red Army soldiers would be executed during the five-month battle.

In one such 'extraordinary event' – a 'betrayal of the Motherland' – an NKVD firing squad had executed a man and buried him in a shell hole for having a self-inflicted wound. But, probably because of drunkenness, they had failed to kill him. So the wounded man had dug himself out of his grave and, somewhat naively, returned to his unit, whereupon he was executed once more; this time successfully.

As the late-summer days of unrelenting fighting passed by, Chuikov described an ever-worsening situation: *'On September 10th, the enemy managed to drive our units back to the outskirts of the city. Our neighbour army, the 62nd, was cut off from us to the right and left. The period of bitter street fighting began.'*

The following day, 11 September, Chuikov was also given command of the 62nd Army and charged with the task of defending the city – a mission which, at that point, must have seemed impossible to achieve. The promotion came in a meeting with General Andrei Yeremenko, Commander of the South-Eastern Front and member of the Politburo, and Commissar Nikita Khrushchev. Chuikov recalled the conversation: *'Yeremenko and Khrushchev said to me, "You must save Stalingrad. How do you feel about that?" "Yes, sir." "No, it isn't enough to obey. What do you think about it?" "It means we'll die. So, we will die." [. . .]'*

General Yeremenko recounted a conversation he had with Stalin at the same time: *'Khrushchev wanted to mine the city. I telephoned Stalin. "What for?" Stalin asked.* [Yeremenko said] *I am not going to surrender Stalingrad. I don't want to mine the city. Stalin said, "Tell him to fuck off then!" [. . .]'*

Two days later, Chuikov visited a dressing station close to the Volga, where ferries were attempting to evacuate the wounded across the mile-wide river: *'The wounded are not being fed, they are lying in the open, they are asking for water. Their bloodstained bandages look like a gaudy theatrical production. I go into an operating theatre. The faces of the doctors and nurses are whiter than their gowns. They are operating on a man with shrapnel in his buttocks. He is groaning. I ask the surgeon, "Why are you cutting away nearly the whole buttock?" "If I leave any flesh, he will die of gangrene." [. . .]'*

In early September, Grossman arrived in Stalingrad from the Volga. He described the sights that greeted him: *'The burned, dead city . . . Inhabitants of a burned building are eating shchi* [cabbage soup] *in a gateway, seated on a pile of belongings. A book entitled "The Insulted and the Injured"* [by Fyodor Dostoevsky] *is lying on the ground nearby. My colleague says to them, "You, too, are insulted and injured." "We are injured, but not insulted," a girl replied.'*

The task facing Chuikov was immense. Heavily outnumbered, overwhelmed in the air, low on ammunition and with his troops low on morale, he had few cards to play. As he addressed his subordinate commanders, perhaps fear was all he had left to motivate them: '*I said to them, "Once you are here, there is no way out. Either you will lose your head or your legs."* . . . *Everyone knew that those who ran would be shot on the spot. That was more terrifying than the Germans.*' So dire was the situation, Chuikov adopted a military code taken from the barbarity of ancient warfare: he had no hesitation in ordering summary executions for cowardice or desertion. He was quite prepared to pull the trigger himself to punish any of his commanders who had abandoned their posts: '*I shot the commander and commissar of one regiment, and a short while later I shot two brigade commanders and their commissars. We made sure news of this got to the men.*'

Chuikov followed the military precept 'time is blood'; fresh troops from the east bank of the Volga were thrown into battle as soon as they landed. The situation worsened on 13 September, when it appeared that the game was up. German infantry took the Mamayev Kurgan, a high point above the city called 'Height 102' on military maps. Control of the hill became vitally important, as it offered a commanding position over the city. With its capture German artillery started firing on the city centre, as well as on the city's main railway station under the hill. They captured the station the next day.

On the same day, the Red Army's 13th Guards Rifle Division, commanded by the charismatic Colonel General Alexander Rodimtsev, already a Hero of the Soviet Union from his exploits in the Spanish Civil War, landed from the east bank of the Volga. His 10,000 men, a force of largely inexperienced new recruits, were immediately hurled into an assault to retake Mamayev Kurgan, which they did on the 16th. They also rushed to defend the railway station. By the following day, almost all the men of 13th Guards had perished, leaving just over 320 survivors.

The hill changed hands several times over the course of the winter. When the battle ended, its soil had been reduced to a black morass of metal and human remains. It stayed black even in the icy depths of winter. The snow kept melting as a result of the many fires and explosions caused by the residue of ordnance. Even in spring, grass refused to grow on the scorched earth. To this day, it is possible to find fragments of bone and metal barely beneath the surface of the hill.

The railway station was defended by one of Rodimtsev's officers, Lieutenant Anton Dragan, who commanded a platoon of fewer than fifty men. When the Germans attacked, an extraordinary struggle ensued for three weeks, during which it is estimated the station changed hands nineteen times.

The guardsmen crawled through ceilings and under floorboards. The close-quarters fighting reduced Dragan's men to a handful. After running out of ammunition, one of them used his bayonet and carved on a wall: 'Rodimtsev's Guardsmen fought and died for their country here.' Under cover of darkness, Dragan and the last five of his men slipped out of the building and managed to make their way through the German lines to the Soviet positions.

Alexander Rodimtsev recalled the situation at the railway station: *'First it was their building, then it was ours, then it was theirs again. It was impossible to say exactly where the front lines were ... The back-and-forth fighting went on day and night ...*

October 1st. These brave troops withdrew from Mamayev Kurgan ... I had nothing left. One battalion had been wiped out and the 34th was in a bad way. I lost some 4,000 men there. That's not an easy thing to accept. One of our guns took out three tanks. Then the guy manning it was badly wounded, but he didn't take one step back right until a German tank ran over him and crushed him. No one retreated or surrendered. Men died, but they did not retreat.'

Many military experts agree that, even considering the many battles yet to come, the desperate defence of the city over those two or three days in the middle of September saved Stalingrad. Significantly, despite the dire circumstances – including his bunker being heavily bombed and flooded with burning oil – Chuikov stayed in the city. Lesser men would almost certainly have relocated their headquarters to the other side of the Volga.

Chuikov used close-quarters guerrilla tactics to unnerve the Germans and reduce the effectiveness of the Luftwaffe's aerial superiority. He reduced the combat zone to what he called 'hand-grenade distance', knowing that any Luftwaffe attacks were just as likely to kill Germans as Soviets. He knew it was a fight to the death and used a range of small-scale weapons, including grenades, flamethrowers and any improvised weapons his men could get their hands on, such as hammers, axes and sharpened spades. The Wehrmacht's soldiers called the battles that ensued a *Rattenkrieg* ('rat war'). The Germans would secure a street by day, set up defensive positions to secure the area, then discover that by the next morning, Red Army riflemen had appeared behind them. They had used attics, cellars and sewers to outflank their enemy.

Vasily Grossman described the success of such tactics: '*Weapons for close-quarter combat have never been used as they have been in Stalingrad ... Our soldiers have become so resourceful ... They can build trenches that are so good that you wouldn't notice the men if you stepped on their heads ... Our soldiers were on the upper floor of a house. Some Germans wound up a gramophone. Our men made a hole in the floor and fired on them with a flamethrower.*'

The deadly attritional nature of the conflict had one simple objective: to bleed the Wehrmacht of its most precious resource, men. The arithmetic was simple: Red Army reserves were only a mile away across the Volga, while the Wehrmacht's were 1,600 miles away; German reserves of men and materiel were limited, while the Soviet Union's were greater; winter would soon come, meaning a repeat of the events of 1941 outside Moscow was highly likely.

A small house in the centre of Stalingrad became an epic story of the battle and typified the street warfare of Stalingrad. Like so many other places in and around the city, it has become a part of Russian and military folklore. The house was a four-storey building in the centre of the city. Part of the ruined building has been preserved and is called 'Pavlov's House' in honour of Yakov Pavlov, the Soviet soldier who led its defence. He had become the leader of his platoon of just two dozen men after his superiors had been killed. On 27 September, he managed to secure the house by lacing it with barbed wire and mines, along with machine-gun posts in the windows. Supply and communication trenches were created, leading from the rear of the house to the bank of the Volga.

The importance of the house derived from the fact that it defended a key section of the Volga riverbank and was at a crossroads, giving the defenders a long line of sight in all directions. The Germans attacked the building several times a day. Each time German infantry or panzers tried to cross the square to close in on the house, Pavlov's men laid down a barrage of machine-gun and anti-tank fire. The defenders, as well as several civilians hiding in the basement, survived the siege for fifty-nine days until they were relieved on 25 November. Vasili Chuikov lauded Pavlov and his men with a very pithy accolade: *'Pavlov's small group of men killed more enemy soldiers than the Germans lost taking Paris.'* He also noted the ethnic diversity of Pavlov's platoon, which contained three Russians, two Ukrainians, two Georgians, an Uzbek, a Kazakh, an Abkhazian, a Tajik and a Tatar. Pavlov himself fought through the rest of the war and was decorated with many awards, including being made a Hero of the Soviet Union.

Alexander Averbukh was a lieutenant in a company of anti-tank riflemen. He and a few of his men became isolated from their battalion: *'It was just me, Captain Lizunov and his runner in the bunker. We decided to leave, one at a time. Lizunov had run about 150 metres but got hit in the thigh. I got to him and lifted him on to my back and crawled 50 metres. I was trying to lift him over the parapet when I got hit in the leg. I had used my bandages, so I had to go without. We kept moving for about two hours. I got hit again to the left side of my chest and in my left arm. I lost consciousness. When I woke up it was four in the morning. I couldn't see Lizunov. I crawled towards a building. It was full of Germans. I didn't have any strength left. I didn't want to be taken alive, so I decided to shoot myself. I lifted my Mauser* [pistol] *but it was full of sand and wouldn't fire.'*

Averbukh managed to crawl back to his command post. However, that was then overrun by a German assault, leaving him isolated once more: *'For the first time in my life, I cried. I crawled another 150 metres and this old man and his daughter picked me up and carried me to their home. The daughter dressed my wounds and gave*

*me some milk. Her name was Zoya. Later, I was sent across the Volga.
I kissed both the man and his daughter goodbye. He cried for me like I
was his own son.'*

Chuikov understood the psychology of war and the importance
of morale. He knew that the ordinary German landser was not a
superman; he bled like other men and his will to fight could be
undermined. One of the most effective weapons in destabilising the
morale of an enemy in battle is the hidden menace of the sniper.
They became an important part of the Red Army's arsenal. In fact,
the exploits of the Red Army's snipers became a major part of the
legend that is Stalingrad.

The most famous sniper was Vasili Zaitsev, the son of a peasant
family from the Ural Mountains, where he learned how to use a
Berdan rifle for hunting (an old Russian Army weapon, in service
at the end of the nineteenth century). His military exploits with a
rifle made him a heroic figure in the Red Army, which led, after
the war, to him becoming a cult figure in military folklore. Prior to
November 1942, he had killed 32 Axis soldiers with a standard-issue
rifle. But during the Battle of Stalingrad, between 10 November and
17 December 1942, he killed 225 enemy soldiers, including 11 of
their snipers.

Zaitsev claimed that the most notable of the eleven was Major
Erwin König, supposedly the head of the Berlin Sniper School,
who, it is alleged, was flown to Stalingrad charged with the specific
responsibility to take out Zaitsev. In his autobiography, Zaitsev
described the duel in detail. The encounter has since been immor-
talised in books and film. Zaitsev claimed that the two protagonists
played a game of cat and mouse for three days, before the Russian
marksman saw a glint of sun in the German's telescopic lens and
delivered the lethal shot. Although there is no doubting Zaitsev's
record of kills, the König story may well have been a piece of
Red Army propaganda. Highly renowned Stalingrad historian Sir
Antony Beevor is convinced, sadly, that the famous story is a myth.

Vasily Grossman wrote an account of an interview he did with
another legendary sniper, Anatoly Chekhov, who was just nineteen
at the beginning of the Battle of Stalingrad. Chekov claimed more

kills than Zaitsev, but found the cold-blooded killing difficult at first: *'When I first got the rifle, I couldn't bring myself to kill a living being: one German was standing there for about four minutes, talking. I let him go. When I killed my first, he fell at once. Another one came out and stooped over the killed one, and I knocked him down, too . . . I was shaking all over: the man was only walking to get some water . . . I felt scared: I'd killed a person! Then I remembered our people and started killing them without mercy . . . I've become a beast of a man: I kill. I hate them as if it's a normal thing in my life.'*

Despite the stubborn resistance and heroic tales, for Chuikov and his forces the situation at the end of September was still perilous. The Wehrmacht controlled the Volga for five miles south of the city. They controlled most of Mamayev Kurgan and the railway station, and had enclosed the Soviet's 62nd Army in a pocket to the north, in the city's 'Factory District'.

15

STALINGRAD: STREET BY STREET, HOUSE BY HOUSE

SEPTEMBER–NOVEMBER 1942

As the cold winds of an approaching winter ruffled the calm waters of the Volga, the Wehrmacht had managed to gain control of 90 per cent of Stalingrad. The Red Army held a sliver of land along the banks of the Volga and, to the north, a wider industrial area called the 'Factory District'. This housed several vital factories that became focal points of the mighty battle: the Krasny Oktyabr (Red October) Steel Plant, the Barrikady (Barricade) Ordnance Factory, the Silikat (Silicate) Factory, and the Dzerzhinsky Tractor Factory. Each would carve its name into Stalingrad folklore.

A second wave of German assaults on the city began on 27 September. Its main objective was to strike at the Krasny Oktyabr Steel Plant and the Tractor Factory, before pushing through to the Volga to encircle Chuikov's 62nd Army.

It was a huge Wehrmacht assault. The German High Command knew that winter was not far away. With the Führer breathing down their necks, they were desperate to destroy the will of the Red Army and break through to the Volga. With so little ground left to take, both objectives must have seemed tantalisingly close. Indeed, a mixed force of panzers, other motorised units and infantry managed to advance over a mile and a half, and came within a mile of the Volga. At certain times, during which the fighting was focused on handfuls of men in separate pockets of hand-to-hand fighting, down to platoon level, some Wehrmacht units got within 200 yards of the river.

However, as before, the defenders, despite the perils of crossing the wide expanse of the Volga, were able to get reinforcements into defensive positions in sufficient numbers to thwart even the most ferocious of attacks. On 28 September, a new Soviet Military Council order, Order No. 171, was issued to the defenders of the city.

> It must be explained to every soldier that the Army is fighting on its last line of defence; there can be no further retreat. It is the duty of every soldier and commander to defend his trench, his position – not a step back! The enemy must be wiped out whatever happens.

Chuikov, employing his standard hyperbole, gave an account of the kind of heroism that Order No. 171 was supposed to invoke: *'Take another example of the wholehearted loyalty of the Soviet People to their country. Between the Krasny Oktyabr and the Barrikady factories runs a gully towards the Volga. The Germans picked this gully for a breakthrough. Lieutenant Zaitsev* [not Vasili Zaitsev the sniper] *and a team of machine-gunners were given the task of holding it. By day it was impossible to raise one's head. The Germans fired at every square yard of soil. Zaitsev brought up his men during the night. The Germans launched an attack, which our machine-gunners met with short bursts of fire until the water inside the gun casings began to boil. One of our gunners was hit. He was replaced by Private Yemelyanov. Zaitsev was fatally wounded. Sergeant Karasev took charge of the platoon. The battle went on until nightfall: 400 enemy dead lay in the gully.'*

Chuikov also recounted the courage of Rifleman Mikhail Panikakha, who was defending a position in the Factory District when a group of German panzers loomed into view: *'Panikakha had already used up all his hand grenades. He had only two Molotov cocktails left. He got up out of his trench and raised his arm to throw one of them when a bullet smashed the flaming bottle above his head, drenching him in flames. Despite the pain and terror, he grabbed the second bottle and ran up to the tank and smashed the bottle against the grille of the engine hatch. A second later an enormous sheet of flame engulfed both the tank and the hero who had destroyed it.'*

He also described the heroics of Junior Lieutenant Vasili Boltenko, who, with his anti-tank weapon and after refusing the order to withdraw, managed to take out four advancing panzers in a single encounter. Chuikov ended his eulogies: *'That is how the soldiers of the 62nd Army fought. It was as if the very earth, soaked in the blood of heroic Soviet soldiers, had called forth courage and steadfastness. Stalingrad had become a symbol of resistance unparalleled in human history.'* Although both florid in tone and propagandist in intent, Chuikov's words reflected an obvious truth: Stalingrad had indeed become an extraordinary symbol of human fortitude and resilience.

Day after day during the first week of October, wave after wave of relentless Wehrmacht onslaughts were halted. There was no doubting the courage and determination of Germany's soldiers, many miles from home and under increasingly demanding pressures, but, as elsewhere along the enormous battlefront from Leningrad to the Caucasus, they had driven their enemy into a corner, in which he was fighting with extraordinary tenacity. The war had become an unstoppable force throwing itself against an immovable object. If there had not been so much hate, there would surely have been much admiration for one another.

On 6 October, the Tractor Factory became the focus of the German attacks. The fighting intensified by the hour, until it reached a crescendo of explosions, gunfire and death. There was no coherent front line; the fighting descended into increasingly brutal firefights between isolated groups.

At the beginning of October, Vasily Grossman crossed to the west bank of the Volga and straight into the heart of the fighting.

'Zholudev's division. Commissar Shcherbina. Tractor Plant.

The command post was buried by an explosion. It became quiet at once. A sergeant dug them out under fire. He worked like a madman, frenziedly, with bubbles on his lips. An hour later, he was killed by a shell. A German "sneezed" [a burst of fire] *with his machine gun. He had crept into the "tube"* [tunnel]. *They dragged him out and tore him to pieces.'*

Alexander Rodimtsev told a less gruesome story, but one that illustrates how soldiers need important distractions, even when the heat of battle is at its most intense: *'Two soldiers came to see me. They had been fighting for fourteen days in a house surrounded by Germans. They asked for food, ammunition, sugar, tobacco. One said, "You know, it's such a peculiar affair, this war in the houses." He smiled. "I don't know if I should tell you this, but a funny incident happened yesterday. The Germans captured a house and there was a barrel of spirits in its basement. Our soldiers became angry about the thought of the Germans drinking the barrel, so twenty men attacked the house, seized the barrel and rolled it away. All this with the whole street held by Germans." [. . .]'*

Several German positions were able to bring their weapons to bear on the vital Volga crossings and landing points. A small wooden pontoon became a crucial supply line. Under cover of darkness, a constant stream of logistics troops, working in single file, carried ammunition, food and medical supplies. But with artillery, dive-bombers and even machine-gun fire a constant threat, the death toll for those carrying essential supplies was as high as it was on the front line. The same was true for the Volga boatmen ferrying materiel in one direction and wounded men in the other. The east bank was also highly vulnerable; kitchens, hospitals, artillery positions and concentrations of reserve troops waiting to cross were under incessant heavy fire.

It was on the east bank that many of the Red Army's women were under threat, but there were also hundreds of women in forward positions on the front line on the west bank. Chuikov was fulsome in his praise for his female comrades: *'Tamara Shmakova* [medical orderly] *saved many lives. Many men are alive today because she hauled them off the battlefield. There were more than a thousand women in the 62nd Army who won decorations: Maria Ulyanova, who was engaged in the defence of Pavlov's House from start to finish; Valia Pakhomova, who carried more than a hundred men to safety; Nadia Koltsova, twice awarded the Red Banner. Was Lyuba Nesterenko not a heroine when, in Lieutenant Dragan's besieged building, she bound the wounds of dozens of injured guardsmen and, bleeding profusely, died with a bandage in her hand alongside a wounded comrade?'* Other than Nesterenko, Chuikov does not reveal what became of the women he mentioned.

Zinaida Golodnova had just graduated as a midwife when she was posted to Stalingrad to join the 62nd Army: *'Early one morning, a soldier and I were ordered to go up to an observation post.*

While returning, a German spotted us and opened fire. We dropped down, holding our breath. I lay there thinking I would die. When things quietened down a bit, we crawled into a shell hole and hid. Tossed into a nearby dugout was a body. I crawled over, blood was pouring from the head; there was no face, only a chin. I called to my comrade, "Look, a soldier that doesn't shave." He replied, "It's a girl, there's her scalp and long hair." [. . .]'

Tamara Umnyagina was a junior sergeant and medical assistant in a guards rifle division: *'Stalingrad. What sort of battlefield is that? It's a city: streets, houses, basements. Try dragging the wounded out of there! My whole body was one single bruise. Everything burned. In Stalingrad, there wasn't a single inch of dirt that wasn't soaked in blood. Russian and German. And gasoline. And grease . . . There was nowhere left, we couldn't retreat. Either we would all die – the country, the Russian people – or we would be victorious. We didn't say it out loud, but everybody understood.*

Reinforcements arrived. Such handsome young fellows . . . I was afraid to get to know them, to talk to them . . . You looked at them and knew they would be killed; two or three days. One time, out of three hundred, only ten were left at the end of the day. I still remember those faces; I see them all.'

The fighting eventually subsided a little. Sheer exhaustion began to translate the clashes into a mindless routine of death. The attackers attacked; the defenders defended. As in a digital war game, the dead became cyphers; both sides were trapped in a void, a vacuum almost beyond pain or reason. A breath was needed. It did not last long, because the horrific imperative of war was still there. The mad game had to continue; there had to be a victor and there had to be a vanquished, but both would lose almost everything.

If conditions were not dire enough for both sides in the morbid ruins of Stalingrad, ever greater demands rained down on the combatants: from Hitler in his Wolf's Lair, in the forests of East Prussia, and from Stalin behind the walls of his Kremlin, in Moscow. A new Wehrmacht offensive was ordered by Hitler, to begin no later than 14 October. Stalin reiterated, yet again, that the city had to be defended at all costs.

The Soviet generals did not need to be clairvoyants to know that yet another attack was coming. The enemy was within sight and within hearing distance; his every move was plain to see.

The Germans were nothing if not methodical, and the Soviets had come to understand how their generals liked to fight. The attack began at dawn on the 14th, heralded by the most intense Stuka dive-bomber attack the Luftwaffe had yet launched. Chuikov described the onslaught: '*October 14th dawned, a day which saw the beginning of fighting of an unprecedented ferocity. Three of the enemy's infantry divisions and two panzer divisions* [even allowing for depleted numbers of tanks and men, the attacking force must have been at least 200 tanks and 40,000 men] *were thrown at our position. Those of us who had already been through a great deal will remember this enemy attack all our lives.*

We recorded some 3,000 sorties by enemy aircraft on that day! Their artillery and mortars bombarded the whole battlefield from morning to night. By midnight, enemy forces had surrounded the Tractor Factory on three sides and were fighting in the workshops. Nearly three thousand German dead and forty tanks were strewn at the walls of the factory. That night, we evacuated three thousand wounded across the river. It would be true to say that October 14th was our most critical day. Our defenders had been split in two, but we had survived.'

With little abatement, the attacks continued for several days, with a focus on the Barrikady Factory and the Krasny Oktyabr Steel Plant. The factory workers had been armed as military detachments, one of which – the Barrikady Detachment – had only five survivors by the evening of the 19th.

Chuikov described the sense of exhaustion felt by the defenders: '*We felt not only that our own ranks were thinning and our strength ebbing, but that the enemy could not go on indefinitely launching his insane attacks* [but the attacks continued]. *They were drowning in their own blood. Their materiel resources were also being exhausted. The Luftwaffe's sorties dropped from three thousand to one thousand a day.*

Nevertheless, despite his losses . . . some inexplicable force drove the enemy to go on attacking. Fresh infantry and panzer units appeared and, regardless of losses, rolled towards the Volga. It seemed as though Hitler was prepared to destroy the whole of Germany for the sake of this one city.'

By 25 October, the Wehrmacht had taken the Silikat Factory, the Tractor Factor, and had overrun parts of the Barrikady Factory, but the Soviet hold on its narrow position next to the Volga was still intact, though precarious. In the area between the Krasny Oktyabr and Barrikady Factories, Wehrmacht machine-gunners were only 400 yards from the Volga. For the Soviets to move along the bank they had to crawl on their hands and knees. The plight of those trying to get across the Volga was now even more hazardous than before.

Vasily Grossman related the experiences of the Siberians of the 308th Rifle Brigade, raised in Omsk as recently as March 1942. They were commanded by Colonel Leonty Gurtyev and fought from the end of September, in defence of the Barrikady Factory.

'*The Germans were on the edge of the plant. A Kazakh was escorting three prisoners. He was wounded. He took out a knife and stabbed the three prisoners to death. A tankist, a big red-haired man, jumped out of his tank in front of Changov's command post when he ran out of shells. He grabbed some bricks and started throwing them at the Germans, effing and blinding. They turned on their heels and ran! . . . The whole of Markelov's regiment was killed or wounded. There were only seven men left. The Germans had taken the whole of the Silikat Plant by the evening of the 3rd . . . We began to defend a destroyed and burning street in front of the Sculpture Park. No one came back from the fighting. They all died on the spot.*

The climax came on October 17th. The attack began at five in the morning and the battle went on all day. They bombed us day and night for three days . . . Kalinin, the deputy Chief of Staff, killed twenty-seven men and hit four tanks with his anti-tank weapon. There were eighty workers and a security company. They had never received any military training. Only three of them survived . . .

The signals platoon commander, Khaminsky, was sitting at the edge of his bunker, reading a book during a heavy bombing raid. Colonel Gurtyev was angry, "What's the matter with you?" "I've nothing else to do," he said, "he's bombing, and I'm reading a book." [. . .]'

The Siberians brought several female medics, clerks and signallers with them from Siberia. One of them gave Grossman an impromptu casualty list of her comrades: *'Lyolya Novikova, a cheerful nurse afraid of nothing, was hit by two bullets in the head. Lysorchuk, Nina, wounded. Borodina, Katya, her right hand smashed. Yegorova, Antonina, she was killed. She went into an attack with her platoon. She was a junior nurse. A sub-machine-gunner shot her in both legs, and she died from loss of blood. Kanysheva, Galya, killed by a direct hit from a bomb. And there are just two of us left: Zoya and I . . . I was wounded by a mortar-bomb fragment near the bunker, and then by a shell splinter near the Volga crossing.'*

Even during the most desperate circumstances, there were some stories that were less gruesome. On one occasion, in the middle of October, Grossman was asked to deliver a relief package of presents from a worthy American women's organisation. He was asked to choose the *'two most courageous women defending Stalingrad'*. A handover ceremony was arranged and the two chosen women, along with several senior commanders, stood to attention, waiting excitedly to receive their gifts. When they opened them, with the bunker shaking from yet another fusillade of bombs, the generous American ladies had sent each of their Allied sisters a very fetching bathing costume with matching beach sandals.

By 26 October, for the Red Army leadership in Stalingrad, in stark military terms, conceding the city and retreating across the Volga had become a glaringly obvious option. But too many had died, and too much was at stake, as Chuikov knew: *'Despite our losses, our fighting spirit was higher than ever. If anyone had ordered us to leave the city, all of us, soldiers, officers, generals, would have treated the order as fake, or as a betrayal, and would not have crossed the Volga.'*

By 27 October, only one ferry was operating and the gullies that ran down to the river, which offered the defenders some cover, were all within the range of Wehrmacht machine guns. But, at last, the Wehrmacht's attacks subsided. They could advance no more; utter exhaustion had set in. It had been a close-run thing. Chuikov said that they had *'come within a hair's breadth of catastrophe'*.

The horrors of the battles of late October 1942 in Stalingrad go a long way towards explaining one of the astonishing statistics of the war on the Eastern Front: the daily death rate. For Axis and Soviet forces combined, but not including the many millions of wounded or captured (or the estimated 18 to 25 million civilian dead), the death rate was close to 10,000 a day over the entire, almost four-year, conflict. If civilian deaths, the wounded and the number of prisoners who died in captivity are all added in, the figure for casualties on the front becomes a staggering 22,500 per day.

Despite his losses and the futility of further suffering and death for his army, Hitler was still obsessed by the need to defeat Stalin and his city and to delight in the humiliation of the inhabitants of the city that had been named for him. Such was his fanaticism, he would listen to no advice, nor could he see what was obvious to everyone else. The killing had to go on.

The Führer saw everything through the distorted lens of his own experiences during and after the Great War: his Iron Cross for bravery; the humiliation of Germany's surrender; the hurt of the draconian treatment of Germany by the Versailles Treaty; the pain of the Fatherland's post-war traumas. The anguish experienced by his beloved *Volk* had blighted his vison and induced a fatal myopia. He saw only vengeance; he was the saviour who would give Germany the revenge it deserved and then lead its people to their rightful destiny as lords of the earth.

At Hitler's unyielding insistence, during the early weeks of November, yet again, the Wehrmacht garnered its rapidly dwindling resources of men and materiel. It would make one final attempt to release the Red Army's tenuous grip on its tiny shard of Mother Russia on the west bank of the Volga. It was, in truth, a city in name only; almost anything that might resemble such a thing had long since been obliterated. There was nothing but a symbolic strip of bloodstained ground, pockmarked by craters and strewn with bodies, rubble and ghastly distortions of twisted steel.

For both sides, the environment of the battle was worsening by the day. Although Stalingrad's geographical position is far to the south, close to both the Black and Caspian seas, it sits near to the great landmass of Central Asia, which brings very hot summers and equally cold winters. The average January temperature is –6°C, with snowfall on two days out of every three. By mid-November, snow had begun to fall, and ice floes had appeared in the Volga. They heralded the icy grip of a winter that would soon creep down from the north. The psychology of the battle had also changed. The Red Army rifleman, the artilleryman, the sapper, they all knew that they had held back the most feared armed force in the world. They knew they could win.

On the German side, the aura of invincibility had been wrenched away from the landsers and panzer troops of the Wehrmacht by the purgatory of the Eastern Front. One of them wrote home to Germany from the pit of his shell hole in Stalingrad's Factory District: *'I cannot understand how men can survive such a hell, yet the Russians sit tight in their ruins, holes and cellars and the chaos of steel skeletons that used to be factories.'*

The Wehrmacht's mighty 6th Army was beaten – and most of them knew it. For the ordinary German soldier looking at the darkening skies of approaching winter over the Steppe, the priority was no longer victory but survival.

The game had also changed in the wider conflict, beyond Stalingrad. On 3 November, an Allied breakout, code-named 'Operation Supercharge', at El Alamein in the Egyptian desert had led to the retreat of Germany's *Panzerarmee Afrika*. Five days later, in 'Operation Torch', an Allied force invaded Vichy-French North Africa, in Morocco and Algeria. In the Pacific, United States Marines were involved in vicious fighting with the forces of the Japanese Empire on Guadalcanal, in the Solomon Islands, and were winning vital ground. The entire axis of the war was beginning to tilt.

With some reinforcements flown in from Germany, the Wehrmacht made its last roll of the dice in Stalingrad on the morning of 11 November. It was led by a massive air assault, followed by head-on infantry attacks and yet more hours of vicious fighting. However, many of the Wehrmacht's battalions were down to 50 per cent of their strength. Hitler wanted panzer commanders to abandon their vehicles and take up the arms of an infantryman. Medical orderlies, drivers, signallers and cooks were sent in to make up the numbers. But unlike previous initiatives, this last throw was weak and ineffective, especially against the growing resolve of the Red Army. The temperature had dropped significantly. The spectre of early December at the gates of Moscow haunted the Germans in their shell holes and improvised shelters. Perhaps the ghost of a Christmas past also made its ominous presence felt in Hitler's Wolf's Lair, in East Prussia.

The Wehrmacht's generals began to plan for another winter when they would lie in wait until a spring offensive could be mounted to finish what they had started. Even Hitler conceded that winter preparations had to begin. However, for the weary men of Germany's far-flung army, winter was going to be spent in very different circumstances than they had imagined.

16

STALINGRAD: VICTORY!

NOVEMBER 1942–FEBRUARY 1943

As the chill of November deepened, Chuikov's defenders were down to about a tenth of their strength. The Volga was freezing, but not yet by enough to give him a bridge to the far bank. His position was about as dire as that of his enemy. However, there was a difference. To the Wehrmacht, Stalingrad was an end in itself, a symbolic trophy of great psychological importance, but to Stavka in Moscow, it was only a means to an end. The end was ambitious and risky. Chuikov had not been told that there was a bigger strategic picture, but indeed there was. He and his forces were to be the bait in a huge bear trap. Chuikov had to hold Stalingrad until the trap was ready. He only just made it.

Zhukov had met with Stalin in Moscow as early as 12 September to begin the planning. A significant weakness in Axis forces had been identified. The Wehrmacht had thrown all its available men and machines into the battle for the streets of Stalingrad. As a result, its extensive flanks on what was, in effect, an occupied peninsula formed by its own spearhead towards the city, were exposed. Critically, they were defended by far less formidable forces – largely Romanian, with support from Italians and Hungarians.

While German reinforcements from the west came sporadically and in small numbers, the Red Army was, in an unremitting tide from the east, able to increase its fighting strength of men and machines in significant numbers.

By 13 November, Zhukov was ready to go to Stalin and request final approval for one of the greatest counter-attacks of the war: *'The morning of November 13th. We saw Stalin. He was in a cheerful mood.*

He listened attentively. By the way he puffed his pipe unhurriedly, we knew he was pleased. We were confident that the pending counteroffensive would be successful and do much for the ultimate liberation of our homeland from the Nazi invaders.'

The statement was bold, but entirely realistic. It would only come to pass after two and a half years and millions more deaths, but it would happen. Zhukov's words marked an extraordinary transformation since the dark days of twelve months earlier, when all had seemed lost. It was also a watershed moment for Germany. In hindsight, the war was lost in the autumn of 1942, but it would take twenty-nine months before the German people were released from Hitler's unrelenting grip.

Zhukov introduced a policy of *maskirovka* ('deception'), to mislead the Germans about Soviet intentions. Defensive fortifications were built in the open to persuade the Germans that the Red Army was digging in, rather than getting ready to attack. Troops, operating under strict radio silence, moved only at night and were camouflaged during the day. Bridges were even built across the Don with their surfaces marginally hidden under water.

Ivan Golokolenko, a Red Army rifleman, listened to Stalin's pre-battle address when it was read to the troops preparing to attack: *'There was something fatherly about it. He said: "Dear generals and soldiers, I address you, my brothers. Today you start an offensive and your actions will decide the fate of the country – whether it remains an independent country or perishes." And those words really reached my heart . . . I was close to tears when the meeting was over. I felt a real upsurge, a spiritual upsurge.'*

The offensive was called 'Operation Uranus', a vast pincer movement from the north and the east. One million soldiers strong, it was launched on the morning of 19 November. It began with a massive artillery barrage followed by an enormous tank, cavalry and infantry advance. The tables had been turned. In 1941, the Wehrmacht's blitzkrieg attack had encircled whole Soviet armies; now the same was about to happen to an entire elite German field army, which would soon be marooned on the banks of the Volga, vainly holding a city that barely existed.

Vasily Grossman had moved 100 miles north of Stalingrad. He was with the Red Army south of the Don, near the small town of Serafimovich, as it crushed the 3rd Romanian Army in the midst of a blizzard and in temperatures of –20°C: *'An image: a strongpoint destroyed by a tank. There is a flattened Romanian. A tank has driven over him. His face has become a bas-relief. Our soldiers are sitting among the corpses, cooking in a cauldron slices cut from a dead horse, stretching their bloodstained hands towards the fire . . . A Russian soldier lay nearby. He had a letter in his hand, "Daddy . . . Come and visit us . . . I miss you very much. I wish I could see you, if only for an hour. I am writing this, and tears are pouring. Nina." [. . .]'*

In just ten days, the Red Army retook the city of Kalach, fifty miles west of Stalingrad. It was a vital strategic position that had fallen to the Wehrmacht in August, and the German's last rail link out of Stalingrad. At Kalach, the Red Army's northern pincer met their comrades from the south-east. The trap was sprung: the Wehrmacht's 6th Army, the heroic victor in the battles of France and Kharkov, was surrounded like a beast in a pit.

Ivan Golokolenko recorded his feelings of elation: *'We felt inspiration. We felt confident that we were capable of beating the enemy successfully, and this operation remained the most memorable, the brightest event. Before that I used to feel depressed, but now it was as if I had opened my wings and I was capable of flying in the sky.'*

Much has been made by historians of the weakness of Germany's Axis allies – Romanian, Italian and Hungarian – on the Eastern Front. However, it should be remembered that although they, on the whole, fought bravely, the three armies were under-equipped and badly led. They were from countries with far less ideological commitment to fascism than their German counterparts, who were driven by the Führer's contagious rhetoric. Put simply, it was Hitler's war, not theirs.

All but cut off – except for a hazardous air route to either Gumrak or Pitomnik airfields – the Wehrmacht in Stalingrad dug in to defend its ground. The beast was badly wounded, but its teeth and claws were still deadly. When Göring assured Hitler that his Luftwaffe could supply the 750 tons per day of supplies the trapped

6th Army needed, the Führer ordered that it hold its position. He declared it a *Festung* ('fortress'), but it became a death sentence for all but a handful.

If Hitler had listened to his commanders on the ground and allowed them a breakout, a significant number of the 6th Army would have survived. Instead, the Führer ordered the launch of *Wintergewitter* ('Operation Winter Storm'), a panzer spearhead, to rescue his beleaguered army. It began on 12 December but fell thirty miles short, on the 30th.

For the next two months, the Red Army's offensive north and west of Stalingrad forced the Wehrmacht backwards from the Don and the Kalmyk Steppe, further and further from the city, so that by 24 January, the German line was 200 miles from the 'fortress' of Stalingrad. Massed outside the city, the Red Army had launched Operation *Koltso* ('Operation Ring'), a noose of steel around at least 250,000 German defenders. For them, life would soon become unbearable.

It was to be a slow death by strangulation. The bitter cold, starvation, disease, and the ever-tighter halter of Soviet weaponry, killed thousands on a daily basis. It was a horror akin to a medieval siege. Eventually, the food supply to the ordinary landser was reduced to less than 200 grams per day – little more than was given to the starving citizens of Leningrad, far to the north. Men were covered in lice; frostbite was widespread; typhus, dysentery and jaundice took hold. It became a living hell.

On 7 January 1943, General Rokossovskiy had ordered a brief ceasefire and offered General Frederick von Paulus, Commander of the 6th Army, generous surrender terms. He also made it clear that the German position was hopeless. Paulus requested permission from Hitler to surrender. The reply read, 'Capitulation out of the question. Every day that the army holds out helps the whole front and draws away the Russian divisions from it.'

Conditions for trapped Soviet citizens were just as bad as they were for the Germans. Vasili Chekalov recorded the desperate situation in his diary: *'The entire area at the shore of the Volga is scoured by craters. Huge craters from tons of bombs alternate with smaller craters*

*from shells and mines. There is not a single living place. Terrible destruc-
tion. Among the ruins I met two women, "Why are you here, why don't
you leave?" "Where am I to go? I'm sick. I had a sixteen-year-old son. I fed
him. I thought, I'll be provided for too, but he was killed."... Her tears
are flowing. "But God doesn't give me death. Where am I going to go? I'll
fall on the road and there'll be no one to pick me up." [...]'*

Nikolai Moskvin was with a partisan group in Belorussia when
he heard the news from Stalingrad that the Red Army had got the
Wehrmacht encircled: *'January 19th. There has been a great victory at
the front! The tide has turned at last. Every one of us wanted to cry out
with all his might, "hoorah!" Stalingrad has turned into a huge trap for
the Hitlerites.'*

After a sustained Red Army offensive captured the last German-
held airstrip in Stalingrad, on 25 January, the Soviets again offered
Paulus a chance to surrender. The General radioed Hitler once
again for permission. He made it clear to Hitler that collapse was
'inevitable' and emphasised that his men were without ammunition or food. He said that at least 18,000 of his troops were
wounded and in immediate need of medical attention. He pleaded
that their condition was so pitiable that effective command was no
longer viable. Once again, Hitler rejected the request out of hand,
and ordered him to hold Stalingrad to the death.

Ivan Golokolenko moved into the centre of Stalingrad as the
garrotte tightened around the neck of the 6th Army: *'26.1.43.
Mamayev Kurgan. The height itself is an eerie sight: there is not a single
place free of craters. It is littered with corpses covered with snow, broken
tanks, mangled guns and crushed water towers.*

*29.1.43. A huge snow field, a German staff column. Dozens of corpses
alone and in piles scattered across the field. Surviving Germans roam
around. In one dugout, I found 23 of them. They sit pitiful, frostbitten
and hungry, and languish in the unknown of their future ... On the way
back, I met a column of prisoners. They walked in a steady stream, filthy,
thin and haggard, wrapping their heads and feet in some dirty rags!
Occasionally it was possible to observe bonfires near the road, around
which small groups of the "conquerors" were warming themselves. At least
20,000 of them passed before my eyes.'*

On 30 January, five days after his second request, Paulus informed Hitler that his men were only hours from collapse. In a futile attempt to revive their shattered morale, the Führer responded by bestowing a host of field promotions on Paulus's officers, and to remind them of their duty to die for their Fatherland. He made Paulus a field marshal, pointing out that there was no known example of a Prussian or German field marshal ever having surrendered. The insinuation was obvious: Paulus was required to commit suicide and, if he declined, he would shame Germany's military history.

In unadorned soldierly detail, Vasili Chuikov described the woeful end of the great battle and the pitiful demise of the Wehrmacht's once-swaggering 6th Army, the 'heroic' conquerors of Western Europe. It would be only the first of many humiliations to come; a trail of defeats that would lead all the way to the *Führerbunker* in Berlin.

'*On January 31st, soldiers of the 64th Army took prisoner Field Marshal von Paulus, commander of the 6th Army, and the whole of his HQ. The fighting in the centre of the city was over. On the evening of the same day, troops of the 62nd Army took prisoner the HQ staff in the north. The German generals were made prisoner by three soldiers of the 62nd Army under an eighteen-year-old Komsomol organiser of a signals regiment, Mikhail Porter, who had fought at Odessa, Sevastopol and Kerch before coming to the Volga.*'

By coincidence, reports from the time suggest that one of the key Red Army personnel at the surrender was Ivan Laskin, the same officer who had commanded the Red Army's 172nd Rifle Division in the courageous defence of Sevastopol, in July 1942.

Captain Nikolai Aksyonov was with the 1047th Regiment, Guards Red Banner Division, on the last day of fighting in the north of the city: '*We took the Barrikady Factory. That was the last stronghold of the northern group. The factory fell at 1.30 p.m. on February 2nd. Just after 3 p.m. all our operations had ended. You can consider 2.30 p.m. an historic moment, the time when the guns stopped firing in the Battle of Stalingrad. The final shot of the great battle rang out at that historic moment. Today the guns are silent, Stalingrad has been defended and thousands of Germans are plodding their way across the Volga.'*

Vasili Chuikov went on to list the German casualties, which he estimated to be at least 1.5 million men (other sources suggest it was perhaps less than half that number): *'The Volga Steppe was full of graves and crosses, more than a hundred thousand of them: 91,000 prisoners, 2,500 officers, 22 generals, and Field Marshal Paulus, now in Russian hands.'*

Ironically, the 91,000 German prisoners who had fought so ferociously to reach the Volga were then marched across it in igno-minious defeat. Chuikov fails to mention what became of them, but they faced yet more horrors in the coming months and years. Many died en route to what were supposed to be prisoner of war camps in the east but were, in fact, NKVD labour camps. They soon became death camps. Only about 5,000 ever returned to Germany. Paulus was treated much better. He was a witness at the Nuremburg Trials in 1945–46 and was allowed to return to Dresden (in Soviet-controlled East Germany) in 1953, where he died three years later.

In Germany, the truth about the disaster at Stalingrad was kept from the population. We will never know Hitler's real feelings when he heard the news of the surrender, but he must have known that not only were his military objectives in ruins, but his expan-sionist dream of a 'Greater Germany' was also over. The Soviet Union had not been shattered by a mighty hammer blow; the vital resources he needed to sustain his future objectives had not been secured; Britain had not capitulated; and America had entered the war. Hitler's army would, eventually, have to fight not on two fronts but on three: the Eastern Front, the Mediterranean, and, after D-Day, northern France and the Low Countries. These were desperate circumstances indeed.

In the ruins of Stalingrad, the Soviet authorities began a census of the civilian survivors. The journalists who arrived after the surrender felt certain that no one could have survived the total destruction of the city. However, almost 10,000 did, 1,000 of whom were children. Sir Antony Beevor's classic account suggests that only nine of the children had parents. How they survived – living like vermin in cellars, shell holes and sewers – was a miracle of human tenacity and courage.

Eleven-year-old Valentina Krutova, along with her younger sister and older brother, was one of the children who survived. With their mother and father missing, they had endured the slow death of their grandmother, whose diseased and decaying body had persuaded the German soldiers not to get too close to the family. Then, when she finally died, the children had to haul her body into the open on a sheet and bury it in a ditch. When the fighting ended, Valentina and her siblings, too weak to move, were huddled together in bed: *'The only thought we had was where to find something to eat. We were so hungry. We simply stayed in bed and were lying all day silently; clinging to each other, hugging each other. Then, one day, we heard a knocking at the door. We could hear shouting* [in Russian], *"Don't knock, maybe there are Germans inside . . . Throw the grenade." But one soldier opened the door. We began to scream, "Don't shoot, we're Russians!" The soldier shouted, "There are children here!" When they came in and saw us, they began to cry.'*

Mortality did not end with the cessation of hostilities. Sick and wounded, military and civilian, were scattered all over the city. There were no medical supplies and almost no food, and it was still the depths of winter. It would take several weeks for the worst of the suffering to end; several years would pass before the process of rebuilding the city could begin.

Inevitably, the war moved on. The front line was soon far to the west, and Chuikov and his army had to catch up. He completed his account of the battle for Stalingrad with words that are both moving and strident: *'Goodbye Volga. Goodbye mutilated and exhausted city. Goodbye comrades-in-arms, who have stayed behind in the earth steeped in our nation's blood. We are going westward, our duty – to avenge you.'*

It was a heartfelt farewell. The comrades to whom the general was saying goodbye numbered over a million casualties. As for the undertaking to 'avenge' his fallen comrades, that vengeance would be wrought with unwavering ferocity all the way to Berlin.

PART FOUR

HELL'S BATTLEFIELD

17

THE TURNING TIDE

MARCH–JUNE 1943

In the natural world, when tides turn, they turn irresistibly. So it was on the Eastern Front throughout 1943. Sometimes the Wehrmacht was able to build sandcastles to hold back the encroaching waves, but that is all they were. There were even times when the Germans were able to push back against the tide with armour and men, but they were fragile islands soon marooned by deep water and eroded away.

With Stalingrad about to be lost, the Axis powers had hurried to get their forces out of the Caucasus. If they were to become encircled, like their colleagues in Stalingrad, the entire Axis southern front could collapse. The High Command had to get its men across the Don and into Ukraine as soon as possible. By 6 February the last German units had crossed the Don bridges and formed a new defensive line from Rostov-on-Don, looking eastwards.

Further to the north, while the battle raged in Stalingrad, the Red Army had launched a series of offensives, beginning on 13 January 1943, which liberated a large area west of the Don, including the key cities of Voronezh, Kursk, Belgorod, Izium and Kharkov. The Red Army tide was in full rip. However, the Wehrmacht soon built one of those tidal barriers that would cause yet more embarrassment and annoyance in Moscow.

Even after more than a year of change and improvement within the Red Army, life as a soldier in an army supposedly built around Soviet egalitarian principles was far from easy, especially if you happened to be Jewish. Vladimir Gelfand was a Jewish Officer who served in Chuikov's 62nd Army in Stalingrad. One of his diary entries read: *'What scoundrels there are, what rabid anti-Semites! It is difficult for us to live here in these ugly conditions. Many other horrific problems exist in our country. People blame Jews for everything; they call us Jews openly. They take out their anger on me and swear and shout "yid" at me.*

Now there was a politruk, also a Jew. They talk to him quite seriously when he comes close to them, they agree with everything, but as soon as he leaves, they rush to shout terrible insults. The anger is stifling me. Now it is dark, and I can't write much, especially since one of these bastards that's lying above me pours all his garbage on my head, I have to move to the edge of the bunk.'

Being Jewish in the Soviet Union had never been easy. Although anti-Semitism was overtly against Soviet principles, in practice it was widespread.

During his meeting with Nazi Germany's Foreign Minister, von Ribbentrop, to discuss a Nazi–Soviet Pact, Stalin had promised him to get rid of 'Jewish domination', especially among the intelligentsia. After dismissing Maxim Litvinov as Foreign Minister in 1939, Stalin had immediately directed incoming Foreign Minister, Vyacheslav Molotov, to 'purge the ministry of Jews', to appease Hitler and to signal to Nazi Germany that the USSR was ready for non-aggression talks.

In the late 1930s and into the 1940s, far fewer Jews were appointed to positions of power within the Soviet state hierarchy than before. Following the Soviet invasion of Poland, Stalin began a policy of deporting Jews to the Jewish Autonomous Oblast and other parts of Siberia. The JAO was located on the Chinese border, in the Soviet Far East, about as far from Moscow as geography would allow.

Historians have speculated about the true motives behind Stalin's anti-Semitism, which may have been motivated, in part, by his belief that Jews were a potential danger because of their ties with the influential Jewish community in America. Whatever the reasons, Soviet Jews were, as ever, never able to rest easily in their homeland.

On 14 February, a brilliant German counter-attack, with massive aerial support from the Luftwaffe, took an overstretched, undermanned and exhausted Red Army by complete surprise. The Germans had committed the cream of the Wehrmacht from the west, including elite SS units like *Das Reich*, *Totenkopf* – and even *Leibstandarte SS Adolf Hitler*, Hitler's personal bodyguard. Much of the lost territory was regained, including the vital city of Kharkov.

With these elite units came terror. Utterly ruthless in battle, they were similarly callous when the fighting was over. During the fighting around Kharkov a *Leibstandarte SS* unit gained the nickname the 'Blowtorch Battalion', after the inhabitants of two Soviet villages were shot and burned. On 12 February, troops of the *Leibstandarte* occupied the villages where retreating Soviet forces had wounded two SS officers. In retaliation five days later, *Leibstandarte* troops killed 872 men, women and children; 233 of them were burned alive in the church of Yefremovka. Ukrainian sources, including surviving witnesses, described the killings at the villages of Yefremovka and Semyonovka.

Vasily Kukhtinov described what happened to his family: *'Those terrible days did not pass my family by. On this bloody day, the Nazis threw a grenade into the house where we hid, and then lit the thatched roof. I was wounded, lost consciousness, and when I woke up, I saw that my mother was dead. Next to her was my bloodied one-year-old sister, Lidochka. Open-mouthed, she stared at our mother's chest and cried. Four of us got out of the house: there was me, I was fourteen, my six-year-old brother, Dima, and my four-year-old brother, Kolya. I carried wounded Lidochka in my arms. Our mother, elder sisters, Katya, Fyokla and Frosya remained forever in the blazing house. My father died in Germany, my elder brother, Ivan, in Belarus. A month later, our little Lidochka died. Many years have passed since the terrible events happened; the grief still hangs like a heavy stone in my soul.'*

Sergei Kovalenko witnessed the atrocity: *The Nazis arrived in small cars. These animals were all in black uniforms. They had skulls on their caps* [SS insignia]. *In the evening, the whole of Semyonovka burned. The heart-breaking screams and cries swept the whole village. Along Krasnaya Street, in Yefremovka, two girls fled. Their mothers, sisters and brothers were killed in front of their eyes. They ran into the gardens. They were shot there. On the morning of February 17th, the*

*police announced that all the men, the elderly and adolescents were to
arrive with shovels to clear the road of snow. For failure to appear – execution. More than 250 people gathered, who were led by guards with
dogs to clear the road. The Nazis went to the villages in white camouflage
uniforms.*

*In their hands they had blowtorches with which they set fire to the
thatched roofs of the huts. They shot everyone in rows, both people and
animals. Then they threw grenades into the cellars, and children into the
wells. Screaming, crying, howling dogs, shots, explosions. Real hell.*

*After lunch, those who cleared the road were ordered to go to the
church for a meeting, where straw was laid on the floor. A machine-gun
burst rang out, bottles of fuel mixture flew, black smoke filled the sky. At
the exit, the Nazis with dogs. There was no salvation. Only seven miracles
managed to escape and survive.'*

The attacks and counter-attacks throughout January and February in Western Russia and Eastern Ukraine were ferocious. Once
again, a Red Army triumph – this time the hugely significant
victory at Stalingrad – had led Stalin to be over-optimistic. The
Wehrmacht's mid-February counter-attack had retaken a large
swathe of newly liberated territory. The fact that the Wehrmacht
had been gravely wounded at Stalingrad did not mean it was dead.
There would be many more months of gruesome battles, some
almost as titanic as Stalingrad had been.

As spring approached, the inevitable muddy thaw – the Russian
rasputitsa – brought a lull to the fighting. Both sides drew breath;
they rested, regrouped and re-equipped. The year of 1943 was going
to be another year of mayhem and slaughter.

By the spring of 1943, the impact of the growing number of
women who were in crucial positions in Soviet forces was beginning to become a significant factor in turning the tide. From 1943
to 1945, there was an average of 2,000 to 3,000 women per field
army, with around 20,000 per battle front, between 2 and 3 per cent
in each case.

Not only did they make an important operational contribution in many areas, they also provided a vital psychological boost.
Having women fighting on the front line, sharing the horrors, the

indignities and the suffering, reinforced the sense that it was a war of survival, a desperate struggle for one's identity, culture and traditions. The Soviets were, in reality, fighting a 'people's war', not the kind of guerrilla/peasant war developed by Mao Tse Tung in the Chinese Civil War – or later, in Vietnam, by Ho Chi Min and the Vietcong – but a 'total war', where the distinction between civilians and soldiers became blurred. For the Soviet population, the war had undoubtedly become both a people's war and a total war. Historians have called it an 'absolute war'; the worst kind of war. To borrow from Lord Acton, 'All wars kill, but absolute wars kill absolutely.'

Tens of thousands of women in the Partisan War in the occupied territories, and more than three-quarters of a million women in the armed forces, had stood shoulder to shoulder with their male comrades in defence of their homeland. Having women on the front line reinforced the obvious reality that the Soviet people were fighting not just for their state, or their way of life, but for their very existence.

One of the most telling contributions made by women was as battlefield snipers. Many became extraordinarily good at one of the deadliest, most cold-blooded skills in a soldier's armoury. It is estimated that as many as 2,000 women snipers were trained during the war. Only a quarter of them survived the conflict.

Military theorists have suggested reasons why women took so well to sniper training, but such explanations, when espoused, lean towards female stereotyping: perhaps they were more patient than their male counterparts; it is said they could breathe calmly and were better able to cope with the cold and the uncomfortable hides necessary for their modus operandi. Whatever the reasons, several of them were so lethal they became legends of the war, and six of them became Heroes of the Soviet Union.

In March 1942, a Central Women's School of Sniper Training was established in Veshniaki, a village a few miles outside Moscow. The school's director was Nora Chegodayeva, a Red Army translator, fluent in French and Spanish, and a graduate of the elite Frunze Military Academy, who had fought as a communist volunteer in the Spanish Civil War. By the end of the war, 1,885 snipers and instructors had graduated.

Major Lyudmila Pavlichenko, a Hero of the Soviet Union, was the top-scoring woman sniper of all time, with 309 confirmed kills, of which 36 were enemy snipers. Not surprisingly, she soon acquired the sobriquet 'Lady Death'. A rifle-club sharpshooter before the war, she had worked as a machinist in the Kiev Arsenal and earned a degree in history. Assigned to a combat role, she was issued with only a fragmentation grenade due to weapons short-ages. However, in August 1941, a wounded comrade handed her his rifle. Pavlichenko then shot her first two enemies, a moment she described as her 'baptism of fire', after which she was officially reassigned as a sniper.

Pavlichenko fought for several weeks during the siege of Odessa, where she recorded 187 kills. At the age of twenty-five, she married a fellow sniper, Alexei Kitsenko, but he was killed soon after the marriage. When the Romanians took control of Odessa, in October 1941, her unit was withdrawn to fight in the siege of Sevastopol. There she trained other snipers, who killed over a hundred Axis soldiers during the battle. In May 1942, newly promoted Lieutenant Pavlichenko was cited by the Southern Army Council for killing 257 Axis soldiers.

Like many of her comrades, she was ruthless about her role and to her dying day had no compassion for her enemies: *We mowed down the Hitlerites like ripe grain ... The only feeling I have is the great satisfaction a hunter feels who has killed a beast of prey.*

In June 1942, Pavlichenko was hit in the face by shrapnel from a mortar shell, after which Stavka ordered that she be evacuated from Sevastopol via submarine. Because of her propaganda value, she was too precious to lose. After she had recovered from her injuries, instead of being sent back to the front, she became a propagandist for the Red Army and, in September 1942, was sent on a tour of Britain, the US and Canada. She became the first Soviet citizen to be welcomed to the White House and met President and Mrs Roosevelt, with whom she began a lifelong friendship.

Even though she was in America as a Soviet ambassador, she was somewhat less diplomatic when fielding questions from the US media: *'I am amazed at the kind of questions put to me by the women press correspondents in Washington. Don't they know there is a war? They asked me silly questions such as do I use powder and rouge and nail polish, and do I curl my hair? One reporter even criticised the length of the skirt of my uniform, saying that in America women wear shorter skirts, and besides my uniform made me look fat. This made me angry. I wear my uniform with honour. It has the Order of Lenin on it. It has been covered with blood in battle. It is plain to see that with American women what is important is whether they wear silk underwear under their uniforms. What the uniform stands for, they have yet to learn.'*

She was also blunt about the contrast in attitudes between the two allies: *'Now [in the US] I am looked upon a little as a curiosity, a subject for newspaper headlines, for anecdotes. In the Soviet Union I am looked upon as a citizen, as a fighter, as a soldier for my country.'*

Less feted, but no less skilful or brave, were riflewomen Mariya Polivanova and Natalya Kovshova, a spotter-and-sniper team killed in action together near Novgorod, in August 1943. Wounded and out of ammunition, they waited until German soldiers clambered into their trench, then detonated their grenades. They were twenty-one and nineteen years old respectively. It is thought the two women may have been responsible for as many as 300 kills. Each was made a Hero of the Soviet Union.

Another sniper and Hero of the Soviet Union was Tanya Baramzina, who had been a teacher before the war. After the invasion, she trained to become a sniper while also training as a nurse. After scoring sixteen kills on the Belorussian Front, she was selected for an airborne raid behind enemy lines. After claiming another twenty German victims, her unit was surrounded, whereupon she took charge of her wounded comrades. She was eventually captured and suffered terrible torture, including having her eyes gouged out, before being blown to pieces at point-blank range by an anti-tank rifle.

One of the most remarkable female heroes of the war was Roza Shanina. Born in humble circumstances, she was the daughter of a milkmaid and a logger. When her parents refused to allow her to go to college, she walked 120 miles through Russia's northern forests to a railway station to catch a train to Arkhangel and enrol in a college.

Three of her brothers were killed during the war, making her determined to enlist. Within Soviet society at the time there were no sensitivities about the loss of multiple siblings. This was in contrast with the American military's 'sole-survivor policy'; the guideline that was the inspiration for the 1998 Spielberg movie, *Saving Private Ryan*. So Shanina was accepted into the Central Women's School of Sniper Training without question. She graduated with honours. An avid letter writer, she began her combat diary as soon as she was deployed as a sniper.

She wrote vivid accounts of combat at the front, including her first 'kill': *'Finally, in the evening, a German showed in the trench. I estimated the distance to the target was not over 400 metres. A suitable distance. When the Fritz, keeping his head down, went towards the woods, I fired, but from the way he fell, I knew I had not killed him. For about an hour the fascist lay in the mud, not daring to move. Then he started crawling. I fired again, and this time did not miss.'*

Shocked by what she had done, her legs gave way and she collapsed into a trench. When she said in shock, *'I've killed a man,'* a female comrade called back, *'That was a fascist you finished off.'* She never felt shock again: *'Day breaks. Walking. Freezing: in my underwear, bra and camouflage, and that's all. Where we are, Fritz is on three sides. I see a guard looming in the distance. But whose? Through the rye, I crept closer. Suddenly a German plane strafed the ground 100 metres from us. At first, I didn't see them, then I did: 100 metres off, motorised artillery and infantry. Eight metres away, a tank crushed a lieutenant, a captain and several soldiers. My rifle jammed. Quickly, I cleared the jam and shot again.*

Here comes the tank directly at me, ten metres away. I feel for my grenades – but they were lost while crawling through the rye. Seven metres out, our 76mm artillery piece hit the tank. Tanks passing by, soldiers throwing grenades at them, all kinds of fire (machine gun, shells), eight shot, the others retreated. After everything, when I saw the dead and wounded, it was terrible. Before his death, the captain gave me a watch.'

Later, Shanina described defending a German counter-attack: *'Very successfully fought back a counter-attack. Fifteen kills for sure, as I was at close range and shot a lot. We watched four artillerymen through ten-fold and six-fold binoculars. When Fritz started to crawl, we could still see their helmets, shot at them. Bullets were ricocheting off their helmets, which we could see well because they were tracer cartridges. First at a distance of 200 metres, then they stood up to full height 100 metres out. When they got within twenty metres, we fled. We were behind an embankment in the woods and escaped easily. We were left alone. Beside me, Captain Aseyev, our artillery division commander, Hero of the Soviet Union, was killed. Day before yesterday, buried female comrade-in-arms Sasha Koreneva. Two more of our female comrades were wounded: Lazarenko Valya and Shmeleva Zina. From our 2nd Battalion there are six left out of seventy-eight. I miss the girls.'*

She was soon a celebrity. Journalist Ilya Ehrenburg wrote: *'Let the Russian mother rejoice who gave birth to, brought up and gave this glorious, noble daughter to the Motherland!'* Magazines portrayed her wearing a skirt with the armour of an ancient Russian warrior while holding a rifle.

Renowned for sniping 'doublets' – two targets hit by two rounds fired in quick succession – she had not only to fight the Germans, but also to cope with being taken out of the front line against her will. She endured the frequently distasteful behaviour of her own comrades: *'For three hours now I've sat and cried. Twelve at night. What good am I? Am I no help? My experience is not wanted. It looks like there are too many support troops, and I will not be called to help. I don't know what to do next. Often, I hear dirty talk. For what do I deserve such useless torture? Everyone shouting raunchy, filthy language.'*

Increasingly worn down by the war and her own unhappiness, her plight began to take its toll. In January 1945, she wrote: *'Frost in the tank, unaccustomed to tank smoke and it hurts my eyes; I can't breathe these fumes. Slept like the dead . . . I'm finally sure that I'm not capable of love . . . Today for me seemed like a month. Nearly vomited at all the body parts. Bandaged the wounded and moved forward . . . Frost, hunger. Went into a unit. The guys threw some filthy compliments at me. Filthy language everywhere. So tired. I went off on my own.'*

She made her last diary entry on 24 January 1945: *'I was with a division. A Lieutenant, Vadim, son of the colonel, a mama's boy and evil. He stuck close to me. I was in the middle of changing my clothes. He walked in without permission . . . He twisted my arms around, threw me down on the couch, kissing me, "Give me a kiss," he was drunk; just then the Colonel walked in – his father. I had tears on my face, crying. "What's going on?" I say. "Just because I'm a girl, does that mean everyone has to kiss me?" He yelled at his son. But after he had left Vadim said, "Understand, I don't want German girls, they're infected, and you're a clean, pretty girl, who I still want to kiss." I said, "You have so many wants. I have to be the one to give in?" [. . .]'*

Later that night, she added: *'Again march at night, now dark, but soon dawn, sitting around the campfire and writing. So bad when no bosses need me. Good, that nobody is giving orders, but still bad – no orders, what to do? I can't seem to find contentment in my heart.'*

Three days later, Shanina was severely injured and was later found by two soldiers, slumped over the body of an artillery officer she was trying to protect. She had been disembowelled, with her chest torn open by a shell fragment. Despite attempts to save her, she died the following day. Perhaps surprisingly, although she had made fifty-nine kills in just ten months and did receive several medals, she was not made a Hero of the Soviet Union.

There were many perks and benefits that went with the award of Mother Russia's highest honour. They included: a union-level personal pension for life, with survivor benefits in the event of the death of the title holder; first priority on the housing list, with a 50 per cent rent reduction, a similar tax exemption and an additional forty-five square metres of living space; an annual return-trip airline ticket, first class; free bus transportation; a free annual visit to a sanatorium or rest home; extra medical benefits, in addition to the country's extensive free medical care; and lavish entertainment benefits at sporting and cultural events, including being excused from the need to queue.

Three female machine-gunners were made Heroes of the Soviet Union. Sadly, all were awarded posthumously. One recipient was a Pole, Anelia Kzhivon, one was a Kazakh, Manshuk Mametova, and one was Ukrainian, Nina Onilova.

Nina Onilova's exploits as a machine-gunner made her a role model for hundreds of women in the Red Army who were in medical or support positions and persuaded them to retrain for combat roles. She was born near Odessa, the daughter of Ukrainian peasants, and brought up in an orphanage following the deaths of her parents. At the outbreak of war, she worked in a textile factory but was inspired to become a machine-gunner after watching *Chapayev*, a highly popular 1930s film based on the life of Russian Civil War commander Vasili Chapayev. The film featured the story of 'Anka', a courageous woman machine-gunner. Anka's exploits led Onilova to take gunnery training lessons in her factory's military training club.

Onilova volunteered for service in the Red Army and was made a medic in the 54th Rifle Regiment but soon used her pre-war training to prove herself as a gunner. In August 1941, in the midst of a German attack during the siege of Odessa, she picked up a comrade's jammed machine gun, quickly cleared it and, with withering fire, used it to repulse a detachment of advancing enemy infantry.

In September, Onilova was badly wounded as the Germans continued their siege, but she chose to remain with her unit. Subsequently, it fell back to positions around Sevastopol in the Crimea. In November, she crawled across twenty-five yards of open ground to destroy a German tank with two Molotov cocktails, for which she was promoted to sergeant and awarded the Order of the Red Banner.

By the spring of 1942, Onilova was a senior sergeant and commander of her own crew. She was seriously wounded for the second time during a German attack in March, in which she single-handedly fought on after the rest of her gun crew were killed.

Taken to a Soviet hospital in the aftermath, she died a week later at the age of just twenty, and was interred at Sevastopol's Communards Cemetery. Though commemorated during and after the war, Onilova was only recognized as a Hero of the Soviet Union in May 1965, on the twentieth anniversary of the war's end.

Anelia Kzhivon became the only non-Soviet recipient of the prestigious award. A machine-gunner in the 1st Polish Division, a unit of Poles affiliated to the Red Army and formed in 1943, she fought in the division's first engagement, the Battle of Lenino, on 12 October 1943. The vehicle Kzhivon was travelling in was attacked by Luftwaffe planes. Injured in the attack, she gave her life rescuing her wounded comrades and managing to secure vital headquarters documents.

Manshuk Mametova was born in Kazakhstan and was studying medicine when war broke out. She joined the Red Army in August 1942. Initially, her gender condemned her to a clerk's job, but she was eventually allowed to train as a machine-gunner, at which she excelled. In her first battle, she earned great praise for delaying her fire until the Germans were right on top of her. At which point, she mowed down a large number with rapid fire.

In October 1943, in Nevel, near the border of Belorussia, after Soviet forces retook the town, a series of German counter-attacks began. In the midst of the battle, Mametova was left on her own when the rest of her comrades were killed. She was hit in the head and knocked out, but regained consciousness and continued firing. Another soldier from her regiment called out, asking her repeatedly to retreat with them, but she refused. She continued firing, inflicting heavy casualties.

Eventually, Mametova was mortally wounded by a barrage of enemy fire but continued fighting until she died of her wounds. She killed more than seventy of the enemy in her final battle. Her remains were discovered by the Red Army when it recaptured Nevel. Her body was buried in the town, where a monument dedicated to her bravery still stands. She was made a Hero of the Soviet Union at the beginning of 1944, the first Kazakh woman to be so honoured.

Vasili Chuikov, a battle-hardened general of the old school, summed up the contribution of Soviet women in the war: *'I can't overlook the very important question which, in my opinion, is still weakly covered in military literature ... the role of women in war, in the rear, but also at the front. Equally with men, they bore all the burdens of combat life and together with us men, they went all the way to Berlin.'*

Andrei Yeremenko, an equally forthright and seasoned general, was also fulsome in his praise, saying that there was hardly *'any military specialism which our brave women did not handle just as well as their brothers, husbands and fathers'*.

18

BLOOD AND IRON: KURSK

JULY 1943

By the summer of 1943, the hell that was the Eastern Front had lasted for two years. But besides the tangible horrors of the battlefield and the civilian atrocities, there was another conflict in progress. It was an ideological battle, which both sides believed was being fought for the hearts and minds of the whole world. Two competing and polar opposite doctrines were fighting to the death. Each thought that brutal totalitarianism would create a better world, and that the war was a necessary purgatory, a cleansing, that could prove which dogma would rid the world of all its ills. Either the enforced racial purity of National Socialism or the draconian egalitarianism of Soviet Communism would be accepted as the dominant global philosophy. Both could not be right. Each side in the conflict believed that their doctrine would become the beacon for the future of the world's nations; the other would be extinguished and discarded by history. In the end, all the pain and suffering yet to come would prove nothing. Both doctrines would be extinguished; both would be dismissed, each of their fanaticisms revealed to be catastrophically wrong, their regimes murderous and evil.

A particularly fearsome part of the pain and suffering yet to come was endured over the long summer months of 1943. In normal times in the western Soviet Union, summer would be a time of long days in the sun, with nature's bounty ripening in the fields. There would be fetes and festivals and the many joys of life in the open air. Even the poorest would be able to find modest fare to eat, and the beer and vodka would flow in abundance.

Although the warm weather and nature's plenty were there that summer, any pleasures that the season may have offered went to waste; there was no one to enjoy them. Instead, people were either fighting, suffering terrible hardships, or dying. Across the huge open spaces, few crops would be harvested, fruit would fall to the ground; instead of ploughshares and tractors, the land would be criss-crossed by tanks and artillery pieces; warmth and clear skies would be replaced by heat and dust. Those months would become known as the days of blood and iron.

On the northern front, a Red Army offensive in January had opened up a seven-mile land bridge to the besieged city of Leningrad. On the central front, following the failure to capture Moscow in December 1941, throughout 1942 the Wehrmacht had been pushed further and further from Moscow. By March 1943, a large pocket of German-held territory stuck out like a sore thumb along the front. It was called the 'Rzhev Salient'.

After the devastating losses at Stalingrad and the growing impetus of Soviet attacks in the south, the Wehrmacht withdrew from the salient from 1 March. The German retreat shortened its defensive line by 230 miles and released 21 divisions, over 300,000 men, at least 100 tanks and over 400 artillery pieces, which were sent to reinforce the southern front. But there was a sting in the tail. The withdrawal was accompanied by a vicious campaign of destruction, the deportation of the able-bodied Soviet population for slave labour, and the wholesale murder of remaining civilians. Entire villages were burned to the ground, wells were poisoned, and swathes of booby traps and mines were placed. Nevertheless, by 22 March, the Rzhev Salient was closed, pushing the German line back over 200 miles from Moscow.

The mood among those who had been fighting since the summer of 1941 had changed dramatically. Nikolai Moskvin was still with the partisans in Belorussia: *'I want to tear out the pages of my diary where I wrote about the collapse of my will. But let them stay there as a lesson in life that it's wrong to jump to conclusions just because things are not going well.'*

Life was incredibly hard for the partisans. Maria Savitskaya-

Radiukevich was a liaison officer between various units: *'I gave birth in '43 . . . By then, my husband and I had joined the partisans. I gave birth to her on a haystack in a swamp. Everything around us was burning. Villages were burned down with people in them . . . They rounded up people in schools, in churches . . . poured kerosene . . . I gathered the charred remains. I gathered my friend's family. Each of us looked for our own. I picked up a small piece, my friend said, "Mama's jacket," and fainted. Some gathered remains in a sheet or pillowcase. My friend had a handbag. What we gathered filled less than half of it. And we put it all in a common grave.*

After that, whatever mission they gave me, I wasn't afraid. My baby was small, just three months old. The commissar would send me off and weep himself. There were wounded men dying in the forest. I had to go. I used to bring medications, bandages, serums from town. There were Germans everywhere; guard posts everywhere. Nobody could pass except me. It's horrible to tell about it now . . . Oh, so hard! I rubbed my baby with salt. She'd go red with a rash and scream her head off. I'd go up to the guard, "Typhus, sir . . . Typhus." They'd shout at me, "Away! Away!" Once we got past the guards, I'd go into the forest and weep my heart out. I was so sorry for my baby. And in a day or two, I'd go again.'

In the south, the post-Stalingrad advance by the Red Army, before the spring thaw set in, had pushed the Wehrmacht back almost 400 miles. The subsequent German counter-attack had regained some territory, but as the ground hardened and the generals prepared their summer offensives, a large, anomalous Soviet 'fist' appeared on the battle map. It was a bulge in the front, approximately 150 miles from north to south and 100 miles from east to west, and became known as the 'Kursk Salient'. Wehrmacht attempts to 'pinch' the salient and win back the ground would lead to the greatest mechanised battles in history.

Both sides prepared for a battle on an enormous scale. Germany concentrated over half a million men, 10,000 guns and mortars, 2,700 tanks and assault guns and 2,500 aircraft to eradicate the bulge and take the city of Kursk. Pre-warned of German intentions by British intelligence, the Red Army dug in and amassed an even more formidable force, including almost 1.3 million men, over

20,000 guns and mortars, 3,600 tanks, 2,650 aircraft, plus a reserve of another half a million men and 1,500 tanks.

The German attack was code-named *Zitadelle* ('Citadel'). Its success was vital to Germany's prospects. After Stalingrad, the Wehrmacht's prestige had suffered a catastrophic blow, both at home and among its Axis allies. Hitler feared that the already tenuous support of his allies would soon disappear altogether. Indeed, Mussolini's power in Italy was waning rapidly. The people, and even his ardent supporters, were turning away from him in droves. Hitler needed a major victory; *Zitadelle* was supposed to give him that victory. Unfortunately, for him, it only added to his long tally of mistakes and misjudgements.

Not realising the long-term consequences, Hitler fell into a cyclical arms race with the Red Army, which made the coming battle even bigger and more ferocious. Conscious that the Soviets were strengthening their defences, he kept delaying *Zitadelle* until he could deploy better-designed weapons, to improve his chances of victory. He waited for new tanks like the 'Panther', new anti-tank weapons and an improved version of the powerful 'Tiger' heavy tank. The delays allowed the Red Army to do exactly the same, giving them time to build their defences yet more robustly.

Several of Hitler's generals counselled him that Germany's only sensible option on the Eastern Front was to concede much or all of its conquests in the Soviet Union, dig in at a reasonable distance from Germany, and fight it out for a draw. This might produce a reluctant peace in the east, which would allow the Wehrmacht to concentrate on defending Western Europe from a massive Allied attack – which, sooner or later, was inevitable.

Any experienced general would have known that by the summer of 1943, Germany was no longer able to win the war in the east. But, for Hitler, a retreat in the hope of eventually suing for peace was tantamount to defeat. He would have to abandon his dream of *Lebensraum* and admit that his ideology had failed to prevail over Soviet Communism. Even if he was aware of the military inevitability, he was never going to accept defeat, whether military or ideological. He rolled the dice one last time, even though it meant countless more deaths and, ultimately, the total destruction of his Fatherland and the complete humiliation of his people.

In Moscow, there had been a similar strategic debate about Kursk. Stalin, impatient as usual, wanted to continue attacking. Stavka disagreed, much to Stalin's annoyance.

Zhukov described the deliberations: '*The Supreme Commander* [Stalin] *was not yet certain whether it was better to counter the enemy with defensive operations or to deliver him a decisive blow. He was afraid that our defences could not take a German blow, as had been the case several times in 1941 and 1942. At the same time, he was not sure that our troops were in a position to defeat the enemy in an offensive action. After repeated discussions* [this is more than a hint about Zhukov's frustration] *Stalin resolved to meet the* [impending] *German attack with all kinds of deeply entrenched defences.*'

Unlike Hitler, Stalin had begun to listen to his generals and, on enough occasions to make a difference, was prepared to bow to their wisdom. It was a crucial shift in Stalin's approach that would prove vital for the outcome of the war. Not only did it mean that his generals' advice was heeded, it also gave them more confidence to be even bolder in offering their opinions. Meanwhile, within the *Führerbunker*, Hitler's generals were being ignored, brow-beaten and humiliated.

The great battle, which opened with massive Wehrmacht pincers to the north and south, eventually began in the early hours of 5 July 1943. Zhukov described the beginning of the great battle: '*At 2:20 a.m., the order was issued. Everyone raced round and round, twisting and twirling, a terrible rumbling was heard and a very great battle began in the Kursk Bulge. The sounds of the heavy artillery, the explosions of bombs and the M-31 rockets* [Katyusha or 'Little Kate'] *and the constant hum of the aircraft engines merged into what was like the strains of a symphony from hell.*'

Zhukov's HQ was only ten miles from the front. Not usually prone to florid passages in his account of the war, the old warhorse employed colourful language more than once in his detailed descriptions: '*We could hear and feel the hurricane-like fire and could not help conjuring up the terrible picture on the enemy's bridgehead . . .*

Fierce enemy attacks began again on the morning of July 7th. The incessant roar of the battle, the gritting noise of tanks and the raving of engines resounded unabated in the air and on the ground.'

The iconic yellow wheatfields of Kursk's ancient countryside were flattened by huge machines of war, their smooth, rolling outlines pockmarked by shell craters. Such was the ferocity of the encounter that the clear skies and fresh morning air were polluted by cordite, dust and smoke. The Red Army's formidable ground defences held in the north, preventing the German panzers from advancing. By 10 July, the northern pincer had been halted. In the south, where the same elite units that had led the Wehrmacht's successful February counter-attack at Kharkov were massed, the Germans had more success. They soon reached the settlement of Prokhorovka, fifty-four miles south-east of Kursk. On 12 July, a mighty clash of iron-clad armaments occurred when two elite units met head-on: the Wehrmacht's II Waffen-SS-Panzer Corps and the Red Army's 5th Guards Tank Army.

The battle became as close to hand-to-hand fighting as was possible in heavily armoured tanks. They fired at one another from point-blank range; most shots from both sides were a direct hit. The distance between the forces was such that tanks were shooting each other from left and right, one after another. The Soviets got close enough to ram the German tanks, to disable their relatively powerful guns from turning. Pavel Rotmistrov commanded the 5th Guards in the battle, and described the fierce fighting: *'Their Tigers and Panthers, deprived in the melee of their advantage in fire-power, were now completely astonished by the Soviet T-34 tanks and even by the lighter T-70s from shorter distances. Smoke and dust swirled all over the battlefield. The earth shook from the powerful blasts. Tanks struck each other and, having grappled, could not cut themselves loose, and fought to the death.'* The 5th Guards suffered significant losses in the attack but succeeded in preventing the Wehrmacht from capturing Prokhorovka and breaking through the third line of defences, the last heavily fortified barrier.

The following account, recently discovered in the Central Archive of the Russian Ministry of Defence, offers a typical example of the intensity of the fighting and the heroism of many of the combatants: *'The tank of T-34 Commander Captain Skripkin sliced into a formation of Tigers and knocked out two enemy tanks, before which an 88mm shell had hit the turret of his T-34 and another pierced the flank armour. The Soviet tank caught fire and the wounded Skripkin was pulled out from his machine by driver Sergeant Nikolayev and radio operator Zyryanov. They took cover in a crater, but one of the Tigers noticed them and moved towards them. Nikolayev and his loader Chernov jumped into the burning machine, started it, and sent it right into the Tiger. Both tanks exploded in the collision.'*

Tanks are heavily armoured, but they are death traps; one of the most dangerous places to be on a battlefield. Their armour plating offers modest protection from attack, but if hit with a weapon of sufficient power – like a specifically designed anti-tank gun, or even a Molotov cocktail – their fuel and/or shells can ignite, incinerating everyone inside. Kursk was in every way a battle of blood and iron. Vassily Grossman quotes tank gun-aimer Trofim Teplenko: *'This was a face-to-face battle. It was like a duel, anti-tank gun against tank. Sergeant Smirnov's head and leg were blown off. We brought the head and leg back and put everything into a little ditch and covered them over.'*

Grossman also quoted extracts from Teplenko's brigade diary: *'A gun-aimer fired at a Tiger* [panzer] *at point-blank range with a 45mm anti-tank gun. It just bounced off. Enraged, the aimer just threw himself at the tank . . . A lieutenant, wounded in the leg, with a hand torn off, was commanding a battery attacked by tanks. After the enemy attack had been halted, he shot himself because he didn't want to live as a cripple.'* The lieutenant's action may seem extreme to us. However, after the war, the Soviet authorities rounded up maimed ex-servicemen and sent them to towns in the Arctic Circle, so that the big cities were not made 'unsightly' by limbless veterans.

Olga Omelchenko, a medical assistant, was at the battle at Prokhorovka: *'The sky thunders, the earth shudders, and you think your heart will explode, and the skin on your back is about to burst. I hadn't thought that the earth could crack. Everything cracked, everything roared. The whole world seemed to be swaying.* She went on to describe how the hand-to-hand fighting *'isn't for human beings . . . Men strike, thrust their bayonets into stomachs, eyes; they strangle one another. Howling, shouts, groans. It's something terrible, even for war.'*

Sergeant-Major Nina Kovelenova, an infantry medical assistant, described sights and sounds that appalled her: *'Once hand-to-hand combat begins, there's immediately this crunching noise: the breaking of cartilage, of human bones. Animal cries . . . It all happened before my eyes . . . Men stabbing one another. Finishing each other off. Sticking a bayonet in the mouth, in the eye . . . In the heart, in the stomach . . . Women don't know such men, they don't see such men at home. It's frightful to think of.'*

Unable to accomplish its objective, *Zitadelle* was cancelled and the Wehrmacht began redeploying its forces to deal with new pressures elsewhere. The Red Army went on a general offensive. By 24 July, the Germans were on the run and had been pushed back beyond *Zitadelle*'s original starting point. The Soviets had finally seized the initiative on the Eastern Front; the long march to Berlin had begun.

The Battle of Prokhorovka has often been named 'the largest tank battle in history'; however, recently opened Soviet archives suggest that the less-well-known Battle of Brody, in 1941, may have involved more tanks, and that the numbers at Prokhorovka may have been exaggerated by Soviet propaganda.

Although the German withdrawal amounted to a Red Army success, it was a pyrrhic victory. Despite outnumbering and out-gunning the Germans, the Soviets suffered many more casualties and a huge loss of vital armament. Definitive casualty figures and losses of materiel are much debated by historians. However, it is estimated there were up to 800,000 Soviet casualties compared to some 200,000 German casualties. Tank losses may have been at least 500 Soviet tanks and at least 300 German panzers.

Historians continue to debate the importance of the Battle of Kursk. Post-battle Soviet propaganda tried to assert that it was another great victory, like Stalingrad. That was clearly not the case; the Wehrmacht chose to disengage, rather than be overwhelmed. Even so, the Red Army held the salient and pushed on afterwards.

In borrowing from other historical accounts, it is perhaps reasonable to suggest the following encounters as the key fulcrums of the war: the defence of Moscow in 1941 was the geopolitical turning point; the defence of Stalingrad was the psychological turning point; and the defence of the Kursk Salient was the military turning point. It is worth adding that all three of the above were Soviet defensive triumphs. From Kursk onwards, all the victories would be Soviet offensive ones.

Zhukov had no doubts about the importance of Kursk: *'The battle was one of the most important engagements of the Great Patriotic War and the Second World War as a whole. Not only were the hand-picked and most powerful units of the Germans destroyed, but the faith of the German Army and the German people in the Nazi leadership and Germany's ability to withstand the growing might of the Soviet Union was irrevocably shattered. Hitler's attempt to wrest the strategic initiative from the Soviet Command had ended in failure. This proved how exhausted Germany was. Nothing could save her now. It was only a matter of time.'*

19

THE MEAT GRINDER

AUGUST–DECEMBER 1943

As the Red Army pushed westwards after the Battle of Kursk, Olga Omelchenko's Chief of Staff summoned her, and said: *'I look at you and think, what made you come to this hellfire? You'll be killed like a fly. It's a war! It's a meat grinder! Let me transfer you to a rear unit?'* She begged him not to, and he relented.

A few days later, during a German attack, two men from Omelchenko's unit *'turned coward'*. She described their fate after they were ordered to be executed: *'In the morning, the whole battalion was lined up, those cowards were brought out and placed before us. Seven men were needed . . . Three men stepped forward. The rest just stood there.'* Several wounded men whom Omelchenko had treated had died because of the cowardice of the two condemned men. *'I took a sub-machine gun and stepped forward. Those two could not be forgiven. Because of them, such brave boys were killed. I carried out the sentence. I forgot everything in the war. My former life. Everything. And I forgot love.'*

Aleksander Slesarev was a young tank commander with the 1st Guards Tank Army. He had fought through the Battle of Kursk and witnessed the liberation of Ukraine that followed: *'We're crossing liberated territory, land that was occupied by the Germans for more than two years. The population is coming out to greet us with joy, In the past, I knew Ukraine only from books, now I can see it with my own eyes: its picturesque nature with lots of gardens.'*

Although Slesarev's bucolic description reflects the euphoria of a long-awaited victory, the reality on the ground was far from joyous. The territories occupied by the Germans had been destroyed almost beyond recognition, its population brutalised beyond belief. The few surviving residents were living in squalor and disease. Mines and live ammunition were scattered everywhere; law and order had broken down long ago. Orphaned children roamed the streets and countryside, where gangs of deserters and criminals held sway. It was survival of the fittest of the most primordial kind.

Women who had had children by German men, who had either raped them or cajoled them for their favours, were abandoned with almost no hope of survival. Their offspring fared little better, many of whom did not make it beyond the first few days of life.

The liberation of Ukraine over the summer of 1943 was a bitter-sweet experience for all who witnessed it. Vasily Grossman recounted the contrasting emotions: 'When our troops enter a village, and the cannonade shakes the air, geese take off and, flapping their wings, fly heavily over the roofs. People emerge from the forest, from tall weeds, from marshes overgrown with tall bulrushes. Old men, when they hear Russian words, run to meet the troops and weep silently, unable to utter a word.'

Vasily Grossman met a young boy, who he thought was about thirteen or fourteen. He recounted their conversation.

'"Where is your father?"

"Killed."

"And mother?"

"She died."

"Have you got brothers or sisters?"

"A sister. They took her to Germany."

"Have you got any relatives?"

"No, they were all burned in a partisan village." [. . .]'

Surrounded by countless lost souls in the midst of a fierce offensive, the renowned journalist could do nothing to help the boy: 'He walked into a potato field, straightening the rags of his torn shirt, his bare feet black from the mud.' Grossman never saw him again.

As he moved through the liberated territory, Grossman heard of the discovery of the bodies at Babi Yar, and the retreating German attempts to hide the atrocity by digging up the bodies and burning them. He was distraught: 'There are no Jews in the Ukraine.

Nowhere, in none of the cities, hundreds of towns, or thousands of villages, will you see the black, tear-filled eyes of little girls; you will not hear the pained voice of an old woman; you will not see the dark face of a hungry baby. All is silence. Everything is still. A whole people has been brutally murdered.'

He wrote words that would prove to be prophetic: *'Every soldier, every officer and every general of the Red Army who had seen the Ukraine in blood and fire . . . understands to the bottom of their souls that there are only two sacred words left to us. One of them is "love", the other is "revenge".'*

By July 1943, Hitler's dream of a 'Greater Germany' was in peril; it seemed his generals had failed him; his army had failed him; his *Volk* had failed him.

On 10 July, Allied forces landed in Sicily, giving them their first foothold on mainland Europe. Hitler's main ally, Benito Mussolini, had seen his popularity in Italy evaporate; he would be overthrown and arrested on 25 July. As a result, the Führer ordered the shortening of the Wehrmacht's defensive position and the evacuation of the Orel Salient, so that he could release forces to the West. They would soon be fighting a series of fierce battles to defend the Italian peninsula.

Now, the Red Army not only held the initiative, but also boasted vastly superior numbers. It had 4.5 million men in its counter-offensive. Almost 360,000 would be lost, with almost 1 million wounded or sick, but that was only a 7.7 per cent loss, a significant improvement on the 13 per cent sacrificed in the breakout from Stalingrad. On the other hand, the Wehrmacht's losses would be 448,000, almost double the 226,000 suffered at Stalingrad. There would be no more major German counteroffensives on the Eastern Front. Machines of war were flooding westwards in huge numbers, from factories beyond the Urals, significantly enhanced by the American Lend-Lease programme, which provided support in military materiel and food. The Red Army now had superiority in men, tanks, guns and aircraft.

Importantly, the Red Army was becoming more mobile, making its imminent 1,100-mile trek to Berlin speedier, its lines of supply more efficient and its momentum more formidable. Over the course of the war, the United States delivered 434,000 jeeps and 3-ton trucks to its Soviet ally. Significantly, its abundant supply of machine tools helped Soviet factories build 2,000 tanks per month – twice the number German factories were able to produce. The relocated heartland of Soviet industry was now concentrated east of the Urals, way beyond the reach of the German Luftwaffe. Meanwhile, Germany's industrial heartland in the Ruhr had been heavily bombed by the RAF since May 1940.

The bombing of cities and civilians had been a feature of the war since its outset, and Allied bombing of German industrial targets was extended to the strategic bombing of cities in the spring of 1942. The strategy was intended to 'de-house' the population, making it impossible for them to work. By the end of the war, more than 50 per cent of most German cities had been destroyed.

The scales had tipped. The Red Army would grow ever stronger, the Wehrmacht ever weaker. Belgorod fell to the Red Army on 6 August, and Kharkov on the 23rd. Both victories were achieved with heavy losses amidst vicious fighting. The battle for Kharkov lasted for ten days before the Germans withdrew, leaving the city in ruins. It was the fourth and last battle of the war for control of the beleaguered city.

Ever more conscious of the inevitability of an Allied invasion of Western Europe, Hitler became less and less focused on the Eastern Front. He knew that the oil of the Caucasus was beyond his reach and that the Lebensraum he craved would never be his. In effect, like Napoleon before him, he abandoned his army, discarding it to fight a series of increasingly desperate rear-guard actions that would lead to many more months of lingering death.

The first defensive line was the Dnieper River, 150 miles west of Kharkov. German plans to construct a heavily fortified line on the west of the Dnieper were only embryonic when the 3rd Soviet Guards Army advanced towards the river on 19 September. After the reversals of the first part of 1943, the OKH had decided to build the Panther–Wotan Line, using the Upper and Lower Dnieper as natural barriers. This was envisaged as an 'East Wall' of defensive positions all the way from the Baltic to the Black Sea. Never much more than a concept, it was too little, too late.

Within twenty-four hours of the Red Army's attack, its 13th Army had made the first crossing of the Dnieper at Chernobyl. Two days later, it had two bridgeheads at Bukrin. Despite the fact that the area around Poltava was defended by elite SS panzer divisions, the Germans made a rapid retreat to Kremenchug, fifty miles to the west. The war on the Eastern Front had taken on a new, previously unimaginable, guise. The Germans were on the run.

As in all wars, the story of the overall strategic battlefields hides a collection of countless intimate, personal stories. One of the myriad in the Battle of Dnieper was that of Sergeant-Major Nina Vishnevskaya, a medical assistant in a tank battalion: '*Medical assistants die quickly. There was no room provided for us in a tank; you had to hang on to the armour plating and avoid having your legs drawn into the caterpillar tread . . . We were five girlfriends at the front: Liuba Yasinskaya, Shura Kiseleva, Tonya Bobkova, Zina Latysh and me. The tank soldiers called us the "Konakovo Girls"* [their hometown in Kalinin].

Before the battle in which Liuba was killed, she and I sat in the evening hugging each other. We talked. It was 1943. Our division was approaching the Dnieper. She suddenly said to me, "You know, I'll be killed in this battle. I have some sort of premonition." I tried to calm her down, "We've been fighting for two years. Bullets are frightened of us." In the morning, we went to the sergeant-major and got him to give us some new sets of underwear. So there she was in this new undershirt. Snow white, with laces . . . It was all soaked in blood . . . White and red together; crimson blood. I remember it to this day.

The four of us carried her in a tarpaulin, she'd become so heavy. We lost many in that battle. We dug a common grave. We put them all in it, as usual, with Liuba on top. There were five of us girls from Konakovo . . . But I alone came back to mama.'

Red Army sappers used all their experience to utilise anything they could lay their hands on to get men and armour across the Dnieper. Small craft, fishing boats, timber and logs lashed together to make makeshift rafts, all transported small groups of riflemen across the river. Such was the scale of the area, the Wehrmacht was unable to defend its vast expanse and, yard by yard, small Soviet bridgeheads became bigger and bigger until they were solidified across a wide stretch.

Anatoly Pavlov, a newly promoted sergeant, crossed the Dnieper with the 68th Guards Rifle Division on 27 September: *'We crossed in the middle of the night. The engineers had found three rowing boats and lashed them together with floorboards. It took all night to get most of the battalion across. There were no Fritzes in sight, but we could hear heavy fighting. We were lucky, the next day, as the engineers brought up pontoons to get our armour across. The Luftwaffe swooped down. It was a massacre. Men and machines flew into the air. Body parts and shrapnel cascaded on to us like hailstones. The Dnieper was blood red for half a mile.'*

By mid-October, the Red Army on the Lower Dnieper had bridgeheads strong enough to launch a massive attack, designed to secure the river's western bank in the southern part of the front. Simultaneously, a major diversion was conducted in the south to draw German forces away both from the Lower Dnieper and from the major city of Kiev.

Soviet forces controlled a bridgehead almost 200 miles long and up to fifty miles wide in some places. In the south, the Wehrmacht in the Crimea was cut off from the rest of the German forces. Any hope of stopping the Red Army had gone. The next objective was Kiev, Ukraine's iconic capital.

On the morning of 3 November, a huge aerial bombardment was followed by a Red Army ground attack. After two days of intense fighting, Soviet troops entered a city still devastated from its capture in 1941, and further punished by the Wehrmacht's scorched earth policy: 7,000 buildings, including 1,000 factories, had been plundered or destroyed; 200,000 civilians had been killed and 100,000 more sent to concentration camps, or to slave labour duties. There were only 80,000 survivors, just 20 per cent of the population's pre-war size.

Vitaly Taranichev was an engineer in a reserve unit behind the front. He wrote a letter home: *'It's one o'clock in the morning, November 7th. At 16:00 hours today we heard the order of our Supreme*

Commander, Comrade Stalin, about the capture of the capital of our Ukraine, the city of Kiev. Natalochka! [an endearing Ukrainian elaboration of 'Natalia'] *I can imagine how delighted you must be to hear the news! The time has passed when the fascists ruled the skies. Everything is working like clockwork; everything is moving forward, towards the west, towards the destruction of fascism.'*

Taranichev had heard the news in a broadcast of a speech given by Stalin in Moscow on 6 November. It was delivered as part of the celebrations of the twenty-sixth anniversary of the Bolshevik Revolution. Stalin wallowed in the news from the front and was fulsome in his praise of the Soviet system and of its people.

The successes of the Red Army would have been impossible without the support of the people, without the self-sacrificing work of the Soviet people in the factories and workshops, collieries and mines, transport and agriculture. In the hard conditions of war, the Soviet people have proved able to ensure for their Army everything at all necessary and have incessantly perfected its fighting equipment. Never during the whole course of the war has the enemy been able to surpass our Army in quality of armaments. At the same time our industry has given the front ever-increasing quantities of war equipment.

The past year marked a turning point not only in the trend of military operations but also in the work of our home front. We were no longer confronted with such tasks as the evacuation of enterprises to the east and the switching of industry to production of armaments. The Soviet State now has an efficient and rapidly expanding war economy.

The Red Army, supported by the entire people, has received uninterrupted supplies of fighting equipment, rained millions of bombs, mines and shells upon the enemy and brought thousands of tanks and planes into battle. One has every ground for saying that the self-sacrificing labour of the Soviet people in the rear will go down in history side by side with the Red Army's heroic struggle and the unparalleled feat of the people in defence of their Motherland.

Although Stalin's words were propagandist, they were far from hollow. He failed to mention Lend-Lease, but his statements were by no means exaggerated, and gave a reasonable summary of the Soviet war effort. More importantly, they reflected a dramatic change in circumstances. Victory heals many wounds and allows many sins to be forgiven. Suddenly, the Supreme Commander had become the wise leader of his people; the great general who had snatched victory from the jaws of defeat. For many, the purges and cruelties of the ruthless dictator were forgotten. Large numbers of those who had doubted the communist vision, particularly in the Red Army, began to think it might have merit after all.

Tamara Torop was a construction engineer. She recorded her feelings at the time: *'My papa . . . My beloved papa was a communist, a holy man. He educated me, "Well, who would I be without Soviet power; a poor man. I'd be a hired hand for some rich kulak* [property-owning peasant]. *Soviet power gave me everything." Papa's long gone. I don't believe it when people say that men like him were stupid and blind; believing in Stalin, believing in Lenin. Believe me, they were good and honest people; they believed not in Lenin and Stalin, but in the communist idea; in socialism with a human face, as they would call it later. In happiness for everyone. For each one. Dreamers, idealists – yes; blind – no. I'll never agree with that. In the middle of the war, Russia began to produce excellent tanks and planes, good weapons, but even so, without faith we would never have beaten Hitler's army. We wouldn't have broken its back. Our main weapon was faith, not fear.'*

The bravery and commitment of individual Soviet soldiers were undeniable: 2,438 Red Army soldiers were awarded the highest honour, Hero of the Soviet Union, during the Battle of the Dnieper. This was more than had been awarded previously.

There were German counter-attacks around Kiev, some of which, for a while, met with some success, including the retaking of the nearby towns of Brusilov and Zhitomir. Huge tank engagements followed over the course of the next month. The scale of the fighting, and the casualties on both sides, added up to numbers that, even today, are difficult to comprehend. The Wehrmacht brought up some reserves, but the Red Army brought up more and retook

Brusilov. By Christmas, the Red Army had won another victory, while the Wehrmacht had suffered another mortal blow.

Significantly, the Red Army now had a firm footing for further southern onslaughts. The year 1944 would see its troops advancing through the Carpathian Mountains and onwards through Romania, Hungary and southern Poland.

20

A PUNCH IN THE GUTS

AUGUST–OCTOBER 1943

Further north, the Soviet advance was focused on the direct route from Moscow to Berlin, the well-trodden east–west road that led, via Minsk and Warsaw, from the Soviet capital to the heart of Hitler's Reich. As it had been for the Wehrmacht in 1941, the ancient city of Smolensk was a vital strategic objective for the Red Army in 1943.

Intended to coincide with the Dnieper offensive in the south, the Battle for Smolensk was a huge Red Army assault against the Wehrmacht's Army Group Centre. Designed to be a body blow to the German Army's midriff, it was a 'punch in the guts' when the enemy was at his weakest.

Heavy losses over twenty-six months of draining battles had reduced the Wehrmacht to a shadow of the formidable force it had been in June 1941, when it had seemed to be a juggernaut that was impossible to stop. Its heart had been torn out; its well-trained and highly disciplined junior officer corps and NCOs had been devastated. Many were dead; some were awaiting death in Soviet gulags; many more were back home in Germany, invalided, maimed, disorientated or demoralised. Most senior officers knew the game was up. Only the honour of the Fatherland, fear of Hitler and his reign of terror, or dread of Soviet reprisals kept them going. They knew what had been done to the people of Eastern Europe; if they were not able to keep the Red Army away from the German heartland, a similar fate awaited their loved ones back home. They knew it was a fight to the death.

The Battle of Kursk was still raging when the Red Army launched Operation Suvorov on 7 August. Significantly, for several months Stalin had been playing down archetypal communist battle cries and slogans and, in ways that would have been unthinkable before the war, had begun using imperial nostalgia and religious metaphors to boost morale. Pointedly, the name of well-known hero of Mother Russia General Alexander Suvorov, the last generalissimo of imperial Russia under Catherine the Great, was now chosen for the Red Army's August offensive.

Stalin had introduced imperial army shoulder straps and insignia for the Red Army, while public reaction to his release of imprisoned clergy and relaxation of religious persecution was such that, in November 1942, on the twenty-fifth anniversary of the October Revolution, Patriarch Sergius had written to Stalin.

> On this 25th anniversary of the Republic of the Soviets, in the name of our Clergy and of all the believers of the Russian Orthodox Church, I salute with cordiality and piety, in your person, the leader chosen by God, the leader of our military and cultural forces, who is guiding us to triumph over the barbarous invasion, to the prosperity of our country in peace, towards a radiant future for its peoples. May God bless by success and glory your valorous exploits.

Operation Suvorov's objective was Smolensk. It lasted fifty-seven days, from 7 August to 2 October. The Soviet attack, numbering 1.2 million men, nearly 1,500 tanks and about 20,000 guns, was opposed by German forces numbering 850,000 men, 500 tanks and almost 9,000 guns and mortars. Yet again, the numbers of combatants involved were extraordinary. As in all the major conflagrations of the Eastern Front, the figures are difficult to grasp – as would be the numbers of casualties at the end of the encounter.

At the beginning of the onslaught, the Wehrmacht held deeply entrenched positions about forty-five miles east of Smolensk. By the end of the operation, the German line would be the same distance to the west of the city. The Red Army's task was a daunting one, but by 14 September it had made good ground. Once again, Hitler ignored his generals' advice and made strategic mistakes that would prove critical. His panicked reaction to the Allied invasion

of mainland Italy on 3 September led him to send vital reinforcements to southern Europe, rather than to the Eastern Front. He
kept elite units on guard duty in peripheral regions of his conquered territories, such as Greece. In truth, the Wehrmacht was
now fighting an unwinnable war in the East.

By 19 September, the Red Army had created a gap in Wehrmacht lines, 150 miles long and 25 miles wide. On 25 September,
after a bold crossing of the northern Dnieper and vicious street
fighting that lasted all night, Soviet troops completed the liberation
of Smolensk. On the same day, another important city, Roslavl, was
recaptured.

Sadly, although Smolensk had been retaken, there was little of it
left in which to celebrate. Under occupation for two years, the ancient
city had been destroyed. As usual, the Germans had left a legacy of
atrocities; a series of war crimes that included mass executions.
Perversely, the few civilians who remained in the city were subjected to continued horrors. The NKVD conducted investigations
of several citizens who may have collaborated with the Germans.
The inquiries led to public hangings in the city in 1945, which
almost the entire population of the city was ordered to witness.

Soviet partisans played an important role in both the Dnieper
and Smolensk offensives. Hidden in the forests, marshes and remote
villages of the vast German-occupied territory, various partisan
units carried out a large number of attacks on the German railway
infrastructure. In June 1943, the Central Committee of the Communist Party of Belorussia proposed a plan for the simultaneous
mass destruction of the railroads in the occupied territories of
the republic. To execute the plan, the Central Headquarters of the
Partisan Movement in Moscow enlisted partisans from Leningrad,
Kalinin, Smolensk, Orel and Ukraine, as well as Belorussian partisans. It became known as the 'Rail War' and was integrated into the
Supreme Command's plans for the Battle of Kursk, the attack on
Smolensk and the offensive to liberate the left bank of the Dnieper
in Ukraine.

The partisans were provided with explosives and fuses; 'forest
courses' offered training in mining and demolition techniques;

TNT was extracted from captured shells and bombs at local ad hoc factories; workshops and smithies made devices for fastening TNT charges to rails. German intelligence recorded over 400 attacks in March of that year, with a peak of 1,100 in July. In August, there were 21,300 rail attacks in Belorussia, which continued almost unabated for the rest of the year. Thousands of locomotives and wagons were destroyed; rails and tracks were sabotaged, and dozens of depots and railheads attacked. The impact on German supply lines was substantial.

At least 100,000 partisans were involved, who were aided by the local population. The mass destruction of Wehrmacht communications made the regrouping of the retreating enemy troops difficult, and it complicated their supply lines, thus making a significant contribution to the success of the 1943 offensives.

However, despite being coordinated by Moscow and local leadership groups, many of the partisans had been living 'wild' for two years. It was a harsh life and a dangerous one. They lived in remote locations – dense forests and insect-infested swamps and marshes – and were ruthlessly hunted down by German patrols. Not only did they die in large numbers in skirmishes, any who were captured faced brutal torture and execution.

A member of the Soviet 31st Army's Political Section, in Belorussia, reported an example of the kind of brutality that was commonplace, both during the Wehrmacht's advance and its retreat: '*Subdivisions of 1162 Infantry Regiment passed through the village of Vidritsa in Shklov, Mogilev Region. Five hundred metres from the village, at the edge of the forest, lay a girl, approximately twenty years of age. The Germans had captured this Soviet girl and, because she was in contact with the partisans, inflicted twenty knife wounds and bruises, having first stripped her naked and raped her. Not one house remained standing in the entire village, where there had been 147 homesteads. It now only exists as a place name.*'

Unlike the unnamed Belorussian girl, whose identity will never be known, and whose fate was typical of tens of thousands of others, Yelena Mazanik was one of the few lucky ones. She survived the war, was made a Hero of the Soviet Union, and lived peacefully in Minsk until she died in 1996 at the age of eighty-two.

Mazanik was born into a Belorussian peasant family and became a waitress in Minsk. After the Germans captured the city, Mazanik infiltrated a Wehrmacht unit using the pseudonym of 'Galina' and worked as a waitress at a dining hall and casino for German officers. Then, in 1943, she began to work as a maid in the mansion of Wilhelm Kube, Nazi Generalkommissar of Belorussia. He was a hated figure, responsible for several atrocities; local partisans had been planning his assassination for some time.

After receiving authorisation from Moscow, partisan detachments in the Minsk area began preparing to liquidate him. In July 1943, they detonated a bomb in a Minsk theatre, killing several dozen German soldiers. However, Kube had left the theatre just minutes before the bomb went off. In September, partisans attacked a banquet for German officers and killed thirty-six high-ranking officials and officers. But again, Kube was not present.

In a series of meetings with partisans, Mazanik agreed to kill Kube, either by using an explosive or poison. Before carrying out the assassination, the partisans made plans for her family to be evacuated from Minsk because of the inevitable retaliation that would follow. Mazanik was given a magnetic bomb no bigger than a cigarette packet and a poison capsule for herself, should she be captured.

On the night of 21 September, Mazanik set the bomb to go off in twenty-four hours. Early the next morning, she wrapped the bomb in her handkerchief: *'I was shaking like a leaf. I had an open-front dress and so placed the bomb under my breast in my underwear. The duty officer was in the small corridor, acting as a guard. I went up to him and said, "Bet you haven't had a cup of coffee today. Go downstairs and someone in the kitchen will give you a cup." Earlier, I had told the cook that the guard was my boyfriend.'*

As Mazanik executed her plan, the rest of her family were packing their possessions into carts and leaving Minsk for partisan-controlled areas of the forest.

'*I ran into the bedroom and took the bomb from under my dress. I knew that the General's bed was the one closer to the door, as I had asked the maid which bed was his and which was his wife's. I wrapped the bomb in the trousers of Kube's son, Willy. I squatted down by the bed and put the bomb between the mattress and springs. Luckily, the bed was not made yet and I jumped up and down on the bed to make sure it wouldn't come out.*'

In the early hours of 22 September, the bomb under Kube's bed went off forty minutes early, killing him. His pregnant wife was not hurt because she had been sleeping in the other bed. A truck had evacuated Mazanik from Minsk and she was never caught. However, the people of Minsk paid a terrible price. In a collective punishment for the assassination, over a thousand innocent civilians were rounded up, forced to dig their own mass grave, and shot.

Years later, when interviewed as an old woman, Mazanik's anger about the German enemy had not subsided: '*If I had the strength, I would do it all again, for my country, for Russia, Belorussia, Ukraine, for my country. Nothing could have stopped me if an enemy came to our land and did what he did, burning people alive. I was present at some of Kube's banquets, held in honour of the leaders who carried out these actions, exterminations. Men who destroyed villages. When they got together and drank schnapps, Kube used to say things like, "I have to admit that Hans has done very well, no one got away, he burned everyone in the village to death, but Fritz didn't do so well this time, a few people slipped through the net, not everyone was eliminated, a few people got away." You just want to kill them, kill them like mad dogs. It was the only country we had, the land where we were born.*'

With the liberation of Smolensk and more and more Belorussian territory, for many partisans the new circumstances meant that their role changed. Nikolai Moskvin's partisan battalion had been put under the leadership of General Ivan Grishin, who had led the liberation of Roslavl. Grishin ordered that Moskvin's men were to join the advancing Red Army. However, they were soon trapped by the Wehrmacht. The veteran was distraught: '*I have one main desire. If it's going to be death, then let it be quick, not with a serious injury, which would be the most frightening thing of all ... My instinct for self-preservation isn't working the way it used to.'* After a near-suicidal breakout charge, which cost dozens of lives, Moskvin and his men did escape the encirclement. However, Soviet discipline was still without mercy. On 13 October, General Grishin issued a grim order: *'For leaving his post without orders, for cowardice, for being panicky and for non-fulfilment of orders, Squad Leader Bacharov is to be shot.'*

As the autumn of 1943 turned wetter and colder, Red Army offensives continued to make progress. In the north, an attack by General Andrei Yeremenko's Kalinin Front towards the Nevel, 320 miles south of Leningrad, took the town within a day. By 31 December, the Red Army had advanced fifty miles and was within striking distance of Vitebsk, where stiff German resistance and the severe winter weather brought an end to Soviet progress.

In the south, the Wehrmacht had been forced out of the Kuban Peninsula, and although it still held the Crimea and Odessa, 1944 would dawn with a strategic position very different from the one twelve months earlier. The position around Leningrad had eased for the beleaguered city; Smolensk, Kiev and Dnepropetrovsk had all been liberated.

Zhukov noted the Soviet Stavka's ambitious plans for 1944: *'The Supreme Command decided to mount an offensive on a front running from Leningrad all the way down to the Crimea.'* In an ironic historical inversion, the Kremlin was laying out an attack which had an uncanny resemblance to the plan hatched by Hitler in the early months of 1941, Operation Barbarossa.

Zhukov outlined the strategy: *'Major offensive operations were to be launched in the South-Western theatre, in order to liberate Ukraine west of the Dnieper and the Crimea. It was decided to totally smash the siege of Leningrad and to push the enemy out of the entire Leningrad region. On the North-Western Front, our troops were to reach the boundaries of the Baltic republics, while the Western Front was ordered to liberate as much of Belorussia as possible.'* It was an ambitious plan that illustrated how the war had changed.

Most importantly, the Red Army was growing in strength by the day, as was its morale and resolve. For the Wehrmacht, the opposite was true. The year 1944 would be another one of relentless fighting and enormous battles, but the military compass of the war pointed in only one direction: westwards, towards Berlin.

21

CIGARS AROUND THE TABLE, MORE DEATH ON THE GROUND

JANUARY–APRIL 1944

By the beginning of 1944, the war on the Eastern Front had become realigned with the war elsewhere. Although the Lend-Lease materiel had been a vital part of the Soviet Union's ability to defend itself, the Red Army had, to all intents and purposes, fought alone since the blitz of Barbarossa.

However, by the time of the first meeting of the 'Big Three' at the Tehran Conference, at the end of November 1943, the interests of Stalin, Churchill and Roosevelt had needed to be redefined and reiterated. Although Roosevelt and Churchill had met several times, and Churchill had flown to Moscow in August 1942, it was becoming important that the three leaders were able to look one another in the eye.

There had been meetings at Foreign Minister level, but they were the lead violins; the three conductors needed to meet to ensure that their three orchestras were, at least loosely speaking, playing the same tune. With the pendulum swinging rapidly towards an Allied victory, it was vital that the three leaders met to agree on a coordinated plan to end the war as quickly as possible.

Crucially, the timing of the promised 'Second Front' in Western Europe needed to be fixed. It had become an issue of increasing frustration for Stalin and the Kremlin, reinforcing the view, widely held throughout Eastern Europe, that the Red Army was fighting alone. Even Lend-Lease was a source of frustration, as expressed by Zhukov: *'In 1943, we received a bit more aid from the United States than in 1942, but it was still far short of what had been promised . . . We wanted to see Nazi Germany defeated as soon as possible and the earliest possible termination of the war, we all looked forward to the Second Front being opened in the immediate future. Of course, we all rejoiced at El Alamein in Tunisia and elsewhere, yet all this fell short of what we had been waiting for from our Allies for so long.'*

There had also been a recent realisation in London and Washington that, with the Red Army on the march westwards, as many of Europe's countries as possible needed to be liberated by Britain and America, before the forces of communism did it for them. Only a few sentences before Zhukov's comment on Lend-Lease, he wrote: *'In the last quarter of 1943, 6.5 million tons of coal, 15,000 tons of oil and 172 million kwh of electricity were produced in the liberated areas alone ... Our country had now switched on its colossal might.'* The fact that the Red Army colossus was about to sweep westwards was suddenly at the forefront of thinking in the war rooms of London and Washington. A Second Front was in everybody's interests – and the sooner the better.

In that context, the other key agenda item for Tehran was the need to lay the groundwork for what would be a new world order after the war; a world order that would be radically different from the world that had gone before. Significantly, Stalin met with Roosevelt prior to the arrival of Churchill. Valentin Berezhkov, Stalin's interpreter, was at the private meeting: *'He [Roosevelt] broached the question of the colonial empires. "I am speaking of this in the absence of our comrade-in-arms, Churchill, since he doesn't like this subject. The United States and the Soviet Union are not colonial powers and I don't think the colonial powers will last long after the end of the war. It is better to discuss this without Churchill's participation since he has no plans, even with regard to India." [. . .]'*

Sergo Beria was given the task of using the latest listening devices to eavesdrop on the private conversations of Roosevelt and Churchill. Interestingly, the duty was not at his father's behest, but that of Stalin himself: *'Sometime later, Stalin sent for me. "You are going to listen to the conversations that Roosevelt will have with Churchill and his own circle. I must know everything in detail, be aware of all shades of meaning. I am asking you all that, because it is now that the question of the Second Front will be settled." Roosevelt said again and again that he would support Stalin in his efforts to destroy the British Empire, as that would correspond to American interests. It seems to me that this was his dominant idea and chief preoccupation.'*

Not only are Beria's and Berezhkov's accounts revealing insights into the machinations of the realpolitik of global affairs, they also summarise the stark reality of what would be Britain's weakness in the post-war world.

The outcome of Tehran was significant in several respects. Stalin was given a promise that the invasion of Western Europe would begin in the summer of 1944. In return for that commitment, Stalin agreed that he would launch a major offensive on the Eastern Front to coincide with the invasion (an offensive that would be code-named 'Operation Bagration') and that he would enter the war against Japan in the Far East.

Zhukov's recollections of the undertakings given at Tehran offer a telling insight into the growing self-confidence of the Red Army; a self-belief that would have stark consequences for post-war Europe and what would soon be called the Cold War.

'By the end of 1943, we had finally overcome our grave situation and with formidable strength and means of war at our disposal, firmly held the strategic initiative. Generally speaking, we no longer required a Second Front in Europe as badly as we had during the earlier two grim years. On his return from the Tehran Conference, Stalin said, "Roosevelt has given his word that extensive action will be mounted in France in 1944. I believe he will keep his word. But even if he doesn't, our own forces are sufficient to complete the rout of Nazi Germany." [. . .]'

The Tehran Conference had ended on 1 December 1943, 892 days since the launch of Barbarossa. In those grim days that had followed the invasion, all seemed lost. In the ensuing twenty-nine months of suffering, the death and destruction had become almost impossible to comprehend. However, at the beginning of 1944, there was only one possible outcome for the war. Although the horror would still go on, and the end of the war was still many months away, January 1944 was the beginning of the end.

Gabriel Temkin was a first-hand witness to the events of those 892 days. A Jewish refugee from Poland, he had witnessed the dishevelled state of the beaten Red Army as it retreated past him, in June 1941. As a refugee, he had been drafted into a labour battalion of the Red Army and had been captured by the Germans and sent to a POW camp, where his chances of survival were slim. His fellow inmates were bribed with bread to inform on any Jews in their midst, but his fellow prisoners did not reveal his identity. He eventually escaped and was cared for by Ukrainian peasants who risked their lives to hide and feed him. In May 1943, he had re-enlisted in the Red Army and through an administrative oversight was allowed to join a combat unit. By 1944, he was a sergeant, serving in a reconnaissance platoon in the 458th Rifle Regiment. For him, the sharp end of the war was a long way from the intrigues of Tehran.

He had seen many things but was shocked by what he witnessed one cold winter morning: 'We arrived in the Korsun-Shevchenkovsky area in mid-February. It was my twenty-third birthday. It was during a blizzard followed by a heavy snowstorm. What I saw the next morning looked like something out of this world. A large valley was covered with greyish-white snow and dotted up to the horizon with hundreds of bodies. That was not altogether uncommon. What was unusual was that all the bodies were naked. The skin of their frozen bodies under the rising sun was less grey, more pinkish, as if they had just gone to sleep after a hot shower. I stood transfixed, watching that unreal, unearthly sight. I could not take my eyes off it. I had seen people before wearing clothing taken from the bodies of fallen German soldiers, but I never thought it was done in such a thorough way.'

Yet another dreadful sight was waiting for him that same early morning: 'Soon after leaving the valley, I came across a local woman emerging from a gully and I noticed something bulky under her shawl. I gave her a curious look and in response, without the slightest hesitation, she lifted her shawl, revealing an axe and a pair of officer's boots with protruding legs cut off above the knees. She liked the boots, she told me, but could not take them off because they were stuck to the frozen legs. Once she got them home and the legs thawed out, they would be easily removed without damaging the boots.'

The bodies at Korsun were the result of an attempt by the Wehrmacht to break out of their encirclement in what was called the 'Korsun-Cherkassy Pocket'. Major Boris Kampov was a *Pravda* war reporter attached to the Red Army's 2nd Ukrainian Front under Marshal Ivan Konev: *'I remember that last fateful night of 16th February. A terrible blizzard was blowing. I rode on horseback. It was so dark; I couldn't see the horse's ears. I mention the darkness and the blizzard because they're an important factor in what happened.'*

Despite the darkness and the blizzard, Soviet forces managed to mount a U-2 aerial bombing raid and a heavy artillery attack on the trapped Germans of the Wehrmacht's 8th Army. The attacks forced the Germans to attempt a mass breakout.

'So that morning they formed themselves into two marching columns of about 14,000 each. Each of them was like an enormous mob. The spearhead and the flanks were formed by the SS of the Wallonia Brigade and the Wiking Division in their pearl-grey uniforms. Inside the triangle marched the rabble of the German infantry, very much down-at-heel. Right in the middle of this, a small select nucleus was formed by the officers.'

Konev's men were lying in wait with massed ranks of infantry, artillery, tanks and Cossack cavalry.

'Then it happened. It was about six o'clock in the morning. Our tanks and artillery appeared and rushed straight into the two columns. What happened next is hard to describe. The Germans ran in all directions. For the next four hours our tanks raced up and down the plain, crushing them by the hundred. Our cavalry competed with the tanks, chasing them through ravines. Hundreds and hundreds of cavalry were hacking at them with their sabres. There was no time to take prisoners. It was a kind of carnage that nothing could stop until it was over. In a small area, over 20,000 Germans were killed. I had been in Stalingrad, but I had never seen such concentrated slaughter.'

The first four months of 1944 saw a Red Army offensive roll the Wehrmacht all the way back to the Danube and into Romania. The retreat cost the Germans large amounts of armour and men, and led them to transfer vital reinforcements from Western Europe. It also led Hitler to cull his generals once more, blaming them for the repeated military failures. With the Red Army rampant, the Allies advancing through Italy, the D-Day Normandy landings imminent, and German cities under constant bombing attacks, the situation facing Germany was dire.

We can only speculate about Hitler's state of mind at this stage of the war, but for his soldiers on the ground, the situation was so desperate they were taking extreme decisions. Boris Kampov witnessed the consequences: '*Over by the woods stood the charred remains of eight large trucks. Captain Omelchenko, a Cossack officer, persuaded us to stop and examine them. "You will see what the Germans are like," he insisted. We ploughed through the deep snow towards the vehicles. Inside were a number of scorched bodies with burned bits of German uniforms sticking to them. "They were trying to get their wounded away," explained Omelchenko. "But when they saw the game was up, they poured petrol over the machines and set fire to them, wounded and all."*'

Kampov encountered many civilians who had witnessed the panicked withdrawal of the Wehrmacht, an elite army reduced to a mob: '*Yufim Sidoryuk, an inhabitant of Krasnoselka, a large village in the Bug area. "They came through in droves; filthy, ragged, some without coats, some in nothing but pants and undershirts. Some rode on horseback, two to a horse. They looked more like a band of ruffians than an army. A hungry, wretched lot. They went from house to house like hungry beasts, picking up anything they could find. One of them came into my place and found a bowl of cabbage. He sat down on the floor and stuffed it into his mouth with both hands like an animal.*'

The loss of vast tracts of German-occupied land in Ukraine meant that the Wehrmacht's 17th Army and the Mountain Corps of its Romanian allies were left isolated in the Crimea. At the beginning of April, a Soviet force over 460,000 strong began the battle to liberate the peninsula. Indicative of the changing fortunes in the war, it took only a month for the Red Army to sweep across the Crimea. Sevastopol fell on 9 May, with German and Romanian survivors escaping by sea.

For some, the liberation of the Crimea did not bring freedom from oppression. For the Crimean Tatars, what followed was catastrophic. On the orders of Stalin, the entire Crimean Tatar population was exiled to Central Asia. Although a great number of Tatar men had served in the Red Army, and took part in the partisan movement in Crimea during the war, the existence of the Tatar Legion in the German Army provided the Soviet leadership with justification for accusing the entire Crimean Tatar population of being Nazi collaborators.

All 240,000 Crimean Tatars were deported en masse to distant parts of the Soviet Union. Any who escaped were shot on sight or drowned in scuttled barges. Within months, half their number had died of cold, hunger, exhaustion and disease. Survivors were eventually relocated and incarcerated in Stalin's gulags.

Sadly, the fate of the Crimean Tatars also befell several other minorities throughout the Soviet Union, including Volga Germans, Chechens, Kalmyks, Ingush, Balkars, Meskhetians and, once they were liberated, Poles and Ukrainians. Perversely, even though Stalin was himself a Georgian, he mistrusted anyone, or any group, whose religion, language or history made them vulnerable to the accusation of collaboration, or the suspicion of disloyalty to Mother Russia, to state socialism, or to his authority as Supreme Commander. Stalin's treatment of ethnic minorities was yet another tragedy piled upon the innumerable tragedies of the war on the Eastern Front.

22

BAGRATION

APRIL-AUGUST 1944

The mighty conflagration that was Stalingrad is rightly defined for what it was: the most profoundly terrible battle in the history of warfare. It was the symbolism of Stalingrad that cast it as a sacrificial altar, to be revered and reviled in equal measure; it was its iconography that made it so memorable. But Stalingrad does not stand alone. There have been countless such battles in the litany of horrors that characterised the war on the Eastern Front.

The battles of Moscow, Kursk and Kharkov were all devastating in terms of casualties, and were of huge strategic importance. But there was an extraordinary battle in the middle of 1944, less well known, that was of enormous significance and at least as big a turning point as Stalingrad. It was called 'Bagration', named by Stalin after fellow Georgian Prince Pyotr Bagration, a general of the Imperial Russian Army during the Napoleonic Wars. Bagration had commanded the Russian left flank at the Battle of Borodino, in 1812, in which he was mortally wounded. His name was a good choice for an offensive launched close to the same ground as in 1812. Napoleon, who rarely praised his enemies, said of his adversary, 'Russia has no good generals. The only exception is Bagration.'

Planning for Operation Bagration began in April 1944, as described by Zhukov: *'At the end of April, the Supreme Command made the final decision on the summer campaign, including the Belorussian operation; it instructed Antonov* [Aleksei Antonov, Stavka Chief of Operations] *to ensure the preparation of the plans and to begin concentrating the troops and materiel for the plan of Operation Bagration (code name for the Belorussian Front).'*

Nikolai Belov, a lieutenant in the 5th Rifle Division who was conscripted into the army in July 1941 and twice wounded in battle, knew that Bagration was imminent when he saw Zhukov arrive at the division's headquarters. His journal entry for 18 June reads: *'There are grounds for thinking that we'll go on to the attack on June 21st or 22nd, which happens to be the third anniversary of the war. It's also four months since we crossed the Dnieper . . . I have been physically poor lately and my nerves are shattered . . . We'll soon be in battle and then I'll forget everything.'*

Central to the offensive was the Soviet military concept of 'deep battle', a military strategy pioneered by Soviet generals in the 1920s and 1930s. Costly in men and resources, and typical of the cynical pragmatism of modern warfare, deep battle meant throwing huge military formations – heavily armoured 'shock' armies – into an enemy's front line in several different locations, often in wave after wave. The objective was to find weak points, break through them, and wreak havoc among the enemy's support and logistics areas.

Deep battle was not unlike blitzkrieg, except that the German concept emphasised the importance of a single strike on a *Schwerpunkt* ('focal point') as a means of rapidly defeating an enemy, whereas deep battle emphasised the need for multiple breakthrough points to exploit the breach quickly. The difference was a matter of expediency: Germany had a smaller population, but a better-trained army, whereas the Soviet Union had a larger population but a less well-trained army. As a consequence, blitzkrieg stressed narrow frontal attacks, where quality could be decisive, while deep battle required wider attacks, where quantity could be used effectively. Regardless of the difference, the end result for the Wehrmacht was that they got a heavy dose of the bitter medicine they had administered to a very different Red Army in 1941.

To make matters worse for the Germans, the Soviets over-estimated German strength when planning Bagration. Stavka believed that at least 850,000 Germans opposed them. This led to a delay while the Soviets amassed more than 5 million soldiers for the offensive. In fact, the combat strength of the Wehrmacht's Army Group Centre was less than half a million. The difference in firepower was even more stark. The Soviets committed more than 4,000 tanks, 34,000 artillery pieces and 4,800 aircraft. Although the figures are widely disputed, the German forces could muster fewer than 800 tanks, around 3,500 artillery pieces and no more than 1,000 aircraft.

Another Soviet military concept, *maskirovka* (which translates into English as 'camouflage'), played an important part in the success of Bagration. Russian military deception was developed in the twentieth century. Measures included concealment, decoys, manoeuvres intended to deceive, and the dissemination of disinformation. The *Soviet Military Encyclopaedia* refers to *maskirovka* as a 'means of securing combat operations and the daily activities of forces; a complexity of measures, directed to mislead the enemy regarding the presence and disposition of forces'.

In Operation Bagration, while the Wehrmacht knew that a summer offensive was likely, deceptive Soviet troop deployments and movements confused the German High Command about its focus of attack. The declining capacity of the Luftwaffe, a vital source of reconnaissance intelligence, meant that aerial information was limited.

Not only was the Wehrmacht significantly outnumbered, outgunned, vulnerable in the air and deceived by *maskirovka*, but its High Command was in a state of panic. Two weeks before Bagration, on 6 June, doomsday had dawned in Normandy. The Allies called it 'D-Day', code-named 'Operation Overlord'. Although the initial Allied landings on the beaches of Normandy had met with stiff resistance, by 12 June all five beaches had been connected, and by the 17th the Allies had reached the west coast of the Cotentin Peninsula, making the Normandy bridgehead secure.

Once again, Soviet partisans were a major nuisance factor. Just before Bagration launched, the partisans conducted a stunning series of attacks on German-held infrastructure. This partisan pressure in the centre, which was aligned with Red Army advances towards Romania from the south, through Ukraine, stretched German forces in its Army Group Centre to the point where the Red Army's Deep Battle strategy was highly likely to succeed.

Germany's Führer played a central role in committing a large part of his once 'invincible' army to almost certain oblivion. Army Group Centre had been his strongest force, but no longer. Hitler had ordered it to 'stand firm' in the face of any Soviet advance. His 53rd Führer Directive, issued on 8 March, had announced that *Feste Plätze* ('fortified places') should be the core of the German defensive line. His concept was that the Soviets would advance past these fortifications, which would, Hitler said, 'fulfil the function of fortresses in former historical times', a notion grimly reminiscent of the horrors of medieval warfare. He went on to command:

> They will ensure that the enemy does not occupy these areas of decisive operational importance. They will allow themselves to be surrounded, thereby holding down the largest possible number of enemy forces and establishing conditions favourable for successful counter-attacks. Local strongpoints will be tenaciously defended in the event of enemy penetration. By being included in the main line of battle they will act as a reserve of defence and, should the enemy break through, as hinges and cornerstones for the Front, forming positions from which counter-attacks can be launched. Each Fortified Area Commandant should be a specially selected, hardened soldier, preferably of General's rank. He will be appointed by the Army Group concerned. Fortified Area Commandants will be personally responsible to the Commander in Chief of the Army Group. Fortified Area Commandants will pledge their honour as soldiers to carry out their duties to the last.

In the event, the Führer Directive became irrelevant. Such was the speed of the Red Army advance, there was no time to create *Feste Plätze*.

Nikolai Moskvin was still with the partisans in Belorussia. He had not seen Red Army troops in battle since 1941, at which point they had been no better than a beaten rabble, but times had changed: *'Now we're in the Soviet rear! The Red Army passed like a typhoon. The enemy has scuttled off in disarray. Four days ago, we were in occupied territory. Today, the front line is two hundred kilometres away from us.'*

The scale of Bagration was similar to the onslaught that was Barbarossa. It was a series of deep battle 'punches' from north to south, which would make the Wehrmacht fight everywhere at once and prevent it from moving its men and armour from one battlefield to another. The first blow would be struck in the north, against the Finns in Karelia, followed by attacks in Belorussia and in the north and south of Ukraine. The main focus would be on the Wehrmacht's midriff, Army Group Centre in Belorussia, where the Red Army's 'punch' would involve classic pincer movements to encircle German forces.

Zhukov was directly involved in the liberation of Minsk, the Belorussian capital: *'At dawn on July 3rd, the 2nd Guards Tank Corps burst into Minsk from the north-east. By the end of the day, a major group of the German 4th Army was cut off from withdrawal and encircled east of Minsk, more than 100,000 officers and men in all. The whole of Minsk was liberated. It was barely recognisable. I had commanded a regiment there for seven years and knew every street and all the main buildings. Now everything was in ruins; where whole apartment buildings had stood, there was nothing but heaps of rubble. The people of Minsk were a pitiful sight, exhausted and haggard, many of them in tears.'*

Vasily Grossman was with General Pavel Batov's 65th Army, part of Marshal Rokossovskiy's 1st Belorussian Front, as it attacked the city of Bobruisk on the Beresina River, ninety miles south-east of Minsk. He described an encounter with an unexpected hero of the advance: *'The first thing we see when we return to the dust and thundering of the main road is a brown camel pulling a cart. It proves to be the famous "Kuznechik". He has already earned three wound stripes and a medal, "For the Defence of Stalingrad".'* Kuznechik travelled with the Red Army all the way to Berlin, and earned his medal. His fame spread far and wide, especially when he was led across the city to spit on the Reichstag.

Larissa Deikun was also with Batov's 65th. As a nurse, she dealt with war at the sharp end. Not only does war scar the body, it also traumatises the soul: '*A wounded man was brought . . . The wound was to the head. You could see almost nothing of him. Just a little. But I obviously reminded him of someone, and he called to me, "Larissa . . . Larissa . . . Larochka . . ." Apparently a girl he loved. And that is my name. I knew I'd never met this man before, yet he was calling me. "You've come? You've come?" I took his hands, bent down . . . "I knew you'd come . . ." Even now I can't talk about it calmly; when I remember it, tears come to my eyes. He said, "When I was leaving for the front, I didn't have time to kiss you . . . kiss me." So I kissed him. A tear welled up, ran off into the bandages, and vanished. And that was all. He died.*'

Bobruisk was in ruins when Batov's men entered. As elsewhere, the Germans had massacred the greater part of the population, especially the Jewish people, who had been confined to a ghetto and, like livestock for the slaughterhouse, systematically murdered in small groups. Now, the German perpetrators were also being slaughtered like sheep. Grossman described what he saw as he entered the city: '*To Bobruisk led the road of revenge. Men are walking over German corpses. Corpses, hundreds and thousands of them, pave the roads, lie in ditches, under the pines in the green barley. In some places, vehicles have to drive over the corpses, so densely they lie on the ground . . . A cauldron of death was boiling here, where the revenge was carried out, a ruthless, terrible revenge.*'

The 'revenge' continued in every village, town and city. Grossman personally witnessed one example in newly liberated Minsk: '*A partisan with a stake killed two Germans. He pleaded with the guards to give him these Germans. He was convinced they were the ones who had killed his daughter and two sons. He broke all their bones and smashed their skulls. He was crying and shouting. "Here you are, for Olya! Here you are for Kolya!" When they were dead, he propped up their bodies against a tree and carried on beating them.*'

The bloody revenge that had been inevitable since the first of the Wehrmacht's atrocities was now in full swing. Just as the hatred born of Nazi ideology, which cast Jews and Slavs as subhuman, had become an infectious plague, now an epidemic of vengeance had taken hold in its turn. Ironically, it was an epidemic fuelled by the conviction within the consciousness of the men and women of the Red Army that a people who could have committed such appalling crimes could not possibly be human.

On 8 July, Zhukov was summoned to Moscow by Stalin: '*We talked about Germany's capacity to wage war on two fronts, against the Soviet Union and the Allied expeditionary forces which had landed in Normandy, and about the role and tasks of the Soviet troops in this concluding phase of the war . . . The question was, what could Hitler's military leaders hope for in the given situation? Stalin's answer was, "They are like a gambler betting his last coin. All their hopes were pinned on the British and Americans. In deciding to wage war against the Soviet Union, Hitler took into account the imperialist circles in Britain and the USA, who totally shared his thinking. And not without reason: they did everything they could to direct the Wehrmacht against the Soviet Union." Molotov* [who had joined the meeting] *added that Hitler would probably attempt to make a separate agreement with the US and British government circles. "That is true," said Stalin, "but Roosevelt and Churchill will not agree to a deal with Hitler. They will try to attain their political aims in Germany by setting up an obedient government, but not by collusion with the Nazis, who have lost all the trust of the people." Then Stalin asked me, "Can our troops begin liberating Poland and reach the Vistula without a stop?"* [. . .]'

Stalin was already planning his post-war domination of Eastern Europe. These were plans that would soon have dire consequences for the people of Poland, especially for those in its capital city, Warsaw.

The Red Army advance travelled at speeds between ten and fifteen miles a day. On 18 July it crossed into Poland, capturing Lublin on the 23rd. On the 28th, Brest-Litovsk was taken. Three days later, it reached the Vistula and was seen not far from Praga, a suburb of Warsaw on the east bank of the river. It had also established a bridgehead on the west bank of the Vistula, at Magnuszew, fifty miles to the south.

At that point, the unfortunate circumstances of another of the Eastern Front's great tragedies were about to unfold. On 1 August, with the sound of gunfire in the distance, the Warsaw Uprising began. It was a courageous struggle for freedom, and one which lasted for sixty-three days. At its end, it would become yet another heartbreaking story of loss and suffering.

By the climax of Bagration at the end of August, it had become the greatest Soviet victory, in numerical terms, on the Eastern Front. For the Wehrmacht, Bagration was an even greater defeat than Stalingrad had been, inflicting more than 400,000 casualties on an army already on its knees. The Red Army had recaptured a vast amount of Soviet territory, moved into the Baltic States, and crossed into pre-war Polish territory. On 17 July, to illustrate the scale of its victory, 60,000 German prisoners, taken from an encirclement east of Minsk, had been paraded through Moscow's Red Square. Even marching at pace, and twenty abreast, the phalanx took nearly three hours to pass Lenin's Mausoleum. Alexander Werth witnessed the column pass: '*Particularly striking was the attitude of the Russian crowd. Youngsters booed and whistled and even threw things at the Germans, only to be immediately restrained by the adults; men looked on grimly in silence. But many women, especially elderly women, were full of commiseration, some even had tears in their eyes, as they looked at these bedraggled "Fritzes". I remember one old woman murmuring "tozhe pognali na voinu (also driven to the war)".*'

Such was the scale of the defeat, the backbone of the Wehrmacht's elite units – their experienced NCOs and junior officers – was shattered by the scale of the losses. Similarly, at senior level, 31 of the 47 German divisional or corps commanders were killed or captured. Of the German generals who were lost in the battle, 9 were killed, 22 were captured, 2 committed suicide and 1 was declared missing in action.

Soviet losses have been more accurately counted, with 180,040 killed or missing, and 590,848 wounded or sick. Sergeant-Major Sofya Kuntsevich was a medical assistant in an infantry company: '*There were such terrible bullet wounds that each needed a whole package. I tore up all my underwear and I told the boys, "Take off your long johns, your undershirts. I've got people dying here." They took everything off, tore it up. I wasn't embarrassed in front of them, they were like brothers to me, and I lived among them like a boy . . . I was wounded three times and had three concussions . . . I wished for just one thing, to live until my birthday, so as to turn eighteen.'*

Deep battle had worked, but at a terrible price.

23

THE TRAGEDY OF WARSAW

OCTOBER 1939–JANUARY 1945

In many ways, Poland was the sacrificial lamb of the Second World War. It was gripped in the jaws of the Nazi–Soviet Pact in 1939, when it was devoured whole by Hitler in the west and Stalin in the east. Five years later, it was once again snared by power politics; this time by the intrigues of the Allies as they prepared the ground for the post-war map of Europe.

Although Polish culture and language have strong identities, the country's geographical position and lack of defendable borders have made it vulnerable to the whims and fancies of its neighbours and the boots of marauding armies. Despite this territorial weakness, the Polish people have always fought hard for their freedom and independence.

During the German occupation, Polish resistance split along ideological lines. The Polish Home Army (*Armia Kragowa*, AK) was pro-Western and supported by Britain and America, while the much smaller Polish People's Army (*Armia Ludowa*, AL) was pro-communist and supported by the Soviet Union.

When the massacre at Katyn was discovered by the Germans, in April 1943, the lengths to which Stalin was prepared to go to ensure that a future Poland would remain within the Soviet sphere of interest became all too obvious.

By 1944, The pro-Western AK numbered at least 250,000, although only a few were well armed. They were scattered across Poland but, as the Red Army advanced into the country in 1944, it rounded up, imprisoned and/or murdered any AK fighters it encountered. The stark reality for the AK was that while the Red

Army was already on Polish territory, the armies of Britain and America were still fighting to break out of the Cotentin Peninsula, over 1,000 miles away in France. In reality, while still fighting the Wehrmacht, the AK had a new enemy, the Red Army.

Typical of the fate of AK fighters was the story of Władysław Filipkowski. He commanded the Polish forces in Lvov, where the AK, with the assistance of the advancing Red Army, took control over the city from the Germans on 27 July. Soon after the liberation, Filipkowski was invited to a conference and arrested by the NKVD as a 'criminal and Polish fascist'. As many as 5,000 of his soldiers were also arrested and were either sent to the Soviet Miedniki gulag or escaped to German-held areas of Poland. Filipkowski was held in several Soviet prisons before he was sent back to communist Poland in November 1947 and set free. However, his son Andrzej, also a former soldier of the AK, was arrested by the communists and held in prisons until the de-Stalinisation thaw of 1956.

By August 1944, Warsaw had already been to hell and back, and more than once. When the Wehrmacht had stormed into Poland in 1939, following the Nazi–Soviet Pact, Hitler had made his intentions very explicit: 'Kill, without pity or mercy, all men, women and children of Polish descent or language.' Warsaw resisted the onslaught for three weeks but was eventually bombed into submission at the cost of 25,000 civilian lives. The ethnic cleansing began immediately, as it did in Soviet-occupied territory. Over 1.5 million Poles were rounded up for forced labour in Germany, and mass executions were commonplace.

One of the main objectives of the German occupation was the eradication of the 400,000 Jews in Warsaw, representing about one-third of the population. As it did throughout its occupied lands, the Wehrmacht decreed a Jewish ghetto on 12 October 1940, the wall of which was sealed on 15 November. Jewish police guarded the inside of the wall, while German troops and Polish police patrolled the outside. Only people with special permits could leave the ghetto, where over 400,000 people were incarcerated.

Conditions inside the ghetto were dire. An average of more than seven people shared each room. Rationing for food had to be introduced, and starvation was widespread. The rations were confined to bread, potatoes and poor-quality fat from various dubious sources. There was, of course, a thriving black market where goods of all sorts could be exchanged for food. Smuggling became a common means of survival. Children crawled through the sewers to get beyond the walls of the ghetto to scavenge for food.

A year before the establishment of the ghetto, in October 1939, forced labour had been made compulsory for all Jewish men and boys aged fourteen to sixty. This was extended to boys aged twelve, in January 1940. As the German war effort intensified, the need for cheap labour increased. By the summer of 1940, the Jewish Council in Warsaw was asked to supply able-bodied Jewish men to work in labour camps; workers were not paid for their efforts. Failure to supply the number demanded led to mass round-ups in the streets.

With over 400,000 people crowded into an area of 1.3 square miles, personal hygiene was all but impossible. Many homes had no running water. Soap was a luxury, and there were just five public bathhouses.

Mary Wattenberg was enclosed in the Warsaw Ghetto from its beginning. The following extracts from her diary reflect the slow but inexorable descent into hell experienced by the Jews of Warsaw.

November 15th, 1940

Today the Jewish ghetto was officially established . . . Work on the walls, which will be three yards high, has already begun. Jewish masons, supervised by Nazi soldiers, are laying bricks upon bricks. Those who do not work hard enough are lashed. It makes me think of our slavery in Egypt. But where is the Moses who will release us from our new bondage? . . .

January 4th, 1941

The ghetto is covered with deep snow. The cold is terrible and none of the apartments are heated. The bitter cold makes the Nazi beasts who stand guard even more savage than usual. Just to warm up, they open fire every so often, and there are many victims among the passers-by . . .

June 12th, 1941

The ghetto is becoming more and more crowded due to a constant stream of new refugees. They are Jews from the provinces, who have been

9. A child has died from hunger in the Warsaw Ghetto, Poland.

10. Red Army riflemen advance through the rubble of Stalingrad,
between 16 and 18 September 1942.

11. T34 tanks advance during the Battle of Kursk, July 1943.

12. A Red Army nurse helps a wounded soldier at the front.

13. Citizens of Odessa greet a Red Army cavalryman after the city's liberation, 10 April 1944.

14. A Red Army tank commander leans over the barbed wire of a German concentration camp to greet a prisoner.

15. The body of a German woman in an SS armoured personnel carrier, the Battle of Berlin, April 1945.

16. A Red Army rifleman walks past a dead SS captain during the Battle of Berlin.

robbed of all their possessions. These people are ragged and barefoot, with the tragic eyes of the starving. Most of them are women and children. They become charges of the community, which sets them up in so-called homes. There they die sooner or later ...

June 26th, 1941

This is the first chance I have had to write since the opening of hostilities. The shock was tremendous. War between Germany and Russia! Who could have hoped that it would come so soon!' ...

July 29th, 1941

The typhus epidemic is raging. Yesterday the number of deaths exceeded two hundred. The doctors are throwing their hands up in despair. There are no medicines and the hospitals are overcrowded ...

September 20th, 1941

The Nazis are victorious. Kiev has fallen. Soon Himmler will be in Moscow. London is suffering severe bombardments. Will the Germans win this war? No, a thousand times no! Germany must be wiped off the face of the earth. Such people should not be allowed to exist ...

Friday 27 February, 1942

Every day when I go to school, I am not sure whether I will return alive. I have to go past two of the most dangerous German sentry posts. There is a guard who has been nicknamed "Frankenstein" because of his notorious cruelty. Apparently, this soldier cannot sleep unless he has had a few victims to his credit. He is a real sadist. This morning, I saw a familiar figure torturing a rickshaw driver, whose vehicle had passed an inch closer to the exit than the regulations permitted. A yellowish liquid dripped from his mouth to the pavement. Soon I realised he was dead, another victim of the German sadist. The blood was so horribly red and the sight of it completely shattered me ...

April 15th, 1942

Mrs Minc, a tenant in our house, related the details of a terrible massacre in Lublin. The Germans ordered all the Jews to gather in the square. The majority did not obey the order and hid in the cellars. Then elite guards began to fire at the windows, and anyone who left his house was shot on the spot. Little children were finished off with revolvers. About half the population was murdered and many more were deported to an unknown destination. Only about two thousand of the original forty thousand were left. They were sent to the Majdanek camp near Lublin. The victims have not yet been picked up. The houses are full of corpses.'

If it had not been bad enough before, the situation within the Warsaw Ghetto soon deteriorated. Marek Edelman, a cardiologist before the war, was an activist within the ghetto. When a new wave of executions began on 18 April 1942, he knew what would soon be the fate of the ghetto: *'Until that day, no matter how difficult life had been, the ghetto inhabitants felt that their everyday life, the very foundations of their existence, were based on something stabilised and durable . . . On April 18th, the very basis of ghetto life started to move from under people's feet . . . By now everybody understood that the ghetto was to be liquidated, but nobody yet realized that its entire population was destined to die.'*

The *Grossaktion* ('Great Action') *Warsaw* was the German code name for the liquidation of the Warsaw Ghetto. It began on 22 July 1942. The Jews were terrorised in daily round-ups, marched through the ghetto and assembled in a square outside the railway station for what was called 'resettlement in the east'. From there, they were transferred in overcrowded cattle trucks to the extermination camp in Treblinka. Up to 7,000 victims travelled twice a day, every day, the first in the early morning, and the second in the mid-afternoon. The deportations lasted until Yom Kippur, on 21 September. Treblinka was equipped with gas chambers disguised as showers for the 'processing' of the mass transportations of people.

Abraham Lewin kept a diary during the tragic events of 1942.

Wednesday 22nd July, 1942

A day of turmoil, chaos, and fear: the news about the expulsion of Jews is spreading like lightning through the town, Jewish Warsaw has suddenly died, the shops are closed. Jews run by, in confusion, terrified. The Jewish streets are an appalling sight – the gloom is indescribable. There are dead bodies at several places. Beggar children are being rounded up into wagons. I am thinking about my aged mother – it would be better to put her to sleep than to hand her over to those murderers.

Thursday 23 July, 1942

Disaster after disaster, misfortune after misfortune. Rain has been falling all day. Weeping. The Jews are weeping. They are hoping for a miracle. The expulsion is continuing. Terrible scenes. A woman with beautiful hair. A girl 20 years old, pretty. They are weeping and tearing at their hair. On Zamenhof Street the Germans pulled people out of a tram and killed them on the spot.

Friday 24 July, 1942

Jews are running as if insane, with children and bundles of bedding. Buildings on Karmelicka and Nowolipie Streets are being surrounded. Mothers and children wander around like lost sheep: where is my child? Weeping. Another wet day with heavy skies: rain is falling. The huge round-up on the streets. Old men and women, boys and girls are being dragged away. The police are carrying out the round-up, and officials of the Jewish community wearing white armbands are assisting them. The round-up was halted at three o'clock. How Jews saved themselves: fictitious marriages with policemen. Guta's marriage to her husband's brother. The savagery of the police during the round-up, the murderous brutality. They drag girls from the rickshaws, empty out flats, and leave the property strewn everywhere. A pogrom and a killing the like of which has never been seen. People get attacks of hysteria; 11,000 people have been rounded up; 100 policemen held hostage.

Saturday 25 July, 1942

Disaster: Terrible scenes in the streets. The police are carrying out elegant furniture from the homes of those who have been driven out. A policeman is crying. He is struck. "Why are you crying?" "My mother, my wife! Wife yes, mother no!" Last night there were a lot of suicides. By yesterday 25,000 had been taken away, with today 30,000. With each day the calamity worsens.'

By July 1942, Mary Wattenberg had been saved from the horror that awaited almost all the people she lived with in the ghetto. Because her mother was an American national, she and her sister, Anna, were sent together with her parents to Pawiak Prison, on 17 July. From there, the family could hear the gunfire, screams and destruction of the liquidation of the ghetto: *'The shootings and the cries coming from the streets are driving us mad. The nights are horrible. Last night forty people were shot under our windows. The slaughter lasted for two hours or more. The murderers finished off their victims with kicks and rifle butts.'* For week after week, Mary and her family listened to Warsaw's Jews being murdered or sent to their deaths in Treblinka.

When 1943 arrived, Mary made a sad entry on 1 January. The night before had been full of nightmares: *'I cannot stop thinking about the stories from Treblinka. I see before me tiled bathhouses filled with naked people choking in the hot steam. How many of my friends and relatives have perished there? How many young, unlived lives? I curse the New Year.'* Just two weeks later, Mary and her family were transferred to Vittel, in the Vosges, in north-east France, where they were held in an internment camp for British and American citizens, in a 'closed zone' under direct German control.

When SS and police units entered the ghetto on the eve of Passover, in April 1943, the streets were deserted. After months of planning, activists had decided to fight back. Many residents of the ghetto had gone into hiding places or bunkers. Their resistance was initiated by the Jewish Combat Organisation (*Żydowska Organizacja Bojowa*, ZOB) under its commander, Mordecai Anielewicz, who wrote an open letter to the inhabitants of the ghetto.

> To the Jewish Masses in the Ghetto
>
> We all remember well the days of terror during which 300,000 of our brothers and sisters were cruelly put to death in the death camp of Treblinka. Six months have passed of life in constant fear of death, not knowing what the next day may bring. We have received information from all sides about the destruction of the Jews in the Government-General, in Germany, in the occupied territories. When we listen to this bitter news, we wait for our own hour to come, every day and every moment. Today we must understand that the Nazi murderers have let us live only because they want to make use of our capacity to work to our last drop of blood and sweat, to our last breath. We are slaves, and when slaves are no longer profitable, they are killed. Everyone among us must understand that, and everyone among us must remember it always.

Armed with home-made pistols, grenades and a few automatic weapons and rifles, the ZOB fighters forced the Germans to retreat beyond the ghetto wall. On the third day of the resistance, the SS began razing the ghetto to the ground, building by building, to force the remaining Jews out of hiding.

Marek Edelman witnessed the destruction: *'Fires were raging over the entire block. Black smoke choked one's throat, burned one's eyes ... The sea of flames flooded houses and courtyards. Thousands of people perished. The stench of burning bodies was everywhere. Charred corpses lay around on balconies, in window recesses, on unburned steps. Thousands committed suicide. They jumped from buildings with their children in their arms.*

Tired beyond all belief, we would fall asleep, anywhere, everywhere and would often catch a German bullet. Nobody even noticed that an old man sleeping in a doorway would never wake up, or that a mother feeding her baby had been dead for three days and that her crying baby's sucking was futile because its mothers arms were cold, her breast dry.'

Jewish resistance fighters made sporadic raids from their bunkers, but the Germans systematically reduced the ghetto to rubble. The German forces killed Anielewicz and those with him in an attack on the ZOB command bunker, which they captured on 8 May. Edelman described what happened: *'On May 8th, detachments of Germans and Ukrainians surrounded our HQ. The fighting lasted two hours. When they realised that they would be unable to take the bunker by storm, they threw in a gas bomb. Whoever survived the bullets, whoever was not gassed committed suicide. Nobody even considered being taken alive. Lutek Rotblat shot his mother, sister, then himself. Thus 80 per cent of the remaining partisans perished, among them Mordecai Anielewicz.'*

Although German forces eventually broke the resistance, individuals and small groups fought the Germans for almost a month.

Marek Edelman was one of a handful who escaped the ghetto: *'All night we walked through the sewers, crawling through entanglements built by the Germans. There were hand grenade booby traps and piles of rubble. In a sewer twenty-eight inches high, it was impossible to stand up straight and the water reached our lips. Every minute someone lost consciousness. Thirst was the worst handicap. Some even drank the thick, slimy sewer water. Every second seemed like months. It took us forty-eight hours to get out.'*

According to the official German report, the Germans captured 56,065 Jews and destroyed 631 bunkers; 7,000 Jews died during the rebellion, and another 7,000 were deported to Treblinka.

After not writing for a while, Mary Wattenberg resumed her diary in June. She was still interned in Vittel.

'June 15th, 1943

We who have been rescued from the ghetto are ashamed to look at each other. Why is it so beautiful in this part of the world? Here everything smells of sun and flowers; in Warsaw there is only blood, the blood of my own people. God, why must there be all this cruelty? I am ashamed. Here I am breathing fresh air and there my people are suffocating in gas and perishing in flames, burned alive. Why?'

In March 1944, Mary and her family boarded a train for Lisbon. After their departure, many of the inmates of Vittel, including Mary's room-mate, were transferred back to Poland to their deaths at Auschwitz. Under a hot sun and brilliant blue sky, the family arrived in New York harbour on 5 March. It was an exhilarating moment for Mary, who was just nineteen. However, the nightmares stayed with her for the rest of her life: *'The feeling of freedom took my breath away. In the last four years I have not known that feeling. Four years of the black swastika; of barbed wire, ghetto walls, executions and, above all, terror – terror by day and terror by night. I found it hard to enjoy my freedom. I imagined it was just a dream; that at any moment I would wake and see the aged men with grey beards, the blooming young girls, and proud young men, driven like cattle to their deaths. I even fancied that I heard the cries of the tortured, and the salty smell of the sea suddenly changed into the nauseating, sweetish odour of human blood.'*

The last chapter in Warsaw's suffering began on 1 August 1944. Ten months earlier, in November 1943, General Tadeusz Komorowski (code-named 'Bór'), commander of the Home Army (AK), had planned a series of local uprisings against the Wehrmacht, timed to precede the liberation of Poland, in advance of the Red Army's attacks westwards. The original plan was hatched by the Polish government-in-exile, in London.

After the Red Army appeared along the east bank of the Vistula

River, Komorowski announced the outbreak of the Warsaw Uprising, on 31 July 1944. The AK anticipated that the uprising would take only a few days and would free Warsaw before the Soviets entered the city. Approximately 45,000 members of the AK, under the command of Colonel Antoni Chruściel (code-named 'Monter'), began the uprising. Only a quarter of the partisans had access to weapons. They were opposed by 25,000 German soldiers equipped with artillery, tanks and planes.

Despite poor tactical coordination and some overzealous, amateurish actions by untrained enthusiasts, Polish forces took over several districts of Warsaw within the first few days, including the Old Town. After the initial success of the AK, German troops slowly recaptured the city, using their superiority in men and weapons, and surrounded the Old Town.

Although there was some substance in Red Army claims that its army was exhausted and its lines of supply too stretched to mount a crossing of the Vistula to liberate Warsaw, the real reason for its sudden pause was Stalin's mendacity. It was clearly in the Kremlin's interest to let the Wehrmacht annihilate the pro-Western AK before sending in the Red Army. Both Churchill and Roosevelt tried to persuade Stalin to help – and they even attempted supply drops into the city – but sadly, humanitarian appeals to Stalin were destined to be futile.

From the beginning of the uprising, German troops systematically took revenge on civilians. The bloodiest action against the inhabitants took place between 5 and 7 August, when at least 40,000 men, women and children were murdered during massacres in the district of Wola. Mass deportations of civilians also took place, with the victims sent to either labour camps or concentration camps.

After more than two weeks of combat, the last Polish soldiers left the Old Town through the sewers on 2 September. Warsaw's ancient heart was destroyed; the district was turned into ruins. Towards the end of September, German forces took control of the rest of Warsaw, systematically razing the city to the ground. The number of victims exceeded 180,000 people. More than 11,000 AK soldiers were captured as prisoners of war, including 'Bór' and 'Monter'.

The uprising became another tragic episode for the Jews of Warsaw. The number of Jews who fought remains unknown, because many of them joined the AK under false names after escaping from the ghetto. On 5 August, one of the AK battalions liberated 348 Jews from Gęsiówka, a concentration camp located in the former Warsaw Ghetto. The majority of them joined the Polish Home Army and fought in the uprising.

Several dozen members of ZOB who had survived the ghetto resistance in 1943 were still in the city when the Warsaw Uprising broke out. Under the command of former ghetto fighters Itzhak Zukerman, Zivia Lubetkin and Marek Edelman, ZOB organized an independent Jewish platoon (ZOB Group). Zukerman became its commander. They all survived the Warsaw Uprising.

By January 1945, fully 85 per cent of Warsaw had been destroyed. The Red Army continued its advance on 12 January. Five days later the 1st Polish Army marched into the ruins of the devastated city, the long-awaited harbingers of Stalin's troops.

•

Warsaw was not alone in its suffering. The Łódź Ghetto was the second largest of Poland's Jewish ghettos. It became a major industrial centre, manufacturing war supplies for the Wehrmacht. The number of people incarcerated in the ghetto was increased further by the Jews deported from other occupied territories.

In early 1944, the fate of the Łódź Ghetto had been decided by the Nazi hierarchy. The initial wave of deportations to Chełmno extermination camp, thirty miles north of Łódź, took place between 23 June and 14 July 1944. When, on 1 August, the Warsaw Uprising began, the fate of those remaining in Łódź was sealed. During the last phase of its existence, 25,000 inmates were murdered at Chełmno, their bodies burned immediately. As the Red Army approached, the remaining Jews were sent to Auschwitz to be killed.

When Łódź was liberated by the Red Army, on 19 January 1945, only 877 Jews were still alive, 12 of whom were children. Of the 223,000 Jews in Łódź who were locked into the ghetto after the invasion of Poland, in April 1940, only about 10,000 survived the

Holocaust in other places. A diary written by an unknown Jewish boy bears witness to the emotions of those trapped in the ghetto. He wrote in the margins of a discarded nineteenth-century French novel by François Coppée, ironically titled *Les Vrais Riches* (*The Truly Rich*), in four languages: Hebrew, Yiddish, Polish and English. The diary is short but intense, spanning May to August 1944. The entries document the news, in June of that year, that deportations were about to begin again after an interval of a year and a half. The confusion and uncertainty of the ghetto population are palpable.

June 12th [written in Hebrew] *I suffer terribly but I still dream of a better future, of a more beautiful life, free and humane . . .*

June 16th [written in Polish] *We are suffering so much . . . Again, they are getting 500 people ready to be sent out of the ghetto. Again, uncertainty overtakes us. Oh! Was all our suffering in vain? If they annihilate us now in their usual manner, why didn't we die in the early days of the war?! My little sister complains that she has lost all will to live – how tragic this is! Why, she is only 12 years old. Will there be no end to our suffering? If so, how? Oh God, oh humanity, where are you? . . .*

July 10th [written in Yiddish] *We are now facing the terrible question of our fate, of our survival. We know that every Jew yet living makes his* [the German beast's] *heart heavier, that he still lusts for our blood. The men, women, children killed, executed, buried alive are still not enough for his insatiable murderous stomach. Now, in his final moments, he's got hold of Hungarian Jewry, solving the problem his way. What then will happen to us?! Can he accept the thought of a few broken Jews – just skulls – still alive? . . . One still wants to live. We all know that after death there is no revenge – and in all of us there burns such hate for the Germans, such yearning for revenge – that we must live on!!! . . .*

July 21st [written in Polish] *At present, mixed feelings possess us; at one moment we are full of hope, in another we are seized by that so well-founded resignation, to the point of feeling choked. Because can one suppose that they would let us live? . . .*

July 25th [written in Hebrew] *Two hours past midnight. I can't sleep because of the bedbugs and my own agitation. For five years I kept my patience, and now it's suddenly gone. One can feel the coming liberation in the air. The Russians have captured Lublin. In Germany there was an attempt on Hitler's life. They want to end a war they definitely oppose. The end is knocking on our doors. Another moment and, if they let us alone, we'll be free. Just the idea makes me cry . . .*

August 3rd [written in English] *When I look at my sister, my heart is melting. She has fought so heroically the last five years. Oh God in heaven, why didst thou create Germans to destroy humanity? I cannot write more. I am resigned terribly and black spirited.'*

The final liquidation of the Łódź Ghetto began four days after the young diarist's last entry. He took the diary with him to Auschwitz, where he perished. The diary was found there after the war and is now stored in the archives of the Yad Vashem Holocaust Memorial Centre, in Jerusalem.

The Red Army liberated the Auschwitz concentration camp complex when a soldier from the 100th Infantry Division entered the camp around nine o'clock on the morning of Saturday, 27 January 1945. There were 7,000 prisoners alive in the three main camps, 500 in the other sub-camps, and over 600 corpses. Tellingly, there were also 837,000 items of women's clothing, 370,000 men's suits, 44,000 pairs of shoes, and 7,000 kg of human hair, estimated by the Soviet War Crimes Commission to have come from 140,000 people. The author Primo Levi described seeing the first four soldiers on horseback approach Auschwitz III, where he had been in the sick bay. They threw *'strangely embarrassed glances at the sprawling bodies, at the battered huts and at us few still alive . . . They did not greet us, nor did they smile; they seemed oppressed not only by compassion but by a confused restraint, which sealed their lips and bound their eyes to the funereal scene. It was that shame we knew so well, the shame that drowned us after the selections, and every time we had to watch, or submit to, some outrage: the shame the Germans did not know, that the just man experiences at another man's crime; the feeling of guilt that such a crime should exist, that it should have been introduced irrevocably into the world of things that exist, and that his will for good should have proved too weak or null, and should not have availed in defence.'*

Georgii Elisavetskii, one of the Soviet soldiers who entered Auschwitz, said in 1980 that when his fellow Red Army soldiers told the inmates, 'You are free, comrades!' they did not respond, so he tried in Russian, Polish, German, Ukrainian. Then he spoke in Yiddish: *'They think that I am provoking them. They begin to hide. And only when I said to them, "Do not be afraid, I am a colonel of the Soviet Army and a Jew. We have come to liberate you" . . . Finally, as if the barrier collapsed . . . they rushed towards us shouting, fell on their knees, kissed the flaps of our overcoats, and threw their arms around our legs.'*

Vasily Grossman, himself Jewish, found what he saw and heard about the death camp at Treblinka almost impossible to commit to paper. In over 15,000 words of gruesome detail he described crimes that are unbearable to read. In one passage he detailed the terrible violations of Josef Hirtreiter, just one of the SS monsters who had free rein in the camps.

'This creature specialised in the killing of children. Evidently endowed with unusual strength, it would suddenly snatch a child out of the crowd, swing him or her about like a cudgel and then either smash their head against the ground or simply tear them in half. When I first heard about this creature – supposedly human, supposedly born of a woman – I could not believe the unthinkable things I was told. But when I heard these stories repeated by eyewitnesses, when I realised that these witnesses saw them as mere details, entirely in keeping with everything else about the hellish regime of Treblinka, then I came to believe that what I had heard was true.'

Despite the feelings of disgust such atrocities evoked in Grossman, he was clear that their horror should not be eschewed, either for the sake of propriety or out of any misplaced sense of decency. It is fitting that the last word on the horrors of the Holocaust should go to him.

'It is infinitely hard even to read this. The reader must believe me, it is hard to write it. Someone might ask: "Why write about this, why remember all that?" It is the writer's duty to tell this terrible truth, and it is the civil duty of the reader to learn it. Everyone who would turn away, who would shut his eyes and walk past, would insult the memory of the dead.'

PART FIVE

GÖTTERDÄMMERUNG

24

THE RED TIDE

SEPTEMBER 1944–FEBRUARY 1945

Although Operation Bagration formally concluded at the end of August, such was its momentum that subsequent offensives unfolded in rapid succession. The Red Army was riding a rip tide; the Wehrmacht, whose defences were no better than lines drawn in the sand, was swept away by relentless waves of men and machines.

Zhukov wrote a summary of the impact of Bagration: '*147 divisions were crushed. As a result, the German defensive line was broken over a 2,200-km* [1,375-mile] *stretch from the western Dvina* [which flows through Latvia into the Baltic Sea at the Gulf of Riga] *to the Black Sea. In some sectors our troops advanced up to 700 km* [430 miles].'

Many in Hitler's regime, including senior men in the Wehrmacht, knew that Hitler was, day by day, condemning Germany to oblivion. After numerous failed assassination attempts – historians have uncovered evidence of at least forty-two – on 20 July 1944, only extraordinary good fortune saved the Führer's life. Led by Colonel Claus von Stauffenberg, Operation Valkyrie was an attempt to kill Hitler and, in a subsequent coup d'état, replace him as leader. Stauffenberg planted a bomb under the conference table in Hitler's Wolf's Lair, in Rastenburg, East Prussia. When the bomb detonated, it killed four people and inflicted injuries on almost all the survivors. However, the heavy solid-oak leg of the table shielded Hitler, who received only minor wounds.

The failure of the assassination attempt and the intended military coup led the Gestapo to arrest more than 7,000 people, 4,980 of whom were executed. Stauffenberg was shot by firing squad. Several others were executed by slow strangulation. Before he was killed,

Stauffenberg's brother, Berthold, was hanged and then revived multiple times. The hangings and multiple resuscitations were filmed for Hitler to view at his leisure. After Valkyrie, there were no more attempts on Hitler's life. The failure of Valkyrie almost certainly condemned Europe to eight more months of suffering.

On 20 August, at the southern extreme of the Eastern Front, the Red Army's 2nd and 3rd Ukrainian Fronts, a force over 1.3 million strong, overwhelmed the largely Romanian Axis forces, making the defeat of their country inevitable. On 23 August, in an anti-Axis coup led by King Michael I, Romania transferred its allegiance to the Allies. In a radio broadcast to the Romanian nation, King Michael ordered a ceasefire, declared Romania's loyalty to the Allies, announced the acceptance of an armistice offered by them, and declared war on Germany. The coup allowed the Red Army to make a rapid advance into Romania. It also led to inevitable Soviet occupation and the capture of at least 130,000 Romanian soldiers, who were transported to Stalin's gulags.

The next Axis domino to fall was Bulgaria, which had never declared war on the Soviet Union. When the 3rd Ukrainian Front approached its border, Bulgaria insisted on its neutrality, ordered the disarming of Wehrmacht troops retreating from Romania, and asked Britain and the United States for an armistice. On 5 September, the Soviet Union declared war on Bulgaria and prepared to invade. Zhukov was sent by Stalin to oversee the invasion. He was asked to consult Georgi Dimitrov, leader of the Bulgarian Communist Party, who told Zhukov: *'Although you are going to prepare for war against Bulgaria, I can assure you that the Soviet forces will not be met with artillery and machine-gun fire, but with bread and salt, according to our old Slav tradition.'*

Zhukov then flew to Pitesti, the headquarters of the 3rd Ukrainian Front. He described what happened next: *'On the morning of September 8th, everything was ready to open fire, but from our observation post we did not see any targets we could shell. When the Red Army advanced, Nikolai Gagen, the 57th Army commander, reported that a Bulgarian infantry division was lined up on both sides of the road, welcoming our troops with unfurled red banners and military music. I immediately phoned Stalin. He told me, "Don't disarm the Bulgarian troops. Let them be while they are waiting for orders from their government." [...]'* A new Bulgarian government was appointed on 9 September, which immediately declared war on Germany. The Bulgarian army later joined the Red Army's advance into Yugoslavia.

For Germany, the situation worsened by the day. In the west, the liberation of Paris, on 29 August, finally brought to an end the already-disgraced Vichy regime of Marshal Pétain. Although Pétain, whom de Gaulle described as 'successively banal, then glorious, then deplorable, but never mediocre', was a collaborator, rather than an ally, Hitler was losing friends as quickly as he was losing territory. In the east, an uprising in Slovakia coincided with the liberation of Paris, ending German dominance of the republic.

On 2 September, Finland accepted an armistice with the Soviet Union. A ceasefire was announced, and Finland ended its ties with Germany, agreeing to disarm any German troops on its territory. German forces in the south of Finland withdrew in haste, while in the north they began to move into Norway. Meanwhile, Allied forces had launched another assault on Western Europe when they landed on the Côte d'Azur, in the South of France, on 15 August. Germany was under attack from all points of the compass, and on four fronts.

The Wehrmacht was not only overwhelmed by vastly superior Allied numbers, but its materiel resources were dwindling at an alarming rate. By September, following the loss of the Romanian oilfields and the devastation wrought by Allied air attacks on its hydrogenation plants that produced oil from coal, German petrol production was at only 8 per cent of what it had been in April. The Red Army, with its boot on the neck of the Wehrmacht, showed no mercy. New offensives on the Eastern Front were launched in quick succession: 8 September, the Eastern Carpathians; 14 September, the Baltic; 28 September, Yugoslavia; 29 October, Hungary. The Soviets committed almost 300 divisions to these offensives, close to 4 million men, more than double the number available to the Wehrmacht in both the east and the west.

Gabriel Temkin was still with 458th Rifle Regiment in the Carpathian offensive, where he witnessed a vision of medieval history: 'Mile-long caterpillars of horse-drawn carts carrying Russian soldiers and their supplies were moving at top speed on all Transylvania–Romanian roads. The only troops getting ahead of us were Red Army cavalry divisions, mainly Cossacks. They disappeared in front of us as quickly as they suddenly appeared, squadron after squadron, galloping through the dust on their splendid horses. Scenes like these had not been seen here since the times of the Huns, Magyars and Mongols when they overran Europe. It was an impressive military operation, bringing us the quickest possible arrival at the Hungarian border. As Möngke Khan [Great Khan of the Mongol Empire, grandson of Genghis Khan, older brother of Kublai Khan] said in a letter to King Louis IX of France in 1254, seven hundred years later we "made near what was far".'

Hungary remained Hitler's last European Axis ally – if the country fell, it would be the final domino in the demise of his partners on the Eastern Front. Its regent, Admiral Miklós Horthy, a political realist who had supported Hitler while simultaneously trying to keep him at arm's length, was caught in an unenviable trap. In January 1943, Hungary's commitment to the war effort, which had never been enthusiastic, had suffered a severe setback. The Red Army, emboldened by its success after the Battle of Stalingrad, cut through the Romanian Army on the Don and destroyed the 2nd Hungarian Army, which suffered 80,000 casualties.

Hitler blamed Hungary's Jews for the defeat and demanded that Horthy punish the 800,000 Jews still living in the country. In response, later claiming that he knew nothing about the death camps, Horthy and his government tried to placate Hitler by supplying 10,000 Jewish deportees for labour battalions. Realising the likelihood that the Allies would defeat Germany, Horthy now began to approach them in the hope of a negotiated surrender.

Unfortunately for the people of Hungary, Hitler was never going to allow the country to leave a huge hole in his defences, in the heart of Europe. In March 1944, while Horthy was in Salzburg negotiating with him, Hitler sent the Wehrmacht into Hungary. As a consequence of the Nazi occupation, another significant element of the Holocaust was put in place. With the collaboration of new Hungarian authorities, Adolf Eichmann began the transportation of 550,000 Hungarian Jews, as well as Jews from Czechoslovakia, Romania and Yugoslavia, to the Nazi death camps.

With the Red Army now starting to fight on Axis territory, the desire for victory within its ranks began to be replaced by a hunger for vengeance. Soon Gabriel Temkin's romantic imagery from medieval history was replaced by scenes of brutality and terror: '*The "Frontovaya Gazeta"* ["Front Newspaper"] *lectured us about how the Hungarian troops, together with their Nazi allies, behaved abominably at Voronezh, on the Don, and at Kiev. "We are entering the enemy's den, we will avenge."* . . . *Ill-discipline worsened as the war progressed and especially when we entered Hungary. The desire "to avenge" was widespread. And the simplest way to avenge was to prevail over the enemy's women. I recall a send-off from one of our commanding officers. "Men! Ahead of you is a city, and there are wine and women there, as much as you desire."* [. . .]'

British Prime Minister Winston Churchill began a ten-day visit to Moscow on 9 October 1944. The 'Big Three' were still carving up post-war Europe, but Roosevelt stayed in Washington. Churchill and Stalin met in private, with only their interpreters present. Just as Roosevelt had tried to isolate Britain in his private meeting with Stalin in Tehran, Churchill tried to do the same to the Americans in Moscow.

Valentin Berezhkov interpreted for Stalin: '*Churchill said, "We have to talk about two countries. One is Greece, the other Romania. We are not too worried about the latter. However, Greece is another matter. Britain must be the leader in the Mediterranean and I hope Marshal Stalin will recognise our central role in Greece, just as I am prepared to recognise Marshal Stalin's role in Romania." Stalin showed understanding, saying Britain would have a serious problem if it didn't control the Mediterranean. "I think," the British prime minister continued, "we should couch these ideas in diplomatic terms, avoiding terms like 'division of spheres of interest', as that would shock the Americans. In my opinion, the United States claims too many rights for itself, leaving limited opportunities for the Soviet Union and Great Britain." Churchill then produced a piece of paper from his breast pocket and pushed it towards Stalin. "I have this naughty document." [. . .]'*

Churchill's piece of paper has been called the 'Percentages Agreement'. It listed five states – Romania, Greece, Yugoslavia, Hungary and Bulgaria – with percentage splits of each, according to the scale of Soviet control and British/American control.

Berezhkov noted: *'There was a long silence. Stalin looked at the numbers carefully, without saying a word. Then he took one of his favourite coloured pencils and put a tick in the paper's top corner. Churchill then said, "Might it not be thought rather cynical if it seemed that we had disposed of these issues, so fateful to millions of people, in such an offhand manner? Let's burn the paper." "No, you keep it." Churchill folded it away and put it in his pocket.'*

As their leaders manoeuvred and schemed, for the troops on the ground there were still many battles to be fought, lives to be lost, bodies to be maimed. In between the two opposing factions, civilians were still caught in the crossfire, and the Holocaust victims were still going to their deaths in droves.

Inevitably, Budapest was the anvil upon which the Red Army hammered its Axis enemies into submission. It also provided a foretaste of what was to come when the avenging armies from the East eventually reached German soil.

The Soviet attack on Budapest began on 29 October 1944, with a force of more than 1 million strong. By 7 November, Red Army and Romanian troops were in the eastern suburbs of the city, just twelve miles from its heart by the Danube. By the end of December, the city was entirely surrounded. Over 30,000 German soldiers and almost 40,000 Hungarians, as well as over 800,000 civilians, were trapped within the city. Hitler refused to allow a withdrawal and declared *Festung Budapest* ('Fortress Budapest'), which was to be defended to the last man.

To make matters worse, Stalin insisted that the city be taken as soon as possible. With his eye firmly on the future division of Europe, and with the 'Big Three' Yalta Conference only weeks away, he wanted as many bargaining chips in his hand as possible.

The urban fighting in the city took on an intensity which resembled Stalingrad, and the city's sewers became part of the battleground. On 17 January 1945, Hitler allowed the defenders to abandon the flat terrain of Pest, and cross the Danube to the hills of Buda, which were easier to defend. The fighting became even more merciless.

Hitler refused to sanction a German breakout, but on the night of 11 February, almost 30,000 German and Hungarian troops attempted to leave the city in three waves. Thousands of civilians accompanied each wave. Entire families, young and old, with whatever possessions they could carry, tried a desperate dash for the countryside. The weather was unforgiving, with snow on the ground and a heavy frost. Unfortunately, the Soviet and Romanian troops were lying in wait in prepared positions.

The first wave managed to surprise the waiting Soviet soldiers and artillery, and many were able to escape. The second and third waves were less fortunate; thousands were killed. Soviet artillery and rocket batteries bracketed the escape area, with deadly results for thousands of escapees. Despite heavy losses, at least 5,000 civilians managed to reach the wooded hills north-west of Budapest and escape towards Vienna. However, only a few hundred German and Hungarian soldiers reached the German lines.

Once Budapest was taken, the Red Army went on the rampage. Hungary was not Germany, but Hungarian soldiers had committed atrocities and they were part of the Axis onslaught that had pillaged Mother Russia. In the mind of the ordinary Soviet rifleman, the Hungarian capital was fair game. Excesses of food and wine led to drunken soldiers running amok through the city. Women and girls were rounded up and locked in Soviet military barracks where they were raped repeatedly. There was also a report that Red Army soldiers had broken into a mental hospital where they had raped and killed female patients aged from sixteen to sixty. The Hungarian writer Gyula Háy was in Budapest in 1945, and observed: *'It was impossible to spend a day or even an hour in Budapest without hearing of brutalities committed by* [Russian] *soldiers.'*

Such was the scale of the appalling behaviour of the Red Army in Budapest, the communists of Köbánya, a suburban district of Pest, sent an appeal to the Soviet Command.

Among the workers of Köbánya, there were very few who sympathised with the Germans, and the majority hate the fascists. But suddenly there was an explosion of insane and frenzied hatred. Drunken soldiers raped women before their children and husbands. They took twelve-year-old girls from their mothers to be raped by groups of ten to fifteen soldiers, among whom were many with venereal diseases. After the first group, others would come, who followed the example of their predecessors. Several of our comrades were killed when they tried to defend their wives and daughters.

The Red Army hierarchy did little to curtail the behaviour of its soldiers. Indeed, indifference went all the way to the Kremlin. When Milovan Djilas, A Yugoslav partisan leader, complained to Stalin about Red Army soldiers raping Yugoslav women (the Red Army, with the support of Marshal Tito's Yugoslav partisans, had been fighting in Yugoslavia since the autumn of 1944), Stalin sent a telling reply.

You have, of course, read Dostoevsky? Do you see what a complicated thing is a man's soul, a man's psyche? Well then, imagine a man who has fought from Stalingrad to Belgrade, over thousands of kilometres of his own devastated land, across the dead bodies of his comrades and dearest ones. How can such a man react normally? And what is so awful in his having fun with a woman after such horrors? You have imagined the Red Army to be ideal, it is not ideal, nor can it be . . . The important thing is that it fights Germans.

Before the Red Army arrived, Budapest had been living with its own horrific events for over a year. The German takeover of the country had brought to power the fascist Arrow Cross Party and its leader, Ferenc Szálasi, who took to the task of supporting Hitler's extermination of the Jewish race with relish.

Gabriel Temkin was in Budapest with the Red Army, where he discovered the atrocities that had been committed by the Arrow Cross against its own people: 'Members of the Arrow Cross became increasingly violent. They would enter Jewish houses, looting, shooting at random, raping. Many Jews were horribly tortured before being dragged to the Danube and shot so that their bodies would be carried away by the river. The favourite method of the Arrow Cross was to handcuff the Jews together in threes, strip them naked, line them up facing the river, then shoot the middle of the three in the back of the head so that the victim would drag the other two with them when they fell into the Danube.'

Thankfully, there were significant numbers of Jewish survivors in Budapest, as Temkin discovered: 'When Pest was taken, we found about 70,000 Jews alive there in the general ghetto, while in the International Ghetto there were about 25,000 survivors. Later on, when Buda was captured, another 25,000 hidden Jews, often with "Aryan" papers, were rescued. In all, some 120,000 Jews of Budapest were saved by the Red Army.'

In and among the stories of horror, there were some examples of the more compassionate face of humanity. Zinaida Vasilyevna, who with her sister, Olga, had ridden with the Cossacks on the Volga in 1942, was a medical assistant in a cavalry squadron: 'Near Budapest . . . It was winter . . . I was carrying a wounded sergeant, the commander of a machine-gun crew. I see this blackish snow . . . charred . . . I realise that it's a deep shell hole, which is what I need. I go down into the hole and there's someone alive and I hear a mechanical scraping . . . I turn and there's a wounded German officer, wounded in the legs, lying there and aiming his sub-machine gun at me . . . When I turned, he saw my face, realised I was a girl and went, "Ha-a-ha" . . . He relaxed and threw aside his gun. So, the three of us are in the same hole. The hole is small, our legs touch. I'm covered with their blood; our blood mingles. The German has such huge eyes and he looks at me with those eyes.

What am I going to do? Cursed fascist! The German just stares at me . . . I remember those eyes even now. I'm bandaging our man and the other one is lying in blood, he's losing blood, one of his legs is completely smashed. A little longer and he'll die. And, before I finished bandaging our man, I tore up the German's clothes and bandaged his leg. The

German says, "Gut, gut." When the ambulance came, I pulled them both out . . . and put them in. The German too.'

Budapest was also the setting for one of the war's most life-affirming stories, one which confirms that, even in the midst of brutal atrocities, there are always those who offer hope and salvation. Swedish businessman Raoul Wallenberg arrived in Budapest at the beginning of July 1944. He had been recruited by the US War Refugee Board (WRB) and travelled to Hungary with the status of a diplomat to the Swedish Legation. Despite having no experience as a diplomat, he led one of the Holocaust's most extensive and successful rescue efforts. His work prevented the deportation of thousands of Hungarian Jews.

By July 1944, the Hungarians and the Germans had deported nearly 440,000 Jews from Hungary. Almost all of them had been sent to Auschwitz-Birkenau, where the SS killed approximately 320,000 of them immediately, upon arrival, and used the rest as forced labourers. Nearly 200,000 Jews remained in Budapest. Validated by the Swedish Legation, Wallenberg issued a *Schutzpass* [a 'certificate of protection'] to Jews in Budapest. He established hospitals, nurseries and a soup kitchen, as well as more than thirty safe houses that formed the basis of the International Ghetto in the city.

After the Arrow Cross Party seized power, during the autumn of 1944, it forced tens of thousands of Budapest's Jews to march westwards to the border with Austria. Wallenberg intervened to release as many people as he could from these columns of lost souls. Wallenberg was not alone. Carl Lutz, the consul general in the Swiss Legation, issued 'Certificates of Emigration', placing nearly 50,000 Jews in Budapest under Swiss protection as potential emigrants to Palestine. Italian businessman Giorgio Perlasca posed as a Spanish diplomat. Closely assisted by Hungarians Laszlo and Eugenia Szamosi, Perlasca issued his own 'Certificates of Protection', validated by nations whose interests neutral Spain represented, and established safe houses, including one for Jewish children.

Wallenberg was last seen with Soviet officials on 17 January 1945. It is presumed that he was detained on suspicion of espionage;

like so many people who had a track record of resisting oppression, Wallenberg was not the sort of man that Stalin would have wanted in his post-war Eastern Europe. He was never seen again. It is difficult to estimate how many people were saved by Wallenberg and his associates, but most sources agree that it was at least 30,000.

After its liberation, Budapest was in ruins, with more than 80 per cent of its buildings destroyed or damaged. Thousands of ethnic Germans within Hungary, along with more than 500,000 Hungarians, were arrested and transported to Soviet forced labour camps. The Battle for Budapest was a final rehearsal before the colossal tumult of the Battle of Berlin.

25

THE JUGGERNAUT

JANUARY–MARCH 1945

Stavka's initial planning for 1945, approved by Stalin in November 1944, anticipated the fall of Berlin in a month and a half. That proved to be too optimistic. Even though it faced overwhelming odds in men and materiel, the Wehrmacht's ability to defend almost-impossible positions was formidable.

The Soviet Union had become an enormous machine of war. The Red Army was its cutting edge, but behind it was an industrial juggernaut of massive proportions. The gauge of Poland's railways was converted to the wider Soviet version, allowing vast quantities of materiel, estimated to have been 132,000 railcars of supplies, to be transported westwards for an almighty assault on Germany. At least 10 million artillery and mortar rounds and almost 40 million gallons of fuel were brought up. Indicative of what that kind of firepower meant is the fact that at both Stalingrad and on the Don Front, fewer than 1 million rounds were fired.

The March on Berlin would in fact take four months and was conducted in four phases: the Vistula–Oder Offensive, from 12 January to 3 February; the East Prussian Offensive, from 13 January to 25 February; the East Pomeranian Offensive, from 10 February to 4 April; and the Battle of Berlin, from 16 April to 8 May.

When the Vistula–Oder Offensive began in the frozen darkness of the early morning of 12 January, the shattered remnants of the Wehrmacht's Army Group South, outnumbered at least 5:1, faced almost 2.5 million refreshed and resupplied Red Army opponents. The Red Army had 6,400 tanks and assault guns; the Wehrmacht could muster only about 1,200 panzers.

Hitler made matters worse when he refused his generals' requests to reinforce their position by bringing in men from elsewhere. At the same time, he ordered that an entire panzer army be sent to Hungary.

The Red Army already had bridgeheads across the Vistula. Its initial target, Frankfurt-an-der-Oder, due west via Łódź, lay less than 300 miles away, across the plains of central Poland.

The attack brought swift results and shocking discoveries. The Front's Military Council report to Stalin after it surveyed Warsaw read:

> The fascist barbarians have destroyed Warsaw. With sadistic cruelty the Hitlerites demolished one block of houses after another. The industrial enterprises have been razed to the ground. Thousands upon thousands of civilians have been exterminated, the rest driven out. It is a dead city.

Zhukov documented the widespread desire for revenge: *'Polish officers and men took the destruction of the city especially hard. I saw battle-scarred Polish soldiers shed tears and pledge there and then to take revenge on their fiendish foe. As for Soviet soldiers, we were all embittered and determined to aptly punish the enemy for the atrocities committed.'*

The Red Army was sweeping across Poland: its tanks at a rate of thirty miles a day; its infantry at twenty miles a day. Łódź and Poznan fell, Breslau soon followed. The German response consisted of a bewildering reorganisation and renaming of its units, the deployment of *Volkssturm* units (a national militia, literally 'People's Storm') and the redesignation of Luftwaffe pilots and Kriegsmarine sailors as infantry.

The Red Army reached the Oder River north of Küstrin on 31 January, and by 3 February it had control of the river at Zehden, south of Stettin. Although the Germans still held bridgeheads east of the river, the Soviets had bridgeheads north of Küstrin and south of Frankfurt-an-der-Oder. In less than three weeks, the Soviets had completed one of the most breathtaking advances of the war, almost 300 miles. From Küstrin, it was only forty miles to Berlin.

The East Prussian Offensive began simultaneously with the Vistula–Oder Offensive, on 13 January, and was conducted northwards towards the Baltic, with the ports of Königsberg and Danzig as the primary objectives. Although the Red Army quickly encircled Wehrmacht forces in several places, the Germans continued to resist for weeks, even when they were many miles behind the front line. Not surprisingly, casualty rates were extremely high among both soldiers and civilians.

Unfortunately, the Red Army advance was unable to save the inmates of the Stutthof concentration camp, twenty-one miles east of Danzig. Stutthof was the first German concentration camp set up outside German borders and had been in operation from 2 September 1939. It would also be the last camp to be liberated by the Allies, on 9 May 1945.

The Germans began evacuating the prisoners from Stutthof on 25 January. There were nearly 50,000 prisoners, the majority of them Jews, in Stutthof and its sub-camps. About 5,000 from the sub-camps were marched to the Baltic coast, forced into the water, and machine-gunned. The rest of the prisoners were marched westwards but were cut off by the Red Army encirclement and so were marched back to the camp. The severe winter weather and the brutality of the SS guards led to thousands of deaths.

In late April, the surviving prisoners were removed to the coast. Once again, hundreds of prisoners were forced into the sea and shot. Over 4,000 were sent by small boats to Germany, some to the Neuengamme concentration camp near Hamburg, and others to camps along the Baltic coast. Many drowned along the way. When the Red Army finally liberated Stutthof, it rescued barely 100 prisoners who had managed to hide.

Steven Springfield was transferred to Stutthof in 1944 with his brother: *The conditions in Stutthof were beyond description. People were dying left and right from hunger. When you woke up in the morning, people were dead next to you, emaciated.* Springfield and his brother were chosen to work in the Danzig shipyard, but their father, who had a limp from childhood scarlet fever, was rejected. Their father died in Stutthof, but the boys were part of the April death march.

'The order came, we are moving out, because the Russians were obviously coming closer . . . The climate was very cold. We were driven on foot, through the German countryside. It was cold. It was snow. My brother could hardly walk. I supported him as much as I could. It got so bad that he pleaded with me to let him go. "Let me die. I . . . I cannot, I . . . I really cannot handle it any more. I . . . I want to die. Leave me here." But it was . . . it was clear that the minute I let him go, he would be shot on the spot, because anybody who couldn't keep up with the march was shot on the spot. You would walk on the road; you could see corpses all over because it was an actual death march. I just couldn't give in. I just couldn't drop my brother. I carried him. I schlepped him. I kept talking to him. I'd say, "We are not too far away from salvation. You can't give up now!" Anyway, somehow, I was able to schlep him to the next camp, which was a place called Gottendorf in eastern Pomerania.'

Lily Mazur-Margules was sent from the Vilnius Ghetto to the Kaiserwald concentration camp, near Riga, in 1943. She was fourteen, her sister was eleven. They were the only survivors of their family. She described what it was like: 'They told us to line up and to get undressed. Naked. Oh, you know, you are only a person as long as you have your clothes on. You can be a professor. You can be a doctor. You can be a scientist. You can be a shoemaker. But as soon as you stand naked, you are lost. You are not a human being any more. This is what I cannot forgive the Germans, that they . . . systematically took away our dignity by undressing us. Many of the girls were young girls. They were virgins. They never saw their parents naked, never saw their mothers naked, but all of a sudden, we . . . we have to get undressed. We were taken, to some place.

They said that they are taking us to bathe, to a general bath. I remember holding my little sister by the hand and we were sharing the shower and I was saying goodbye to her because I was sure that the gas will come out any moment. And I . . . was talking to her to soothe her because she was very afraid, and I was telling her, "Don't worry. Mama . . . Mama is looking for us from Heaven." And we were standing there. I was just like saying goodbye and then all of a sudden, the water appeared.'

Lily Mazur-Margules was on the April death march with the Springfield brothers: *'You had to stay at the front. If you fell to the back, you would be shot. I saw young girls walk and walk and all of a sudden they became frozen. They straightened their legs and arms like frozen mummies and fell on their faces into the snow. The Germans didn't have to shoot them . . . One of my friends started to feel bad, so with someone on her other side we started to drag her. One of the guards noticed. He just took her away into the field and shot her there and then.'*

Again, in among the horrors of the battlefield and the terrors of the Holocaust, there were occasional moments of decency. One of them, born of tragedy, was recounted by Efrosinya Breus, a Red Army doctor, who was in East Prussia during the drive to the Oder. She and her husband had joined up together.

'We were already passing through East Prussia. Everybody was talking about victory. He was killed . . . Killed instantly . . . by shrapnel . . . an instant death . . . in a second. I didn't allow them to bury him at once. I wanted us to have one more night. To sit next to him. To look . . . to caress.

I decided I would take him home. To Belarus, hundreds of miles away. Everybody thought I'd lost my mind with grief. No! No! I went from one general to the next and got as far as Rokossovskiy [Marshal Konstantin Rokossovskiy had been given command of the 2nd Belorussian Front in November 1944]. *At first, he refused . . . Some sort of abnormal creature! So many men had been buried in common graves in foreign lands. I managed to get another meeting with him. "Do you want me to kneel before you?" "I understand you . . . But he's already dead . . ." "We had no children. Our house burned down. No photographs are left. There's nothing. If I bring him home, there will at least be a grave. And I'll have somewhere to go back to after the war." He said nothing, paced the office. Paced. "Have you ever loved, Comrade Marshal? I'm not burying my husband; I'm burying my love." He said nothing.*

"Then I too want to die here. Why should I live without him?" He said nothing for a long time. Then he came up to me and kissed my hand. I was given a special plane for one night. I boarded the plane . . . Put my arms around the coffin . . . and fainted . . .'

Vasily Grossman arrived at the small Polish town of Skwierzyna (Schwerin-an-der-Warthe in German), which had been part of the German province of Brandenburg since 1938. The town was occupied by the 8th Guards Army. He described the scenes he witnessed: *'Everything is on fire. Looting is in full swing. An old woman has thrown herself from a window of a burning building. We enter a house, there's a pool of blood and in it an old man shot by the looters. A German woman, dressed in black, with dead lips, is speaking in a barely audible rustling voice. She has brought with her a teenage girl with black velvety bruises on her neck and face, a swollen eye, with terrible bruises on her hands ... Horrifying things are happening to German women. Women's screams are heard from open windows.'* What Grossman described was only the beginning.

The East Prussian Offensive merged into the East Pomeranian Offensive in early February. Stalin continued to concentrate on ensuring that German units from the Baltic were prevented from outflanking the assault on Berlin. His insistence on securing the Red Army's flanks delayed the assault on Hitler's capital, originally planned for February, until April. Stalin's decision to delay the attack became a source of argument between his generals, and a subject of future debate among military historians. One view was that Berlin could have been taken much earlier, while others argued that an early attack would have left the Red Army vulnerable to Wehrmacht counter-attacks.

Although the Wehrmacht was, in reality, already beaten, the fighting was no less intense than the slaughter of previous years. With their Fatherland and their loved ones at their backs, most of the German landsers fought like cornered animals. At the same time, the Red Army riflemen were different soldiers from the ones who had taken flight as the blitzkrieg overwhelmed them, during the first weeks of Barbarossa. Even so, the fear of battle was still too much for some, as Soviet officer Vladimir Gelfand recorded in his diary: *'Another self-shot lieutenant! He was the first officer I saw shot because of cowardice. He shot himself in the left hand. Young, awarded the Order of the Red Banner and the Medal for the Defence of Stalingrad,*

the rewards were taken away from him, his personal property was confis-
cated, he was deprived of all benefits and shot like a dog. "To the traitor of
the Motherland, fire!" He firmly closed his eyes, and at the same moment
three automatic bullets smashed into his head. He collapsed to the ground,
streams of gushing blood pouring from his head.'

Marshal Rokossovskiy launched the East Pomeranian Offensive
on 10 February. However, after an initial advance of twelve miles, it
was halted by intense German resistance. On 26 February, he used
more tanks east of Neustettin, which produced a further penetration of twenty-five miles. By 2 March, the Wehrmacht's 2nd Army
found itself completely cut off and, two days later, Soviet tanks
reached the Baltic. The German 2nd Army withdrew in disarray
into Danzig, where it was besieged.

Danzig finally fell at the end of March and, a week after the
fall of the city, the Soviets declared the East Pomeranian Offensive
complete. According to Soviet figures, in the Battle for Danzig the
Germans lost 49,000 soldiers: 39,000 dead and 10,000 captured. In
1945, the Red Army was doing to the Wehrmacht what the Wehrmacht had done to the Red Army in 1941.

Zhukov offers a comprehensive summary of the strategic position in the spring of 1945: *'Our troops had liberated all of Hungary,*
and much of Czechoslovakia; they had entered Austria and liberated
Vienna [the Viennese offensive began on 13 April, with the city
falling two months later] *and took up advantageous positions for*
advancing deeper into Austria and southern Germany.

In the Western Theatre, our Allies had forced the Rhine in February
and March, and the eastern bank of the Oder and the Neisse from the
Baltic to Görlitz. We had a jumping-off point for the final defeat of
the [Wehrmacht's] *Berlin Group and the storming of Berlin . . . Nazi*
Germany had no strength left to continue fighting; it faced its doom.'

On 7 March, Zhukov was summoned back to Moscow to meet
with Stalin. By then, Stalin must have known that Zhukov would
be cast as the Soviet Union's military saviour. He may have wanted
to reassure himself of the general's loyalty – perhaps he was genu-
inely grateful – but in any case, he wanted to tell Zhukov about the

outcome of the Yalta Conference. The 'Big Three' had met from 4 to 11 February, during which time they had formalised the Allies' agreement for the map of post-war Europe. Stalin also wanted to confirm with Stavka the details of the assault on Berlin.

To Zhukov's surprise, the visit produced a rare glimpse of the ordinary man hidden behind the public face of the dictator: *'I went to Stalin's country house. He was not in the best of health. He asked me a few questions about the situation in Pomerania and on the Oder, then said, "Let's stretch our legs a little. I feel sort of limp." From the way he looked, talked and moved, I could tell he was extremely fatigued. As we were strolling through the park, Stalin suddenly started telling me about his childhood. We spent at least an hour chatting. On our way back, I said, "Comrade Stalin, I've been meaning to ask you for a while about your son, Yakov. Have you heard anything about him?" [. . .]'*

Yakov Dzhugashvili (Stalin's family name) was the eldest of Stalin's three children, born when Stalin was a young revolutionary in his mid-twenties. As a youth, Yakov was shy, reserved and unhappy, and tried to commit suicide several times. He studied to become an engineer, but his father insisted that he train as an artillery officer. Yakov completed his training just weeks before Barbarossa. Sent to the front, only six weeks after the outbreak of hostilities, he either surrendered or was captured by the Germans near Vitebsk and was held as a prisoner at the Sachsenhausen concentration camp. After the capture of German Field Marshal von Paulus at Stalingrad, the Germans offered to exchange Yakov for him. This was flatly refused by Stalin, who said, 'Just think how many sons ended in camps! Who would swap them for Paulus? Were they worse than Yakov?' It is thought that Hitler also sought to exchange his nephew, Leo Raubal, for Yakov but that was turned down as well.

Zukhov waited for a response: *'Stalin did not answer at once. We took a good hundred steps, before, in a subdued voice, he said, "Yakov won't be set free. The fascists will shoot him first. From what we know, they are keeping him separate from the other POWs and are putting pressure on him to betray his country." Stalin was silent for a minute, then said firmly, "No, Yakov will prefer any kind of death to betrayal." [. . .]'*

It is not clear if Stalin knew of his son's fate, but if he did, he did not reveal it to Zhukov. In fact, almost two years previously, on 14 April 1943, Yakov had thrown himself on to the electric fence at Sachsenhausen and was subsequently shot.

Stalin continued his introspective mood with Zhukov: '*At the table, Stalin sat silent for a long time, not touching his food. Then said bitterly, "What a terrible war. How many lives of our people has it carried away? There are probably very few families of us left who haven't lost someone close to them."* [. . .]'

By 20 March, Vladimir Gelfand's battery was in a Red Army bridgehead on the west bank of the Oder. Although most of the ethnic Germans in the area had fled, some remained. They were easy prey for the young men of the Red Army: '*The German women are afraid, but in order to avoid being abused by older fighters, begged to sleep with those who are younger. Andreyev was lucky, he was young. The girl chose him to sleep with him. But when he began, she shook her head and whispered sheepishly, "Es ist nicht gut* ["It's no good"], *ich bin noch Jungfrau* ["I'm still a virgin"]." *Her words further inflamed our hero, and he began to be more insistent. She refused for a long time until he took out the gun. Then she calmed down and, trembling, lowered her underwear . . . Grasping at him tightly, she began to push towards him. So, working together, they came to the goal and she soon smiled. He dressed her in a civilian dress, and she went out to her friends cheerful.*'

Perhaps Gelfand had put a veneer on the encounter to disguise the rape of an innocent girl at gunpoint. Even so, there must have been many encounters between vulnerable German women and Soviet soldiers, with almost as many outcomes as there were encounters. Tens of thousands were undoubtedly rapes, many of which were grossly brutal, but there must also have been many pragmatic deals done for the sake of survival, desperate quid pro quos of mutual interest. German women had to make appalling choices as the Red Army approached their homes. Taking flight was one choice, suicide was another; but many chose what must have appeared at the time to have been the least worst option and sought out a 'protector' who would shield them from mass rape and death.

During the Red Army's relentless advance westwards, not all the incidents were horrific, not all the stories were tales of sadness and grief. Macha Rolnikas, the young Jewish girl who had described so graphically the brutality of the German occupation of Vilnius in June 1941, was, miraculously, after almost five years of Nazi captivity, still alive. She had survived the Vilnius Ghetto and the terrors of the Stutthof concentration camp. In the camp, she was beaten repeatedly and came close to death several times: *'They advise us to watch out for a certain man named Max. Max is the devil in the disguise of a human being. He has already beaten some to death. He is also a prisoner, locked up for eleven years for having killed his wife and children. The SS love him for his unequalled cruelty. Max beats us brutally. We are covered in bruises. I call these bruises "Max's autographs".*

Horrible, I slept covered by a corpse. It was very cold, and I curled up against my neighbour's back. I slipped my arms under her armpits. I thought she even moved to squeeze my arms. And in the morning, I discovered that she was dead.

The supervisor chose eight of us and declared that we were the team of "undertakers" . . . In our barracks, forty to sixty women die every day. A cart to which some prisoners are harnessed arrives. Two of them take the dried-up and frozen bodies by the arms and feet, swing them and throw them on the heap of naked bodies. The crematorium is working day and night. Next to it heaps of bodies are piling up. Every day, nearly a thousand people die in the camp.'

Macha's diary is undated. However, in what must have been April 1945, with the Red Army nearby, she and her fellow survivors were forced to leave on a death march: *'So this is the end. Now that freedom is near, I am at the end of my tether. If only I had some strength . . . The days go by and we can't see the end of the road. We walk and walk. We are given nothing to eat. I have begun to swell up. The side I sleep on during the night is completely swollen. One eye is puffed up and I can no longer open it during the day . . . In order to feel my powerlessness a bit less and not to think of the torture that is caused by each step, I go on writing my journal in my head.'*

Macha describes how she eventually collapsed. Despite the pleadings of her friends, she could not go on and they had to leave her. She expected a bullet or a slow death from hunger, but a stranger appeared, gave her a walking stick, and forced her to get up: *'She tells me not to be foolish now that freedom is so close.'* With the will to live reignited, Macha was able to move again, but almost immediately a guard appeared and forced them into a barn where there were already many women: *'Will they set it on fire? We will be burned alive!'*

Her diary continues: *'A siren. Why this uproar? Why is everyone crying? Why are they running? They are going to trample me. Help me get up. Don't leave me alone ... And I can't get up ... I can hear men's voices. Soldiers of the Red Army. It is them. They rush into the barn. "Do you need help, little sister?" Two soldiers cross their arms and make a chair and carry me. Ambulances arrive. One soldier carries me, the other gives me some bread, the third one gives me his gloves. One of them takes out a dirty handkerchief and, like with a little girl, he wipes away my tears. "Don't cry, little sister, we won't allow any harm to come to you ever again." And on his cap shines the red star. It's been such a long time since I've seen it!'*

Meanwhile, the soldiers of the Red Army were still waiting to begin the attack on Berlin. Vladimir Gelfand was stationed at the Soviet bridgehead beyond the Oder, west of Küstrin, when he received breaking news from the international press that shocked and saddened the people of the United States and its allies: *'The post has just brought the most tragic news to me of all foreign reports: Roosevelt has died* [12 April]. *I respected and appreciated him always for his charming, intelligent nature, for his exceptional popularity among Americans. He alone managed to turn American politics sharply and thoroughly against fascism. Eternal memory to Roosevelt, my favourite foreign figure. Weighed down by the bitterness of loss, I bow my head.'*

26

VENGEANCE

APRIL–MAY 1945

Berlin's doom and that of the rest of the Third Reich became an orgy of vengeance. Given the horrors that had been daily occurrences since June 1941, it is perhaps not surprising that the final days of the war were similarly chilling. Many of the horrific acts perpetrated during Germany's advances eastwards, on both military and civilian targets, were repeated during the Soviet Union's advance westwards. The need to take revenge for everything that had happened between 1941 and 1943 created a storm of hatred, which meant that the brutality of those years was repeated in 1944 and 1945.

Women were raped, brutalised and murdered in enormous numbers. Men and children were made to watch the rapes, then they were shot. Fearing retribution, thousands of Nazis – leading figures, SS soldiers and camp guards – committed suicide rather than fall into the hands of the Russians. Many civilians, at least 7,000 in Berlin alone, did the same. It was a horror story that continued into the heart of Berlin and left a bitter legacy in Germany – a legacy that, ironically, may last far longer than the thousand years of Hitler's mythical millennium Reich.

Fyodor Bogratyov, who had kept his diary going since his rapid retreat to Moscow in 1941, was still serving as a sapper: *Then we crossed the Oder and entered the Land of Death. There it was – the cursed Germany! The villages were burning; everything was destroyed. There were no Germans, everyone had run away. Fights were going on day and night. The Germans dropped leaflets from planes. They read: "Murder, death, blood, the whole of Berlin is so fortified. There are so many lines of defence that it is impossible to take it, it is better to surrender." It was the latest provocation by Hitler and Göring. Our soldiers laughed.'*

Battle-hardened by the war he had lived through since September 1941, Nikolai Inozemtzev had also reached the German border, in northern Poland: '*On a clear sunny morning, we cross the Polish–German border. I stop the car and fire a salvo. We are in Germany! This gives wings to the advancing army, forcing one to forget about fatigue and difficulties. Two to three kilometres from the border are huge food depots in the forest. Canned food of all kinds: cheese, biscuits, sausage, beer; anything. The guys are laughing, Nowhere is a single soldier visible. Their cities are burning in the distance, while we drink French champagne and German liquor, eat Danish cheese, Bulgarian cans of food and Dutch chocolate.'*

The final Red Army directive on the eve of the crossing of the East Prussian border urged the retribution that was to come.

On German soil there is only one master – the Soviet soldier. He is both the judge and punisher for the torments of his fathers and mothers, for the destroyed cities and villages . . . Remember your friends who are not there. Instead of them are the next of kin of our killers and oppressors.

As he moved deeper into Germany, Inozemtzev's reports became more harrowing: '*More burning German cities, traces of fleeting battles on the roads, groups of captured Germans who are surrendering in huge numbers. They are alone, they are afraid, devastated villages, hundreds and thousands of abandoned bicycles on the roads, cattle, roaring loudly – there is no one to milk them. There are corpses of men, women and children in apartments. Terrible scenes of mass rape . . .*

After what they did to us, I do not feel sorry for the Germans. Let them shoot them and do whatever they want with them. Even so, these rapes undermine the dignity of the army as a whole and each Russian individual is humiliated. In addition, it will inevitably entail a decline in discipline and reduce the combat effectiveness of the army. All these licentious animal instincts will be extremely difficult to get rid of later.'

Lieutenant Nina Sakova was a paramedic with the advancing Red Army: '*I got to Germany . . . All the way from Moscow. The first*

*thing I saw on German soil was a handmade sign, "Here she is – accursed
Germany!" We entered a village . . . The shutters were all closed. They
had dropped everything and fled. Goebbels had persuaded them that
the Russians would come and hack, stab and slaughter. We opened the
doors of the houses. There was no one, or they all lay killed or poisoned.
Children lay there. Shot, poisoned.'*

Leonid Rabichev graduated from a military academy in 1942.
In December of the same year, he became a lieutenant and platoon
commander of the 100th Separate Airborne Surveillance Army
Company, part of the 31st Soviet Army. As the Red Army moved
west, he fought in the liberation of several cities, including Rzhev,
Smolensk, Orsha, Minsk and Grodno. The fighting was horrendous
and, in his memoirs, he described countless military terrors.

However, what he saw in German East Prussia shook him to
his core: *'On carriages and on foot, old men, women and children were
moving along all the country's roads and highways. Our tank crews,
infantrymen, artillery troops drove them on and, in order to clear a path,
were tossing their carriages, with furniture, suitcases and horses, into the
ditches along the roads. They pushed the old men and boys to one side,
and, having forgotten their duty and honour, threw themselves by the
thousands on the women and young girls.*

*Women, mothers and their daughters, are lying to the right and left
along the road and in the front of each stands a laughing armada of men
with their pants down. Bleeding and losing consciousness, the women
are dragged off to the side and the children who rush to help them are
shot. There are guffaws, snarling, laughter, cries and moans. And their
commanders, their majors, and colonels, are standing on the road. Some
chuckle to themselves, while some are conducting it, or rather, are regu-
lating matters.*

*Everything is allowed, nothing is punished, no one is responsible. It's
just a mindless mob. And the colonel, the one who was directing, couldn't
hold out any longer and takes his place in line, while a major shoots any
witnesses, the hysterical struggling children and old men.'*

Author Lev Kopelev was a communist idealist and committed Bolshevik. He volunteered for the Red Army at the outbreak
of war and served as a propaganda officer and also, through his

knowledge of German, as a translator. In late January 1945, he was in Allenstein, East Prussia, after its capture by the Red Army. Kopelev blamed Soviet propaganda for the behaviour of the Red Army: '*Millions of people had been brutalised and corrupted by the war. Our propaganda: bellicose, jingoistic and false. I had believed that such propaganda was* necessary *on the eve of war, and all the more so for the war's duration, but I had come to understand that from seeds like these come poisoned fruit.*

The city is corrupting soldiers: trophies, women, drinking. We were told that the division commander, Colonel Smirnov, had personally shot a lieutenant who had organised his soldiers to stand in line to rape a woman lying in a gateway. At the headquarters we heard about another terrible incident. Several Russian girls, who had been deported to Germany, worked as waitresses in our headquarters. Being civilians, they did not wear uniforms, but they were lavishly supplied with captured clothes. One of them, the most beautiful among them, young, well built, cheerful, had been wearing her golden hair in waves, falling to her shoulders, the way the German women do. Yesterday, she was carrying a bucket of soup across the street. Several drunken soldiers were wandering around. They saw her, "Hey, German bitch!" and a burst from a machine gun hit her in the back. She died on the spot, crying, "Why, what for?" [. . .]'

As many historians have pointed out – including Stephen Fritz and Catherine Merridale, who have focused on the psychology of the war – the humiliation and brutalisation of the German people, especially the mass rape of German women, was more an expression of national/racial potency than sexual virility. Having been cast as inferior *Untermenschen* by the Germans, and dehumanised and degraded as a consequence, the Soviet's mass rape of the women of the aggressors, especially in front of their menfolk, symbolised the collective righting of a terrible wrong. It was a sort of ethnic cleansing by sexual torture, which did, in many cases, lead to murder.

Men of the Red Army were expressing their collective power over impotent German men; men who had once lauded their superiority but were now unable to prevent the ultimate humiliation of their women. The German people were being 'taught a lesson' that would live with them and their nation for as long as the death and destruction inflicted on the Soviet population would live in the memories of the people of the Motherland.

Anna Ratkina was a junior sergeant and a telephone operator. Like many women in the Red Army, she had little sympathy for German women: *'Of course I remember a German woman who had been raped. She was lying naked with a grenade between her legs . . . Now I feel ashamed, but I didn't then. In the first few days we had one feeling, and afterwards, another . . . after several months . . . Five German girls came to our battalion . . . to our commander. They were weeping. The gynaecologist examined them: they had wounds. Jagged wounds. Their underwear was bloody . . . They had been raped all night long. The soldiers had stood in line . . .'*

By this point of the war, wary that his plan for a future communist-controlled eastern Germany was in danger of being seriously undermined, Stalin insisted on improvements in the behaviour of his army.

'We formed up our battalion . . . We told those German girls, "Go and look, and if you recognise someone, we'll shoot him on the spot, regardless of his rank." But they sat there and wept . . . They didn't want more blood . . . Then each one got a loaf of bread. Of course, all of this is war . . . You think it was easy to forgive? To see intact white houses with tiled roofs. With roses . . . I myself wanted to hurt them . . . Of course, I wanted to see their tears . . . It was impossible to become good all at once. Fair and kind. As good as you are now. To pity them. That would take me dozens of years.'

Ilya Ehrenburg was still the most vociferous of the Soviet propagandists and was continuing to pour poison into the ears of the Soviet soldiers as they marched into Germany: *'Germany is a witch . . . We are in Germany. German towns are burning. I am happy. The dead are knocking on the doors of Unter den Linden and all the other cursed streets of this cursed city. We shall put up gallows in Berlin . . . An icy wind is blowing along the streets of Berlin; a terror that is driving them and their females to the west . . . It's too late. Germany, you can whirl around in circles and burn and howl in your deathly agony; the hour of revenge has struck!'*

Soviet vengeance was particularly painful for the inhabitants of

Demmin, a town in Pomerania, northern Germany. When retreating Wehrmacht troops destroyed the bridges over the Peene River, the advancing Red Army was delayed in the town. Their blood up, their minds seeking retribution, their bodies hungry for food and female conquest, this was a toxic mix among soldiers who had been advancing at up to twenty-five miles a day. Rape, pillage and brutal executions were the consequence.

Almost the entire centre of the town was burned to the ground. The carnage led to the mass suicide of at least 1,000 people. The suicides included drowning, hanging, wrist-cutting and shooting. Most bodies were buried in mass graves. After the war, all discussion of the suicides was taboo under the new East German communist regime, which led to a silence that continued until the reunification of Germany in 1990. And Demmin was not alone: Neubrandenburg witnessed more than 600 suicides; there were over 680 in Neustrelitz, at least 1,000 in Stolp (now Polish Słupsk), and 600 in Lauenburg (now Polish Lębork).

Ilya Ehrenburg was told to put an end to his provocative tirades on 14 April, when the Kremlin realised that his vitriol was hardly conducive to its plan to create a pro-communist East Germany, dominated by Moscow, after the war. However, the damage had been done by then. The genie of hate was out of the bottle.

•

The stage was now set for the final onslaught on Berlin. Supported in the air by 7,500 aircraft, the Red Army deployed 2.5 million troops, over 6,000 tanks and over 40,000 artillery pieces for the advance on the German capital. In stark contrast, fewer than 1 million Germans stood in their way, many of them from untested training units, Hitler Youth, police, sailors, Luftwaffe ground crew and the *Volkssturm* of old men and those previously discarded as unfit for combat.

The Germans did have significant numbers of tanks, especially powerful Tiger tanks with their 88mm shells. But they were short of fuel and ammunition, and many soldiers had not been paid for months. Apart from the SS diehards, bolstered by the fanatical zeal of assorted foreign units, including the formidable Nordland Division of Scandinavian fascists and the Charlemagne Division of French Nazis, German morale had been shattered by endless defeats and the gradual destruction of the Fatherland by Allied bombing.

The letters German soldiers received from home must have made grim reading, with many families from the west already under Allied control. However, despite the overwhelming odds, the Wehrmacht would make the Red Army pay for every yard of German soil in buckets of blood. As they had so many times before, Stalin and his generals were more than willing to pay the price by sacrificing the blood of their men and women in wave after wave of frontal assaults.

Stalin was in a hurry. The Americans and British had recently crossed the Rhine, on 22 and 23 March respectively, and by 11 April the Americans had reached the Elbe River, just eighty miles from Berlin. The Soviet leader was appalled by the thought that the Americans might capture Berlin before him. To speed up his campaign, he split the command of the Berlin operation between Marshal Zhukov in the centre and Marshal Konev in the south. Shrewdly, Stalin made the capture of the city a race between his two most senior commanders, men who were great rivals and who were both eager to win the prize of the conquest of the German capital.

Zhukov was to punch into Berlin from the centre and north, while Konev was asked to attack from the south-east, before swinging north, swallowing the German capital in the jaws of a gigantic pincer movement. Stalin sent a message to Zhukov as he was preparing to attack: 'Hitler is spinning a web to stir up a disagreement between the Russians and the Allies. This web must be swept aside by the capture of Berlin by Soviet forces. We can do this and must do this. Hit the Germans without mercy and you will soon be in Berlin.'

On 15 April, the colossal attack began with one of the most powerful artillery barrages in history. So numerous were the Red Army's artillery pieces, it was able to deploy rows of them: over 250 pieces for every 1,000 yards of the front line, which amounted to one every four yards.

Vasili Chuikov's 62nd Army, the heroes of Stalingrad, had been redesignated the 8th Guards Army. It had fought through Poland as part of Zhukov's 1st Belorussian Front. There was no love lost between the two men. Chuikov described what the onslaught was like: *'The command was given to the men in the trenches to bring forward the colours . . . 03:00 hours, Berlin time. The second hand on the Front Commander's watch completed its sweep, and, in an instant, night became day. A volcanic rumble resounded as 40,000 guns began to fire. The Oder valley seemed to rock. Fountains of dust and smoke shot up to the sky.'*

Over 1 million shells were hurled against the Wehrmacht positions west of the Oder. However, the defenders were well dug in; it took Zhukov and Chuikov three days to break the German resistance, far longer than Zhukov had planned. He used powerful searchlights to blind the German defenders, but they were less than effective in the gloom of a cold day; their glare was as much of an impediment to his own forces as it was to the Germans. The searchlights were also an easy target. When they burst into life, the Germans poured fire on them, killing many of the female operators.

Zhukov, never one to hold back men and machines, used his tanks as battering rams against the Wehrmacht defences. Soviet soldiers died at three times the rate of the Germans. Soviet T-34 tanks were especially vulnerable to the *Panzerfaust* (the German anti-tank bazooka), and many volleys were fired by young Germans hiding in destroyed buildings or in trenches and ditches. Many of the Hitler Youth, some as young as fourteen or fifteen, were given *Panzerfausts*, but no rifles, which were much too scarce.

It was an attritional battle, with huge casualties on both sides. Inevitably, the resolute, but outnumbered, German defenders began to be overwhelmed by wave after wave of Red Army shock troops. On 19 April, the 1st Belorussian Front eventually broke through the final defensive line of the Seelow Heights, east of Berlin. Nothing but pockets of devastated German formations stood between the Red Army and Berlin. Sergeant Nikolai Vasilyev, Commander of the 6th Artillery Battery, 266th Rifle Division, described the scene: *'Towards evening our battery reached the heights, and we saw an*

*enormous city. We were overwhelmed by a feeling of joy and jubilation.
It was the last enemy line and the hour of reckoning had come . . . Our
medical instructor, Malanya Yurchenko, wrote on the battery shells: "For
Stalingrad, for the Donbass, for Ukraine, for the orphans and widows.
For mothers' tears!" [. . .]'*

By the night of 19 April, the German defence east of Berlin had,
in effect, ceased to exist. There were pockets of resistance, but they
were more like groups of urban guerrillas than an army. Chuikov
summed up the hopelessness of the German position: *'The enemy's
main forces, decimated and scattered, were making their last stand in
pillboxes, underground shelters and cellars. The Nazi government was
fully informed through every available channel of communication that
no alternative was offered but unconditional surrender.*

*The lives of thousands upon thousands of German youths, German
soldiers whom fate had so far spared in this long and hopeless war, could
still be saved. The lives of thousands of Germans hung in the balance. But
Hitler continued to keep them in submission and threw more lives into
the meat grinder . . . And he mercilessly threw yesterday's schoolchildren
into battle, condemning them to death under shelling and under the
tracks of tanks. Imagine a crowd of about 400 boys, clad in black school
uniforms, not one over fifteen, walking down the street towards our lines.
Hitler sent these children against our tanks. They were close to our position. They carried Panzerfausts, which can tear a man to pieces. We sent
up flares to stop them, but they rushed towards us. We had to open fire.
The death throes of the Nazi regime began, its ringleaders fully revealing
their cowardice and cruelty.'*

Vasily Grossman travelled from Moscow to Berlin on 20 April,
to report on the death throes of the German capital. With his usual
lucid prose, he described what he saw as he journeyed through
occupied Germany: *'The trees along the road: apple, cherry, all are
in bloom. The dachas of Berliners. Everything is wallowing in flowers:
tulips, lilac, apricot blossom. The birds are singing. Nature does not
lament these last days of war . . . In the town of Landsberg near Berlin,
children are playing at war. Our troops are finishing off German imperi-
alism in Berlin, but here, boys with wooden swords and lances, with long
legs, their hair cut short with blond fringes, are shouting in shrill voices,*

*stabbing one another, jumping, leaping wildly. Birth is being given to a
new war. It is eternal, undying.'*

To the south-east, Konev's front had had more success than
Zhukov's. So, by 22 April, the German forces defending Berlin were
entirely encircled. As the Red Army tightened its noose, significant
numbers of German units – including the Wehrmacht's 9th Army,
led by General Theodor Busse – ignored Hitler's direct orders, and
attempted to escape to the south-west. Busse's primary objective was
survival. But importantly, survival as prisoners of the Western Allies
rather than the Soviet Union. He gave the order for the 9th to break
out. As it did so, thousands of refugee Berliners went with them.

Another appalling battle was about to take place. Bitter fighting
ensued in and around Halbe, a forested area thirty-five miles south
of Berlin. The effect of Soviet artillery fire, supported by massive
air attacks, was devastating. The German troops suffered very heavy
losses. More than 40,000 died in the Halbe breakout. Thousands
of civilians also died; the exact number will never be known. One
local witness remembers how the narrow paths leading through the
forests were piled high with corpses. It took the local population
months to clear the site. Even today, multiple corpses continue to
be found each year in and around Berlin, most of them in Halbe.
Some 25,000 German soldiers managed to break through to the
Elbe, where they surrendered to the American troops.

In Berlin itself, the vicious fighting, street by street, building by
building, continued for several days, but the situation was hopeless. Even so, Goebbels was still making bellicose radio broadcasts,
declaiming groundless propaganda that promised new weapons
to magically snatch victory from the jaws of defeat. He also issued
cruel threats to a people who, in their blind devotion to Hitler
and his perverse ideology, had lost everything, 'Any German who
offends against his self-evident duty to the nation will lose his
honour and his life.'

The police and SS had checkpoints on the roads out of the city
and roamed the streets looking for deserters. Any they found, or
any hapless citizens they rounded up, were executed on the spot.
Many were strung up to deter others. The bodies of both soldiers

and civilians, perhaps as many as 10,000, were left dangling like rag dolls from any convenient lamppost. Many had crude signs around their necks, proclaiming *Deserteur* ('Deserter'), *Feigling* ('Coward'), *Verräter* ('Traitor') or *Schwächling* ('Weakling').

On 30 April, Chuikov's men reached the Reichstag, the old German parliament, the iconic symbol of the German state. Since an arson attack in 1933, which Hitler had made use of to consolidate his power, the building had been largely unused; dictators, after all, have little use for parliaments. Even so, its profound symbolism meant that it was the prime target for the Red Army. Chuikov was well aware of its significance: *'North of the Imperial Chancellery, near the Brandenburger Tor, stood the Reichstag, a tall, domed building. It had been damaged by bombs and now was a huge empty shell, easy to defend. Every step cost us lives and a superhuman effort. The fighting for this last vestige of the Third Reich was marked by the mass heroism of the Soviet troops. They went into combat in the brilliant spring sunshine. They wanted to live. And it had been for the sake of life and happiness on earth that they had ploughed their way through fire and death from the Volga to Berlin.'*

Contemporary writings about the final days of Berlin often use phrases such as 'entering the lair of the fascist Beast'. But the 'Beast' was no more. He was a pathetic shell of a man, broken in mind and body, with a handful of pitiful sycophants around him, still cowed by the venom he was able to summon in moments of blind fury, still bent to his will. Although some fanatical Nazis still roamed Berlin's streets, most of Hitler's acolytes had slunk away to escape the deadly retribution that awaited them, abandoning the Berliners to their fate.

Left behind, cowering in the ruined buildings, were the pitiful human remnants of a city that, just a few years earlier, had stood on the brink of ruling the world – or so they had been told. Perhaps not entirely innocent, they may well have been swept along by Nazi hysteria and been proud of their Reich's conquests, but now they were alone and defenceless. Old men, children and women were the only ones who remained. They would pay the price that so many of the guilty would manage to avoid.

Like Stalingrad, Berlin was a potent symbol, despite its pathetic state. The war was over, but Stalin demanded more blood to crush an already devastated city and to annihilate a Wehrmacht that had long since bled to death. Similarly, Hitler insisted on yet more sacrifice to defend a cause he had lost at least two years earlier. Their appetite for destruction cost the Red Army over 80,000 dead and at least 300,000 wounded or sick. The Wehrmacht and its ragtag assortment of support echelons suffered an estimated 100,000 fatalities, 220,000 wounded and at least half a million prisoners, many of whom were marched off to Soviet death camps, never to return. It is also estimated that at least 125,000 civilian Berliners died during the taking of the city and that at least 1 million were rendered homeless.

While the Nazi hierarchy were making their plans to escape, Hitler decided to await his fate in his bunker. It is certain that he had already decided to take his own life. He demanded that his body be consumed in the flames of several cans of petrol, so that not even his corpse would fall into the hands of the enemy. By then his mental and physical decline had become severe. He trusted none but a few personal aides and openly berated the German people for having let him down and for failing to deliver the glories that he believed his ideological vision and military prowess had offered them.

As early as 19 March, in what became known as his 'Nero Order' – 'Destructive Measures on Reich Territory' – he had demanded the total destruction of Germany's infrastructure.

All military transport and communication facilities, industrial establishments and supply depots, as well as anything else of value within Reich territory, which could in any way be used by the enemy immediately or within the foreseeable future for the prosecution of the war, will be destroyed.

Fortunately for Germany's future, Albert Speer, Hitler's otherwise loyal Minister of Armaments and War Production, was horrified by the order and refused to carry it out, keeping the decision from his Führer until the last days of the war.

Hitler's blind faith in his warped version of Social Darwinism had led him to turn on his own *Volk*, the people he had originally claimed were the 'Master Race': 'If the war is lost, so too is the *Volk*.' By an ironic inversion of 'survival of the fittest', the surviving Germans were the weakest ones; the best of them, the heroic ones, had died fighting for the Fatherland, leaving the useless residue of the German race to survive. They were the scum, and therefore not worth saving. On the day of his suicide, he was reported as saying, 'If the German people lose the war, then they will have proved themselves unworthy of me.'

The situation inside the *Führerbunker*, Hitler's concrete tomb deep under the garden of the new Reich Chancellery, was macabre. On 20 April, the day of the Führer's fifty-sixth birthday, he had recorded his last newsreel, inspecting a twenty-strong group of Hitler Youth who had won meaningless Iron Crosses for attacking Red Army tanks. The Führer, holding his trembling left arm behind his back, walked down the row of little boys, patting them on their cheeks. In the footage, several of the boys, in high-pitched voices still not broken, tell their stories. They are immaculately dressed, and all are clean-shaven, reflecting their youth.. That evening, Hitler's mistress, Eva Braun, organised a champagne party to celebrate his birthday. The only present was a sack of money from his soldiers; his ironic comment was simply to reflect that it seemed a little lighter than in previous years.

The civilian population of the city was already bearing the brunt of the Red Army's revenge. Though the first wave of elite Soviet troops was generally considered to be disciplined, it was the second wave, fuelled by large stocks of alcohol found in the city, that indulged in orgies of rape and violence.

By 25 April, Vladimir Gelfand was on the banks of the Spree River, just south-east of Berlin: *'It was strange, the day before yesterday, I was in the suburbs of Berlin, riding a bicycle. I met with a group of German women carrying suitcases and bundles. Suddenly they all rushed to me with tears. It was difficult for them to carry their belongings and so I offered them my bike. They nodded their heads, and suddenly they looked at me with such emerald eyes, so damn sharply, that somewhere in the depths of my heart a light of compassion appeared, and I convinced myself of the need to know the cause of these women's suffering.*

In broken German, I asked them where they lived, and why they had left their home. They spoke with horror about the grief on the first night of the Red Army's arrival. They lived not far from where we were, so I went with them. They lived well. A huge two-storey house with luxurious furnishings, magnificent interior decoration and painted walls and ceilings. When our soldiers came, they pushed everyone into the basement.

"They were poking here," explained the beautiful German woman, pulling up her skirt, "all night, and there were so many of them. I was a girl," she sighed, and cried. "They ruined my youth. Among them were old; there were young and pimply, and everyone climbed on me, everyone poked. There were no less than twenty of them, yes, yes," and she burst into tears. "They raped my daughter," the poor mother interjected, "they can still come and rape my girl again."

Her daughter rushed to me, "You'll sleep with me. You can do whatever you want with me, but you're the only one! I'm ready to be with you, I agree to whatever you want, but save me from such a thing with a lot of people!" Her grief and suffering were beyond shame. Her mother begged me. "Don't you want to sleep with my daughter? Your Russian comrades who were here, everyone wanted! They may come again, or in their place twenty new ones will appear, and then my grief will be unbearable!" The girl began to hug me, to beg, smiling broadly through her tears. She tried to resort to everything that is in the art of a woman and played the part well.'

Gelfand completed his diary entry for 25 April by suggesting that his military duty led him to decline the desperate plea from the German woman and her mother. Perhaps he did accept but did not want to admit to it in writing. Either way, he did not say what became of the German women, with or without his protection. Gelfand's account is just one of what must have been thousands of similar tragic encounters.

A combination of Soviet denials, the profound embarrassment of German women, and the shame of the German men who were forced to witness the humiliation of their womenfolk, meant that the scale of the mass rape and murder which took place in the city first killing their six children with cyanide, Goebbels and his committed suicide at 20:30. For those in the *Führerbunker*, bels' death – the last of Hitler's disciples – finally dispelled the sianic power that their beloved Führer had exerted over them.

Early the following morning, on 2 May, with battling still conning in the Reichstag, where elite SS units were fighting to the man, Chuikov, by now exhausted, was asleep: *'At 05:50, I was akened and told that a delegation had come from Goebbels. I sprang and hurriedly washed my face.'* The delegation told Chuikov of oebbels' suicide. At the same time, a call came in from Red Army orward units, reporting that German soldiers were lining up in olumns to surrender: *'At 06:00 hours, May 2nd, Commander of 56th Panzer Corps, General Weidling, accompanied by two generals of his staff crossed the line and surrendered.'*

Weidling was taken to Chuikov's command post, where he drafted a surrender note: *'Weidling handed me the paper in silence. It read, "On April 30th, the Führer committed suicide, thus abandoning us who swore loyalty to him. According to the Führer's order, we, the German troops, were to continue fighting for Berlin despite having run out of ammunition and regardless of the general situation, which makes further resistance senseless.*

I order: cease resistance forthwith.

Weidling, General of Artillery, former Commandant of the Berlin Defence Area".'

Some pockets of SS resistance continued to fight for the rest of the day, but the skirmishes eventually petered out. Fighting in Prague continued until at least 11 May but, to all intents and purposes, Germany was a conquered nation. The Red Army had achieved what, five years earlier, had seemed impossible. Chuikov recorded the momentous realisation: *'So the war was over. The men of the 8th Guards Army had travelled a long way from Stalingrad to Berlin . . . What our soldiers and all Soviet people had been through during the war had never been experienced by any other nation. It was the bloodiest war in history.'*

Grossman wrote his own account of the day's events: *'May 2nd. The day of Berlin's capitulation. It's difficult to describe it. A monstrous*

was kept largely hidden for many years. Only recent research and the testimony of a few brave survivors have revealed the true nature of the trauma. It is estimated that as many as 2 million German women were raped during the last six months of the war, around 100,000 of them in Berlin. The horror also extended to Soviet women who had been forced into slave labour in Germany. In a sad absurdity, in the eyes of many Red Army soldiers, the Soviet girls had become guilty by association with the Germans, and many of them were brutalised along with German victims.

Hitler's deterioration, both mentally and physically, escalated as he became more and more isolated in his bunker. By 27 April, marooned under a small patch of ground, his disintegration expressed itself in either uncontrollable rages or menacing silences.

Much as Hitler might have indulged in fantasies of being the ultimate Teutonic warrior, he was not the Siegfried of heroic German legend, and Braun was no Brünhilde. The final act of their shameful opera was far from a Wagnerian idyll. In a wretched final scene in a squalid underground vault, there was no warrior's death for him, no glorious immolation for her; just a bullet and a cyanide capsule. There was no funeral pyre by the Rhine, no Rhinemaidens and no Valhalla, just a shallow scrape in the ground and several cans of petrol to obliterate their bodies.

Not surprisingly, within hours of his death, Hitler's sordid demise became shrouded in mystery. It soon became the subject of a stream of conspiracy theories, many of which suggested that he had escaped from his bunker and survived. Much of the intrigue was created by the Soviet obsession with secrecy. Definitive proof, from dental records and forensic detective work, was kept concealed in Moscow and only made available in recent years. Consequently, there is now little doubt that the accounts given at the time were accurate and that Hitler met his ignominious end as a charred carcass in a hole in the ground.

Soviet interpreter Yelena Rzhevskaya played a central role in the process of recovering and examining Hitler's body: *'There was something portentous about Adolf Hitler being dissected under the watchful eye of Dr Faust* [Faust Shkaravsky, Soviet forensic expert]. *The autopsy* was performed by a female doctor, Major Anna Marants, and took place in Berlin-Buch [a Berlin suburb] on May 8th, 1945.' Shortly after the autopsy, Rzhevskaya was given 'a second-hand burgundy red box with a soft lining and covered with satin, the kind of thing made to hold a bottle of perfume or cheap jewellery'. The box contained teeth and a lower jaw, which, backed by Hitler's dental records, provided the irrefutable evidence of his death.

Later that day, after briefly celebrating the German surrender, Rzhevskaya was walking down the stairs in the small house in Buch where the autopsy had been carried out: 'Suddenly, it was as if something had jolted me and I clutched at the bannister. Never am I going to forget the feeling that electrified me at that moment. God Almighty, is this happening to me? Is this me standing at the moment Germany surrenders, with a box in my hands containing the indisputable remnants of Adolf Hitler!'

Along with Hitler's Iron Cross and some other personal effects, the contents of Rzhevskaya's burgundy box were only revealed with the collapse of the Soviet Union in 1991. In 1970, under the orders of Yuri Andropov, then the head of the KGB [the successor to the NKVD], the rest of Hitler's remains were exhumed from where they had been buried on a Soviet military base in Magdeburg. The remains, along with those of Eva Braun and of Goebbels and his family, were cremated once more, the residues pulverised and scattered in a nearby river.

•

Chuikov was at his command post on the southern bank of the Spree, late in the evening of 30 April. There had been fierce fighting all day as, building by building, the government offices of the Nazi regime were taken, one by one: 'I was urgently summoned to the telephone. General Glazunov, Commander of the 4th Guards Rifle Corps, his voice animated with excitement, reported, "Lieutenant-Colonel Seifert of the German Army is at our forward position with a white flag. He has a letter for the Soviet Command." [...]'

Seifert's letter was the beginning of a protracted process of negotiation. Chuikov had agreed to receive a delegation from the

German High Command and was waiting [...] 03:55 hours [on 1 May] the door opened and a [...] an Iron Cross and a Nazi swastika on his sleeve [...] was General Krebs, Chief of Staff of German Land [...] a Panzer Corps Colonel and an interpreter. Not w[...] Krebs said, "I'll speak of extremely secret matters. Yo[...] eigner to be told that on April 30th, Hitler departed thi[...] will; he has committed suicide.'

Unfortunately, despite the fact that soldiers and [...] still dying throughout Berlin, Krebs was not there [...] unconditional surrender that the Allies insisted up[...] he was attempting to buy time and gain acceptance [...] post-Hitler Nazi government, with Goebbels as its Cha[...] Grossadmiral Dönitz as its President. At the same time, the[...] were trying to negotiate a separate peace with Britain and [...]

Chuikov made several calls to Zhukov, and Zhukov [...] same with Stalin. When Zhukov made the first call, Stalin [...] his summer cottage: 'The call was answered by a duty gener[...] said, "Comrade Stalin has just gone to bed." "Please wake him up[...] matter is urgent." In a little while Stalin was on the line and I rep[...] to him about Hitler's suicide and the letter from Goebbels proposing [...] armistice. Stalin answered, "Now he's done it, the bastard. Too bad [...] couldn't be taken alive. There can be no talks, either with Krebs or any[...] other Hitlerites; only unconditional surrender." [...]'

When dawn came on May Day, an auspicious day in the Soviet calendar, the German position became more and more convoluted. Fanatical factions within the regime, allied to SS units on the ground, were actively resisting any attempts to surrender. Still unable to agree to an unconditional surrender, Krebs left the negotiations at 13:08, leading to an inevitable outcome, as recorded by Chuikov: 'The Command was given to open maximum intensity fire and finish off the enemy as quickly as possible.'

Even though their position was hopeless, and their Führer was dead, diehard adherents of his Reich continued to fight. It was the last spasm of a convulsion of brutality and hate that had begun in the early-morning darkness of 22 June 1941. In the evening of 1 May, *concentration of impressions. Fire and fires, smoke, smoke, smoke. Enormous crowds of* [German] *prisoners. Their faces are full of drama. There's sadness, not only personal suffering but the suffering of the citizens of a beaten nation. This overcast cold and rainy day is the day of Germany's ruin: in smoke, in flames, amid hundreds of corpses in the street. Corpses squashed by tanks, squeezed out like tubes ... Prisoners: policemen, officials, old men and next to them schoolboys, almost children ... A dead old woman is sitting on a mattress by a front door, leaning her head against the wall. A child's little legs in shoes and stockings are lying in the mud. It was a shell, or a tank ran over her.'*

Following the deaths of Hitler and Goebbels, and Berlin's capitulation, events moved rapidly around Europe. On 4 May, German forces in north-west Germany, the Netherlands and Denmark surrendered. On 6 May, German troops besieged in Breslau (Polish Wrocław) surrendered. The following day, on 7 May, General Alfred Jodl signed the German instrument of surrender in Rheims. Finally, on 8 May, a second ceremony, demanded by Stalin, took place in Berlin. As the Soviet people had borne the brunt of the war, he insisted that the final surrender should be in the presence of the High Command of the Red Army. So, in a very modest former Wehrmacht officers' mess hall in Karlshorst, a garden suburb of Berlin, German Field Marshal Wilhelm Keitel signed a second surrender document in the presence of Marshal Zhukov, who thus had the honour of being the figurehead of the Soviet victory.

Zhukov had few qualms about the price paid by the Red Army soldiers under his command who took Berlin: *'They died in the laps of nurses, lay on makeshift stretchers, in courtyards, on staircases, bleeding profusely, fighting for breath, whispering their last words. They died silently and suddenly. They died to bring forward the end of the war and the victory by a few moments. It was not only orders that threw them into that fantastic assault.'*

Similarly, Marshal Konev, Zhukov's great rival for the prize of being the conqueror of Berlin, had no doubts about the need for victory, no matter the cost to those under his command: *'I happened to hear arguments that the fighting in Berlin could have been conducted with less fury, fierceness and haste, and therefore fewer casualties. There is an outer logic to this, but it ignores one thing: the actual situation, the actual strain of the fighting, and the actual state of the men's morale. These men burned with a passion and a desire to end the war as soon as possible. Those who want to judge how justified or unjustified were the casualties must remember this.'*

With hindsight, what is apparent is that, in order to defeat the German colossus, the Soviet Union needed generals like Chuikov, Zhukov, Konev and several others, who were utterly ruthless in pursuit of their military objectives. What is also obvious is that, without the unbridled willingness of the men and women of the Soviet Union, both combatants and civilians, the ruthlessness of their generals would have meant nothing.

For those at the sharp end of the great conflagration, the end of hostilities produced a wide range of emotions. Tamarah Lazerson survived the Kovno (Kaunas) Ghetto in Lithuania but lost both parents. Her diary entry for 9 May reads: *'Yesterday Germany surrendered unconditionally. The war is over. Red flags fly triumphantly over Kovno. At long last, the ugly fascists have been decisively defeated . . . Whatever may come, I am delighted that the dictator has been brought to his knees. The arrogant fiend who touted "Germany, Germany, above all" now has to stoop to the barbarians of the East – the USSR.'*

Olga Vasilyevna, who with her sister, Zinaida, had ridden with the Cossacks on the Volga in August 1942, recalled the first moments of normality at the end of the conflict: *'The last days of the war . . . I remember this . . . We were driving and suddenly there was music somewhere. A violin . . . For me, the war ended that day . . . It was such a miracle; suddenly music!'*

Anastasia Voropaeva was a corporal and a searchlight operator with her unit in Germany. She came across some Russian girls who had been freed from forced labour camps: *'One of them was pregnant. The prettiest one. She had been raped by the boss she had worked for, who had forced her to live with him. She went along crying, beating her stomach. "I won't bring a Fritz home! I won't!" The other girls tried to reason with her . . . but she hanged herself . . . along with her little Fritz.'*

Sofya Kuntsevich welcomed the end of hostilities: *'When I see a common grave, I kneel before it. Before every common grave . . . always on*

my knees . . . I got as far as Berlin. I put my signature on the Reichstag:
"I, Sofya Kuntsevich, came here to kill war." [. . .]'

Many of the signatures, inscriptions and graffiti scratched on the walls of the Reichstag by Red Army soldiers were retained during its restoration, in the 1990s. Written in Cyrillic script, they include such slogans as *'Hitler kaputt'* and the names of individual soldiers. One of them was *'Boris Victorovich Sapunov'*. Boris was the first soldier to find his name when the restoration was complete. He said: *'We weren't proud, we were just drunk. And afraid that we could still be shot, right at the end.'*

Reflecting the mood of vicious revenge, some of the graffiti was offensive, and was removed, but, tucked away in the building's south-eastern corner, one obscure, faded expletive remains. Perhaps the restorers thought that one ordinary soldier's crudity should stand as testament: *'The Belorussian, I fuck Hitler in the arse.'*

27

AFTERMATH

MAY 1945–

At the end of the war, in May 1945, there were two fates for Germany. In the west, in the territories occupied by the US, Britain and France, the recovery became part of the general European revival. It was a renewal instigated by the Marshall Plan, in which the US transferred over $12 billion (equivalent to over $129 billion as of 2021) in its economic recovery programmes to Western European nations. The period from 1948 to 1952 brought the fastest period of growth in European history. Industrial production increased by 35 per cent and agricultural production significantly outstripped pre-war levels. The destitution of the immediate post-war years disappeared, and Western Europe enjoyed twenty years of unprecedented growth. In what soon became West Germany, the single major trauma that remained was the one that Germans still live with: the huge burden of guilt for the aggression and brutality of its armed forces and the genocide of the Holocaust and other crimes against humanity.

The Germans in the east, in what soon became part of the Soviet Eastern Bloc as the German Democratic Republic (East Germany), had a different destiny. They too had to live with the guilt of their behaviour during the war, but their fate meant that they had to live within an oppressive regime until the collapse of the Soviet Union and German reunification. The East German economy did recover, but slowly and strictly along communist lines. Peace came, but only within the strictures of an authoritarian society.

In the first instance, the traumas of the Red Army occupation – the looting, rape and violence – took many months to dissipate.

In many cities, the Red Army's hierarchy was either unwilling or unable to control the behaviour of its men. The problem was exacerbated by the conduct of nearly 2 million released Russian POWs and forced labourers. Gangs of them roamed the streets and coalesced into significant groups of armed bandits, who hid in the countryside and forests. Reports suggested that, as late as 1948, bandits were still operating in the woods around Berlin.

It took the Red Army far longer to restore order among its men than it had taken to conquer Germany's homeland. The Chief of Police of Merseburg, a town in Saxony, East Germany, reported the following crimes, by 'persons in Soviet uniform', for the period 1 January to 3 May 1946: '34 murders, 345 robberies after breaking and entering, 328 robberies on the street, 60 train robberies, 123 stolen cows, 212 assaults and injuries (10 ending in death) and 162 rapes.'

Looting was commonplace. Ordinary Red Army soldiers – humble peasants, poorly paid factory workers, who had never seen anything even resembling the luxuries available to the German people – regarded everything the Germans owned as a spoil of war. Truckloads of booty flooded back to the east. The postal service was overwhelmed. Watches, cameras and jewellery became a form of currency. Even the great Zhukov was said to have helped himself to the goods and chattels of the vanquished. He was accused of sending home to Moscow seven freight cars of furniture and carpets to furnish his several apartments in the city, in addition to countless expensive trinkets, including diamonds and gold.

During Stalin's post-war witch-hunts, intended to denounce those around him who had become too powerful, he had Zhukov's dacha searched. The report read, 'It is a museum.' The 'museum' included 17 gold rings, 323 furs, 400 metres of velvet and silk, 44 carpets, and so many paintings that 'some even hung in the kitchen'. Over his bed, there was 'a huge canvas depicting two naked women . . . but not a single Soviet book'. Also found were 'twenty unique shotguns from Holland and Holland', the renowned UK gunsmith. Unlike many others, Zhukov was not tortured, nor was he sent to a gulag, but his 'luxuries' were confiscated, and he was sidelined to minor military roles in Ukraine, and then in the Urals.

Germany's total defeat led to an ideological/philosophical purging: 'Nazism' and 'Hitler' became words never to be spoken. The immediate past and its wickedness became taboo, and a policy of 'de-Nazification' was strenuously pursued by the post-war Allied administrations. Whether in the liberal democracy of West Germany, or in communist East Germany, Hitler's fanaticism was purified from the German psyche.

International efforts were made to pursue those who had been guilty of committing the worst atrocities during the war. The Nuremberg Trials defined and began to codify a legal framework for prosecuting those accused of 'genocide' and 'crimes against humanity'. Nevertheless, only a handful of Nazis were punished for the countless crimes that had been committed in the east as part of Barbarossa. Several took their own lives, rather than face retribution, and an unknown number managed to escape to safe havens, mainly in South America. The vast majority of the perpetrators of some of the most gruesome acts of barbarity eventually managed, after arrest and relatively short prison sentences, to revert to civilian life. Some even avoided capture and recrimination altogether, denying any guilt to their dying days. Several leading generals cooperated with the Allies and managed to reinvent themselves as members of a 'clean' Wehrmacht.

It is thought that Bruno Dey, a ninety-three-year-old pensioner and former SS Guard at the Stutthof concentration camp, who was convicted of being an accessory to murder in a Hamburg court in July 2020, may be the last surviving German war criminal to be brought to trial. He was convicted on 5,232 counts and sentenced to two years' suspended probation. He was sentenced according to German juvenile criminal law, as he was only seventeen when he committed his crimes. Journalistic sources suggest that there may be fourteen cases still being investigated. However, it is thought that few, if any, will ever go to court.

•

Operation Barbarossa spelled the end of the Nazi–Soviet Non-Aggression Pact, described as 'a pact with Satan to drive out the Devil'. Significantly, while Germany's ruthless despot (the 'Satan' of the pact) was but a charred cadaver, his 'Thousand Year Reich' obliterated, Stalin (the 'Devil' of that deceitful deal) was still in the Kremlin and widely glorified as the saviour of the Motherland. In June 1945, he resurrected a tsarist title and made himself 'Generalissimo of the Soviet Union'. Instead of rebuilding the nation's internal infrastructure and enhancing its social system to the benefit of its hard-working people, he chose to advance his grandiose ambitions by devoting vast expenditure to the arms and space races of the Cold War. It was an attempt to keep pace with the United States – a nation which, in both military and economic terms, was the most powerful in the world – but it was a challenge the Soviet Union could never meet, and the expenditure bled the country white. Meanwhile, Beria and his henchmen were still in control of the NKVD and its notorious prison at Lubyanka, with their elaborate machinery of oppression, torture and murder. The country was an armed camp and Stalin more powerful than ever.

Lamentably, the oppression and suffering of the people of Eastern Europe did not end in 1945. Lyudmila Kashechkina was a partisan during the war. She was captured and tortured; beaten, kicked and whipped, and given what she called a 'fascist manicure' where needles were inserted under her fingernails. She was stripped, electrocuted and racked on wooden rollers so that her joints were dislocated. She witnessed an SS guard smash the skull of a young child on an iron water pump. She was sent to a labour camp in France, from which she escaped and joined the French Resistance and was awarded the Croix de Guerre.

After the war, she returned home to Belarus, anticipating what should have been a warm welcome for one of her country's genuine heroes: *'I came back home . . . I remember . . . the first stop on our land . . . We all jumped off the train and kissed the ground . . . I arrived in Minsk, but my husband wasn't there. He had been arrested by the NKVD; he was in prison . . . They tell me, "Your husband is a traitor." But my husband and I worked together in the underground. The two of us. He was a brave man. He's a true communist. His interrogator started yelling at me, "Silence, French prostitute, Silence!" They had many questions about him: He had lived under the occupation, why didn't he die? How did he stay alive? They didn't take into consideration that we fought, sacrificed everything for the sake of victory. And we won . . . The people won! But Stalin didn't trust the people. That was how our Motherland repaid us. For our love, for our blood.*

My husband was released after six months. When he was captured by the fascists, they smashed his skull, broke his arm, but the NKVD made him an invalid for good. They broke his ribs, injured his kidney . . . I took care of him for years. But I wasn't allowed to say anything against them; he wouldn't hear of it . . . "It was a mistake, that's all." And I believed him.'

Valentina M—va did not want to reveal her full name as she told her post-war story: '*Even after the war, I lived in fear. Lived in hell . . . It was a warm September* [in 1945], *I remember the sun. I remember the fruit. A lot of fruit. My neighbour called me from downstairs, "Valya! Valya!" I rushed downstairs, and there was my husband . . . my Ivan . . . my dearest little husband . . . He had come back from the front! Alive! I kiss him. I stroke his shirt, his hands . . . He stands as if turned to stone. He doesn't smile, he doesn't hug me. Perhaps he's shell-shocked, deaf? It doesn't matter, I'll take care of him. Many wives have husbands like it.*

We had one night. Just one night. The next day they came for him. He had gone through Romania, Czechoslovakia. He brought back honours. He had already been through two interrogations. He had been marked because he had been a prisoner. He had been wounded and captured at Smolensk in the first days of the war but had escaped and joined the Ukrainian partisans. When Ukraine was liberated, he had gone to the front and was in Czechoslovakia on victory day and recommended for a medal. His interrogator yelled at him, "Why are you alive? Why did you stay alive?" He was taken away.

He came home seven years later. He had been in the Kolyma labour camp [in the far east of Siberia]. *Our son had grown up. I had become "an enemy of the people". My entire life was wasted. I keep silent. My husband keeps silent. We're afraid even now. We're frightened . . . And we'll die scared. Bitter and ashamed.'*

Stalin's pre-war paranoia, a time of fearsome darkness that had gripped the country, and had only abated temporarily during the war, came back with a vengeance as soon as the war was over. The tragic stories of Lyudmila and Valentina were not unusual. There were countless examples of soldiers and civilians who, rather than being lauded for what they had achieved, were hunted down and punished for having survived.

Freed from direct involvement in fighting the Wehrmacht, the NKVD went on a post-war rampage. It carried out mass arrests, deportations and executions. The targets included both supposed and actual collaborators with Germany and various anti-communist resistance movements, like those in Poland, Ukraine and the Baltic States. Its punitive actions continued until the early 1950s. In Western Ukraine between 1946 and 1949, an estimated 500,000 people were deported into exile in Soviet Siberia or Central Asia.

Although the war against Germany was over, the Red Army was still fighting. After having extracted territorial concessions from Roosevelt at the Yalta Conference, in exchange for an undertaking to invade Japanese-occupied territories in Asia, Stalin launched his invasion of Manchuria on 9 August 1945. One and a half million Soviet personnel were committed to the attack and although the Japanese Army fought tenaciously, the fighting was soon over.

As in Europe, the Soviets dismantled Japanese industries and enterprises in the area and transported them back to continental Russia. Similarly, the behaviour of the soldiers of the Red Army in Asia was as reprehensible as its conduct in Germany. The property of the Japanese was looted, and Soviet soldiers attacked and raped Japanese civilians. One such atrocity took place at Gegenmiao, in Inner Mongolia, where over a thousand Japanese women and children were raped and murdered. More than 1,800 Japanese women had taken refuge in the Tibetan Lamasery. On the morning of 14 August, after they had raised a white flag, in just two hours, over half the refugees were shot, run over by tanks, or bayoneted by Soviet soldiers.

Mankichi Oshima was a nine-year-old boy at the time of the massacre. Gegenmiao was a long way from Berlin, but Mankichi's story was very familiar: *'We tried to hide from the soldiers and ran towards a trench together with my mother and sister. We ducked down with some other evacuees, but the Soviet soldiers came down into the trench as well. As the soldiers chased us, the adults started to commit suicide and kill the children. I was waiting for my turn to be killed when my father and older brother found us. My younger sister had already been killed, and we had to leave her body behind as we escaped.'*

As the Red Army advanced, many Japanese women married local men to protect themselves from persecution by Soviet soldiers. According to Soviet historians, many Japanese civilians committed mass suicide as the Red Army approached. Mothers were forced by the Japanese military to kill their own children before killing or being killed themselves; the Japanese Army often took part in the killing of its own civilians.

•

Away from the tragedies of war, nature dealt the Soviet Union a severe blow in the summer of 1946. A major famine began to hit the country in July, reaching a peak between February and August 1947 before subsiding, although deaths from famine were still being recorded in 1948. A severe drought was the major cause of the crisis, but the havoc wrought by the war was also a major contributor. By the end of the conflict, in May 1945, almost a whole generation had gone, industry and agriculture had been all but annihilated, and hunger and disease were rampant.

The grain harvest in 1946 was barely 40 per cent of the yield in 1940. There was a significant decrease in the number of able-bodied men in the rural population, accompanied by a shortage of agricultural machinery and horses. The politics of the Kremlin also made matters worse. In order to consolidate control of its new Eastern Bloc, Stalin's government continued to export food to Soviet-occupied Europe.

It is estimated that at least 1 million people died in the famine, but it could have been many more. The figures rival the losses on some of the bloodiest battlefields of the Eastern Front. In Moldova between 1946 and 1947, there were at least 115,000 deaths. Thirty-four cases of cannibalism were reported over the same period, although the figure was likely to have been much higher. In Ukraine, there were between 400,000 and 500,000 child and teenage deaths and there was an escalation in cannibalism. Disease soon followed and teams had to be created to collect bodies, which were put into mass graves.

Valentin Caşu, a Ukrainian of Romanian descent, lived in Chernivtsi, Western Ukraine: '*I fought for the Soviet Union, even against the country of my ancestors. I was once proud of our collective farms and trusted Stalin, but now everyone in our village is starving. I am a trained soldier and know how to survive, but I'm worried about the old people and the children.*' Three-quarters of Caşu's village of 300 had died by the spring of 1946.

In Russia itself, at least 500,000 people perished. Two state decrees were passed on 5 June 1947, the 'Laws of Spikelets' (ears of wheat). The laws made attacks on state property punishable by five to twenty-five years in prison. For even very small thefts of a few ears of wheat, the punishment was up to one year in prison. For stealing a few pounds of grain, a person could be sent to the gulags for up to ten years. Stanislav Obolensky lived through the famine in Russia: '*It was the ultimate tragedy. After what we had lived through, to have won our freedom, then for us to die of hunger in our tens of thousands was the greatest sadness of all.*'

After the war, ill health and fatigue led Stalin to spend increasing amounts of time away from Moscow, especially amidst the warmth of his summer dacha at Lake Ritsa in Abkhazia, close to the Black Sea, in the beautiful mountains of Georgia. It was one of five he kept in the south. Apparently, such was his fear of his rivals, each dacha had to be fully prepared for a sudden visit, and he never told anyone in the Kremlin which of the five he was using.

From 1946 onwards, Stalin made only three speeches, all very brief. However, his ruthlessness and paranoia remained as intense as ever. He had several of his doctors arrested on suspicion of disloyalty, and subsequently tortured to produce confessions incriminating themselves. In 1951, he initiated the Mingrelian Affair, a purge of the Georgian branch of the Communist Party, which resulted in over 11,000 deportations.

During this time, Stalin also exhibited growing anti-Semitism and removed several leaders of the Jewish community around him and in his Soviet satellite states. He began his anti-Semitic purge by repressing his wartime allies, the Jewish Anti-Fascist Committee. In January 1948, Solomon Mikhoels, the chairman of the JAC, was assassinated on Stalin's personal orders, in Minsk. Mikhoels was arrested and killed under the supervision of Stalin's Deputy Minister of State Security, Sergei Ogoltsov. His murder was disguised as a hit-and-run car accident, and his body dumped on a roadside in the city.

In November 1948, the Soviet authorities launched a campaign to liquidate what was left of Jewish culture. The leading members of the JAC were arrested. They were charged with treason, 'bourgeois nationalism' and planning to set up a Jewish republic in the Crimea to serve American interests. Repressive action was taken to eradicate Jewish history: the Museum of Environmental Knowledge of the Jewish Autonomous Oblast (established in November 1944) and the Jewish Museum in Vilnius (established at the end of the war) were both closed down. The Historical-Ethnographic Museum of Georgian Jewry (established in 1933) was shut down at the end of 1951. Stalin's anti-Semitism may have been motivated by his fear that Jews were a potential danger because of their ties with a pro-Western Israel in the Middle East, despite his support for an independent Jewish state in the early years after the war.

In November 1952, the Slánský trial took place in Czechoslovakia. Fourteen senior Communist Party figures, eleven of them Jewish, were accused and convicted of being part of a vast Zionist-American conspiracy to subvert Eastern Bloc governments. All fourteen defendants were found guilty, eleven of them were sentenced to death and executed by public hanging; the remaining three received life sentences.

Following eight more years of Stalin's tyrannical post-war rule, his wearying burden on the Soviet people and those around his empire was eased a little in 1953. After suffering a cerebral haemorrhage on 1 March, Stalin died four days later. There were suggestions that Lavrentiy Beria had had him murdered. Indeed, Beria himself claimed responsibility. According to Molotov's memoirs, Beria declared that he had 'done [Stalin] in' and 'saved [us] all'. However, there is no real evidence to support Beria's assertion. In fact, his own arrest and execution were only months away.

Despite what he had done to those he ruled, the mourning of Stalin's death was an extraordinary outpouring of emotion. His body was embalmed and placed on display in Moscow's Hall of Columns, in the Trade Union Building, for three days. The crowds were such that a crush killed 100 people. People wept openly in the streets. In sub-zero temperatures, hundreds of thousands waited to file past his black-framed catafalque.

By the time of his death, the victory on the Eastern Front that his people had brought him had left Stalin able to govern a mighty empire, one even more expansive and powerful than that of the tsars. The new Soviet Union and its satellite and aligned states controlled huge areas of the globe. Quite apart from distant allies in Cuba, Africa and South-East Asia, the Generalissimo held sway over a vast Eastern Bloc. It stretched from the border with West Germany in the west to the Bering Straits in the east, a distance of eleven time zones. In the north, it reached from the frozen wastes of the Arctic to the Black Sea, the Caucasus and the Gobi Desert in the south.

Importantly, Soviet territorial gains in the Far East, and the demise of Japan, laid the foundations of the geopolitics of Asia well into the twenty-first century. Mao Tse Tung's communist victory in the subsequent civil war in China led to the rise of the People's Republic in 1949, while the ideological division of the Korean peninsula led to the 1950–53 Korean War and a political stalemate that has lasted for seventy years. More broadly, communist movements flourished across Asia, with major consequences in countries that were still part of European empires, such as Vietnam, Laos, Cambodia and Malaya.

Stalin's last speech was delivered to the 19th Party Congress of the Communist Party of the Soviet Union on 14 October 1952. He ended the speech with a call for the success of the communist parties in the capitalist world:

> Long live the peace between the peoples!
>   (*Prolonged applause.*)
> Down with the arsonists of war!
>   (*Everyone stood up. Stormy, prolonged applause that became an ovation. Shouts of 'Long live Comrade Stalin!', 'Long live the great leader of the working people of the world, Comrade Stalin!', 'The great Stalin!', 'Long live peace between the peoples!'*)

He was a revolutionary to the last, but his rallying cry came to nothing. As we approach the middle years of the twenty-first century, there are a mere handful of countries in the world with communist principles. However, all but one of them have, to a certain extent, embraced private ownership and wealth, leaving perhaps North Korea as the only country that could be described as 'Stalinist'.

The Soviet leaders who followed Stalin were less ruthless, but also less perceptive. The Soviet sphere of influence declined, the Soviet Union lost most of its non-Russian states and the Eastern Bloc disintegrated. However, in time, a new Russian tsar appeared – a leader who, just like Stalin, has risen to enormous power on a wave of national pride and love for Mother Russia.

Neither the applause for the 'Great Stalin' nor the words of his final rallying cry to communists around the world offer us any great insight into the enigma that is Russia and its people. When looking at the legacy of Barbarossa, it is clear that Stalin and Hitler left indelible imprints on their domains, leaving marks – stigmas, even – that will always be prominent in the long legacies of their countries. And yet, neither man – neither Stalin (a Georgian, not a Russian) nor Hitler (an Austrian, not a German) – defines the country he ruled.

In the context of Russia's recent history, Stalin's geopolitical legacy was a potent brew. His terrors, the state system he built and the extraordinary events he presided over during the war on the Eastern Front are, overwhelmingly, the critical experiences of the modern Russian people. However, it is in the voices of the ordinary Soviet citizens – people whose lives, families and futures were swept away in the ferocious onslaught of Barbarossa – that we truly begin to understand the impact of the campaign in the East. The witness testimonies in this book, many of them long forgotten, some of them previously undiscovered or ignored in the West, are the antidote to the horror and brutality of war. Their testimonies – which variously express bravery, resignation, stoicism, devotion to their Motherland, ruthlessness in war, generosity in peace, pride in their intellectual heritage – reveal to us the individual and shared experiences of the people who lived through 'the bloodiest war in history'. Perhaps, in very simple terms, it is Barbarossa – Russia's 'Great Patriotic War' – that bares the soul of the nation.

ACKNOWLEDGEMENTS

There are many to thank who, despite the limitations of my own contribution, have made this book possible and rendered it moderately coherent and plausible. Russian historian, documentary-maker and academic Victor Belyakov and his research associates in various Russian archives have produced a rich vein of original letters and diaries which constitute important new material for the book. I am also indebted to the many authors who have gone before me in attempting to tell the extraordinary story of the Eastern Front. I have drawn on their excellent work to help me piece my account together. I have readily borrowed several of their quotes from the witness material they have gathered because they are so powerful. They are all listed in the Select Bibliography and referenced in the Endnotes. I thoroughly recommend them all to anyone who would like to delve into more detail about the war.

An author is a voice in the wilderness without a publisher. Over the years, Alex Clarke, Publishing Director at Wildfire, has become my mentor and good friend. I suppose his support for my modest works may lead some to question his literary judgement! Nevertheless, he is the rock around which this book is formed and I will always be grateful to him for his encouragement and wise counsel. Alex is also surrounded by a great team. Shan Morley Jones, the nicest, most astute and benign copyeditor an author could wish for, has, once again, turned a dog's breakfast of a manuscript into a vaguely edible repast; Serena Arthur, Wildfire's Editorial Assistant, has, with a calm reassurance and a permanent smile, done all the hard work in honing all the many details required to transform a crude manuscript into a finished article. More broadly within Headline, of which Wildfire is a part, Publicity Manager, Rosie Margesson, and Head of Marketing, Jo Liddiard, have worked wonders in generating interest in the book and in convincing people that it is a far better piece of work than it actually is.

Finally, without the ones I love, who put up with my limitations, bad temper and idiosyncrasies, this book would never have been started, let alone finished. To Lucy, my patient and ever-encouraging wife, to my sons, Adam (and his wife, Michelle), Charlie and Jack, and my grandchildren, Sam and Jess, my very grateful thanks.

WITNESSES

(The witnesses are listed in order of first appearance.)

Introduction

Lyubov Shaporina. Apart from being the founder of Leningrad's Puppet Theatre, Shaporina was an artist, designer and translator. Her diary, published for the first time in 2011, covers the period from the 1920s to the 1960s and addresses a wide range of subjects, including politics, economics, religion, life in her country's cities and villages, the siege of Leningrad, political repression, the activities of the NKVD, literary life, music, painting and theatre. She died in 1967, at the age of seventy-eight.

Volha Barouskaya. The location of the massacre described so graphically by Barouskaya is currently a forested area behind the Zialiony Luh district of Minsk, next to the city's ring road.

Lavrentiy Beria. After the war, Beria organised the communist takeover of the state institutions in Central and Eastern Europe. After Stalin's death, in March 1953, Beria became First Deputy Premier of the Soviet Union. In a coup led by Khrushchev, in 1953, Beria was arrested on multiple charges of rape and treason. Marshal Zhukov was the arresting officer. Beria was sentenced to death and executed in December 1953. A violent sexual predator and ruthless assassin, he went to his death wailing and pleading for mercy. None was forthcoming. Quotes from Beria are from his son's book. See below.

1. A Pact with Satan to Drive out the Devil

Vyacheslav Molotov. An old Bolshevik and protégé of Stalin, Molotov served as Foreign Minister in 1935–49, and again in 1953–6. After the war, Molotov was involved in negotiations with the Western Allies. He retained his place as a leading Soviet diplomat and politician until March 1949, when he fell out of Stalin's favour. His relationship with Stalin deteriorated further. However, after Stalin's death, in 1953, Molotov was resolutely opposed to Khrushchev's de-Stalinisation policy and defended Stalin's legacy until his death in 1986 at the age of ninety-six.

Sergo Beria. After the war, Sergo graduated from the Leningrad Military Academy of Communications. While working on his diploma, he designed the first Soviet air-to-sea KS-1 *Kometa*-class cruise missile and became one of the country's top military engineers. His master's and doctoral dissertations were based on his projects, for which he also received the Order of Lenin and the Stalin Prize. After the arrest and execution of his father, in 1953, Sergo was placed in solitary confinement for a year, and deprived of all ranks, awards and academic degrees. In 1954, together with his mother, he was sent into 'administrative exile' in the Urals, where he was nevertheless given a three-room apartment and the right to work on his rocket designs. Son and mother also changed their surname to Gegechkori (his mother's maiden name), convinced that 'with the surname Beria people would tear us apart'. From 1990 to 1999, Sergo worked as a chief designer at the Kiev Research Institute. In 1999, he wrote *Beria, My Father*, translated by Brian Pearce and published in English by Duckworth in 2001, in which he desperately tried to rehabilitate his father, whom he loved dearly. He firmly believed that all his father's actions had been in the interests of the state. Sergo died in Kiev in 2000, aged seventy-five.

Valentin Berezhkov. In 1945, Valentin turned to journalism and from 1969 to 1988 was Chief Editor for the Soviet monthly journal *USA-Economics, Politics, Ideology*. Berezhkov received a doctorate from the Institute of USA and Canada Studies in 1974 and taught at Moscow State University and the Moscow State Institute of International Relations. From 1978 to 1983 he served in the Soviet Embassy in

Washington as First Secretary. He also taught at the Monterrey Institute of International Studies, Claremont College, and Occidental College in California. He wrote seven books, including, in 1991, his last book, *I was Stalin's Interpreter*, which was reissued in the United States, in 1994, as *At Stalin's Side*. He died in 1998, in Los Angeles, at the age of eighty-two.

Georgy Zhukov. In 1939, military veteran Zhukov had been given command of an army group and won a decisive battle over Japanese forces at Khalkhin Gol, for which he had won the first of his four Hero of the Soviet Union awards. In February 1941, he had been appointed as Chief of the Red Army's General Staff but was replaced following Barbarossa. After his defence of both Leningrad and Stalingrad, he planned several major offensives, including the Battle of Kursk and Operation Bagration. In 1945, Zhukov commanded the Battle for Berlin and took the German surrender. After the war, Zhukov's success and popularity led to Stalin seeing him as a threat. He was stripped of his positions and relegated to minor commands. After Stalin's death, in 1953, Zhukov supported Khrushchev's bid for Soviet leadership and, in 1955, was appointed as Defence Minister. In 1957, he lost favour again and was forced to retire. Zhukov's memoirs in two volumes were first published in Russian in Moscow, in 1974. In 2013, they were published in English as *Marshal of Victory*, edited by Geoffrey Roberts, and translated by Svetlana Frolova, published by Stackpole Books in the USA and Pen & Sword Military in the UK. Zhukov died in 1974 at the age of seventy-seven.

Dawid Sierakowiak. Based on his last diary entry, and recent research, it is thought that Dawid died towards the end of 1943 of tuberculosis, starvation and exhaustion, the syndrome known as 'ghetto disease'. Dawid's diary was discovered by a Polish gentile, Waclaw Szkudlarek, who originally lived in one of the apartments that was evacuated to create the ghetto. Szkudlarek only returned to his home after the Red Army liberated the city, five years later. At least two of the notebooks that Dawid kept as his diary have been lost. The first two notebooks were published in Poland in 1960, edited by Holocaust scholar Lucjan Dobroszycki, also a survivor of the Łódź Ghetto. In 1967, a leading

Łódź journalist, Konrad Turowski, purchased the three surviving notebooks and was preparing them for publication when an outbreak of
anti-Semitism under the then communist regime in Poland blocked
the publication. Years passed before a full version of all five surviving
notebooks was finally published and made available to the public, in
1998.

3. A Warm Sunny Morning

Nikolai Evseev. Nikolai escaped from the siege of Sevastopol and survived the war.

Dimitri Pavlov. After Stalin's death, Dimitri Pavlov and other commanders were rehabilitated. In 1965, he was reinstated as a Hero of the
Soviet Union and his other honours were returned. It was not until the
Gorbachev era that it was declared publicly that Pavlov had not been
the main culprit in the defeat of June 1941 and that the orders given
to him could not have been fulfilled by anyone.

Semyon Timoshenko. The failure of the 1942 Kharkov counter-attack
and Zhukov's success in defending Moscow during December 1941
had persuaded Stalin that Zhukov was a better commander than
Timoshenko. Stalin removed Timoshenko from front-line command
in July 1943, but he retained his senior position in the military hierarchy. After the war, he held various military posts and, in 1960, was
appointed Inspector General of the Defence Ministry, a largely honor-
ary post. He died in Moscow in 1970 at the age of seventy-five.

Dimitri Masslinikov. Dimitri was one of the few survivors of the 13th
Regiment in June 1941. Most of its men were able to escape from
being encircled by the German advance at Bialystok, but when they
were trapped again near Minsk, only a few dozen escaped. Masslinikov
was one of them. Gravely wounded, he hid in a ditch until he was
found by some local partisans, who managed to get him back to a
Red Army unit. He spent the rest of the war in a hospital in Armenia.

Vasily Kuznetzov. The remnants of Kuznetzov's 3rd Army fought its
way back to Soviet lines, earning him much praise from Stalin. He

continued with several commands throughout the war, including the Battle for Berlin, where his 1st Belorussian, 3rd Shock Army was involved in the street battles in the German capital. One of its units, the 150th Rifle Division, stormed the Reichstag and hoisted the Victory Banner above the building. It was raised by three Soviet soldiers: Alexei Berest, Mikhail Yegorov and Meliton Kantaria.

Ivan Boldin. General Boldin had a series of commands until the end of the war. His memoirs, *Pages of Life*, were published by the Soviet Ministry of Defence Publishing House, in 1961. Boldin died in Kiev, in 1965, at the age of seventy-two.

Elena Skrjabina. She and her family survived the siege of Leningrad when they were evacuated across the frozen Lake Lagoda, eventually arriving in Pyatigorsk in the Caucasus. When that city fell to the invading German Army, they escaped once more, to Ukraine, where she was conscripted into a labour battalion and ended in a forced labour camp in the Rhineland. At the end of the war, she was able to emigrate with her two sons to the United States, where she became a professor of French at the University of Iowa. Her diary recording her wartime experiences in the Soviet Union was translated by Norman Luxenburg and published in English as *Siege and Survival: The Odyssey of a Leningrader* by Southern Illinois University Press, in 1971.

Misha Volkov. Misha's diary is kept in the Russian State Archive of Social and Political History, Moscow.

Konstantin Simonov. Konstantin wrote accounts throughout the war all the way to Berlin. After the war, he continued as a journalist and writer. He died in Moscow, in 1979, at the age of sixty-three. Simonov's words as used in the 1942 Soviet propaganda poster 'Kill Him' were extracted and adapted from his much longer poem '*Ubey Yego*' ('Kill Him'), published in *Pravda* on 19 July 1942.

4. Crisis in the Kremlin

Anastas Mikoyan. After the war, Mikoyan remained in positions of power. When Stalin died, in 1953, he backed Khrushchev and his de-Stalinisation policy and became First Deputy Premier under Khrushchev. In 1964, Khrushchev was forced to step down in a coup that brought Leonid Brezhnev to power. Mikoyan served as Chairman of the Presidium of the Supreme Soviet, the nominal Head of State, from 1964 until his forced retirement in 1965. He died in 1978, at the age of eighty-two.

Colonel Ivan Fedyuninsky. The colonel survived the war and was made a general in 1955. His memoirs, *Underground on Alert*, were published by Military Memoirs Moscow, in 1961. Fedyuninsky died in 1965, at the age of seventy-seven.

Elena Kudina. Valentina survived the war. She was interviewed by Nobel Prize winner Svetlana Alexievich for her outstanding anthology *War's Unwomanly Face*, which was published in English for the first time in 1988, by Progress Publishers, Moscow. The anthology is now available as a Penguin Modern Classic, *The Unwomanly Face of War* (English translation by Richard Pevear and Larissa Volokhonsky).

Nikolai Moskvin. Nikolai survived the first Battle of Smolensk. He was later injured in a battle near the city and hid in the woods until he was rescued by local villagers, with whom he stayed to help with the autumn harvest. Behind German lines, but in the remote countryside, he was temporarily out of harm's way and survived the war. His diary is in the State Archive of the Smolensk Oblast.

Gabriel Temkin. Gabriel survived the early days of the invasion, in June 1941, and was soon drafted into the Red Army. But, as a foreigner (Polish), and Jewish, he was assigned to a labour battalion. He was captured digging trenches for the defence of Stalingrad in the Don Valley, in July 1942, and sent to a prisoner of war camp, where his 'Aryan appearance' saved his life. He escaped from the camp and rejoined the Red Army, working as a German translator. He settled in Poland after the war with his wife, Hannah, but then moved to America. He died in Florida, in 2006, at the age of eighty-five. His parents and siblings perished in the Łódź Ghetto.

5. Smolensk

Panteleimon Ponomarenko. After the occupation of Belorussia, in 1941, Ponomarenko became one of the leaders of the local partisan groups. During this time, it is claimed he clashed with Polish partisans. After the war he became a member of the Soviet Politburo and an ambassador. Ponomarenko died in 1984, at the age of eighty-one.

Andrei Yeremenko. Marshal Yeremenko continued to hold senior military commands. In 1955, he was given the rank of Marshal of the Soviet Union. In 1958, he was made Inspector General for the Ministry of Defence, a largely ceremonial role that allowed him to retire that same year. His diaries, *Stalingrad, Memoirs of a Front Commander*, were published by Voenizdat, in Moscow, in 1961. Yeremenko died in 1970, at the age of seventy-eight.

Nikolai Amosoff. Nikolai survived the war, became an acclaimed Ukrainian heart surgeon and best-selling author. He died in 2002, at the age of eighty-nine. In 2008, he was voted second in Ukraine's list of 'Greatest Compatriots'.

Vasili Chekalov. It is not known what became of Chekalov after Stalingrad. The last entry in his diary is dated 29 January 1943. It reads: *'Tried to rest, but the continuous stream of prisoners* [German] *did not even let you close your eyes, and then Khizhnyakov called and asked for a farewell evening I had to arrange. The beginning of the evening was delayed, and only about midnight when a small "evening" began. Much to my regret, I drank an extra 100 grams. That spoiled my mood. I never went back to my dugout.'*

Nikolai Inozemtzev. Nikolai survived the war to become an economist and journalist. He became Deputy Editor-in-Chief of Pravda, the Party newspaper, Director of the Institute of World Economy and International Relations, and, in 1981, was elected to membership of the Central Committee of the Communist Party of the Soviet Union. Inozemtzev died in 1982, at the age of sixty-one.

6. Leningrad: The Great Siege Begins

Valeri Krukov. Valeri survived the war; his family were never heard of again. By the end of the war, Valeri had become a senior lieutenant in the Red Army. There is no known record of what became of him after 1945.

Yuri Ryabinkin. When his mother and sister were evacuated from the city, they were unable to carry him and had to leave him behind. It is not known for certain what became of Ryabinkin, although it is highly likely that he died where his mother had to leave him. His mother died during her evacuation on a bench at Vologda railway station (400 miles east of Leningrad). His father, who had been arrested during the 1936–37 Terrors, perished somewhere in a gulag. His sister, Ira, spent the rest of the war in a children's home and was later brought up by an aunt.

Dimitri Likhachev. Dimitri, his wife and twin daughters survived the siege of Leningrad. In 1943, he and his family were exiled to Kazan, Tatarstan. By the end of the war they had returned to Leningrad. He became a highly respected historian and linguist and a leading dissident. He wrote prodigiously, including heart-rending recollections of the siege of Leningrad. He died in 1992, at the age of ninety-one.

Maria Mostovskaya. Maria survived the siege of Leningrad and the war.

Ivan Fedulov. Ivan survived the war.

Alexandra Aresenyeva. Alexandra survived the siege of Leningrad and the war.

7. Leningrad: Starvation

Lydia Ginzburg. Lydia wrote a number of highly respected literary criticisms after the war. She died in Leningrad, at the age of eighty-eight, in 1990.

Olga Berggolts. Olga broadcast on the radio to the people of Leningrad throughout the siege. Her voice and words became a source of strength for the city. Before the siege, she had become critical of the regime and was arrested, beaten and imprisoned, as a result of which the baby she was carrying was stillborn. Her husband was imprisoned and shot. She was released and exonerated in 1939. In March 1942, she became so malnourished that, despite her protests, her friends forced her to leave Leningrad across Lake Ladoga's Road of Life. She recovered in Moscow and returned to Leningrad in April. She continued to write after the war. Olga died in Leningrad, in 1975, aged sixty-five. Her memory lives on at the Piskaryovskoye Memorial Cemetery, the resting place built to hold the 470,000 victims of the siege, where her words are engraved on a wall: 'No one is forgotten, nothing is forgotten.' Her diaries have been published in Russian in various collections, from *Leningrad Speaks* (1945) to *Olga, Forbidden Diary* (2010).

Vera Rogova. Vera survived the war.

Ivan Krylov. Ivan survived the war.

Vera Inber. Vera survived the war. Her diary was translated into English by Serge Wolff and Rachel Grieve and published as *Leningrad Diary* by Hutchinson, in London, in 1971. She died in 1972, at the age of eighty-two.

Anna Govorov. Anna's fate is unknown.

Aleksandra Liubovskaia. Alexandra survived the siege of Leningrad and the war.

Alexander Dymov. Alexander survived the siege of Leningrad and the war.

Dimitri Lazarev. Dimitri survived the siege of Leningrad and the war.

Elena Taranukhina. Elena survived the siege of Leningrad.

Maria Ivanova. Maria survived the siege of Leningrad.

Vasily Yershov. Vasili's diary is kept in the Bakhmeteff Archive at Columbia University, in New York.

Karl Eliasberg. Karl continued to conduct after the war. In 1964, there was a reunion for Karl and twenty-four of the original musicians with a performance in Shostakovich's presence. The survivors played in their same seats. Karl later wrote: *'I cannot explain the feeling I had. The glory of fame and the grief of loss, and the thought that maybe the brightest moments of your life are gone. The city now lives a peaceful life, but no one has the right to forget the past.'* He died in 1978, at the age of seventy.

Andrei Krukov. Andrei survived the siege of Leningrad. He became a musicologist and leading authority on the performance of Shostakovich's Seventh Symphony during the siege. He wrote several books about music during the siege, including *The Musical Life of Wartime Leningrad*, published by Kompozitor, in Leningrad, in 1985. He told his story and shared his diary with Michael Jones for his book *Leningrad: State of Siege*. Andrei's powerful words about surviving the siege are used by Jones to end the epilogue of his excellent account of the psychology of the siege.

Pavel Luknitsky. Pavel survived the siege of Leningrad. His account of it, *Leningrad Operates*, was published in three volumes, in Russian, in 1971.

8. The 'Brutal Dog' Let Loose

Yitskhok Rudashevski. After Yitskhok was murdered in the Ponary Massacre in 1943, his diary was discovered by his cousin, Sore Voloshin, a young woman who had escaped the massacre and joined a partisan group. Returning from the war, Sore found the diary in his hiding place. The diary is now stored in the archives of the Yivo Institute for Jewish Affairs, in New York. Originally written in Yiddish, it was published in English as *The Diary of the Vilna Ghetto* by the Ghetto Fighters' House, in Israel, in 1973.

Laimonas Noreika. Laimonas was interviewed about his recollections of the war in 2004. The recording is held in the United States Holocaust Museum. Laimonas died in 2007, in Vilnius.

Ephraim Oshry. Ephraim survived the Kaunas Ghetto and the war. He moved to Rome, then Canada and then New York with his second wife, Frieda. They had six sons and three daughters. He died in New York, in 2003, at the age of ninety-five.

Macha Rolnikas. Macha survived the Vilnius Ghetto before being moved to the Stutthof concentration camp for employment as an 'undertaker'. As a result of her 'employment', she survived in the camp until the Red Army liberated Stutthof, in 1944. She was reunited in Vilnius with her older sister and father; her younger siblings and mother had perished. Following the end of the war, Macha moved to the Soviet Union, first to study at the Maxim Gorky Literature Institute, and later to Leningrad, where she married. Her diary, *I Must Tell*, was first published in 1964, in Yiddish, Hebrew and Lithuanian. Macha died in 2016, at the age of eighty-nine.

Frida Michelson. After the Rumbula Massacre, Frida lived in the forest for the next three years. In 1950, she was deported to Siberia by the Soviet authorities but managed to get to Israel, in 1971. During the 1960s, she wrote down her memories of the war, in Yiddish, the original copy of which is in the Jews of Latvia Museum. Frida died in 1982, at the age of seventy-six.

Max Kaufmann. Max survived the war. He wrote down his memories in 1947, which were published in German, in Munich, under the auspices of the American Military Government of Occupation. Largely unnoticed for many years, his recollections were translated and finally made available in English, in 2010. He hoped his diary would serve as a dedication to the innocents of Latvia, 'May these few words be the flowers on their graves.' Max died in 1987, at the age of ninety.

Martyrs of Nowogródek. One of the Sisters survived the horror. Before reporting to the police station, Sister Maria Stella had asked one member of the community, Sister Maria Malgorzata Banas, who worked as a nurse in the local public hospital, to stay behind at the convent, to take care of the church and its pastor. She was the best candidate because she wore civilian clothing for her job. It was days before she and the townspeople knew that the other Sisters had been killed. Eventually, Banas located their grave, quietly tending it and the parish church during the war years and during the post-war Soviet occupation. She died in 1966.

The nuns who died (with their birth names and ages) were: Sister Maria Stella, Superior (Adelaide Mardosewicz, age 54), Sister Mary Imelda (Jadwiga Żak, age 50), Sister Mary Rajmunda (Anna Kukułowicz, age 50), Sister Maria Daniela (Eleanor Jóźwik, age 48), Sister Maria Kanuta (Józefa Chrobot, age 47), Sister Maria Gwidona (Helena Cierpka, age 43), Sister Maria Sergia (Julia Rapiej, age 42), Sister Maria Kanizja (Eugenia Mackiewicz, age 39), Sister Maria Felicyta (Paulina Borowik, age 37), Sister Maria Heliodora (Leokadia Matustzewska, age 37), Sister Maria Boromea (Veronika Narmuntowicz, age 26).

In September 1991, the canonisation process for the eleven sisters was officially opened, and on 28 June 1999, Pope John Paul II proclaimed that they were martyrs. They were beatified on Sunday, 5 March 2000.

Maria 'Masha' Bruskina. Maria went unacknowledged for many years after the war. Soviet anti-Semitism led her to be mentioned only as 'the unknown girl'. However, in 2009, a new memorial plaque, bearing her name, was placed at her execution site.

Dina Pronicheva. Dina's testimony is reproduced in Arad Yitzhak's comprehensive survey *The Holocaust of Soviet Jewry in the Occupied Territories of the Soviet Union*, Yad Vashem Studies, Volume XXI, published in Jerusalem, in 1991. Dina died in Moscow in 1977.

Raya Dashkevich. Raya's account can be found among the written testimonies at the Yad Vashem Holocaust Remembrance Centre in Jerusalem. There is also an account in Gil Samuil's book *Their Blood is Speaking Even Today*, published in New York, in 1995. Raya's husband died fighting the Germans. She became an accountant after the war. In 1991, she attended a Babi Yar memorial, which was also attended by American President George Bush. Written by Elizabeth Shogren, a report of Raya's visit to Babi Yar in 1991 was published in *The Los Angeles Times*, 30 September 1991. Raya died in 2003.

Ivan Bondarenko. The Ukrainian priest continued his life as a local priest after the war. He died in 1953.

9. Moscow: Enemy at the Gates

Konstantin Rokossovskiy. Rokossovskiy went on to take part in the counteroffensives at Stalingrad and Kursk. He was instrumental in planning and executing part of Operation Bagration, one of the most decisive Red Army victories in the war, after which he was made Marshal of the Soviet Union. After the war, he became Defence Minister in the newly established Polish People's Republic. He was dismissed in 1956, when a new regime came to power, and he returned to the Soviet Union, where he lived out the rest of his life until his death in 1968, aged seventy-one. An English edition of Rokossovskiy's diary, *A Soldier's Diary*, was published in 1970 by Progress Publishers, Moscow.

Ivan Shabalin. Shabalin was killed on 20 October when trying a night breakout from the encirclement. His diary was found by a German officer and translated for military intelligence. It was distributed to local German commanders to emphasise the demoralised state of the Soviet forces. The original diary was lost during the war.

Fyodor Bogratyov. It is not known what became of Fyodor at the end of the war. He was in Berlin on 2 May 1945 and left on the 4th. His last entry reads: '*We are 62 kilometres from Berlin at the barracks of our fellow Russians,* [German] *slaves and prisoners. We're waiting to be released home.*'

Mikhail Ivanovich. Mikhail survived the war. He stayed in state security and rose in the ranks of the KGB (which evolved from other agencies, such as the NKVD, in 1954). He was interviewed in 1971 for a collection of military memoirs and archival documents, and expressed no regrets about his actions in the NKVD.

Irina Tupikova. It is not known what became of Irina after her diary ends in January 1943.

Yelena Rzhevskaya. Yelena lived in Moscow after the war, where she continued her career as a writer. She was allowed to publish her memoirs in the 1960s. She died in April 2017, aged ninety-seven.

10. Moscow: 'Marshal Mud' and 'General Winter'

Vasily Grossman. Vasily reported on the Red Army's wartime story all the way to Berlin, in 1945. His accounts of the horrors of the Holocaust were among the first to be published. They are disturbingly graphic and vivid. After the war, Vasily fell foul of the Soviet regime and he became disillusioned with many of its policies. Although he was never arrested, many of his works were not published until after his death, in 1964, at the age of fifty-eight.

Oleg Kurganov. Oleg survived the war and continued to work as a photojournalist. He also became a scriptwriter and, in the 1970s, was involved in a series of television dramas about the war. He died in 1997, at the age of ninety. Kurganov's diary, *Eternal Flame*, was published by *Pravda*, in Moscow, in 1945.

11. Eyes South

Vladimir Gelfand. Vladimir survived the war. He had joined the Red Army in 1942 and reached the rank of first lieutenant. He fought in the Caucasus and at Stalingrad, and was in Berlin in 1945. After the war he became a teacher specialising in Russian history and literature. His diaries, spanning the years 1941 to 1946, were published in Swedish, German and Russian after the war. Gelfand died in 1983, at the age of sixty.

Ivan Laskin. Colonel Laskin went on to fight at Stalingrad and to organise the surrender of Field Marshal Paulus and his 6th Army. In 1943, then a general, he was arrested on trumped-up charges and taken to Lubyanka Prison in Moscow, the headquarters of the NKVD, and then to the notorious Sukhanovo Prison. He was not released until

1952, and was 'rehabilitated' the next year. In 1966, he was allowed to be presented with the American Government's Distinguished Service Cross. Laskin died in 1988, at the age of eighty-seven.

Boris Borisov. Boris survived the war and continued to live in Sevastopol. He wrote several accounts of the war, including *The Feat of Sevastopol*, published in 1957, and *Men of Sevastopol Do Not Surrender*, published in 1961. He died in 1980.

Oleksiy Gudzovsky. Oleksiy's letters are in held in the National Archives of Ukraine, in Kiev.

12. The Fulcrum

Albina Gantimurova. Albina survived the war. She was interviewed by Nobel Prize winner Svetlana Alexievich for her outstanding anthology *War's Unwomanly Face*, which was published in English for the first time in 1988, by Progress Publishers, Moscow. The anthology is now available as a Penguin Modern Classic, *The Unwomanly Face of War* (English translation by Richard Pevear and Larissa Volokhonsky).

Alexei Surkov. Alexei survived the war, after which he continued to write. He was particularly prolific as a poet, popular with the soldiers of the Red Army. Surkov died in 1983, at the age of eighty-three.

Ilya Ehrenburg. Ilya survived the war and continued to write prodigiously. He stayed loyal to the Soviet system, and his views became the subject of much intellectual debate. Much of his wartime writing was published as part of the Soviet propaganda campaign, especially his notorious 'Kill them all' article in *Red Star* on 13 August 1942. Ehrenburg's accounts of the war were published in two separate collections: *War* (in two volumes) and *Series on the War Years*, published by Novyi Mir, in Moscow, in 1943 and 1964 respectively. He died in 1967, at the age of seventy-six.

Elena Kovalevskaya. Elena survived the war. She was interviewed by Nobel Prize winner Svetlana Alexievich for her outstanding anthology

War's Unwomanly Face, which was published in English for the first time in 1988, by Progress Publishers, Moscow. The anthology is now available as a Penguin Modern Classic, *The Unwomanly Face of War* (English translation by Richard Pevear and Larissa Volokhonsky).

Sydir Kovpak. Kovpak was twice awarded the status of Hero of the Soviet Union and survived the war to become a Deputy of the Supreme Soviet of the USSR. He wrote several accounts of his life as a partisan, including *From Putivil to the Carpathian Mountains*, which was published immediately after the war, in 1945. The English translation was published by Politvydav Ukrainy, Kiev, in 1973. He died in 1967, at the age of eighty.

Dmitri Medvedev. Dmitri wrote his memoirs as *Stout Hearts: It Happened near Rovno*, published by Foreign Languages Publishing House, in 1948. His memoirs were published in English by the University Press of the Pacific, in 2002. Dimitri died in 1954, at the age of fifty-six.

Klara Tikhonovich. Klara survived the war. She was interviewed by Nobel Prize winner Svetlana Alexievich for her outstanding anthology *War's Unwomanly Face*, which was published in English for the first time in 1988, by Progress Publishers, Moscow. The anthology is now available as a Penguin Modern Classic, *The Unwomanly Face of War* (English translation by Richard Pevear and Larissa Volokhonsky).

Antonia Kondrashova. Antonia survived the war. She was interviewed by Nobel Prize winner Svetlana Alexievich for her outstanding anthology *War's Unwomanly Face*, which was published in English for the first time in 1988, by Progress Publishers, Moscow. The anthology is now available as a Penguin Modern Classic, *The Unwomanly Face of War* (English translation by Richard Pevear and Larissa Volokhonsky).

Alexandra Khramova. Alexandra survived the war. She was interviewed by Nobel Prize winner Svetlana Alexievich for her outstanding anthology *War's Unwomanly Face*, which was published in English for the first time in 1988, by Progress Publishers, Moscow. The anthology is now available as a Penguin Modern Classic, *The Unwomanly Face of War* (English translation by Richard Pevear and Larissa Volokhonsky).

Paulina Kasperovich. Paulina survived the war. She was interviewed by Nobel Prize winner Svetlana Alexievich for her outstanding anthology *War's Unwomanly Face*, which was published in English for the first time in 1988, by Progress Publishers, Moscow. The anthology is now available as a Penguin Modern Classic, *The Unwomanly Face of War* (English translation by Richard Pevear and Larissa Volokhonsky).

Zoya Kosmodemyanskaya. Zoya's fate became widely known after the publication of Pyotr Lidov's article 'Tanya' in the *Pravda* newspaper, in January 1942. The author learned of the Petrishchevo execution by chance, from a local elderly peasant who had witnessed it. In February of the same year, Zoya was posthumously awarded the title of Hero of the Soviet Union.

Pyotr Lidov. Pyotr was killed in a German air raid on Poltava air base, in Ukraine, in June 1944.

13. Protect the Oil.

Ivan Tyulenev. General Tyulenev remained the commander of the Transcaucasian Front for the rest of the war. He published several books about the war. He died in Moscow, in 1978, at the age of eighty-six. Tyulenev wrote several accounts of the war, including *Soviet Cavalry Fighting for the Fatherland* and *Through Three Wars*, published in 1957 and 1960 respectively, in Moscow.

Vasili Chuikov. After the war, General Chuikov was Chief of the Group of Soviet Forces in Germany. He was made Deputy Minister of Defence in 1960. In 1961, he became head of the Soviet Civil Defence Forces. Chuikov died in 1982, at the age of eighty-two.

Mitrofan Nedelin. The 'Lieutenant Nedelin' mentioned by Chuikov may well have been Mitrofan Nedelin, who was an artillery commander in the area in 1942. He eventually became a major general and, in 1959, Chief Marshal of Artillery. In 1960, Nedelin was killed in an explosion at the Baikonur Cosmodrome, when a test rocket exploded, killing 120 people. The catastrophe was named after him. He was fifty-six.

Zinaida Vasilyevna. Zinaida survived the war. She was interviewed by Nobel Prize winner Svetlana Alexievich for her outstanding anthology *War's Unwomanly Face*, which was published in English for the first time in 1988, by Progress Publishers, Moscow. The anthology is now available as a Penguin Modern Classic, *The Unwomanly Face of War* (English translation by Richard Pevear and Larissa Volokhonsky).

Marina Chechneva. Marina continued to fly after the war, including setting speed records and in competitive flying. She published five books about her career. She died in 1961, at the age of sixty-one. Chechneva's diary, *The Aircraft Take off into the Night*, was published by Military Education, in Moscow, in 1962.

Polina Gelman. Polina continued her career as a military officer after the war and trained to be a translator. Her story was included in *Heroines: Issue I. Essays on Women – Heroes of the Soviet Union*, published by Politizdat, in Moscow, in 1969. She died in 2005, at the age of eighty-six.

Alexandra Popova. Alexandra survived the war. She was interviewed by Nobel Prize winner Svetlana Alexievich for her outstanding anthology *War's Unwomanly Face*, which was published in English for the first time in 1988, by Progress Publishers, Moscow. The anthology is now available as a Penguin Modern Classic, *The Unwomanly Face of War* (English translation by Richard Pevear and Larissa Volokhonsky).

14. Stalingrad: The Great Battle Begins

Nikita Khrushchev. The record of Khrushchev's contemporaries during the Battle of Stalingrad suggests that he was highly regarded by them. He went on to lead the Soviet Union from the mid-1950s until 1964. He died in 1971, at the age of seventy-seven.

Andre Borodin. As Director of the Museum of Defence Tsaritsyn-Stalingrad, Borodin was asked to compile the casualty figures for the battle. (Tsaritsyn was the name of the city from 1589 to 1925.)

Alexander Rodimtsev. After Stalingrad, General Rodimtsev fought at the Battle of Kursk and in Operation Bagration. After the war, he was a commander in Siberia and a military attaché in Albania. Rodimtsev died in Moscow, in 1977, at the age of seventy-two.

Alexander Averbukh. Alexander was interviewed in Moscow, in 1942, while he was recuperating and waiting to receive his award, the Order of the Red Banner. It is not known what became of him after 1942, nor the fate of Captain Lizunov and his runner, whom he tried to save in Stalingrad.

Anatoly Chekhov. Chekhov's exploits were remarkable. From October 1942 to 28 January 1943, Chekhov killed 256 enemy German soldiers and officers. For his heroism and skill, Chekhov was nominated to the rank of Hero of the Soviet Union. However, the plane that was carrying the paperwork for the award was shot down while on its way to Moscow, meaning that he was denied the award. He died in 1965.

15. Stalingrad: Street by Street, House by House

Vasili Boltenko. Vasili survived Stalingrad. Apart from being mentioned in General Chuikov's memoirs, he told his own story in an interview that was conducted in May 1943 and included in Jochen Hellbeck's copious anthology *Stalingrad, the City that Defeated the Third Reich*, published in New York by the Perseus Book Group, in 2015.

Zinaida Golodnova. Zinaida survived the war.

Tamara Umnyagina. Tamara survived the war. She was interviewed by Nobel Prize winner Svetlana Alexievich for her outstanding anthology *War's Unwomanly Face*, which was published in English for the first time in 1988, by Progress Publishers, Moscow. The anthology is now available as a Penguin Modern Classic, *The Unwomanly Face of War* (English translation by Richard Pevear and Larissa Volokhonsky).

Leonty Gurtyev. Following the liberation of the city of Stalingrad, Gurtyev's division fought in the Battle of Kursk. However, on 8 August 1943, during the battle for the recapture of Orel, a shell exploded at

the officers' observation post and Gurtyev, using his body to protect
General Alexander Gorbatov, died from shrapnel wounds.

16. Stalingrad: Victory!

Ivan Golokolenko. Ivan survived the war. He was interviewed by
author and documentary maker Laurence Rees for his 2008 BBC TV
series and book *World War Two: Behind Closed Doors: Stalin, The Nazis,
and The West.*

Nikolai Aksyonov. Nikolai survived the war.

Valentina Krutova. Valentina and her siblings survived the war.

17. The Turning Tide

Vasily Kukhtinov. Vasily survived the war and gave his account to a
Ukrainian inquiry, in 2007.

Sergei Kovalenko. Sergei survived the war and gave his account to a
Ukrainian inquiry, in 2007.

Lyudmila Pavlichenko. Lyudmila took a degree in history after the
war and worked as a historian for the Soviet Navy. After struggles with
her mental health and alcohol, she died in Moscow in 1974, aged just
fifty-eight. A joint Ukrainian-Russian feature film, *Battle for Sevastopol*,
was made about her in 2015.

Roza Shanina. After Roza's death, her diary, consisting of three thick
notebooks, was kept for twenty years by the war correspondent Pyotr
Molchanov. An abridged version was published in the Russian literary magazine *Yunost*, in 1965, and the diary was transferred to the
Regional Museum of Arkhangel. Several of her letters have also been
published. Her diary has recently been translated into English by A.
G. Mogan and published as an e-book, *Stalin's Sniper: The War Diary
of Roza Shanina*. There are several Roza quotes in Lyuba Vinogradova,
Avenging Angels: Soviet Women Snipers on the Eastern Front (1941–45),
translated from the Russian by Arch Tait and published by MacLehose
Press, in 2017.

18. Blood and Iron: Kursk

Maria Savitskaya-Radiukevich. Maria survived the war. She was interviewed by Nobel Prize winner Svetlana Alexievich for her outstanding anthology *War's Unwomanly Face*, which was published in English for the first time in 1988, by Progress Publishers, Moscow. The anthology is now available as a Penguin Modern Classic, *The Unwomanly Face of War* (English translation by Richard Pevear and Larissa Volokhonsky).

Pavel Rotmistrov. Marshal Rotmistrov commanded mechanised forces in Germany in 1945, and retired in 1962. He died in Moscow, in 1982, at the age of eighty.

Trofim Teplenko. Vasili Grossman does not tell us what became of Trofim.

Olga Omelchenko. Olga survived the war. She was interviewed by Nobel Prize winner Svetlana Alexievich for her outstanding anthology *War's Unwomanly Face*, which was published in English for the first time in 1988, by Progress Publishers, Moscow. The anthology is now available as a Penguin Modern Classic, *The Unwomanly Face of War* (English translation by Richard Pevear and Larissa Volokhonsky).

Nina Kovelenova. Nina survived the war. She was interviewed by Nobel Prize winner Svetlana Alexievich for her outstanding anthology *War's Unwomanly Face*, which was published in English for the first time in 1988, by Progress Publishers, Moscow. The anthology is now available as a Penguin Modern Classic, *The Unwomanly Face of War* (English translation by Richard Pevear and Larissa Volokhonsky).

19. The Meat Grinder

Aleksander Slesarev. Aleksander's letters were published as *Letters to and from the Front 1941–1945*, in Smolensk, in 1991.

Nina Vishnevskaya. Nina survived the war. She was interviewed by Nobel Prize winner Svetlana Alexievich for her outstanding anthology

War's Unwomanly Face, which was published in English for the first time in 1988, by Progress Publishers, Moscow. The anthology is now available as a Penguin Modern Classic, *The Unwomanly Face of War* (English translation by Richard Pevear and Larissa Volokhonsky).

Anatoly Pavlov. Anatoly may have survived the war. His diary ends in 1944. The reason for this – death, casualty, capture – is not known.

Vitaly Taranichev. Vitali's letters are held in the archives of the Soviet Komsomol in Moscow.

Tamara Torop. Tamara survived the war. She was interviewed by Nobel Prize winner Svetlana Alexievich for her outstanding anthology *War's Unwomanly Face*, which was published in English for the first time in 1988, by Progress Publishers, Moscow. The anthology is now available as a Penguin Modern Classic, *The Unwomanly Face of War* (English translation by Richard Pevear and Larissa Volokhonsky).

20. A Punch in the Guts

Patriarch Sergius. After the German invasion of the Soviet Union in 1941, Stalin, needing the moral support of the Church during the war, scaled back the anti-religious campaign of the 1930s. In the early hours of 5 September 1943, Stalin met with the leaders of the Russian Orthodox Church and promised some concessions to religion, in exchange for their loyalty and assistance. Among the concessions were the permission to open the Moscow Theological Seminary and Academy, the release of imprisoned clerics, and the restoration of some church property. In return, the Soviet government put the Church under the control of its secret services. The most important concession was the permission to gather the Episcopal Council and to elect a new Patriarch. On 8 September 1943, at a Council of Bishops, Sergius was elected Patriarch of Moscow. He died eight months later, on 15 May 1944, at the age of seventy-six.

Yelena Mazanik. After the assassination of Wilhelm Kube, Mazanik was invited to Moscow, ostensibly to meet Stalin, but was told to report to the Lubyanka, the NKVD's office and prison. She was shown into a large office, where she was interrogated by Beria's deputy, Sergei Kruglov. As she looked around, she saw a pair of boots poking out from behind a screen and knew that someone was there listening. Kruglov asked her questions which annoyed her: had she ever had sex with Kube? Kruglov then demanded to know who gave the orders for the assassination. The grilling lasted for about an hour, after which she was given a protocol to sign. She refused, adding that they could kill her but she would not sign anything. Eventually, she was made a Hero of the Soviet Union and allowed to leave Moscow. She was told later that the NKVD had planned to kill her and put another woman in her place to present to Stalin. She had had a merciful reprieve.

General Grishin. On 27 April 1943, Grishin became Chief of Staff of the 11th Guards Army. In June, he became 49th Army Commander. During August and September, Grishin led the army in the Battle for Smolensk. His forces received a twenty-gun artillery salute in Moscow for their capture of Roslavl. Four rifle divisions were awarded the honour 'Roslavl', while Grishin was awarded the Order of Suvorov 1st class. During the offensive, the army had captured Grishin's home village of Vnukovichi, where he learned that German troops had shot his father, mother and other relatives. Grishin died in Moscow in 1951, at the age of fifty.

21. Cigars Around the Table, More Death on the Ground

Boris Kampov. Major Kampov's account of the massacre at Korsun appears in Alexander Werth's classic 1964 history of the Eastern Front, *Russia at War*. As Kampov became a renowned writer after the war under the pseudonym Boris Polevoi, Werth suspected that Kampov may have romanticised part of his account. This doubt is perhaps reinforced by the fact that such details do not form part of the official reports of either the Red Army or the Wehrmacht. In support of Kampov's version, it is interesting to note that the overall context of the events matches quite closely the account of Gabriel Temkin.

22. Bagration

Nikolai Belov. Nikolai did not survive the war. He fought all the way to Berlin and became a highly decorated veteran. However, although he witnessed the fall of the city, on 4 May he was sent to Tangermünde on the Elbe, where he was killed the next day in what was almost the last skirmish of the war. A month later, the daughter who had been conceived while he was home on leave was born. His journal, *Diary from the Front*, 1941–1944, was published in Russian, in 1997.

Larissa Deikun. Larissa survived the war. She was interviewed by Nobel Prize winner Svetlana Alexievich for her outstanding anthology *War's Unwomanly Face*, which was published in English for the first time in 1988, by Progress Publishers, Moscow. The anthology is now available as a Penguin Modern Classic, *The Unwomanly Face of War* (English translation by Richard Pevear and Larissa Volokhonsky).

Alexander Werth. Alexander was born in St Petersburg in 1901. He left Russia with his family in the wake of the Bolshevik Revolution, in 1917, and became a British citizen in 1930. During the war, he was the BBC's correspondent in the Soviet Union and witnessed many of its events first hand. His memories of the war formed the basis of his 1964 book, *Russia at War*, which is still regarded as the definitive eyewitness account of the war. He died in Paris, in 1969, at the age of sixty-eight.

Sofya Kuntsevich. Sofya survived the war. She was interviewed by Nobel Prize winner Svetlana Alexievich for her outstanding anthology *War's Unwomanly Face*, which was published in English for the first time in 1988, by Progress Publishers, Moscow. The anthology is now available as a Penguin Modern Classic, *The Unwomanly Face of War* (English translation by Richard Pevear and Larissa Volokhonsky).

23. The Tragedy of Warsaw

Mary Wattenberg (Mary Berg). Mary's survival and her journey to America meant that her story became one of the few first-hand accounts of the Warsaw Ghetto to have been handed down for future generations. It is not only a story of the horror and deprivation of the ghetto, but also a moving account of the way in which people strove to create some semblance of normality; indeed, to hold on to civilised life itself. Her memoir was serialised in American newspapers in 1944, making it one of the earliest accounts of the Holocaust to be written in English. American publishers declined to publish the manuscript, saying that the market 'was flooded with books about concentration camps and Nazi persecution'. It was eventually published in February 1945 but went out of print in the 1950s before being republished in 2006. Mary was active in telling the story of the Warsaw Ghetto in the early 1950s, on radio, and making appearances to publicise the horrors of the Holocaust. She then dropped out of public view, refusing to participate publicly in any Holocaust-related events. She died in York, Pennsylvania, in April 2013, at the age of eighty-eight. Her identity was discovered after her death when a part-time antiques dealer bought her scrapbook at an estate sale because he was interested in her photos of aircraft. Later, at the request of one of Mary's nephews, he donated the material to the US Holocaust Memorial Museum, in Washington, where it is now available online.

Marek Edelman. Marek was the last surviving leader of the Warsaw Ghetto Uprising and the last survivor of the Warsaw Uprising. He chose to stay in Poland despite harassment by the communist authorities. When, in the face of oppression from Poland's communist government, his wife and children emigrated from Poland to France in 1968, Edelman decided to stay in Łódź, saying, 'Someone had to stay here with all those who perished here.' He published his memoirs, *The Ghetto Fights: Warsaw 1943–45*, which have been translated into six languages, including English. He died in 2009, at the age of ninety.

Abraham Lewin. Abraham was a writer, teacher and historian who, before the war, taught in the Jehudyiah Girl's Gymnasium. In the ghetto, he was one of the co-founders of the Underground Ghetto Archive. He was killed in January 1943 during fighting in the ghetto. His wife, Luba, was deported to Treblinka death camp in August 1942, where she perished. His only daughter, Ora, died in Warsaw during 1943.

Mordecai Anielewicz. Mordecai died in the Warsaw Ghetto. The contents of his open letter have survived in the testimony of others.

Unknown diarist. The diary of the Łódź Ghetto was written by a young man who never gave his name. He was apparently connected to circles in the ghetto that may have had access to a radio or to newspapers, because he was very aware of the progress of the war. There are several theories as to why he wrote in different languages – he may have used Hebrew when he didn't want his younger twelve-year-old sister to understand. His English is very flowery and formal. The entries in Yiddish and Polish, the languages he apparently spoke most fluently, seem to be the most uninhibited and raw.

Primo Levi. Levi was an Italian-Jewish chemist and partisan. After the war, he became an author. His account of his year in Auschwitz, *If This Is a Man*, was first published in 1947.

Georgii Elisavetskii. Elisavetskii was put in charge of Auschwitz and made responsible for the welfare of its survivors. It is not known what became of him after the war.

24. The Red Tide

Georgi Dimitrov. Dimitrov was the first communist leader of Bulgaria, which he led along repressive Stalinist lines from 1946 until his death in July 1949. Dimitrov died in a sanatorium near Moscow. The rapid decline in his health led to speculation that Stalin had had him poisoned. Stalin feared a plan supported by Dimitrov (although with less enthusiasm by Tito) that Bulgaria and Yugoslavia should form a Federation of the Southern Slavs. If successful, such a federation would have been an entity powerful enough to thwart the Kremlin's attempts to control that area. The proposed alliance with Bulgaria never happened.

Gyula Háy. Gyula became better known by his anglicised name, Julius Hay. He was a playwright and author. His account of Budapest is from his autobiography. He died in Switzerland in 1975, aged seventy-five.

Raoul Wallenberg. More than a decade after his disappearance, a Soviet government report, published in 1956, suggested that Wallenberg had died on 17 July 1947, while detained in the infamous Lubyanka Prison in Moscow. The report suggested that Wallenberg died of a 'cardiac infarction', but subsequent research suggests that he may have been executed. In October 2016, seventy-one years after his disappearance, Sweden declared Wallenberg legally dead.

25. The Juggernaut

Steven Springfield. The Springfield brothers survived the war and after being liberated by the Red Army went to live in the United States. Steven was interviewed and his testimony recorded for posterity by the United States Holocaust Memorial Museum in Washington, in 1990.

Lily Mazur-Margules. The Mazur sisters survived the war and after being liberated by the Red Army went to live in the United States. Lily was interviewed and her testimony recorded for posterity by the United States Holocaust Memorial Museum in Washington, in 1996.

Efrosinya Breus. Efrosinya survived the war. She was interviewed by Nobel Prize winner Svetlana Alexievich for her outstanding anthology *War's Unwomanly Face*, which was published in English for the first time in 1988, by Progress Publishers, Moscow. The anthology is now available as a Penguin Modern Classic, *The Unwomanly Face of War* (English translation by Richard Pevear and Larissa Volokhonsky).

26. Vengeance

Nina Sakova. Nina survived the war. She was interviewed by Nobel Prize winner Svetlana Alexievich for her outstanding anthology *War's Unwomanly Face*, which was published in English for the first time in 1988, by Progress Publishers, Moscow. The anthology is now available as a Penguin Modern Classic, *The Unwomanly Face of War* (English translation by Richard Pevear and Larissa Volokhonsky).

Leonid Rabichev. Leonid won two Orders of the Patriotic War and the Order of the Red Star. In 1960, he became a member of the Artists' Union of the USSR as well as a renowned poet, writer and graphic artist. His war memoirs, *The War Will Excuse Everything*, were published, in Russian, by Awallon, in 2003. He died in 2017, at the age of ninety-four.

Lev Kopelev. Because of his open criticism of the behaviour of Red Army soldiers, Kopelev was arrested in 1945 and sentenced to a ten-year term in a gulag for fostering 'bourgeois humanism' and for 'compassion towards the enemy'. Released in 1954, he was rehabilitated in 1956. Still an optimist and believer in idealistic communism, he rejoined the Soviet Communist Party. He taught in the Moscow Institute of Polygraphy and the Institute of History of Arts, from 1957 to 1969. In 1980, while he was on a study trip to West Germany, his Soviet citizenship was revoked. He became a Professor at the University of Wuppertal. In 1990, Soviet premier Mikhail Gorbachev restored Kopelev's Soviet citizenship. He died in Germany, in 1997, at the age of eighty-five. His account of his wartime experiences was translated by Anthony Austin and published as *No Jail for Thought* by Penguin Books, in 1977.

Anna Ratkina. Anna survived the war. She was interviewed by Nobel Prize winner Svetlana Alexievich for her outstanding anthology *War's Unwomanly Face*, which was published in English for the first time in 1988, by Progress Publishers, Moscow. The anthology is now available as a Penguin Modern Classic, *The Unwomanly Face of War* (English translation by Richard Pevear and Larissa Volokhonsky).

Nikolai Vasilyev. Nikolai's words were quoted by Georgy Zhukov in the second volume of his memoirs. Zhukov does not say what became of Nikolai.

Tamarah Lazerson. Tamarah survived the Kovno Ghetto by hiding when it was liquidated. Left deeply scarred after the war, she was reunited with her brother and later married and emigrated to Israel. Her diary, which she began when she was thirteen, is kept in the United States Holocaust Memorial Museum Collection in Washington. The museum does not hold a current record for Tamarah. If she is still alive in Israel, she will be ninety-two.

Olga Vasilyevna. Olga survived the war. She was interviewed by Nobel Prize winner Svetlana Alexievich for her outstanding anthology *War's Unwomanly Face*, which was published in English for the first time in 1988, by Progress Publishers, Moscow. The anthology is now available as a Penguin Modern Classic, *The Unwomanly Face of War* (English translation by Richard Pevear and Larissa Volokhonsky).

Anastasia Voropaeva. Anastasia survived the war. She was interviewed by Nobel Prize winner Svetlana Alexievich for her outstanding anthology *War's Unwomanly Face*, which was published in English for the first time in 1988, by Progress Publishers, Moscow. The anthology is now available as a Penguin Modern Classic, *The Unwomanly Face of War* (English translation by Richard Pevear and Larissa Volokhonsky).

Boris Sapunov. Boris became a historian at the Hermitage Museum in St Petersburg. He found his name on a visit to Berlin in October 2001. It is at a height of 1.5 metres on the south wall in the north wing of niche D. His story was reported in the German media at the time of his visit. He died in 2012, at the age of ninety.

27. Aftermath

Lyudmila Kashechkina. Lyudmila survived the war. She was interviewed by Nobel Prize winner Svetlana Alexievich for her outstanding anthology *War's Unwomanly Face*, which was published in English for the first time in 1988, by Progress Publishers, Moscow. The anthology is now available as a Penguin Modern Classic, *The Unwomanly Face of War* (English translation by Richard Pevear and Larissa Volokhonsky).

Valentina M—va. Valentina survived the war. She was interviewed by Nobel Prize winner Svetlana Alexievich for her outstanding anthology *War's Unwomanly Face*, which was published in English for the first time in 1988, by Progress Publishers, Moscow. The anthology is now available as a Penguin Modern Classic, *The Unwomanly Face of War* (English translation by Richard Pevear and Larissa Volokhonsky).

Mankichi Oshima. Mankichi's account of the Gegenmaio Massacre was reported in Japan's national newspaper, *The Mainichi*, in August 2017. At the time, he was eighty-one years old.

Valentin Caşu. There is no record of what became of Valentin.

Stanislav Obolensky. There is no record of what became of Stanislav.

ENDNOTES

Note on sources

A significant number of the witness accounts listed below have come from sources where the material has already been accurately translated into English. For new material and for published material that only exists in the Cyrillic alphabet, extracts from the witness material have been translated for this book by Victor Belyakov and his researchers in Russia. Further clarifications and nuances in English have been added by the author. All source books, where the title only exists in Cyrillic, have also been translated into English for ease of reference. Several state archives have been used in researching this book, not just in the various Russian state archives, but also those of Belarus, Ukraine, Latvia and Lithuania. The various Holocaust libraries, in both the United States and Israel, have been an important source of material. They are all listed in the Endnotes.

Frequently cited sources are abbreviated as follows.

BMF Sergo Beria (translated by Brian Pearce), *Beria, My Father* (London: Duckworth, 2001).

BoR Marshal Vasili Ivanovich Chuikov (translated by Harold Silver), *The Beginning of the Road* (London: MacGibbon & Kee, 1963).

EoTR Marshal Vasili Ivanovich Chuikov (translated by Ruth Kisch), *The End of the Third Reich* (London: MacGibbon & Kee, 1967).

IW Catherine Merridale, *Ivan's War: Life and Death in the Red Army 1939–1945* (London: Faber & Faber, 2005).

MoV Georgy Zhukov (translated by Svetlana Frolova, edited by Geoffrey Roberts), *Marshal of Victory*, in two volumes, *Vol. I: 1896–1941, Vol. II: 1941–1945* (Barnsley: Pen & Sword Military, 2013).

UFW Svetlana Alexievich (translated by Richard Pevear and Larissa Volokhonsky), *The Unwomanly Face of War* (London: Penguin Modern Classics, 2017). First published in English as *War's Unwomanly Face* (Moscow: Progress Publishers, 1988).

WaW Vasily Grossman (edited and translated by Antony Beevor and Luba Vinogradova), *A Writer at War, Vasily Grossman with the Red Army, 1941–1945* (London: Harvill Press, 2005).

For all other sources, full citation appears in the first instance within each chapter, with a recognisable shortened form thereafter.

Preface: The 'Soul' of Russia

page

xxxiii **Dostoevsky said of it, 'It's frightening how free'** – '10 masterful quotes about the Russian soul you need to know', *Russia Beyond*, 29 December 2017. https://www.rbth.com/arts/327188-10-masterful-quotes-about-russian (accessed January 2020).

Introduction: Drawing the Ideological Battle Lines

page

3 *'Leningrad USSR, On the 22nd'* – Michael Jones, *Leningrad: State of Siege* (London: John Murray, 2008), pp. 66–68. Shaporina's diary, *A Diary in Two Volumes*, was published in 2011 by NLO, Moscow. There are significant extracts in Veronique Garros, Natalia Korenevskaya and Thomas Lahusen (eds), translated by Carol A. Flath, *Intimacy and Terror, Soviet Diaries from the 1930s* (New York: New Press, 1995).

3 **For my part, I would like to assure you, comrades** – all Stalin's writings and speeches can be found at https://www.marxists.org/reference/archive/stalin/works/decades-index.htm. They are indexed by decade from September 1901 to October 1952 (accessed December 2019).

4 *'The great, great Dostoevsky'* – Jones, *Leningrad*, pp. 66–68.

4 *'I was very scared when I heard women yelling'* – Barouskaya's testimony can be heard in a recording by Radio Free Europe (Belarus Service), 2 June 2017, at https://www.rferl.org/a/belarus-soviet-union/28524493.html (accessed November 2019).

4 *'There will be some innocent victims'* – Simon Sebag-Montefiore, *Stalin: The Court of the Red Tsar* (London: Phoenix, 2004), p. 222.

1. A Pact with Satan to Drive out the Devil

page

15 *'September 1938, Budapest, We're living through'* – Laurel Holliday, *Children's Wartime Diaries* (London: Piatkus, 1996), p. 138.

15 *'In the month of July'* – Ben Hecht, *Perfidy* (New York: Julian Messner, 1961), p. 133.

16 Hitler . . . called the Soviet Union 'the greatest danger' – https://
www.history.com/topics/world-war-ii/german-soviet-nonaggression-pact
(accessed February 2020).

17 The protocol was startlingly blunt – Political Archive of the Federal
Foreign Office, Berlin. The full text of the pact can be seen at https://
www.1000dokumente.de/index.html?c=dokument_de&dokument=
0025_pak&object=facsimile&pimage=1&v=100&nav=&l=de (accessed
December 2019).

18 'Down to the last moment my father tried to persuade Stalin' – BMF,
p. 81.

18 'Stalin was reasoning' – Valentin Berezhkov (translated by Sergei
Mikheyev), At Stalin's Side (New York, NY: Birch Lane Press, 1994),
p. 31.

18 'While bombs had not yet begun to explode' . . . 'If we did not collapse
already in 1939' – MoV Vol. I, p. 210.

18 'Terrible, interesting, strange news!' – Alan Adelson (ed), translated by
Kamil Turowski, The Diary of Dawid Sierakowiak (Oxford: Oxford
University Press, 1998), p. 27.

19 'Friday 1st September' – Adelson, Sierakowiak, p. 68.

19 'September 6th: Oh God' – Adelson, Sierakowiak, p. 70.

21 Boris Yeltsin released top-secret files to Polish President Lech
Walesa – The secret NKVD files were released in 1992. In April 2010,
Russian President Dmitry Medvedev released them online: http://web.
archive.org/web/20080505093030/http:/www.electronicmuseum.ca/
Poland-WW2/katyn_memorial_wall/kmw_resolution.html (accessed
March 2020).

2. Facing the Blitzkrieg

page

24 'The weight of the human and materiel potential of the USA' –
Hitler's Political Testament: Dictated to Bormann from February to April
1945 (Hamburg: Albrecht Knaus Verlag, 1981), p. 78.

26 'In the spring of 1941' – MoV Vol. I, p. 247.

26 'Stalin was convinced' – MoV Vol. I, p. 250.

3. A Warm Sunny Morning

page

28 'A wonderful Crimean evening' – Pyotr Knyshevski et al, The Hidden
Truth of War, 1941: Unknown Documentaries (Moscow, 1992),
pp. 330–31.

29 'Get the staff together this morning' – IW, p. 74.

30 *'Our defences were poor'* – diary entry for 25 June 1941. Masslinikov's diary is in the State Archive of the Russian Federation in Moscow, 7537/16.

30 *'Kuznetsov informed me with a tremble in his voice'* – Alexander Werth, *Russia at War* (London: Pan Books, 1964), p. 154.

30 *'The atmosphere was incredibly hot'* – Werth, *Russia*, pp. 152–3.

31 *'No one answered. I kept calling.'* – *MoV Vol. I*, p. 281.

31 Citizens of the Soviet Union – The text of Molotov's speech on 22 June 1941 can be found at http://www.historicalresources. org/2008/08/26/molotov-reaction-to-german-invasion-of-1941/ (accessed December 2019).

32 *'Molotov sounded hesitant and hasty'* – Colin Cross, *Adolf Hitler* (London: Hodder and Stoughton, 1973), p. 355.

33 *'I was a boy, fifteen years old'* . . . *'I lived through German rule'* – *IW*, p. 78.

33 *'We will put up with any hardships'* . . . *'Our indignation has no limits'* . . . *'The feeling of unlimited love for their Motherland'* – *IW*, p. 79.

34 *'We passed columns of refugees from Lvov'* . . . *'We walked without a break'* . . . *'I still can't understand'* – *IW*, p. 83.

35 *'After about three hours, above the forest'* – Konstantin Mikhailovich Simonov, *One Hundred Days of War* (Moscow: Rusich World at War Series, 1999), p. 37.

35 *'[. . .]"We have given everything to the war"'* – Simonov, *One Hundred Days*, p. 43.

35 *'Moving east, we drove into such a wilderness'* – Simonov, *One Hundred Days*, p. 54.

36 *'It was so poignant'* – Simonov, *One Hundred Days*, p. 56.

36 *'Bitter and angry, the colonel said'* – Simonov, *One Hundred Days*, p. 62.

37 *'We took a truck and drove along a forest path'* – Simonov, *One Hundred Days*, p. 70.

38 *'It was a hot summer day'* – Simonov, *One Hundred Days*, p. 76.

4. Crisis in the Kremlin

page

40 'The rascal was able to walk through Red Square on a rainy day' – Simon Sebag-Montefiore, *Stalin: The Court of the Red Tsar* (London: Phoenix, 2004), p. 83n.

41 *'They began by asking Zhukov questions'* – Anastas Mikoyan (translated by Katherine T. O'Connor and Diana L. Burgin), *Memoirs of Anastas Mikoyan: The Path of Struggle*, Vol. 1 (Madison, CT: Sphinx Press, 1988), p. 125.

41 *'Stalin would not calm down'* ... *'If these men had been property owners'* – BMF, p. 70.

41 *'We decided to visit him'* – Chris Bellamy, *Absolute War* (London: Macmillan, 2007), p. 227.

41 **'Pretend inferiority and encourage his arrogance'** – Bellamy, *Absolute War*, p. 228.

42 *'Stalin and our military men had not appreciated'* – BMF, p. 70.

43 *'We did not foresee the large-scale surprise offensive'* – MoV Vol. I, p. 283.

43 *'There were over 563,000 Communists in the Red Army and Navy'* – MoV Vol. I, p. 295.

43 *'In early July, when the enemy had occupied Minsk'* – MoV Vol. I, p. 330.

44 **Comrades! Citizens! Brothers and sisters!:** all Stalin's writings and speeches can be found at https://www.marxists.org/reference/archive/stalin/works/decades-index.htm. They are indexed by decade from September 1901 to October 1952 (accessed March 2020).

46 *'It is hard to describe the enormous enthusiasm'* – Alexander Werth, *Russia at War* (London: Pan Books, 1964), p. 149.

46 *'But when Stalin began to speak'* – UFW, p. 22.

46 *'Stalin did not describe the situation as tragic'* – Werth, *Russia*, pp. 166–7.

47 *'Our situation is very bad'* ... *'It is possible that we are not completely beaten'* ... *'It seems that I didn't do a good job'* – IW, pp. 86–7.

47 *'Some in trucks, many on foot'* – Gabriel Temkin, *My Just War* (Novato, CA: Presidio Press, 1998), p. 38.

47 *'Sometimes bottlenecks were formed by troops'* ... *'We thought we surely had enough'* – Werth, *Russia*, p. 148.

5. Smolensk

page

49 *'The enemy aimed to cut the Western Front in two'* – MoV Vol. I, p. 409.

49 *'The retreat has caused blind panic'* – IW, pp. 96–7.

49 *'Our unit was surrounded'* – Martin Dean, *Collaboration in the Holocaust: Crimes of the Local Police in Belorussia and Ukraine, 1941–44* (London: Palgrave Macmillan, 2003), p. 26.

50 *'He made a salute to, I suppose, Hitler'* ... *'The boys understood'* – IW, p. 99.

50 'if we do not intend to win ourselves to death' – David Glantz and Jonathan House, *When Titans Clashed: How the Red Army Stopped Hitler* (Lawrence, KS: University Press of Kansas, 2015), p. 72.

51 *'We first tried this superb weapon'* – IW, p. 96.

51 *'On July 16th almost the whole of Smolensk fell'* – MoV Vol. I, p. 422.

52 *'Soviet Army, 5 kms west of Roslavl, We are retreating'* – Nikolai

Amosoff (translated and adapted by George St George), *PPG-2266 A Surgeon's War* (Chicago: Regnery, 1975), p. 61.

52 '*We were near a small village*' – Chekalov's diary was kept by his family for sixty years before being published in Russian, in Moscow, by the Russian Humanist Society, in 2004 (edited by V. A. Kuvakin and A. G. Kruglov). 23.08.41, pp. 6–7.

53 '*That the enemy's offensive was halted at Smolensk*' – *MoV Vol. II*, p. 23.

54 Dovator broke through the German positions: Daniel Johnson, 'Lev Dovator: the most dangerous cavalry in the Great Patriotic', *Global News*, 27 December 2019.

56 '*After unrelenting and bitter battles*' – *MoV Vol. II*, p. 62.

56 'We have underestimated the Russian Colossus' – David Stahel, *Operation Barbarossa and Germany's Defeat in the East* (Cambridge: CUP, 2009), p. 388.

57 '*September 27, 1941. Nice sunny day*' . . . '*The order comes*' – Inozemtzev's wartime diary, *I Shall Establish Myself*, was compiled by Petr Cherkasov and published, in Russian, in the periodical *IMEMO*, Vol. 1, in 2003. 27/9/41, pp. 3–4.

6. Leningrad: The Great Siege Begins

page

60 '*We lived in a little wooden house*' . . . '*I joined a battalion of volunteers*' – Krukov's account of the war (translated by J. Fineberg) was published as a chapter in *Heroic Leningrad: Documents, Sketches and Stories of its Siege and Relief* (Moscow: Foreign Languages Publishing House, 1945), pp. 31–2.

61 '*A strained relationship has grown up*' – Michael Jones, *Leningrad: State of Siege* (London: John Murray, 2008), p. 89.

61 '*They came at night, searched*' – Anna Reid, *Leningrad, Tragedy of a City Under Siege* (London: Bloomsbury, 2011), p. 32.

61 '*Every leader in every paper shouts out*' – Jones, *Leningrad*, p. 91. Yuri's diary emerged in 1970 in response to a newspaper appeal as part of research by the authors Ales Adamovich and Daniil Granin. Their book was translated by Hilda Perham and published in English under the title *A Book of the Blockade* (Moscow: Raduga Publishers, 1983).

61 '*Where's Mama?*' – Reid, *Leningrad*, pp. 272–3.

62 '*The destruction of the Badaev warehouses*' – Jones, *Leningrad*, pp. 44–5.

63 '*The rumours of children's evacuation were frightening*' – Dimitri Likhachev (translated by Bernard Adams and edited by A. R. Tulloch), *Reflections on the Russian Soul: A Memoir* (St Petersburg: Central European University Press, 2000). Likhachev's memories of Leningrad are collected in the chapter 'The Blockade', pp. 216–61.

63 'Suddenly we heard that the Germans were dropping paratroopers' –
    Michael Jones, *Leningrad: State of Siege* (London: John Murray, 2008),
    p. 98.

64 'A plane flew right over us' . . . 'A plane circled and came back' – Jones,
    Leningrad, p. 99.

64 'The station was on fire' – Jones, *Leningrad*, p. 99.

64 'One day, returning from the Pushkin House' – Likhachev, *Reflections*,
    'The Blockade', pp. 216–61.

65 Our beloved Leningrad . . . a dump for corpses – Jonathan Dimbleby,
    Russia, A Journey to the Heart of a Land, (London: BBC Books, 2008),
    pp. 78–9.

7. Leningrad: Starvation

page

66 'St Petersburg must be erased' – Hitler Directive 1601. Quoted (in a
    Russian translation from the German) at http://www.hrono.ru/
    dokum/194_dok/19410922.php (accessed December 2020).

66 'Leningrad must die' – The speech in full can be read at 'Adolf
    Hitler – speech in the Löwenbräukeller' – http://der-fuehrer.org/reden/
    english/41-11-08.htm (accessed December 2020).

67 You begin to realise that as you sit at home – Lydia Ginzburg
    (translated by Alan Myers, edited by Emily van Buskirk), *Notes from the
    Blockade* (London: Vintage, 1995), pp. 24–5.

67 'One wanted to squeeze oneself into the ground' – Anna Reid, *Leningrad,
    Tragedy of a City Under Siege* (London: Bloomsbury, 2011), p. 143.

67 'Houses burned for weeks' – Dimitri Likhachev (translated by Bernard
    Adams and edited by A. R. Tulloch), *Reflections on the Russian Soul:
    A Memoir* (St Petersburg: CEU Press, 2000). Likhachev's memories of
    Leningrad are collected in the chapter 'The Blockade', pp. 216–61.

68 'We were stationed at 500-metre intervals' . . . 'We all took a military
    oath' . . . 'We laboured day and night' – Michael Jones, *Leningrad: State
    of Siege* (London: John Murray, 2008), p. 221.

70 '7 p.m. The situation is catastrophic' . . . 'I cried for the first time' –
    https://erenow.net/ww/the-900-days-the-siege-of-leningrad/42.php
    (accessed April 2020).

70 'The bathrooms didn't work' – Likhachev, *Reflections*, 'The Blockade',
    pp. 216–61.

70 'The first time I saw a body' – *Heroic Leningrad: Documents, Sketches and
    Stories of its Siege and Relief*, translated by J. Fineburg (Moscow:
    Foreign Languages Publishing House, 1945), p. 76.

70 'so identical . . . Everyone is shrivelled' – Alexis Peri, *The War Within:
    Diaries from the Siege of Leningrad* (Cambridge, MA: Harvard
    University Press, 2017), p. 156.

70 *'I saw nurses dragging the corpses of the dead'* – Likhachev, *Reflections*, 'The Blockade', pp. 216–61.

71 *'We lead a primitive life'* . . . *'Much respected Citizen Editor'* – Michael Jones, *Leningrad: State of Siege* (London: John Murray, 2008), p. 214. Alexander Dymov's story was researched by the authors Ales Adamovich and Daniil Granin. Their book was translated by Hilda Perham and published in English under the title *A Book of the Blockade* (Moscow: Raduga Publishers, 1983).

71 *'But first I'll give him one good meal'* – https://erenow.net/ww/the-900-days-the-siege-of-leningrad/41.php (accessed March 2020).

72 *'A dystrophic walked along'* – Reid, *Leningrad*, p. 354.

72 *'Finally, we were at the gates of the mortuary'* – Reid, *Leningrad*, p. 228.

72 *'The cannibalism has begun!'* – Likhachev, *Reflections*, 'The Blockade' pp. 216–61.

73 *'Comrade Ivanov was killed today'* – *Heroic Leningrad*, p. 79.

74 *'I came back from the queues'* – Elena Taranukhina was interviewed in the 1990s about her experiences in Leningrad during the siege. Her words can be heard on the BBC Sound Archives, 'My Century: The Siege of Leningrad', 18 January 1999. https://www.bbc.co.uk/sounds/play/p033xc6l (accessed March 2020).

74 *'The rest have died'* – Jones, *Leningrad*, p. 216.

75 *'I remember the body of a woman: naked'* – Likhachev, *Reflections*, 'The Blockade', pp. 216–61.

75 *'Zhenya died on December 28th'* – Tanya Savicheva's diary is on display in the Museum of the History of St Petersburg. Extracts can be viewed online at https://www.pravmir.com/article_238.html (accessed April 2020).

75 *'In hunger people showed their true selves'* – Likhachev, *Reflections*, 'The Blockade', pp. 216–61.

76 In that moment, we triumphed – Jones, *Leningrad*, p. 261.

76 *'The suffering was on an unprecedented scale'* – Epilogue to Jones, *Leningrad*, pp. 293–6.

76 *'Such was the image of my own unhappy, proud, besieged city'* – https://erenow.net/ww/the-900-days-the-siege-of-leningrad/44.php (accessed February 2020).

8. The 'Brutal Dog' Let Loose

page

81 Adolf Hitler! We are linked and united with you alone! – Ronald Smelser, *Robert Ley: Hitler's Labour Front Leader* (Oxford: Berg Publishers, 1992), p. 67.

85 *'June 1941. The first great tragedy'* . . . *'It is Yom Kippur Eve'* – curated

by Bilhah Shilo, extracts from Yitskhok Rudashevski's diary can be found at https://www.yadvashem.org/education/educational-materials/artifacts/diary.html (accessed January 2020).

86 '*On the concrete forecourt of the petrol station*' . . . '*Those horrific events have been burned on to my memory*' – documents and photographs relating to the massacre can be found at https://rarehistoricalphotos.com/kovno-garage-massacre-lithuania-1941/ (accessed January 2020).

87 '*There were Germans present on the bridge to Slobodka*' – Ephraim Oshry (translated by Y. Leimam, edited by Bonnie Goldman), *Annihilation of Lithuanian Jewry* (New York, NY: Judaica Press Inc., 1995), p. 3.

87 '*A woman crawling on all fours*' – Macha Rolnikas, *I Must Tell* (reconstructed diary 1941–45), translated and published by Daniel H. Shubin (2018). Extracts from the diary can be found at https://spartacus-educational.com/GERrolnikas.htm (accessed December 2019).

88 '*The columns of people were moving on and on*' – Frida Michelson (translated and edited by Wolf Goodman, adapted by David Silberman), *I Survived Rumbula* (New York, NY: United States Holocaust Museum, 1982), pp. 77–8.

89 '*The bloody evacuations began*' – Max Kaufmann (translated by Laimdota Mazzarins, edited by Erhard Roy Wiehn and Gertrude Schneider), *Churbn Lettland: The Destruction of the Jews of Latvia* (Konstanz: Hartung-Gorre Verlag, 2010), p. 62. The whole text is available online at http://www.shamir.lv/images/Kaufmann_st(3).pdf (accessed February 2020).

90 Estonia is the only country in Eastern Europe where: 'Estonia, an oasis of tolerance', *The Jewish Chronicle*, 25 September 1936, pp. 22–3.

90 '*When I came home, there were two men in our apartment*' – Eugenia Gurin-Loov, *Holocaust of Estonian Jews 1941* (Tallinn: Eesti Juudi Kogukond (Estonian Jewish Community), 1994), p. 224.

92 '*My God, if sacrifice of life is needed*' . . . '*There is a greater need for a priest*' – the story of the Nuns of Nowogródek has been taken from the account by Sisters Theresa Gorska and M. Noela Wojatowicz of the Holy Family of Nazareth, *Blessed Martyrs of Nowogródek* (Philadelphia: Holy Family University, 2000).

93 '*I am tormented by the thought*' . . . '*When they put her on the stool, the girl turned*' – Maria's story and the testimony of Pyotr Borisenko are told in Daniel H. Weiss and Nechama Tec, 1997, 'A Historical Injustice: The Case of Masha Bruskina', *Holocaust and Genocide Studies*, Vol. VII, Issue 3, 366–77.

94 '*I watched what happened*' – Hofer's account is included in Michael Berenbaum's book *Witness to the Holocaust* (New York, NY:

HarperCollins, 1997). The full testimony can be found at https://phdn. org/archives/einsatzgruppenarchives.com/hofer.html (accessed April 2020).

95 *'Dina is not a Russian name'* ... *'The policeman ordered me to strip'* – from the testimony of Dina Pronicheva. See https://www.yadvashem. org/education/educational-materials/learning-environment/babi-yar/ written-testimonies.html (accessed March 2020).

95 *'I stood at my father's side'* – from the memoir of Raya Dashkevich. See https://www.yadvashem.org/education/educational-materials/ learning-environment/babi-yar/written-testimonies.html (accessed March 2020).

96 *'The Germans didn't take women soldiers prisoner'* – UFW, p. 123.

9. Moscow: Enemy at the Gates

page

98 *'What's going on, Comrade Commander?'* – Konstantin Rokossovskiy, *A Soldier's Diary*, (Moscow: Progress Publishers, 1970), pp. 145–6.

99 *'14.10.41. The enemy has encircled us'* – After the war Shabalin's diary, which had been translated into German for military intelligence, was translated back into Russian, handed over to the Soviet authorities in Berlin and is now held in the State Archive of the Russian Federation. The daily newspaper *Izvestia* published an abridged version in 2005. The newspaper's archive can be found at www.izvestiya.ru (accessed March 2020).

99 *'We drove along a major road'* ... *'In Moscow, panic'* – Diary of Fyodor Bogratyov, a Private in the Great War 1941–1945. 5–17/X-1941, p. 20.

100 *'He didn't look very well'* – MoV Vol. II, p. 8.

100 *'As we drove across the Protva River'* – MoV Vol. II, p. 13.

100 *'I saw only an old woman rummaging'* – MoV Vol. II, p. 16.

101 'prepare to take the industrial enterprises of Moscow out of commission' – Chris Bellamy, *Absolute War* (London: Macmillan, 2007), p. 286.

102 *'My father told me that he had said to Stalin'* – BMF, p. 76.

102 *'ostensibly to coordinate the supplies of oil for the army'* – Valentin Berezhkov (translated by Sergei Mikheyev), *At Stalin's Side* (New York, NY: Birch Lane Press, 1994), p. 329.

102 *'It was necessary, absolutely necessary'* – Mikhail Ivanovich was interviewed in 1971 for a collection of military memoirs and archival documents, compiled by K. I. Bukov, M. M. Gorinov and A. N. Ponomarev, and later published, in Russian, as *Moscow Military Memoirs and Archival Documents 1941–1945* (Moscow: Mosgorarckhiv, 1995), p. 73.

103 *'The building was all but deserted'* – Bellamy, *Absolute War*, p. 291.

103 *'It was a very nervous time'* – diary entry for 27 October 1941. Irina Tupikova's diary is in the State Archive of the Russian Federation in Moscow, 7527/19.

103 *'I was still in Moscow on October 1st'* – Yelena Rzhevskaya (translated by Arch Tait), *Memoirs of a Wartime Interpreter* (Barnsley: Greenhill Books, 2018), p. 5.

104 *'A steamer was moored waiting for us'* – Rzhevskaya, *Memoirs*, p. 7.

104 *'Something like 250,000 people'* – *MoV Vol. II*, pp. 24–5.

104 *'The Moscow Motor Works started making machine guns'*, *MoV Vol. II*, p. 25.

10. Moscow: 'Marshal Mud' and 'General Winter'

page

106 *'I don't think anyone has ever seen such terrible mud'* – *WaW*, p. 52.

106 *'Life for the people was terrible'* – *WaW*, pp. 39–40.

107 *'However much they write in the newspapers about their atrocities'* – *IW*, p. 111.

108 *'Losses were being replaced'* – *MoV Vol. II*, p. 31.

108 *'With a tsarina-like generosity she gives'* – *WaW*, pp. 53–4.

109 **'May you be blessed by great Lenin's victorious banner!'** – all Stalin's writings and speeches can be found at https://www.marxists.org/reference/archive/stalin/works/decades-index.htm. They are indexed by decade from September 1901 to October 1952 (accessed November 2019).

109 *'I returned to the capital on 7th November'* – *BMF*, p. 76.

111 The enemy knows that December can bring ferocious frosts – Oleg Kurganov, writing in *Pravda*, 29 November 1941.

111 *'Bourgeois historians put all the blame on mud'* – *MoV Vol. II*, p. 41.

112 *'Stalin asked, "Are you sure"'* – *MoV Vol. II*, p. 34.

112 *'Deep snow greatly hampered the concentration'* – *MoV Vol. II*, p. 49.

113 *'Late on January 5th I was summoned'* – *MoV Vol. II*, p. 52.

11. Eyes South

page

115 *'Everyone had to go forward, forward'* – Konstantin Mikhailovich Simonov, *One Hundred Days of War* (Moscow: Rusich World at War Series, 1999), p. 81.

116 *'Singles, small groups and large divisions'* – the full text of the diaries, in Russian, can be found at http://militera.lib.ru/db/gelfand_vn/02.html (accessed and translated January 2020). 21.07.42.

117 *'a hellish cacophony'* . . . *'Heat!'* . . . *'Lemonade, kvass, seltzer water'* . . . *'We never managed'* – Pyotr Knyshevski et al, *The Hidden Truth of War, 1941: Unknown Documentaries* (Moscow, 1992), pp. 334–7.

118 *'Shells whined overhead and exploded'* – Ivan Laskin, *Towards a Turning Point* (Moscow: Voenizdat, 1977), p. 42.

119 *'Russia my country, my native land!'* – Alexander Werth, *Russia at War* (London: Pan Books, 1964), pp. 365–6.

119 There are forty-six of us left . . . *'They ran with maddened eyes'* – https://warfarehistorynetwork.com/2016/12/27/sturgeon-catch-1942-the-siege-of-sevastopol/ (accessed January 2020).

119 *'Taking rifles and cartridges from dead soldiers'* – Werth, *Russia*, p. 367.

120 *'The majority of our commanding officers are cowards'* – *IW*, p. 132.

120 *'They shared their last crusts with us'* – *IW*, p. 132.

12. The Fulcrum

page

121 'If I don't get the oil of Maikop and Grozny' – speech by Adolf Hitler, 1 April 1942, quoted in Ian Kershaw, *Hitler 1936–1945: Nemesis* (London: Allen Lane, 2000), p. 541.

123 The people of our country, for all the love and respect: http://soviethistory.msu.edu/1943-2/the-nazi-tide-stops/no-one-steps-back/ (accessed April 2020).

124 *'He openly recognises the catastrophic situation'* – *IW*, p. 136.

124 *'Stalin's famous order No. 227'* – *UFW*, p. 37.

125 If you don't want to give away / To a German, with his black gun: Simonov's poem 'Kill Him' is quoted in Alexander Werth, *Russia at War* (London: Pan Books, 1964), p. 417.

125 My heart is as hard as stone, / My grievances and memories: The full poem 'I Hate' was published in *Pravda*, 12 August 1942.

126 One can bear anything . . . The Germans are not human: Werth, *Russia*, pp. 411–14.

126 *'I discovered what hatred was'* – *UFW*, p. 44.

128 *'As a guerrilla, I swear before all'* – Nik Cornish, *Soviet Partisan 1941–44*, (Oxford: Osprey, 2014), p. 31.

128 *'According to incomplete figures, hundreds of thousands'* – *MoV Vol. II*, pp. 359–60.

128 *'Our role is to distract, annoy and enrage'* – Dmitri Medvedev, *Strong in Spirit* (Moscow: Terra-Knizhnyy, 1952), p. 61.

129 *'I heard words . . . Poison . . .'* – *UFW*, p. 197.

129 *'My mother was taken by the Gestapo'* – *UFW*, p. 253.

130 *'There was a woman, Zajarskaya'* – *UFW*, p. 256.

130 *'We had the Chimuk brothers in our detachment'* – *UFW*, p. 257.

132 '*She was the bravest soldier I knew*' – https://nasledie.pravda.
ru/1119686-elena_kolesova/ (accessed and translated May 2020).

132 '*What can I do when the enemy is so close?*' – a full account, including
her final words, can be read at https://www.encyclopedia.com/women/
encyclopedias-almanacs-transcripts-and-maps/kosmodemyanskaya-
zoya-1923-1941 (accessed June 2020).

133 Her eyes, arched by the black wings of her eyebrows: Pyotr Lidov's
tribute to 'Tanya' is quoted in S. Krasilshchik (ed), translated by Nina
Bouis, *World War II: Dispatches from the Soviet Front* (Madison, CT:
Sphinx Press, 1985), p. 79.

13. Protect the Oil

page

134 '*Even the smallest railway stations were cluttered*' – Alexander Werth,
Russia at War (London: Pan Books, 1964), p. 565.

135 '*Many years have passed since all this happened*' – *BoR*, p. 32.

135 '*Early on the morning of July 22nd*' – *BoR*, p. 35.

136 '*Those were hard and dreadful days*' – *WaW*, p. 130.

137 '*The first baptism in combat*' – *UFW*, p. 146.

137 '*We stopped for a snack near a burned-out T-34 tank*' – *BoR*, p. 57.

138 A year has passed, every day of which sowed death – the letter is
held in the State Archive of the Russian Federation in Moscow.

139 '*I felt nothing for the Germans I was attacking*' – Anna Noggle, *A
Dance with Death – Soviet Airwomen in World War II* (College Station,
TX: Texas A&M University Press, 1994), p. 74.

140 '*We had been fighting for one thousand nights*' – Noggle, *Dance with
Death*, p. 42.

140 '*The planes they gave us were Po-2s*' ... '*You approach a target*' – *UFW*,
p. 194.

141 '*The entire Caucasian theatre of war became a complex of defences*'
– Werth, *Russia*, p. 569.

14. Stalingrad: The Great Battle Begins

page

145 Nothing but tears. Regiments disappeared – https://stalingradfront.
com/tours/ (accessed May 2020).

146 '*The day passed quietly*' – Chekalov's diary was kept by his family for
sixty years before being published in Russian, in Moscow, by the
Russian Humanist Society, in 2004 (edited by V. A. Kuvakin and A. G.
Kruglov). 23.08.42, p. 20.

147　'*August 23rd proved to be a tragic day*' – *BoR*, p. 61.

147　'*For the past few days and still right now*' – *IW*, pp. 149–50.

148　'*Now there is nowhere further to retreat*' – *WaW*, p. 133.

148　'*A clear, cold morning in Dubrovka*' – *WaW*, pp. 134–5.

148　'*Sixteen guardsmen, led by Lieutenant Kochetkov*' – *BoR*, p. 59.

149　'*On September 10th, the enemy managed to drive our units*' – *BoR*, p. 70.

150　'*Yeremenko and Khrushchev said to me*' – *BoR*, pp. 75–6.

150　'*Khrushchev wanted to mine the city*' – https://erenow.net/ww/ stalingrad-city-that-defeated-third-reich/24.php (accessed July 2020).

150　'*The wounded are not being fed*' – *BoR*, pp. 73–4.

150　'*The burned, dead city*' – *WaW*, p. 135.

150　'*I said to them, "Once you are here"*' – *BoR*, p. 81.

151　'*I shot the commander and commissar of one regiment*' – *BoR*, p. 82.

152　'*First it was their building*' – Jochen Hellbeck, Stalingrad, the City that Defeated the Third Reich (New York, NY: Perseus Books, 2015), pp. 302 and 309.

153　'*Weapons for close-quarter combat have never been used*' – *WaW*, p. 155.

154　'*Pavlov's small group of men killed more enemy soldiers*' – *BoR*, p. 158.

154　'*It was just me, Captain Lizunov and his runner*' . . . '*For the first time in my life, I cried*' – these words are taken from an interview with Averbukh conducted by a *politruk* from his company, Innokenty Gerasimov, on behalf of the Soviet Historical Commission (established in 1942). The stenographer, Alexandra Shamshina, was part of the delegation that conducted interviews in Stalingrad with many other eyewitnesses of the battle, beginning in January. Details about the Commission can be seen at https://erenow.net/ww/stalingrad-city-that-defeated-third-reich/26.php (accessed May 2020).

155　'*When I first got the rifle*' – *WaW*, p. 157.

15. Stalingrad: Street by Street, House by House

page

158　It must be explained to every soldier – *BoR*, pp. 155–6. Chuikov refers to Order No. 171, which includes a reference to 'not a step back' from Order 227. It is difficult to explain the anomaly, especially as he quotes from Order 171 text that is not part of Order 227. There is no historical record of a Military Council Order 171 of 28 September 1942.

158　'*Take another example of the wholehearted loyalty*' – *BoR*, p. 158.

158　'*Panikakha had already used up all his hand grenades*' – *BoR*, p. 159.

159　'*That is how the soldiers of the 62nd Army fought*' – *BoR*, p. 160.

159 'Zholudev's division. Commissar Shcherbina. Tractor Plant' – WaW, p. 172.

159 'Two soldiers came to see me' – WaW, pp. 173–4.

160 'Tamara Shmakova saved many lives' – BoR, pp. 232–3.

160 'Early one morning, a soldier and I were ordered to go' – Roger D. Markwick and Euridice Charon Cardona, *Soviet Women on the Frontline in the Second World War* (Basingstoke: Palgrave Macmillan, 2012), pp. 82–3.

161 'Stalingrad. What sort of battlefield is that?' – UFW, p. 323.

162 'October 14th dawned, a day which saw the beginning' – BoR, p. 180.

162 'We felt not only that our own ranks were thinning' – BoR, p. 190.

163 'The Germans were on the edge of the plant' – WaW, pp. 177–9.

164 'Lyolya Novikova, a cheerful nurse' – WaW, p. 183.

164 'two most courageous women defending Stalingrad' – WaW, pp. 188–9.

164 'Despite our losses, our fighting spirit was higher than ever' . . . 'come within a hair's breadth' – BoR, pp. 197–8.

166 'I cannot understand how men can survive' – Antony Beevor, *Stalingrad* (London: Viking Press, 1998), p. 232.

16. Stalingrad: Victory!

page

168 'The morning of November 13th. We saw Stalin' – MoV Vol. II, pp. 119–20.

169 'There was something fatherly about it' – http://ww2history.com/ key_moments/Eastern/Soviets_launch_Operation_Uranus (accessed April 2020).

170 'An image: a strongpoint destroyed by a tank' – WaW, pp. 192–3.

170 'We felt inspiration' – http://ww2history.com/videos/Eastern/Stalingrad (accessed April 2020).

171 'Capitulation out of the question' – https://www.history.com/ this-day-in-history/von-paulus-to-hitler-let-us-surrender (accessed May 2020).

171 'The entire area at the shore of the Volga is scoured by craters' – Chekalov's diary was kept by his family for sixty years before being published in Russian, in Moscow, by the Russian Humanist Society, in 2004 (edited by V. A. Kuvakin and A. G. Kruglov). 13.01.43, pp. 33–4.

172 'January 19th. There has been a great victory at the front!' – IW, p. 160.

172 '26.1.43. Mamayev Kurgan. The height itself is an eerie sight' – Ivan Ivanovich Golokolenko, *My Fight Against the Foreign Armies* (Moscow: Voenizdat, 1980), p. 231.

173 'On January 31st, soldiers of the 64th Army took prisoner' – BoR, p. 259.

173 'We took the Barrikady Factory' – Jochen Hellbeck, *Stalingrad, the City*

that Defeated the Third Reich (New York, NY: Perseus Books, 2015), p. 351.

174 'The Volga Steppe was full of graves and crosses' – BoR, p. 263.

175 'The only thought we had was where to find something to eat' – Laurence Rees, War of the Century (London: BBC Books, 1999), pp. 142–3.

175 'Goodbye Volga. Goodbye mutilated and exhausted city' – BoR, p. 267.

17. The Turning Tide

page

180 'What scoundrels there are, what rabid anti-Semites!' – the full text of the diaries, in Russian, can be found at http://militera.lib.ru/db/gelfand_vn/02.html (accessed and translated April 2020). 29.12.42.

181 'Those terrible days did not pass my family by' ... 'The Nazis arrived in small cars' – Pavel Bragin, 'Colonel "Blowtorch": How Himmler's favorite eliminated the population of the Kharkiv villages of Efremovka and Semonovka', Kharkiv News, 12 August 2020. Text available, in Russian, at https://mykharkov.info/news/polkovnik-payalnaya-lampa-kak-lyubimchik-gimmlera-istrebil-naselenie-harkovskih-sel-efremovki-i-semenovki-68005.html (accessed October 2020).

184 'We mowed down the Hitlerites like ripe grain' – https://www.history.co.uk/article/lyudmila-pavlichenko-lady-death-historys-deadliest-female-sniper (accessed April 2020).

185 'I am amazed at the kind of questions put to me' ... 'Now I am looked upon a little as a curiosity' – https://www.mentalfloss.com/article/565151/retrobituaries-lyudmila-pavlichenko (accessed April 2020).

186 'Finally, in the evening, a German showed in the trench' – all the quotations from Roza's diary in this chapter are extracted from https://rozasdiary.com/ (accessed January 2020).

187 'Let the Russian mother rejoice' – https://allthatsinteresting.com/roza-shanina (accessed January 2020).

190 'I can't overlook the very important question' – Chris Bellamy, Absolute War (London: Macmillan, 2007), p. 521.

18. Blood and Iron: Kursk

page

193 'I want to tear out the pages of my diary' – IW, p. 161.

194 'I gave birth in '43' – UFW, pp. 43–4.

196 'The Supreme Commander was not yet certain' – MoV Vol. II, p. 168.

196 'At 2:20 a.m., the order was issued' ... 'We could hear and feel the hurricane-like fire' – MoV Vol. II, p. 182.

197 'Their Tigers and Panthers, deprived in the melee' – John Erickson (foreword by Marshal Sokolov), Main Front: Soviet Leaders Look Back on World War II (London: Brassey's, 1987), p. 131.

198 'The tank of T-34 Commander Captain Skripkin' – https://warfarehistorynetwork.com/2016/09/02/the-battle-of-kursk-showdown-at-prokhorovka-and-oboian/ (accessed May 2020).

198 'This was a face-to-face battle' ... 'A gun-aimer fired at a Tiger' – WaW, p. 233.

198 'The sky thunders, the earth shudders' – UFW, p. 132.

199 'Once hand-to-hand combat begins' – UFW, p. 66.

200 'The battle was one of the most important engagements' – MoV Vol. II, pp. 194–5.

19. The Meat Grinder

201 'I look at you and think' – UFW, p. 135.

201 'turned coward' ... 'In the morning ... I took a sub-machine gun' – UFW, p. 137.

201 'We're crossing liberated territory' – IW, p. 195.

202 'When our troops enter a village' – WaW, p. 248.

202 '"Where is your father?"' ... 'He walked into a potato field' – WaW, p. 249.

203 'There are no Jews in the Ukraine' – WaW, p. 251.

203 'Every soldier, every officer and every general' – WaW, p. 248.

205 'Medical assistants die quickly' – UFW, p. 85.

206 'We crossed in the middle of the night' – Anatoly Pavlov's letters are held in the State Archive of the Russian Federation in Moscow, 7427/19. Extracts have been translated for this book.

207 'It's one o'clock in the morning' – IW, p. 197.

207 The successes of the Red Army would have been impossible: all Stalin's writings and speeches can be found at https://www.marxists.org/reference/archive/stalin/works/decades-index.htm. They are indexed by decade from September 1901 to October 1952 (accessed January 2020).

208 'My papa ... My beloved papa was a communist' – UFW, p. 172.

20. A Punch in the Guts

211 On this 25th anniversary of the Republic of the Soviets: for Sergius' letter and an analysis of the relationship between Church and Soviet

state during the Great Patriotic War, see https://www.socialist.net/religion-in-the-soviet-union.htm (accessed December 2019).

213 *'Subdivisions of 1162 Infantry Regiment passed through'* – report dated 23 August 1943. The report is held in the State Archive of the Russian Federation in Moscow, 7567/18.

214 *'I was shaking like a leaf'* . . . *'I ran into the bedroom'* . . . *'If I had the strength'* – Mazanik's story is given more detail in Kazimiera J. Cottam, *Women in War and Resistance: Selected Biographies of Soviet Women Soldiers* (Nepean, ON: New Military Publishing, 1998), pp 362–5.

215 *'I have one main desire'* – *IW*, p. 222.

216 *'For leaving his post without orders'* – John A. Armstrong (ed.) *Soviet Partisans in World War II* (Madison, WI: University of Wisconsin Press, 1964), p. 737.

216 *'The Supreme Command decided'* . . . *'Major offensive operations were to be launched'* – *MoV Vol. II*, p. 231.

21. Cigars Around the Table, More Death on the Ground

page

218 *'In 1943, we received a bit more aid'* . . . *'In the last quarter of 1943'* – *MoV Vol. II*, p. 229.

219 *'He broached the question of the colonial empires'* – Valentin Berezhkov (translated by Sergei Mikheyev), *At Stalin's Side* (New York, NY: Birch Lane Press, 1994), p. 239.

219 *'Sometime later, Stalin sent for me'* – *BMF*, pp. 92–3.

220 *'By the end of 1943, we had finally overcome'*, *MoV Vol. II*, p. 229.

221 *'We arrived in the Korsun-Shevchenkovsky area'* . . . *'Soon after leaving the valley'* – Gabriel Temkin, *My Just War* (Novato, CA: Presidio Press, 1998), p. 157.

222 *'I remember that last fateful night'* . . . *'So that morning they formed themselves'* . . . *'Then it happened'* – Alexander Werth, *Russia at War* (London: Pan Books, 1964), pp. 699–701.

223 *'Over by the woods stood the charred remains'* – Boris Polevoi (the post-war nom de plume of Boris Kampov), *From Belgorod to the Carpathians* (London: Hutchinson, 1945), p. 113.

223 *'Yufim Sidoryuk, an inhabitant of Krasnoselka'* – Polevoi, *From Belgorod*, p. 136.

22. Bagration

page

225 *'At the end of April, the Supreme Command'* – *MoV Vol. II*, p. 266.

226 *'There are grounds for thinking'* – *IW*, p. 238.

227 *maskirovka* . . . 'means of securing combat operations' – The *Soviet Military Encyclopaedia* in eight volumes was published by Voenizdat, the publishing house of the Soviet Ministry of Defence, between 1976 and 1980.

228 'fulfil the function of fortresses' . . . They will ensure that the enemy does not occupy: sometimes referred to as Order 11, the Führer Directive can be read at http://der-fuehrer.org/reden/english/wardirectives/53.html (accessed February 2020).

228 '*Now we're in the Soviet rear!*' – *IW*, p. 240.

229 '*At dawn on July 3rd, the 2nd Guards Tank Corps*' – *MoV Vol. II*, p. 279.

229 '*The first thing we see when we return*' – *WaW*, p. 273.

230 '*A wounded man was brought*' – *UFW*, p. 121.

230 '*To Bobruisk led the road of revenge*' – *WaW*, p. 273.

230 '*A partisan with a stake killed two Germans*' – *WaW*, p. 276.

231 '*We talked about Germany's capacity to wage war*' – *MoV Vol. II*, p. 281.

232 '*Particularly striking was the attitude of the Russian crowd*' – Alexander Werth, *Russia at War* (London: Pan Books, 1964), p. 862.

232 '*There were such terrible bullet wounds*' – *UFW*, p. 196.

23. The Tragedy of Warsaw

page

235 'Kill, without pity or mercy' – https://allthatsinteresting.com/nazi-occupied-poland (accessed February 2020).

236 '*November 15th, 1940. Today the Jewish ghetto*' – Mary Wattenberg (edited by Susan Lee Pentlin), *The Diary of Mary Berg, Growing up in the Warsaw Ghetto* (London: One World Publications, 2013), p. 28.

238 '*Until that day, no matter how difficult*' – Marek Edelman, *The Ghetto Fights, Warsaw 1943–45* (London: Bookmarks, 2014), p. 30.

238 '*Wednesday 22nd July, 1942. A day of turmoil*' – Abraham Lewin (edited by Antony Polonsky), *A Cup of Tears – A Diary of the Warsaw Ghetto* (London: Fontana, 1990). Extracts from the diary, including entries for 22 to 25 July, can be read at http://www.holocaustresearchproject.org/ghettos/al-diary.html (accessed February 2020).

239 '*The shootings and the cries coming from the streets*' – Wattenberg, *Diary of Mary Berg*, p. 173.

240 '*I cannot stop thinking about the stories from Treblinka*' – Wattenberg, *Diary of Mary Berg*, p. 208.

240 To the Jewish Masses in the Ghetto: https://www.jewishvirtuallibrary.org/the-last-letter-from-morde (accessed June 2020).

241 '*Fires were raging over the entire block*' – Edelman, *Ghetto Fights*, p. 42.

241 'On May 8th, detachments of Germans and Ukrainians' ... 'All night we walked through the sewers' – Edelman, Ghetto Fights, p. 44.

242 'June 15th, 1943. We who have been rescued' – Wattenberg, Diary of Mary Berg, p. 222.

242 'The feeling of freedom took my breath away' – Wattenberg, Diary of Mary Berg, p. 246.

245 'June 12th. I suffer terribly but I still dream' – https://www.yadvashem. org/articles/general/the-final-days-of-the-lodz-ghetto.html (accessed May 2020).

246 'strangely embarrassed glances at the sprawling bodies' – Primo Levi (translated by Stuart Woolf), If This Is a Man (London: Abacus 1987), p. 79.

247 'They think that I am provoking them' – Dan Stone, The Liberation of the Camps: The End of the Holocaust and Its Aftermath (London: Yale University Press, 2015), p. 45.

247 'This creature specialised in the killing of children' – Robert Chandler (ed), translated by Elizabeth Chandler and Olga Mukovnikova with contributions by Yury Bit-Yunan, Vasily Semenovich Grossman, The Road: Stories, Journalism, and Essays (New York, NY: NYRB Classics, 2010), p. 101.

247 'It is infinitely hard even to read this' – WaW, p. 301.

24. The Red Tide

page

251 '147 divisions were crushed' – MoV Vol. II, p. 293.

252 'Although you are going to prepare for war against Bulgaria' – MoV Vol. II, p. 297.

252 'On the morning of September 8th, everything was ready' – MoV Vol. II, p. 298.

253 'successively banal, then glorious' – https://detritusofempire.blogspot. com/2019/08/time-capsule-such-complicated-treason.html (accessed June 2020).

254 'Mile-long caterpillars of horse-drawn carts' – Gabriel Temkin, My Just War (Novato, CA: Presidio Press, 1998), p. 191.

255 'The "Frontovaya Gazeta" lectured us' – Temkin, My Just War, p. 194.

255 'Churchill said, "We have to talk about two countries"' ... 'There was a long silence' – Valentin Berezhkov (translated by Sergei Mikheyev), At Stalin's Side (New York, NY: Birch Lane Press, 1994), p. 304.

257 'It was impossible to spend a day' – Norman Naimark, The Russians in Germany (Cambridge, MA: Harvard University Press, 1995), p. 70.

258 Among the workers of Köbánya: Krisztián Ungváry (translated by

Ladislaus Löb), *Battle for Budapest, 100 Days in World War II* (London: I. B. Tauris, 2002), Kindle edition.

258 **You have, of course, read Dostoevsky?:** Richard Overy, *Russia's War*, (London: Penguin Books, 1998), p. 262.

259 '*Members of the Arrow Cross became increasingly violent*' . . . '*When Pest was taken, we found*' – Temkin, *My Just War*, p. 209.

259 '*Near Budapest . . . It was winter*' – UFW, p. 151.

25. The Juggernaut

page

263 **The fascist barbarians have destroyed Warsaw:** https://polandin. com/40901511/soviet-report-on-wwii-destruction-of-warsaw-revealed (accessed April 2020).

263 '*Polish officers and men took the destruction of the city especially hard*' – MoV Vol. II, p. 319.

264 '*The conditions in Stutthof were beyond description*' . . . '*The order came, we are moving out*' – oral history interview with Steven Springfield, conducted by Linda G. Kuzmack, 30 March 1990, US Holocaust Memorial Museum Collection: https://collections.ushmm.org/search/catalog/irn504712 (accessed May 2020).

265 '*They told us to line up and to get undressed*' . . . '*You had to stay at the front*' – oral history interview with Lily Margules, conducted by Regine Beyer, 27 August 1996, US Holocaust Memorial Museum Collection: https://collections.ushmm.org/search/catalog/irn504928_ (accessed April 2020).

266 '*We were already passing through East Prussia*' – UFW, p. 229.

267 '*Everything is on fire. Looting is in full swing*' – WaW, pp. 326–7.

267 '**Another self-shot lieutenant!**' – the full text of the diaries, in Russian, can be found at http://militera.lib.ru/db/gelfand_vn/05.html (accessed and translated April 2020). 16.02.45.

268 '*Our troops had liberated all of Hungary*' – MoV Vol. II, p. 338.

269 '*I went to Stalin's country house*' – MoV Vol. II, p. 339.

269 '**Just think how many sons ended in camps!**' – Simon Sebag-Montefiore, *Stalin: The Court of the Red Tsar* (London: Phoenix, 2004), p. 454.

269 '*Stalin did not answer at once*' . . . '*At the table, Stalin sat silent*' – MoV Vol. II, pp. 339–40.

270 '*The German women are afraid*' – Gelfand diary entry for 20.03.45.

271 '*They advise us to watch out for a certain man*' . . . '*So this is the end*' . . . '*She tells me not to be foolish*' . . . '*Will they set it on fire?*' . . . '*A siren*' – Macha Rolnikas, *I Must Tell* (reconstructed diary 1941–45), translated and published by Daniel H. Shubin (2018). Extracts from

the diary can be found at https://spartacus-educational.com/
GERrolnikas.htm (accessed May 2020).

272 *'The post has just brought the most tragic news'* – Gelfand diary entry
for 28.04.45.

26. Vengeance

273 *'Then we crossed the Oder and entered the Land of Death'* – *Diary of
Fyodor Bogratyov, a Private in the Great War 1941–1945.* 10/IV-1945,
p. 53.

274 *'On a clear sunny morning, we cross the Polish–German border'* –
Inozemtzev's wartime diary, *I Shall Establish Myself,* was compiled by
Petr Cherkasov and published, in Russian, in the periodical *IMEMO,*
Vol. 1, in 2003. 9/1/45, p. 37.

274 On German soil there is only one master: https://historymadeeeasier.
com/war/ (accessed July 2020).

274 *'More burning German cities, traces of fleeting battles'* – 21/1/45, p. 42.

274 *'I got to Germany . . . All the way from Moscow'* – *UFW,* p. 304.

275 *'On carriages and on foot, old men, women and children'* – *IW,*
pp. 267–8.

276 *'Millions of people had been brutalised and corrupted'* – *IW,* p. 263.

277 *'Of course I remember a German woman who had been raped'* . . . *'We
formed up our battalion'* – *UFW,* p. 307.

277 *'Germany is a witch . . . We are in Germany'* – Karl Bahm, *Berlin 1945:
The Final Reckoning* (London: Amber Books, 2001) p. 137.

279 *'Hitler is spinning a web to stir up a disagreement'* – *MoV Vol. II,*
p. 347

280 *'The command was given to the men in the trenches'* – *EoTR,* pp. 178–9.

280 *'Towards evening our battery reached the heights'* – *MoV Vol. II,* p. 378.

281 *'The enemy's main forces, decimated and scattered'* – *EoTR,* p. 194.

281 *'The trees along the road: apple, cherry, all are in bloom'* – *WaW,*
pp. 333–4.

282 'Any German who offends against his self-evident duty' – https://
warfarehistorynetwork.com/2016/12/05/battle-of-berlin-third-reich-
death-knell/ (accessed May 2020).

283 *'North of the Imperial Chancellery, near the Brandenburger Tor'* – *EoTR,*
p. 225.

284 All military transport and communication facilities – Hugh Trevor-
Roper (ed), *Blitzkrieg to Defeat: Hitler's War Directives 1939–1945* (New
York, NY: Holt, Rinehart and Winston, 1971), pp. 206–7.

285 *'If the war is lost, so too is the Volk'* – https://www.historyplace.com/
worldwar2/defeat/enter-bunker.htm (accessed May 2020).

285 'If the German people lose the war' – Robert Waite, 1971, 'Adolf Hitler's Guilt Feelings: A Problem in History and Psychology', *Journal of Interdisciplinary History*, Vol. 1, No. 2, 229–49.

285 'It was strange, the day before yesterday' – the full text of the diaries, in Russian, can be found at http://militera.lib.ru/db/gelfand_vn/05.html (accessed and translated May 2020). 25.04.45.

287 'There was something portentous about Adolf Hitler being dissected' ... 'a second-hand burgundy red box' ... 'Suddenly, it was as if something had jolted me' – Yelena Rzhevskaya (translated by Arch Tait), *Memoirs of a Wartime Interpreter* (Barnsley: Greenhill Books, 2018), p. 228.

288 'I was urgently summoned to the telephone' ... 'At 03:55 hours the door opened' – EoTR, p. 229.

289 'The call was answered by a duty general' – MoV Vol. II, p. 390.

289 'The command was given to open maximum intensity fire' – EoTR, p. 252.

290 'At 05:50, I was awakened' ... 'At 06:00 hours' ... 'Weidling handed me the paper' – EoTR, pp. 256–8.

290 'So the war was over' – EoTR, p. 263.

290 'May 2nd. The day of Berlin's capitulation' – WaW, p. 338.

291 'They died in the laps of nurses, lay on makeshift stretchers' – MoV Vol. II, p. 414.

291 'I happened to hear arguments that the fighting in Berlin' – Marshal Konev, *Years of Victory* (Forest Grove, OR: University Press of the Pacific, 2005), p. 115.

292 'Yesterday Germany surrendered unconditionally' – Laurel Holliday, *Children's Wartime Diaries* (London: Piatkus Books, 1995), p. 134.

292 'The last days of the war ... I remember this' – UFW, p. 157.

292 'One of them was pregnant. The prettiest one' – UFW, p. 306.

292 'When I see a common grave, I kneel before it' – UFW, p. 196.

293 'We weren't proud, we were just drunk' – Andreas Kluth, 'The Graffitti That Made Germany Better', *The Atlantic*, 3 July 2014.

27. Aftermath

page
295 'persons in Soviet uniform' ... '34 murders, 345 robberies' – Norman Naimark, *The Russians in Germany, 1945–49* (Cambridge, MA: Harvard University Press, 1995), p. 92.

295 'It is a museum' ... 'some even hung in the kitchen' ... 'a huge canvas' ... 'twenty unique shotguns' – Geraldine Norman, 'Stalin and the Spoils of War', *Independent* Sunday Culture section, 25 June 1995.

297 'I came back home ... I remember ... the first stop on our land' – UFW, p. 294.

298   *'Even after the war, I lived in fear'* – UFW, p. 298.

300   *'We tried to hide from the soldiers'* – Oshima is quoted in 'Survivor of 1945 "Gegenmiao" massacre continues to tell tale', *The Mainichi* (*Japan Daily News*), 11 August 2017.

301   *'I fought for the Soviet Union'* – Irina Bezborodova, *Foreign prisoners of war and internees in the USSR*, National History no. 5 (Bucharest: Institute of Historical Studies, 1997), p. 23.

301   *'It was the ultimate tragedy'* – Stéphane Courtois et al (eds), *The Black Book of Communism: Crimes, Terror, Repression* (Cambridge, MA: Harvard University Press, 1999), p. 234.

303   **Beria declared that he had 'done [Stalin] in' and 'saved [us] all'** – Simon Sebag-Montefiore, *Stalin: The Court of the Red Tsar* (London: Phoenix, 2004), p. 640.

304   **Long live the peace between the peoples!**: all Stalin's writings and speeches can be found at https://www.marxists.org/reference/archive/stalin/works/decades-index.htm. They are indexed by decade from September 1901 to October 1952 (accessed June 2020).

Witnesses

page

315   *'Tried to rest, but the continuous stream of prisoners'* – Chekalov's diary was kept by his family for sixty years before being published in Russian, in Moscow, by the Russian Humanist Society, in 2004 (edited by V. A. Kuvakin and A. G. Kruglov). 29.01.43, p. 37.

318   *'I cannot explain the feeling I had'* – Ed Vulliamy, 'Orchestral manoeuvres (part two)', *Observer* Music section, 25 November 2001.

321   *'We are 62 kilometres from Berlin'* – Diary of Fyodor Bogratyov, a Private in the Great War 1941–1945. 4/VI-1945, p. 71.

SELECT BIBLIOGRAPHY

Alexievich, Svetlana, *The Unwomanly Face of War* (London: Penguin Books, 2017)

Axell, Albert, *Russia's Heroes* (London: Constable, 2001)

Axell, Albert, *Marshal Zhukov, The Man Who Beat Hitler* (London: Longman, 2003)

Barskova, Polina, *Besieged Leningrad: Aesthetic Responses to Urban Disaster* (DeKalb, IL: Northern Illinois University Press, 2017)

Bellamy, Chris, *Absolute War* (London: Macmillan, 2007)

Berenbaum, Michael, *Witness to the Holocaust* (New York: Harper Collins, 1997)

Berezhkov, Valentin, *At Stalin's Side* (New York, NY: Birch Lane Press, 1994)

Beria, Sergo, *Beria, My Father* (London: Duckworth, 2001)

Cottam, Kazimiera, *Women in War and Resistance: Selected Biographies of Soviet Women Soldiers* (Nepean, ON: New Military Publishing, 1998)

Chuikov, Marshal Vasili Ivanovich, *The Beginning of the Road* (London: MacGibbon & Kee, 1963)

Chuikov, Marshal Vasili Ivanovich, *The End of the Third Reich* (London: MacGibbon & Kee, 1967)

Cumins, Keith, *Cataclysm, The War on the Eastern Front 41–45* (Solihull: Helion & Company, 2011)

Dimbleby, Jonathan, *Russia, A Journey to the Heart of a Land* (London: BBC Books, 2008)

Edelman, Marek, *The Ghetto Fights, Warsaw 1943–45* (London: Bookmarks, 2014)

Edwards, Robert, *First Winter on the Eastern Front* (Mechanicsburg, PA: Stackpole Books, 2018)

Erickson, John, *The Road to Berlin* (London: Yale University Press, 1999)

Erickson John, *The Road to Stalingrad* (London: Cassell Military, 2003)

Ezergaillis, Andrew, *The Holocaust in Latvia 1941–1944* (New York, NY: US Holocaust Memorial Museum, in association with the Historical Institute of Latvia, 1996)

Fineberg, J. (translator), *Heroic Leningrad, Documents, Sketches and Stories of its Siege and Relief* (Moscow: Foreign Languages Publishing, 1945)

Fritz, Stephen, *Ostkrieg, Hitler's War of Extermination in the East* (Lexington, KY: University Press of Kentucky, 2011)

Grossman, Vasily, *A Writer at War* (London, Harvill Press, 2005)

Hay, Julius, *Born 1900: Memoirs* (Chicago, IL: Open Court, 1975)

Hellbeck, Jochen, *Stalingrad, the City that Defeated the Third Reich* (New York, NY: Perseus Books, 2015)

Jones, Michael, *Leningrad: State of Siege* (London: John Murray, 2008)

Kirchubel, Robert, *Atlas of the Eastern Front 1941–45* (Oxford: Osprey, 2016)

Kopelev, Lev, *No Jail for Thought* (London: Penguin Books, 1977)

Lewin, Abraham, *A Cup of Tears – A Diary of the Warsaw Ghetto* (London: Fontana, 1990)

Likhachev, Dimitri, *Reflections on the Russian Soul: A Memoir* (St Petersburg: CEU Press, 2000)

Markwick, Roger and Cardona, Euridice, *Soviet Women on the Frontline in the Second World War* (Basingstoke: Palgrave Macmillan, 2012)

Mawdsley, Evan, *Thunder in the East, The Nazi-Soviet War 1941–1945*, 2nd edition (London: Bloomsbury, 2016)

Merridale, Catherine, *Ivan's War, Life and Death in the Red Army 1939–45* (London: Faber & Faber, 2005)

Michelson, Frida, *I survived Rumbula* (New York, NY: United States Holocaust Museum, 1982)

Naimark, Norman, *The Russians in Germany, 1945–49* (Cambridge, MA: Harvard University Press, 1995)

Overy, Richard, *Russia's War* (London: Penguin Books, 1998)

Peri, Alexis, *The War Within: Diaries from the Siege of Leningrad* (Cambridge, MA: Harvard University Press, 2017)

Rees, Laurence, *War of the Century* (London: BBC Books, 1999)

Rees Laurence, *World War Two: Behind Closed Doors: Stalin, The Nazis and The West* (London: BBC Books, 2008)

Reid, Anna, *Leningrad, Tragedy of a City Under Siege* (London: Bloomsbury, 2011)

Rokossovskiy Konstantin, *A Soldier's Duty* (Moscow: Progress Publishers, 1970)

Rzhevskaya, Yelena, *Memoirs of a Wartime Interpreter* (Barnsley: Greenhill Books, 2018)

Salisbury, Harrison, *The 900 Days, The Siege of Leningrad* (Boston, MA: Da Capo Press, 1969)

Skrjabina Elena, *Siege and Survival: The Odyssey of a Leningrader* (Carbondale, IL: Southern Illinois University Press, 1971)

Sokolov, Boris, *Myths and Legends of the Eastern Front* (Barnsley: Pen & Sword, 2019)

Stone Dan, *The Liberation of the Camps: The End of the Holocaust and Its Aftermath* (London: Yale University Press, 2015)

Temkin, Gabriel, *My Just War* (Novato, CA: Presidio Press, 1998)

Wattenberg, Mary, *The Diary of Mary Berg, Growing up in the Warsaw Ghetto* (London: One World Publications, 2013)

Werth, Alexander, *Russia at War* (London: Pan Books, 1964)

Zhukov, Georgy, *Marshal of Victory Vol. I: 1896–1941* (Barnsley: Pen & Sword Military, 2013)

Zhukov, Georgy, *Marshal of Victory Vol. II: 1941–1945* (Barnsley: Pen & Sword Military, 2013)

Osprey Publishing: Campaign

(Books in this series are illustrated with full colour 3D 'bird's eye views', battle scenes, maps and black-and-white photographs.)

Antill, Peter, *Berlin 1945: End of the Thousand Year Reich*, Campaign 159 (Oxford: Osprey, 2005)

Antill, Peter, *Stalingrad 1942*, Campaign 184 (Oxford: Osprey, 2007)

Forczyk, Robert, *Moscow 1941*, Campaign 167 (Oxford: Osprey, 2006)

Forczyk, Robert, *Sevastopol 1942*, Campaign 189 (Oxford: Osprey, 2008)

Forczyk, Robert, *Warsaw 1944*, Campaign 205 (Oxford: Osprey 2009)

Forczyk, Robert, *Leningrad 1941–44*, Campaign 215 (Oxford: Osprey, 2009)

Forczyk, Robert, *Demyansk 1942–43*, Campaign 245 (Oxford: Osprey, 2012)

Forczyk, Robert, *Kharkov 1942*, Campaign 254 (Oxford: Osprey, 2013)

Forczyk, Robert, *Kursk 1943 (Northern Front)*, Campaign 272 (Oxford: Osprey, 2014)

Forczyk, Robert, *The Caucasus 1942–43*, Campaign 281 (Oxford: Osprey, 2015)

Forczyk, Robert, *Kursk 1943 (Southern Front)*, Campaign 305 (Oxford: Osprey, 2017)

Forczyk, Robert, *The Dnepr 1943*, Campaign 291 (Oxford: Osprey, 2016)

Forczyk, Robert, *Smolensk 1943*, Campaign 331 (Oxford: Osprey, 2019)

Healey, Mark, *Kursk 1943*, Campaign 16 (Oxford: Osprey, 1992)

Kirchubel, Robert, *Operation Barbarossa 1941 (1): Army Group South*, Campaign 129 (Oxford: Osprey, 2003)

Kirchubel, Robert, *Operation Barbarossa 1941 (2): Army Group North*, Campaign 148 (Oxford: Osprey, 2005)

Kirchubel, Robert, Operation *Barbarossa 1941 (3): Army Group Center*, Campaign 186 (Oxford: Osprey, 2007)

Zaloga, Steven, *Bagration 1944*, Campaign 42 (Oxford: Osprey, 1996)

Osprey Publishing: Elite

(Each book in this series focuses on a single army or elite unit, military tactics or a group of famous commanders.)

Sakaida, Henry, *Heroines of the Soviet Union 1941–45*, Elite 90 (Oxford: Osprey, 2003)

Sakaida, Henry, *Heroes of the Soviet Union 1941–45*, Elite 111 (Oxford: Osprey, 2004)

Osprey Publishing: Essential Histories

(Books in this series study the origins, politics, fighting and repercussions of one major theatre of war, from both military and civilian perspectives.)

Jukes, Geoffrey, *The Second World War (5) The Eastern Front 1941–1945*, Essential Histories 24 (Oxford: Osprey, 2002)

Osprey Publishing: Men at Arms

(A series of illustrated reference books on the history, organisation, uniforms and equipment of the world's military forces.)

Thomas, Nigel, *World War II Soviet Armed Forces (1): 1939–41*, Men at Arms 464 (Oxford: Osprey, 2010)

Thomas, Nigel, *World War II Soviet Armed Forces (2):1942–43*, Men at Arms 468 (Oxford: Osprey, 2011)

Thomas, Nigel, *World War II Soviet Armed Forces (3): 1944–45*, Men at Arms 469 (Oxford: Osprey, 2012)

Zaloga, Steven, *The Red Army of the Great Patriotic War 1941–45*, Men at Arms 216 (Oxford: Osprey, 1984)

Osprey Publishing: Warrior

(A series of illustrated books that focus on the motivation, training, everyday life, weaponry and equipment used by combatants.)

Cornish, Nik, *Soviet Partisan 1941–44*, Warrior 171 (Oxford: Osprey, 2014)

Rottman, Gordon, *Soviet Rifleman 1941–45*, Warrior 123 (Oxford: Osprey, 2007)

INDEX